ARCO

MASTER THE

CLERICAL EXAMS

ARCO

MASTER THE
CLERICAL EXAMS

Christi M. Heuer

Sharon S. Saronson, MSE

John J. Niesz

5th Edition

PETERSON'S

A ⓝelnet. COMPANY

An ARCO Book

ARCO is a registered trademark of Peterson's, and is used herein under license by Peterson's.

About Peterson's, a Nelnet company
Peterson's (www.petersons.com) is a leading provider of education information and advice, with books and online resources focusing on education search, test preparation, and financial aid. Its Web site offers searchable databases and interactive tools for contacting educational institutions, online practice tests and instruction, and planning tools for securing financial aid. Peterson's serves 110 million education consumers annually.

An American BookWorks Corporation Project

For more information, contact Peterson's, 2000 Lenox Drive, Lawrenceville, NJ 08648; 800-338-3282; or find us on the World Wide Web at www.petersons.com/about.

Editor: Therese DeAngelis; Production Editor: Linda Seghers; Manufacturing Manager: Ivona Skibicki; Composition Manager: Gary Rozmierski.

ISBN-13: 978-0-7689-2335-3
ISBN-10: 0-7689-2335-2

Printed in the United States of America

10 9 8 7 6 5 4 3 2 1   09 08 07

Fifth Edition

ANOTHER RECOMMENDED TITLE

ARCO Master the Civil Service Exams

Contents

Before You Begin

HOW THIS BOOK IS ORGANIZED

ARCO Master the Clerical Exams gives you a structured, step-by-step tutorial program that can help you master all the basics you need to score high on federal, state, and local clerical exams. It covers key points and gives you the practice you need to do well on these exams.

Although we cannot predict exactly what your exams will be like, this book can help you prepare for the most probable question types. The instructional chapters will prepare you for questions you're likely to face. The model exams are not actual exams, but they will give you excellent opportunities to practice and prepare for your clerical exam. Other features of this book include details about the jobs you may be eligible for, information on announcements concerning the clerical exams, sample questions from previous exams, and where to get started finding a clerical job in federal, state, or local government.

ARCO Master the Clerical Exams is written for civil service candidates who have limited time but who want to prepare for their exam efficiently. If you already know what type of career you wish to pursue, this book will help you prepare for any of the major exams. If you don't know what type of job you'd like to apply for, this book can also be useful. It will not only help you prepare for your exam, but it will also provide information about various types of careers available in civil service so you can begin to narrow your choices. *ARCO Master the Clerical Exams* provides you with the following information:

- **"Top 10 Strategies to Raise Your Score"** gives you a preview of some of the test-taking strategies you'll learn in this book.

- **Part I** provides a review of the types of careers available in three sectors of civil service: federal civilian employment and state and local civil service. We also review the specifics of finding a clerical position. Each sector has its own requirements and tests, but certain types of questions will appear on most of the exams in all sectors.

For example, most tests include questions to assess your understanding of vocabulary and grammar. You will also be tested for basic mathematics skills. Many clerical tests measure your ability to memorize and remember information accurately. We've provided a sampling of different test types you will encounter, as well as a review section to help you practice. Also in this section, we explain how clerical exams are scored and we offer general test-taking tips that will help you score higher on test day.

- **Part II** is a diagnostic test, which provides an opportunity for you to practice the most common types of test questions you may encounter and assess your readiness to take the clerical exams. Take this test before you review the rest of the book. It will help you find out where your skills are strongest and where they need improvement.

- **Part III** consists of eight full-length practice tests, drawn either from official sample examinations or from models that are closely patterned after the actual exams. Timing, level of difficulty, question styles, and scoring methods all conform to the examinations for which they're meant to prepare you. As a special feature of this book, we include explanations of all the correct answers to these tests.

- **Two Appendixes** provide information on where to find federal, state, and local civil service jobs. We also include a review of the jobs available in the Department of Homeland Security.

SPECIAL STUDY FEATURES

ARCO Master the Clerical Exams is designed to be as user-friendly as it is complete. To this end, we have included several features that will help make your test preparation more efficient.

Overview

Each chapter begins with a bulleted overview listing the topics that will be covered in the chapter. This allows you to quickly target the areas in which you are most interested.

Summing It Up

Each chapter ends with a point-by-point summary that captures the most important points contained in the chapter. This is a convenient way to review key points.

Bonus Information

As you work your way through the book, keep your eye on the margins to find bonus information and advice. You will see this information presented in the following forms:

NOTE

Notes highlight critical information about a career as a clerical worker and the application process.

TIP

Tips provide valuable advice for effectively handling both the job search and the application and examination processes.

ALERT!

Alerts do just what the title says—they alert you to common pitfalls or misconceptions in test-taking for clerical civil service exams.

YOU'RE WELL ON YOUR WAY TO SUCCESS

You have made a decision to pursue a career as a clerical worker. *ARCO Master the Clerical Exams* will help you select the field in which you're best suited to work and will guide you in finding, applying for, and landing the job of your dreams. Good luck!

GIVE US YOUR FEEDBACK

Peterson's, a Nelnet company, publishes a full line of resources to help guide you through the clerical exams and application process. Peterson's publications can be found at your local bookstore or library, and you can access us online at www.petersons.com.

We welcome any comments or suggestions you may have about this publication and invite you to complete our online survey at www.petersons.com/booksurvey. Or you can fill out the survey at the back of this book, tear it out, and mail it to us at:

> Publishing Department
> Peterson's
> 2000 Lenox Drive
> Lawrenceville, NJ 08648

Your feedback will help us to provide personalized solutions for your career advancement.

TOP 10 STRATEGIES TO RAISE YOUR SCORE

1. **Mark your answers by completely blackening the answer space of your choice.**

2. **Mark only ONE answer for each question,** even if you think that more than one answer is correct.

3. **If you change your mind about the answer, erase completely.** Leave no doubt as to which answer you have chosen.

4. **If you do any figuring on the scratch paper—and you will for the math questions—be sure to mark your answer on the answer sheet.**

5. **Check often to be sure that the question number matches the answer space number and that you have not skipped a space by mistake.**

6. **Answer first those questions that seem easiest to you.** Then go back and give a little more time to the questions that seem harder.

7. **Guess if you can.** There is no penalty for a wrong guess. If you do not know the answer, eliminate the answers that you know are wrong and guess from among the remaining ones. If you have no idea whatsoever of the answer choose an answer other than the first. The first choice is generally the correct answer less often than the other choices.

8. **Keep track of time.** Don't be tied to your watch, but do glance at it. If time for any section is about to run out, mark all the remaining spaces with the same answer. By the law of averages, you should pick up an extra point or two.

9. **Don't panic.** If you cannot finish a section, don't worry. If you are accurate in the questions that you do answer, and if you guess on the remainder, you can do very well.

10. **Check and recheck.** If you finish any section before time is up, check to be sure that each question is answered in the right space and that there is only one answer for each question.

PART I

CLERICAL EXAM BASICS

All About
Clerical Careers

EXPLORING YOUR OPTIONS

Clerical work offers the proverbial "foot in the door" to thousands of occupations in government and in the private sector. Clerical work, in its own right, is clean and pleasant. Best of all, entry-level clerical work can open numerous different paths to supervisory and administrative postions or to nonclerical jobs within the organization.

Clerical work is an ideal entry point at which to begin a career. Mature adults can also reenter the job market after years of absence via clerical positions. There also is opportunity for career change into less physically strenuous office work for those whose previous work demanded a degree of strength and stamina, so it lends itself to those seeking semiretirement as well.

An alert clerical worker is in an ideal position to learn about the operations of the place in which he or she is employed. If the workplace is a government office, the clerical worker learns the functions of the office, the services delivered, the chain of command, the daily operations, and the ultimate mission of that office and the larger agency. If the workplace is an office of an organization that provides a service to the public, the clerical worker's learning beyond the job at hand is similar to that of a government clerical worker. If the organization produces a product, the clerical worker learns about the product itself, the business of producing and distributing the product, and the advertising, marketing, and sales of the product. Constant exposure to the business allows the clerical worker to absorb knowledge of the company beyond his or her assigned duties. The job itself provides the education and background for moving ahead.

From a clerical job in government, you may naturally progress into higher-level, more complex clerical work with ever greater responsibility, or you might expand into different aspects of office work. Promotion might entail taking on supervisory duties with an eventual role in the ranks of administration.

A clerical job in the private sector opens even more avenues for growth and diversification. As the clerical worker becomes more familiar with the firm, he or she may go into manufacturing itself, into the business aspects of the company, or into the field as a member of a sales force. A clerical worker in one business tends to be exposed to many other businesses in the course of daily work. You may find that the business of a client or customer offers greater fulfillment than your present company, and you may move upward by moving to another company altogether.

Under the umbrella term "clerical work," you will discover hundreds of different jobs: filing, typing, stock-taking, tabulating, distribution, bookkeeping, data entry, word processing, statistical, stenographic—and the list goes on and on.

TIP

The U.S. Office of Personnel Management Web site, http://opm.gov/, provides valuable information for job seekers, including information on veterans' preferences and online applications.

As varied as the types of jobs is the nature of employers of clerical workers. The federal government offers a wide range of clerical employment; so do state, county, and municipal governments. The U.S. Postal Service, an independent agency of the federal government, employs many clerical workers for processing and distributing mail. And jobs with private employers are so numerous that they are difficult to categorize.

FEDERAL CLERICAL JOBS

Until recently, applicants who passed the civil service test for federal government positions were placed on standing registers of eligibles maintained by the Office of Personnel Management (OPM). Applicants also had to complete a standard federal employment application form, the SF-171, to apply for all jobs. Today, some federal agencies fill their jobs the way private industry does: by allowing applicants to contact the agency directly for job information and application processing. However, there are significant differences between the job application process for private-sector work and that of the federal government because of the laws, executive orders, and regulations that govern federal employment.

Today, the OPM no longer maintains registers of eligible candidates. Applicants can mail or fax a resume to the hiring office listed on a job announcement, or they can apply online using their resume at USAJobs, *http://www.usajobs.opm.gov*.

Job seekers do not need a rating from OPM to enable them to apply for nonclerical vacancies. The SF-171 is also obsolete. Instead, an optional application for federal employment, the

OF-612, is available for those who do not have a current resume. In addition to clerical exams, a few positions require a written test.

Jobs in more than sixty different clerical fields are filled using results of the Federal Clerical Exam. Employees who have these jobs, like many others in the federal government, are paid using the General Schedule (GS), which assigns different "grades" to jobs according to the level of responsibility, experience, or education required. The exact pay level of a specific position should appear on the job announcement.

Each clerical field includes job positions at several levels. Generally, all you need to qualify for entry-level positions is a high school diploma or comparable job experience, although some entry-level positions also require specific skills, such as typing or shorthand. As you gain experience, you become eligible for promotion to a higher-level position that may be more specialized and may involve administrative work. You can also start out at a higher-grade level if you already have the required specialized experience or additional education. Experience gleaned from summer or part-time jobs can play a factor as well, so many applicants are eligible for entry at higher pay grades than GS-2 without requiring additional education.

Except for the position of clerk-stenographer (which has a GS-3 entry-level pay grade), the entry level pay grade for clerical jobs is commonly GS-2. Initial hires are usually at either the GS-2 or GS-3 level.

Salaries for federal employees under the General Schedule are comparable to nonfederal pay levels in similar occupations. Competent employees receive periodic pay increases. Promotions are based on the ability to handle increased responsibility and a demonstration that you have increased your level of experience and skill.

Paydays are every two weeks. As in the private sector, your net pay will reflect deductions for federal, state, and local taxes as required, as well as for retirement savings. Group health insurance and life insurance are available; the federal government pays 72 percent of the average health insurance premium. Vacation benefits begin at thirteen days per year for most new full-time employees and increase with the length of time you work. Most full-time federal government employees also earn thirteen days of paid sick leave each year, regardless of how long they have been on the job.

On-the-job training for increasingly responsible positions is often provided, and employees are encouraged to continue their own career education. In addition, the federal government sponsors formal training courses and sometimes pays for outside training that is directly related to improving job performance.

Here is a review of some of the more common clerical jobs available with the federal government.

TIP

Federal, state, and municipal agencies looking for employees often contact professional societies, veterans' organizations, trade associations, and unions. Check with organizations to which you belong to find leads on job offerings.

Clerk

The general title "clerk" covers many specific positions in which typing, stenography, and data-entry skills are either not required or are not an important aspect of the job. Opportunities at the entry level in these fields are more limited than for typing, stenography, and data-entry jobs because more of them require specialized experience or training. However, entry-level opportunities do exist.

Thousands of general clerks, such as mail and filing clerks and miscellaneous clerks, perform a variety of typical office and record-keeping tasks. Most of these positions are filled at entry level. Sales store checker positions are also available with the federal government; these positions are similar to those of private retail businesses and are usually on military bases or in agency supply stores.

Jobs in these fields are usually above the entry level: personnel support, supply, transportation, stock control, accounting, payroll, and finance. Payroll clerks, for example, keep records and perform other duties related to issuing paychecks; cash processing clerks handle and track cash disbursements.

Postal Service Worker

As in other branches of the federal government, the title "clerk" in the U.S. Postal Service refers to a number of different job functions. One group of clerks is comprised of window clerks, distribution clerks, machine-operating distribution clerks, and mark-up clerks. All of them directly handle mail in some way, and all are chosen according to their scores on Postal Exam 473, the Postal Clerk and Carrier Exam. Mark-up clerk candidates must also qualify on a computer-administered alpha-numeric typing test, Examination 715.

A second group of clerks in the Postal Service perform more traditional clerical functions. These are clerk-typists and clerk-stenographers, as described above. All candidates for these positions must take Examination 710, which is a test of clerical aptitude and verbal abilities, and they must qualify on Examination 712, a typing test administered on a computer. Candidates for a clerk-stenographer position must also earn qualifying scores on Examination 711, the stenography test.

People are most familiar with the Postal Service window clerk, whom you see behind the counter in your local post office selling stamps, accepting packages, and performing other customer service duties. However, most postal clerks are distribution clerks who work behind the scenes sorting incoming and outgoing mail in workrooms. Only in small post offices do clerks perform both kinds of work.

When mail arrives at the post office, it is dumped onto long tables, where distribution clerks and mail handlers separate it into groups of letters, parcel post material, and magazines and newspapers. Clerks feed letters into stamp-canceling machines or cancel by hand. The mail is then shunted to other sections of the post office, where it is sorted according to destination.

Clerks first separate the mail into primary destination categories (local, nearby states, distant states, and large cities); then by one or more secondary distribution categories. In post offices with electronic mail-sorting machines, clerks push a button corresponding to the letter's destination, and the letter drops into the proper slot.

Clerks at post office windows provide a variety of services in addition to selling stamps and money orders. They weigh packages to determine proper postage and check the size, shape, and condition of packages for mailing. They register and insure mail and answer questions about postage rates, mailing restrictions, and extra services. They also help customers file claims for damaged or lost packages. In large post offices, window clerks might provide only a few of these services; these positions are called registry, stamp, or money order clerks.

Distribution clerks work indoors handling sacks of mail weighing as much as 70 pounds. They sort and distribute mail using memorization. Machine distribution clerks must learn computer codes for automatic mail routing. They are on their feet all day and are required to stretch, reach, and throw heavy bundles. The work of a distribution clerk is more routine than that of other Post Office clerks, but the starting salary is higher. Distribution clerks begin at GS-6, while other clerks and carriers usually begin at GS-5.

Although the amount of U.S. mail is expected to grow as the population does and as the number of new businesses increases, modernization and installation of new equipment in post offices will likely increase the amount of mail each clerk can handle. For example, post offices now have machines that semiautomatically mark destination codes on envelopes. These codes are read by computer-controlled letter-sorting machines, which automatically drop each letter into the proper slot corresponding to its destination. Clerks read addresses only once—at the time they are coded—instead of several times.

Applicants for distribution clerk positions must be physically able to perform the duties described in a job announcement. Any physical condition that may create a hazard for the worker or for other employees can be grounds for disqualification. Clerks must have at least 20/30 vision (rated by the Snellen vision test) in one eye. Wearing eyeglasses or contact lenses is permitted. Deaf or hard-of-hearing applicants can qualify for clerk positions. Appointment hinges on completion of a physical exam, a drug test, and a psychological interview. Letter-sorting machine operators must also take Exam 473.

STATE AND LOCAL CLERICAL JOBS

Following the lead of the Federal Government, every state has instituted some form of civil service or merit-based hiring procedure. In matters of internal hiring, each state has complete autonomy; no higher authority tells a state which positions must be filled by examination or which examination to use. However, in the interests of efficiency and fairness in hiring, nearly all states fill clerical positions through civil service examinations.

TIP

If "Optional Fields" or "Options" is listed on the front page of a civil service job announcement, it refers to related positions that can be filled through the same announcement. You may apply for these positions simultaneously with the primary position.

In addition to administering examinations to fill job vacancies in state government, many states offer their testing services to counties and municipalities as well. Thus, a person qualifying on a state-administered clerical examination may, if he or she wishes, have name and ranking listed on any number of eligibility rosters in counties or towns in which the person might be willing to work. In other states, state testing is only for state positions, and counties and municipalities have their own individual arrangements or independent systems.

As testing arrangements may vary from state to state, so procedures and the tests themselves may also vary. In general, state-administered clerical exams test the skills and abilities needed for specific jobs or families of jobs. Where applicable, typing and stenographic tests are part of the testing package. Since budgetary restraints limit available state personnel, most state examinations are of the multiple-choice variety for easy scoring.

County Clerical Employment

TIP

Your state's official Web site may list job opening announcements in state government. Some of these sites allow you to apply electronically. Check city or county Web sites as well; they may offer similar information.

In some states, county subdivisions serve as convenient geographical and political units but have relatively little operational governmental function. In such states, county clerical testing is limited to selection of personnel for county offices, most often health departments and court systems. In those states, most nonmunicipal government services are distributed among the state, townships, towns, and boroughs. Where the state is the main coordinating body, the state may test and compile eligibility lists for its constituent local governments.

Other states place a great deal of power and autonomy with their counties. The counties operate and administer their own highway systems, police divisions, hospitals, educational units, prisons, and recreational areas. Where the counties deliver such services, they also tend to offer support and assistance to local governments within their borders, so they may assume the testing function for county-wide employment at various levels. A single clerical exam administered by a county might be used to establish eligibility lists for towns, incorporated villages, school districts, and library districts within that county. Applicants taking county exams can specify which local entities they would like to be considered for and can have their names placed on a number of lists on the basis of one exam score.

Counties also have a great deal of discretion in test development and in choosing which tests to administer. Any given county may decide at any time to purchase an examination from a commercial test developer, to use a state-developed exam, or to join a consortium of neighboring counties and have an examination specially developed according to the specifications of the cooperating counties. The county may also change its examination from administration to administration, seeking the best tool for choosing the most appropriate and productive employees.

Variations in subjects and formats are greatest among law enforcement and correctional examinations. Subjects of clerical examinations are limited by the nature of clerical work itself. Even so, there are differences in approach to clerical testing, according to job descriptions and from county to county.

For example, Westchester County in New York administers an examination for the entry-level job title "jr. typist." This is a two-part examination testing only typing speed and accuracy and spelling. Rank-order certification is based on this 90-question, 10-minute spelling test and five-minute plain-paper-copy typing test. With this certification, applicants may seek employment with local governments, school districts, and libraries throughout the county. The hiring bodies may, of course, require candidates to demonstrate other skills and abilities as well.

Clerical Employment in the Courts

The job title "court clerk" is generally not a title filled by entry-level clerical workers. The court clerk is usually a senior employee of the court with a number of years of service as a court officer and considerable legal knowledge. The court clerk does perform many clerical duties, but they are only secondary to administrative and even paralegal responsibilities. Where the court clerk position is a promotional one, the employee will have passed clerical-type exams at earlier stages of employment testing. The court clerk exam will be a test of legal knowledge.

In those areas where "court clerk" is the title applied to any clerical worker in the court system, the court clerk exam will, of course, be more typical of clerical examinations. More often, clerical workers in the courts fill job titles like "file clerk," "office clerk," and "clerk-typist." For example, in the Unified Court System of New York, which staffs state and municipal courts, a typical job designation is "senior appellate office typist." In announcing the opening of this job title, the Unified Court System of New York published the following job description:

> Senior Appellate Office Typists work with a limited degree of independence on a variety of office clerical and typing tasks in the Appellate Divisions or Appellate Terms of the Supreme Court. They may also serve as receptionists, information clerks, work in Appellate Division law libraries, or perform other related duties.

Municipal Clerical Positions

If you were not aware of this fact before, you most certainly now are convinced that clerical positions appear at every governmental level and in every locality. Big cities are no exception. Most big cities operate their own civil service systems, develop and administer their own examinations, and maintain their own eligibility lists. The job titles can be simple and all-inclusive or they can be highly specialized.

The city of New York tends to administer a separate exam for each job title as the list of eligibles for that title is exhausted or expires. But the exams used to test for related positions are very similar. Numbers of questions, timing, subjects tested, and proportion of questions on each subject vary little. Only the words and figures change.

The municipal office aide exam in this book is an actual office aide examination given by the city of New York some years ago. Some question styles have changed over the years. Some new styles have been introduced; old, discredited question styles have been discarded. If you are taking a New York City exam, it will be similar, but not exactly the same as this. If your exam is for a city other than New York, you can expect less similarity.

Another city's exam may resemble a federal or state exam. Whatever the format, however, clerical skills are clerical skills, and much of the subject matter will be the same. Emphasis and question form may differ, but for all of these exams, you must demonstrate the ability to perform clerical duties.

Try the municipal office aide exam in this book even if you are not taking a New York City exam. It will give you good practice in taking a varied exam that is not divided into discrete segments. Any test-taking practice will help you prepare for the exam you will take.

CLERICAL JOBS IN THE PRIVATE SECTOR

ALERT!
Read the job announcement carefully before you send in your application. Often the announcement lists supplemental forms or information you must submit along with the application. Without this information, your application will be dismissed as incomplete, no matter how qualified you are.

Civil service testing—that is, testing for positions in the public sector—is standardized and uniform within each governmental jurisdiction. Testing in the private sector, by contrast, is highly individualized. A private employer has the option to test or not to test, to devise tailor-made tests for positions within the company, or to purchase ready-made exams from a commercial test publisher.

Most often a small, private employer will rely on school records, recommendations, a personal interview, and, if relevant, typing and stenography tests. Large corporations often screen applicants with clerical tests of their own, to avoid the time and effort of checking references and interviewing applicants who are unqualified.

Within the private sector, most clerical exams are administered by employment agencies—both temporary agencies and agencies that specialize in placing permanent employees. The agencies gain and maintain their reputations by sending qualified prospects to their clients. One way for an agency to verify the competence of people seeking employment is by testing their skills.

SUMMING IT UP

- Taking a clerical position in a federal, state, or local office or in the public sector can be a means to achieve a higher-level position. With experience and increased responsibility, clerical workers often move up to administrative or supervisory positions. Clerical work can be ideal for those just starting their careers, those seeking to reenter the job market after a long absence, or those who are semiretired.

- Depending on your experience, education, and skills, you can begin as a clerical worker for the federal government at a higher pay grade than entry level. Applicants for federal clerical positions can submit a resume or fill out an optional application for federal employment, the OF-612.

- Exam requirements for state and local government positions vary greatly. Most states have a civil service or merit-based hiring system. All have complete autonomy in hiring decisions, but nearly all require applicants to take a civil service exam. The exam may be devised by the state, specific cities or municipalities, or counties; developed by cooperating groups of counties; or purchased from a commercial testing firm.

- Although civil-service testing is relatively standardized, testing in the private sector is highly variable. Private employers are free to devise their own tests, to purchase tests from other firms, or to hire employment agencies to devise and administer tests. They may also opt not to test at all.

Civil Service Test Requirements

OVERVIEW

- **Preparing for the Civil Service Tests**

- **Summing it up**

PREPARING FOR THE CIVIL SERVICE TESTS

Most federal, state, and municipal units have recruitment procedures for filling civil service positions. They have developed a number of methods to publicize job opportunities. Places where you can obtain such information include:

- The offices of the state employment services. There are almost 2,000 throughout the country. These offices are administered by the state in which they are located, with the financial assistance of the federal government. You can find the address of the one nearest you using a quick online search.

- Your state Civil Service Commission. Address your inquiry to the capital city of your state.

- Your city Civil Service Commission. These departments may also be called the Department of Personnel. You will be able to identify it under a listing of city departments.

- Your municipal building and your local library.

- Complete listings are carried by such newspapers as *The Chief-Leader* (published in New York City), and by other city- and state-wide publications devoted to civil service employees. Many local newspapers run a section on regional civil service news.

- State and local agencies looking for competent employees will contact schools, professional societies, veterans organizations, unions, and trade associations.

- School boards and boards of education, which employ the greatest proportions of state and local personnel, will have information about job openings.

You will find more in-depth information at the end of this book.

The Format of the Job Announcement

When a position is open and a civil service examination will be administered for it, a job announcement is posted. This announcement contains everything an applicant has to know about getting the job.

The announcement begins with a job title and salary. A typical announcement describes the work, the location of the position, the education and experience requirements, the kind of examination required, and the system of rating. It may also mention about veteran preference and age limit. It tells you which application form to fill out, where to get the form, and where and when to file it.

Study the job announcement carefully. It will answer many of your questions and help you decide whether you are interested in the position and are qualified for it.

There is no point in applying for a position and taking the examination if you do not want to work where the job is located. The job may be in your community or hundreds of miles away at the other end of the state. If you are not willing to work in a distant location, study other announcements that will give you an opportunity to work in a place of your choice. A civil service job close to your home has an additional advantage, since local residents usually receive preference in appointments.

The words **Optional Fields**—sometimes just the word **Options**—may appear on the front page of the announcement. You then have a choice to apply for that particular position in which you are especially interested. This is because the duties of various positions can be quite different, even though they bear the same broad title. A public relations clerk, for example, does different work from a payroll clerk, although the positions are considered broadly in the same general area.

Not every announcement has options, but the precise duties are described in detail, usually under the heading **Description of Work.** Make sure that these duties are in the range of your experience and ability.

Most job requirements provide a **deadline for filing** an application. Others bear the words, **No Closing Date** at the top of the first page; this means that applications will be accepted until the needs of the agency are met. In some cases, a public notice is issued when a certain number of applications has been received. No application mailed past the deadline date will be considered.

Every announcement has a detailed section on **education and experience requirements** for the particular job and for the optional fields. Make sure that in both cases, you meet the minimum qualifications. If you do not meet the given standards for one job, there may be others open for which you stand a better chance of making the grade.

If the job announcement does not mention **veteran preference,** it would be wise to inquire whether such a provision exists in your state or municipality. There may be none, or it may be limited to disabled veterans. In some jurisdictions, surviving spouses of disabled veterans are given preference. All such information can be obtained through the agency that issues the job announcement.

Applicants may be denied examinations and eligible candidates may be denied appointments for any of the following reasons:

- intentional false statements
- deception or fraud in examination or appointment
- use of intoxicating beverages to the extent that ability to perform the duties of the position is impaired
- criminal, infamous, dishonest, immoral, or notoriously disgraceful conduct

The announcement describes the **kind of test** given for the particular position. Pay special attention to this section. It tells you what areas will be covered in the written test and lists the specific subjects on which questions will be asked. Sometimes sample questions are provided.

Usually, the announcement states whether the examination is to be **assembled** or **unassembled.** In an assembled examination, applicants assemble in the same place at the same time to take a written or performance test. The unassembled examination is one in which an applicant does not take a test; instead, he or she is rated on education and experience and whatever records of past achievement the applicant provides.

In the competitive (assembled) examination, all applicants for a position compete with one another; the higher the grade, the better the chance of being appointed. Also, competitive examinations are given to determine desirability for promotion among employees.

Civil service written tests are rated on a scale of 0 to 100, with 70 usually being the passing mark.

Background Investigation

Any person who is employed by the federal government must submit to a background investigation to ensure good character and loyalty to the United States. The scope of the investigation may vary depending on the type of position you are applying for. Law enforcement positions that require access to classified documents will also require a full security clearance.

If you have concerns that your background investigation could be a stumbling block in your application process, you may be wise to take the following steps to reduce the chances that you and/or your potential employer will be surprised by information found during the investigation process:

1. **Order a copy of your credit report.** If you see something in your credit report that you do not recognize or that you disagree with, you may want to dispute the information with the creditor and/or credit bureau before it counts against you in the application process or you have to explain it to an interview panel. For example, another person's name may appear on your credit report—this can happen when someone mistakenly records the wrong Social Security number on a credit application. Reviewing your credit report also ensures that you have not been an unwitting victim of identity theft.

2. **Check court records.** If you have an arrest record or have been involved in court cases, go to the county where it took place and inspect the files. Make sure the information is correct and up to date.

   Sometimes court records indicate a felony conviction even though the crime was reduced to a misdemeanor, or it was reported as a misdemeanor conviction when the charge was reduced to an infraction. This may happen if a signature that was required to reduce the charges was not obtained or recorded by the court. Don't rely on what your attorney may have told you. If you think a conviction was expunged or dismissed, get a certified copy of your report from the court.

3. **Check DMV records.** Request a copy of your driving record from the Department of Motor Vehicles in any state where you have or had a driver's license to ensure that all information is accurate.

4. **Order a background check on yourself.** If you want to see what an employer's background check might uncover, you can hire a company that specializes in producing such reports to conduct one for you. That way, you can discover whether the databases vendors use contain erroneous or misleading information. Check the Yellow Pages under "Investigators," or use one of the many online search services.

5. **Ask to see a copy of your personnel file from your previous job.** Some states have laws that enable you to see your employment file even if you do not work for that employer anymore. You may also want to ask whether your former employer has a policy about the release of personnel records, since many companies limit the amount of information they disclose.

6. **Alert family, friends, neighbors and colleagues about the background check.** When your personal and professional associates are aware that they might be asked to provide information about you, it helps alleviate suspicions on their

part and alerts you to possible problems. Their knowledge of the situation will ease their apprehension, making them feel more comfortable with the interviewer—and setting a better tone for the interview. It will also give them time to consider dates and events that they may be asked to recall, so that their responses are more prepared and accurate. In addition, their prior knowledge gives them permission to disclose information about you to the investigator. Forewarning others can shorten the time it takes for the background check to be completed.

SUMMING IT UP

- The first step in preparing to take a civil service exam is finding positions you are interested in. Federal and state employment services post job announcements listing everything you need to know, including title, salary, duties, geographic location, experience and skills required, and type of exam required.

- Take special care in filling out the application form for a job you are interested in. Follow directions exactly and be truthful and thorough in your responses.

- Depending on the position, you may be asked to submit to a background investigation. It's a good idea to check your own records to be sure the information is accurate. This includes credit reports, driving records, school records, financial reports, and any legal or criminal records. Let your friends and family know in advance that they may be contacted during this investigation.

Federal, State, and Local Tests

OVERVIEW

- About civil service tests
- Federal testing
- State testing
- Local testing
- Clerical employment tests for court-related and private-sector positions
- Summing it up

ABOUT CIVIL SERVICE TESTS

Before we discuss the different types of tests you might encounter, here is some general information about civil service tests. To be considered for most civil service jobs, especially entry level, applicants may be required to take a test. Test grades are used to place applicants on job referral lists, often called "registers." These lists or "registers" of successful applicants are then sent by civil service to those agencies with vacancies to fill. The agency then contacts the highest-scoring applicants for job interviews.

What are the civil service tests like? Different kinds of tests are given for different types of jobs. Most civil service tests are "paper-and-pencil" multiple-choice exams. If you are applying for typing, word processing, or secretarial jobs, also take a typing skills test, usually on a PC. Except for typing skills, most of these tests are not speed tests.

The tests are usually graded by computer. All questions on a test are valued equally; no question counts more than any other. Passing grades range from 70–99. The number of questions you must answer correctly to pass depends on the kind of test you're taking, but on most, you must answer 60–70 percent of the questions correctly to pass.

The typing skills test given to secretarial job applicants is graded for speed and accuracy. To pass the skills test, you must type at least 40 wpm, after penalties for errors. You would normally subtract 1 wpm for each error. The faster and more accurately you type, the higher your score will be. The results of this test, combined with your multiple-choice test score determines your final grade.

It takes about two weeks for you to receive your grade. Once that grade is issued to you, your name goes on the "register" to be referred for vacancies. Your grade notice will tell you when your grade expires—usually in about a year. Permanent state employee grades do not expire, but if there is a significant change in the test, the grade will be cancelled.

If you want to retake the test, you must wait six months, except in cases where tests are specifically exempt from this rule. You should be cautious, however. If you retake the test, your new score will replace the old score, regardless of which grade is higher.

FEDERAL TESTING

Exam Selection Procedure

Examinations for clerical jobs are administered by individual federal agencies when they are ready to hire. Sometimes examinations will be announced and administered for all clerical occupations at one time; in other cases, separate examinations for specific jobs are announced. See Appendix A at the back of this book for more specific information. Clerical examinations are given frequently because of the large number of available jobs.

Selection Requirements

Selection requirements for the clerical occupations in the Federal Government are based on studies of the training, experience, and skills required for successful job performance at the different grade levels. Job applicants must meet the education or experience requirements, show evidence of having the required skills, and, for entry at GS-2 through 4 (GS-3 through 5 for clerk-stenographers), pass a job-related written test.

RATINGS

Applicants who meet the minimum experience and education requirements and skill levels are given numerical ratings based on their written test scores. Applicants must pass the written test in order to receive a rating. Qualified veterans of the military service have 5–10 points added to their qualifying ratings.

WRITTEN TESTS

The written tests for clerical occupations measure the verbal and clerical skills needed for success in these jobs. In general, the same written test battery is used for all clerical jobs except data transcriber and sales store checker. This battery consists of two tests: a Verbal Tasks Test and a Clerical Tasks Test.

Because of these possible differences in requirements, you should check the specific examination announcement for each position in which you are interested to confirm the type of test battery you will have to take.

As long as a modified examination was not used, once you have passed the written test you do not have to take it again to apply for other clerical jobs. Nor do you have to reestablish that you meet the minimum experience or education requirements, or that you have the required skills. (However, your rating can expire after a certain period of time; if it does, the expiration date will be shown on the rating form.)

Skill Requirements

- When a job requires typing skill, you must be able to type accurately at 40 words per minute.

- When dictation skill is required, you must be able to transcribe dictation accurately at 80 words per minute. GS-2 data transcribers must be able to type accurately at 20 words per minute, and GS-3 and GS-4 data transcribers must be able to type accurately at 25 words per minute.

- Stenographer applicants may use any system of taking and transcribing dictation they wish.

Skill requirements may be measured in several different ways. The most frequently used method is the proficiency certificate. These certificates may be issued by schools and other authorized training organizations and by some state employment services. If this is the case, you are told where to obtain a certificate if you do not already have one. Applicants with proficiency certificates usually do not have to take further tests to demonstrate their skill levels.

Another method that is sometimes used is self-certification by applicants. In this process, an applicant signs a statement that he or she meets the skill requirements for the job. Agencies usually require applicants who have self-certified their skills to take a performance test before they are hired.

The Federal Clerical Examination

The Federal Clerical Examination consists of two separately timed sections, a Verbal Tasks Test and a Clerical Tasks Test. A few agencies and occupations are exempt from some of the standard regulations governing federal hiring in the civil service. In these cases, jobs do not have to be listed on USAJobs, and applicants may have to fill out different forms or follow different procedures than usual. Excepted-service agencies include those in the legislative and judicial branches of the federal government, as well as several agencies in the executive branch.

The Federal Verbal Tasks Test

WHAT THE TEST IS ABOUT

The Verbal Tasks Test includes questions in spelling, meaning, and relationship of words; recognition of sentences that are grammatically correct; and reading, understanding, and using written material.

These test tasks relate to a variety of job tasks, such as proofreading and correcting typed copy, using instruction manuals, organizing new files of related materials, and carrying out written instructions.

The test includes 85 questions—25 on word meaning, 20 on word relationships, 20 on spelling, 10 on grammar, and 10 on reading. Each page of the test has a few questions of each type. For each question, you will select the best answer from among a set of suggested answers.

HOW THE TEST IS ADMINISTERED

Each applicant receives a copy of the test booklet with sample questions and an answer sheet. You are allowed three minutes to study the directions and answer the sample questions. You then use a separate answer sheet for recording answers to the test. Exactly 35 minutes are allowed for the test.

Here are official directions and sample questions. You may allow yourself more than three minutes to study these now, since you are not actually in a testing situation.

EXERCISE 1

Sample Answer Sheet

1. Ⓐ Ⓑ Ⓒ Ⓓ Ⓔ   3. Ⓐ Ⓑ Ⓒ Ⓓ Ⓔ   5. Ⓐ Ⓑ Ⓒ Ⓓ Ⓔ
2. Ⓐ Ⓑ Ⓒ Ⓓ Ⓔ   4. Ⓐ Ⓑ Ⓒ Ⓓ Ⓔ

Directions: Study the sample questions carefully. Each question has four suggested answers. Decide which one is the best answer. Find the question number on the Sample Answer Sheet. Show your answer to the question by darkening completely the space corresponding to the letter that is the same as the letter of your answer. Keep your mark within the space. If you have to erase a mark, be sure to erase it completely. Darken only one answer for each question. Do NOT darken space (E) for any question.

1. *Previous* means most nearly

   (A) abandoned
   (B) former
   (C) timely
   (D) younger

2. Just as the procedure of a collection department must be clear-cut and definite, the steps being taken with the sureness of a skilled chess player, so the various paragraphs of a collection letter must show clear organization, giving evidence of a mind that, from the beginning, has had a specific end in view.

   The paragraph best supports the statement that a collection letter should always

   (A) show a spirit of sportsmanship
   (B) be divided into several paragraphs
   (C) be brief, but courteous
   (D) be carefully planned

3. Decide which sentence is preferable with respect to grammar and usage for a formal letter or report.

   (A) They do not ordinarily present these kind of reports in detail like this.
   (B) A report of this kind is not hardly ever given in such detail as this one.
   (C) This report is more detailed than what such reports ordinarily are.
   (D) A report of this kind is not ordinarily presented in this much detail.

4. Find the correct spelling of the word and darken the proper answer space. If no suggested spelling is correct, darken space (D).

   (A) athalete
   (B) athelete
   (C) athlete
   (D) none of these

5. SPEEDOMETER is related to POINTER as WATCH is related to

   (A) case
   (B) hands
   (C) dial
   (D) numerals

exercises

ANSWER KEY AND EXPLANATIONS

1. B	2. D	3. D	4. C	5. B

1. **The correct answer is (B)** Word meaning questions consist of one given word followed by four different words labeled (A), (B), (C), and (D). You are to select the word which has the closest meaning to the word given in the question. It may help if you remember that you are looking for the best match among the choices given, but not necessarily a perfect match.

   Answering these questions depends upon your knowledge of vocabulary, but here are some tips if you do not recognize the correct answer immediately.

   - If you have a general idea about what the given word means but are having trouble choosing an answer, try using the word in a short sentence. Then substitute each of the answer choices in the same sentence to see which one seems to best fit the sentence.

   - Try to break the given word into parts to see whether the suffix (ending) or the prefix (beginning) of the word gives a clue about its meaning.

   You could have used the above tips to answer sample question 1. The correct answer to this question is choice (B), "former." If you did not know the meaning of "previous" but you remembered that the prefix "pre" usually means "before," that clue could help you to select choice (B) as the correct answer.

2. **The correct answer is (D).** The reading questions consist of a paragraph followed by four statements. Read the paragraph first, then select the one statement which is based on information given in the paragraph.

   - Do not worry if you are unfamiliar with the subject discussed in the paragraph. You do not need to have any knowledge about the subject of the paragraph, since the answer to the question is always given in the paragraph itself.

   - Do not worry about whether the correct statement or any of the incorrect statements are true. The important thing is that the correct answer is the only statement that says the same thing as is said in the paragraph. Some of the other statements may be true, but they are not based on the content of the paragraph.

   - To select the correct statement, first eliminate choices which clearly conflict with the paragraph. Then, if you still have two or more choices, look for the specific section of the paragraph that covers the information given in each one of the choices.

   - Compare the given facts carefully, until you can eliminate the remaining incorrect choices.

   For sample question 2, choice (D) is correct because it is the only choice that states the basic point made in the paragraph. Choice (A) is meant to draw attention if you did not read the paragraph carefully and remembered only that chess, which is similar to a sport, is mentioned. Choice (B) would draw attention because the word "paragraphs" is mentioned; however, the reading paragraph did not specify that a collection letter should have any particular number of paragraphs. Similarly, the reading paragraph did not say anything about being brief or courteous, so choice (C) is incorrect.

3. **The correct answer is (D).** Grammar questions give four versions of a single sentence. Each sentence expresses the same thought, but only one of them is grammatically correct.

- Most of the incorrect sentences are obviously poorly constructed.

- Others have such errors as using singular verbs with plural nouns.

- In the more difficult questions, pay attention to smaller details, like the misuse of punctuation, which can make a sentence very difficult to understand.

To answer these questions, first eliminate the sentences you are sure are incorrect. Then compare the remaining ones until you can choose one as being more correct than the others.

- It is possible that one sentence will seem to be correct because it uses the same informal grammar that people often use when talking. However, this type of sentence structure is not suitable for writing.

In sample question 3, choice (D) is correct. Choice (A) uses the plurals "these" and "reports" with the singular "kind." Choice (B) uses "not hardly ever" instead of the correct "never." Choice (C) inappropriately inserts "what" into the sentence.

4. **The correct answer is (C).** Spelling questions give three spellings of a common word, labeled (A), (B), and (C). Each question also offers the option of "none of these" as choice (D). You must decide which one of the three given spellings is correct or whether none of them is correct.

- Sometimes it helps to answer these questions by looking away from the given choices and writing the word yourself on the margin of your test booklet. Then check to see whether the spelling you believe is correct is one of the choices.

In sample question 4, choice (C) is correct.

5. **The correct answer is (B).** Word relationship questions give two words that are related in some way, and then give the first word of a second word relationship which you are to complete. You are given four choices to complete that relationship. The correct choice is the word that completes that relationship in the way most similar to the relationship in the first pair of words.

To answer these questions, look at the first pair of words and decide what the relationship is between the words. Then choose the answer that best completes that same relationship for the second pair of words.

- Remember that the correct answer completes an analogous relationship, not because it is about the same subject as the first pair of words.

For sample question 5, consider what a pointer does on a speedometer. It is used to indicate speed at a particular moment. A watch uses hands, choice (B), for the same general function. Choice (A) is incorrect because the watch case has nothing to do with this function. Choices (C) and (D) are wrong because, although the dial and the numerals are involved indicating the time, they do not perform the specific function that the hand does.

The Federal Clerical Tasks Test

WHAT THE TEST IS ABOUT

The Clerical Tasks Test is a test of speed and accuracy in completing four clerical tasks. You have 120 questions to answer within a short time. The test contains 30 questions on name and number checking, 30 on arranging names in correct alphabetical order, 30 on simple arithmetic, and 30 on inspecting groups of letters and numbers. The questions are arranged in groups or cycles of five questions of each type.

HOW THE TEST IS ADMINISTERED

Each applicant receives a copy of the test booklet with sample questions and an answer sheet. You are allowed ten minutes to study the directions and answer the sample questions printed on the two pages.

Use the separate answer sheet for recording answers to the test. Exactly 15 minutes are allowed for this test.

HOW TO ANSWER THE TEST QUESTIONS

Directions for answering all four types of questions on the Clerical Tasks Test are provided with the sample questions. Below is additional specific information on how to answer each type of question Look first at the sample questions on the test and then study the information here until you understand how to answer the questions. (Here, you do not have to limit yourself to the ten minutes allowed in the actual test situation.)

The Clerical Tasks Test is a test of speed in carrying out these relatively simple clerical tasks, so you should work quickly. However, the test also measures accuracy, and you are penalized for wrong answers in the total test score. This means you need to be careful as you work and that wild guessing is not a good idea. Do not be so concerned about accuracy that you work more slowly than you should. Remember that both speed and accuracy are important to achieve a good score.

The question types in this test appear on each page of the test. You may find it easier to answer all questions of one type rather than switching from one question type to another. This is perfectly acceptable, but take extra caution when filling in answers on the answer sheet.

EXERCISE 2

Sample Answer Sheet

1. Ⓐ Ⓑ Ⓒ Ⓓ Ⓔ　　　7. Ⓐ Ⓑ Ⓒ Ⓓ Ⓔ　　　12. Ⓐ Ⓑ Ⓒ Ⓓ Ⓔ
2. Ⓐ Ⓑ Ⓒ Ⓓ Ⓔ　　　8. Ⓐ Ⓑ Ⓒ Ⓓ Ⓔ　　　13. Ⓐ Ⓑ Ⓒ Ⓓ Ⓔ
3. Ⓐ Ⓑ Ⓒ Ⓓ Ⓔ　　　9. Ⓐ Ⓑ Ⓒ Ⓓ Ⓔ　　　14. Ⓐ Ⓑ Ⓒ Ⓓ Ⓔ
4. Ⓐ Ⓑ Ⓒ Ⓓ Ⓔ　　　10. Ⓐ Ⓑ Ⓒ Ⓓ Ⓔ　　　15. Ⓐ Ⓑ Ⓒ Ⓓ Ⓔ
5. Ⓐ Ⓑ Ⓒ Ⓓ Ⓔ　　　11. Ⓐ Ⓑ Ⓒ Ⓓ Ⓔ　　　16. Ⓐ Ⓑ Ⓒ Ⓓ Ⓔ
6. Ⓐ Ⓑ Ⓒ Ⓓ Ⓔ

This exercise contains four kinds of questions. There are some of each kind of question on each page in the booklet. The time limit for the test will be announced by the examiner.

If you finish the sample questions before you are told to turn to the test, it is a good idea to study the code given above for (A), (B), (C), (D), and (E). This code is repeated on every page.

Directions: In each line across the page there are three names, addresses, or codes that are very much alike. Compare the three and decide which ones are EXACTLY alike. On your answer sheet, mark:

(A) if **ALL THREE** names, addresses, or codes are exactly **ALIKE**
(B) if only the **FIRST** and **SECOND** names, addresses, or codes are exactly **ALIKE**
(C) if only the **FIRST** and **THIRD** names, addresses, or codes are exactly **ALIKE**
(D) if only the **SECOND** and **THIRD** names, addresses, or codes are exactly **ALIKE**
(E) if **ALL THREE** names, addresses, or codes are **DIFFERENT**

1. Davis Hazen　　　David Hozen　　　David Hazen
2. Lois Appel　　　Lois Appel　　　Lois Apfel
3. June Allan　　　Jane Allan　　　Jane Allan
4. 10235　　　10235　　　10235
5. 32614　　　32164　　　32614

Directions: For each question there is a name, number, or code in a box at the left and four other names, numbers, or codes in alphabetical or numerical order at the right. Find the correct space for the boxed name or number so that it will be in alphabetical and/or numerical order with the others and darken the answer space of your choice on your answer sheet.

6. | Jones, Jane |

(A) →
      Goodyear, G. L.
(B) →
      Haddon, Harry
(C) →
      Jackson, Mary
(D) →
      Jenkins, William
(E) →

7. | Kessler, Neilson |

(A) →
      Kessel, Carl
(B) →
      Kessinger, D. J.
(C) →
      Kessler, Karl
(D) →
      Kessner, Lewis
(E) →

Directions: In the following questions, solve each problem and find your answer among the list of suggested answers for that question. Choose (A), (B), (C), or (D) for the answer you obtained: or if your answer is not among these, darken (E) for that question.

8. Add: 22
        +33

(A) 44
(B) 45
(C) 54
(D) 55
(E) none of these

9. Subtract: 24
            − 3

(A) 20
(B) 21
(C) 27
(D) 29
(E) none of these

10. Multiply: 25
             × 5

(A) 100
(B) 115
(C) 125
(D) 135
(E) none of these

11. Divide: 6)126

(A) 20
(B) 22
(C) 24
(D) 26
(E) none of these

Directions: Find which suggested answer contains numbers and letters all of which appear in the question. If no suggested answer fits, darken (E) for that question.

12. 8 N S 9 G T 4 6
13. T 9 7 Z 6 L 3 K
14. Z 7 G K 3 9 8 N
15. 3 K 9 4 6 G Z L
16. Z N 7 3 8 K T 9

Suggested Answers

(A) = 7, 9, G, K
(B) = 8, 9, T, Z
(C) = 6, 7, K, Z
(D) = 6, S, G, T
(E) = none of these

ANSWER KEY AND EXPLANATIONS

1. E	5. C	8. D	11. E	14. A
2. B	6. E	9. B	12. D	15. E
3. D	7. D	10. C	13. C	16. B
4. A				

Sample Questions 1–5. Memorizing the answer choices for this question type may be helpful in increasing your speed. In these questions, you compare three names or numbers and decide which are exactly alike. You then select your answer from a set of choices that describe whether all of them, some of them, or none of them are alike. These choices are labeled (A), (B), (C), (D), and (E) and are given at the top of the first page of the Sample Questions for the Clerical Tasks Test and are repeated on each page of the test booklet.

- These choices remain the same for all questions of this type in the test, so if you memorize them, you can save them when choosing your answers.

Sample Questions 6–7. For the alphabetizing questions, remember that the most important rule for putting the names in order is to consider each letter in the complete last name in strict alphabetical order, exactly as it appears.

- This is true even when the name includes more than one capital letter (as in DeLong), or involves prefixes which may be spelled differently in different names (as in McDuff and MacDuff).

- Ignore punctuation, such as apostrophes and hyphens, that appear in a name (as in O'Hara).

- When two last names are identical in every way, then alphabetize according to the first and second names given, following the same rules.

Sample Questions 8–11. The key to the arithmetic questions is to avoid careless errors. Remember that the correct answer may not be included as one of the given alternatives. In this case, you would darken choice (E) on the answer sheet.

- Answers will always be exact (no decimal places), so if the answer you get is not exact, work the problem again.

Sample Questions 12–16. There are several different ways of approaching the letter and number inspection questions. You should use the method that works best for you.

One method is to work from the answer choices to the questions. Look at each answer choice and, one at a time, compare each letter or number it contains with the question until you can accept or reject it. Here is how you would use this method to answer Sample Question 12:

- Start by looking at the first number given in choice (A), which is a 7.

- Quickly scan question 12 for this number. Since it does not include a 7, choice (A) can be rejected.

- Next consider the first letter in choice (B), which is an 8. Scanning question 12 confirms that an 8 is present. Moving on to the next number in choice (B), the number 9, scanning of the question confirms its presence also, as well as the next letter in choice (B), the letter T. There is no Z, however, so choice (B) is then rejected.

- Using the same process of elimination for choice (C), no number 7 is found, and this choice is rejected.

- One by one, all of the letters and numbers in choice (D) are found, so choice (D) is marked as correct on the separate answer sheet.

- If all the letters and numbers in choice (D) do not appear in question 12, then choice (E), "none of these," would be the correct answer.

You may be able to save time using this method by scanning for two of the given letters or numbers at one time.

Another method is to look at the particular question and quickly and memorize all the numbers and letters it contains. Then, glance at each choice to select the one that is a good possibility based on your memory of the numbers and letters.

- Carefully double-check this choice with each of the numbers and letters given in the question.

- If you use this method, be sure to spend only a few seconds memorizing the numbers and letters in the question, or you will waste too much time on each question.

Whichever method you choose, remember that any of the answer choices may be used to answer more than one of the five questions included in the set on each page. Also, note that the letters and numbers in the answer choices and questions do not have to be in the same order. Finally, unlike the situation for the first five sample questions on the Clerical Tasks Test, the answer choices for these questions do not remain the same throughout the test. Therefore, it will not help you to memorize any of the answer choices for with these sample questions.

Exam 710—Sample Questions for Clerk-Typist and Clerk-Stenographer

The following questions are samples of the types of questions that will be used on Examination 710. Study these questions carefully. Each question has several suggested answers. You are to decide which one is the *best answer*. Next, on the Sample Answer Sheet, find the answer space that is numbered the same number as the question, then darken the space that is lettered the same as the answer you have selected.

EXERCISE 3

1. (A) (B) (C) (D) (E)   9. (A) (B) (C) (D) (E)   16. (A) (B) (C) (D) (E)
2. (A) (B) (C) (D) (E)   10. (A) (B) (C) (D) (E)   17. (A) (B) (C) (D) (E)
3. (A) (B) (C) (D) (E)   11. (A) (B) (C) (D) (E)   18. (A) (B) (C) (D) (E)
4. (A) (B) (C) (D) (E)   12. (A) (B) (C) (D) (E)   19. (A) (B) (C) (D) (E)
5. (A) (B) (C) (D) (E)   13. (A) (B) (C) (D) (E)   20. (A) (B) (C) (D) (E)
6. (A) (B) (C) (D) (E)   14. (A) (B) (C) (D) (E)   21. (A) (B) (C) (D) (E)
7. (A) (B) (C) (D) (E)   15. (A) (B) (C) (D) (E)   22. (A) (B) (C) (D) (E)
8. (A) (B) (C) (D) (E)

CLERICAL APTITUDE

Directions: For each question there is a name, number, or code in a box at the left and four other names, numbers, or codes in alphabetical or numerical order at the right. Find the correct space for the boxed name or number so that it will be in alphabetical and/or numerical order with the others and darken the answer space of your choice on your answer sheet.

1. | Roggen, Sam |

(A) →
Rogers, Arthur L.
(B) →
Roghani, Fada
(C) →
Rogovin, H.T.
(D) →
Rogowski, Marie R.
(E) →

2. | 05076012 |

(A) →
05076004
(B) →
05076007
(C) →
05076010
(D) →
05076021
(E) →

3. | CBA—1875 |

(A) →
CAA—1720
(B) →
CAB—1819
(C) →
CAC—1804
(D) →
CAD—1402
(E) →

Directions: In each line across the page there are three names, addresses, or codes that are very much alike. Compare the three and decide which ones are EXACTLY alike. On your answer sheet, mark:

    (A)   if **ALL THREE** names, addresses, or codes are exactly **ALIKE**
    (B)   if only the **FIRST** and **SECOND** names, addresses, or codes are exactly **ALIKE**
    (C)   if only the **FIRST** and **THIRD** names, addresses, or codes are exactly **ALIKE**
    (D)   if only the **SECOND** and **THIRD** names, addresses, or codes are exactly **ALIKE**
    (E)   if **ALL THREE** names, addresses, or codes are **DIFFERENT**

4.	Helene Bedell	Helene Beddell	Helene Beddell
5.	E T. Wedemeyer	F T. Wedemeyer	E T. Wedmeyer
6.	3214 W Beaumont St.	3214 Beaumount St.	3214 Beaumont St.
7.	BC 3105T-5	BC 3015T-5	BC 3105T-5
8.	4460327	4460327	4460327

Directions: Choose the word that is correctly spelled and darken its letter on your answer sheet.

9.   **(A)**   accomodate
     (B)   acommodate
     (C)   accommadate
     (D)   none of the above

10. **(A)**   manageble
     (B)   manageable
     (C)   manegeable
     (D)   none of the above

Directions: In the following questions, solve each problem and find your answer among the list of suggested answers for that question. Choose (A), (B), (C), or (D) for the answer you obtained, or if your answer is not among these, darken (E) for that question.

11. $32 + 26 =$

    (A) 69
    (B) 59
    (C) 58
    (D) 54
    (E) none of the above

12. $57 - 15 =$

    (A) 72
    (B) 62
    (C) 54
    (D) 44
    (E) none of the above

13. $23 \times 7 =$

    (A) 164
    (B) 161
    (C) 154
    (D) 141
    (E) none of the above

14. $160/5 =$

    (A) 32
    (B) 30
    (C) 25
    (D) 21
    (E) none of the above

exercises

VERBAL ABILITY

Questions 15–17 test your ability to follow instructions.

Directions: Each question directs you to mark a specific number and letter combination on your Sample Answer Sheet. The questions require your total concentration because the answers that you are instructed to darken are, for the most part, NOT in numerical sequence (i.e., you would not use number 1 on your answer sheet to answer question 1; number 2 for question 2; etc.). Darken the number and space specifically designated in each test question.

15. Look at the letters below. Draw a circle around the middle letter. Now, on your Sample Answer Sheet, find number 16 and darken the space for the letter you just circled.

 R   C   H

16. Draw a line under the number shown below that is more than 10 but less than 20. Find that number on your Sample Answer Sheet and darken space A.

 5   9   17   22

17. Add the numbers 11 and 4 and write your answer on the blank line below. Now find this number on your Sample Answer Sheet and darken the space for the second letter in the alphabet.

 _____

Answer the remaining test questions on the Sample Answer Sheet in numerical sequence (i.e., number 18 on the Sample Answer Sheet for question 18; number 19 for question 19, etc.).

Directions: Choose the sentence below that is most appropriate in grammar, usage, and punctuation for a business letter or report. Darken its letter on your answer sheet.

18. **(A)** He should of responded to the letter by now.
 (B) A response to the letter by the end of the week.
 (C) The letter required his immediate response.
 (D) A response by him to the letter is necessary.

Directions: Questions 19–20 consist of a sentence containing a word in boldface type. Choose the best meaning for the word in **boldface** type and darken its letter on the your answer sheet.

19. The payment was **authorized** yesterday. **Authorized** most nearly means

(A) expected
(B) approved
(C) refunded
(D) received

20. Please **delete** the second paragraph. **Delete** most nearly means

(A) type
(B) read
(C) edit
(D) omit

Directions: In questions 21–22 below, read each paragraph and answer the question that follows it by darkening the letter of the correct answer on your answer sheet.

21. Window Clerks working for the Postal Service have direct financial responsibility for the selling of postage. In addition, they are expected to have a thorough knowledge concerning the acceptability of all material offered by customers for mailing. Any information provided to the public by these employees must be completely accurate.

The paragraph best supports the statement that Window Clerks

(A) must account for the stamps issued to them for sale.
(B) have had long training in other Postal Service jobs.
(C) must help sort mail to be delivered by carriers.
(D) inspect the contents of all packages offered for mailing.

22. The most efficient method for performing a task is not always easily determined. That which is economical in terms of time must be carefully distinguished from that which is economical in terms of expended energy. In short, the quickest method may require a degree of physical effort that may be neither essential nor desirable.

The paragraph best supports the statement that

(A) it is more efficient to perform a task slowly than rapidly.
(B) skill in performing a task should not be acquired at the expense of time.
(C) the most efficient execution of a task is not always the one done in the shortest time.
(D) energy and time cannot both be considered in the performance of a single task.

exercises

ANSWER KEY

1. B	6. E	11. C	15. B	19. B
2. D	7. C	12. E	16. C	20. D
3. E	8. A	13. B	17. A	21. A
4. D	9. D	14. A	18. C	22. C
5. E	10. B			

Exam 711—Sample Questions for Clerk-Stenographer

Only stenographer competitors take a stenography test. The sample passage on the next page shows the length of material dictated. Sit down with your pencil and notebook.

INSTRUCTIONS FOR DICTATION

Directions: Have someone dictate the sample passage to you. It should take 3 minutes. Take notes on your own paper.

Directions to person dictating: This practice dictation should be dictated at the rate of 80 words a minute. Each pair of lines is dictated in 10 seconds. Do not dictate the punctuation except for periods, but dictate with the expression the punctuation indicates. Use a watch with a second hand to enable you to read the exercise at the proper speed. Turn the page to begin.

DICTATION

3 MINUTES

> **Directions to the person dictating:** Exactly on a minute start dictating. Finish reading each two lines at the number of seconds indicated below.

I realize that this practice dictation	
is not a part of the examination	10 sec.
proper and is not to be scored. (Period)	
When making a study of the private	20 sec.
pension structure and its influence on	
turnover, the most striking feature is its	30 sec.
youth. (Period) As has been shown, the time	
of greatest growth began just a few years	40 sec.
ago. (Period) The influence that this	
growth has had on the labor market and	50 sec.
worker attitudes is hard to assess,	
partly because the effects have not yet fully	1 min.
evolved and many are still in the	
growing stage. (Period) Even so, most pension	10 sec.
plans began with much more limited gains	
than they give now. (Period) For example,	20 sec.
as private plans mature they grant	
a larger profit and a greater range of gains to	30 sec.
more workers and thereby become more	
important. (Period) Plans that protect accrued pension	40 sec.
credits are rather new and are being	
revised in the light of past trends. (Period)	50 sec.
As informal and formal information on pension	
plans spreads, the workers become more	2 min.
aware of the plans and their provisions	
increase. (Period) Their impact on employee attitudes	10 sec.
and decisions will no doubt become	
stronger. (Period) Each year, more and more workers	20 sec.
will be retiring with a private pension,	
and their firsthand knowledge of the benefits to	30 sec.
be gained from private pensions will spread	
to still active workers. (Period) Thus, workers	40 sec.
may less often view pensions as just	
another part of the security package	50 sec.
based on service and more often	
see them as unique benefits. (Period)	3 min.

After dictating the test, pause for 15 seconds to permit the test-taker to complete notetaking.

EXERCISE 4

1. Ⓐ Ⓑ Ⓒ Ⓓ Ⓔ   10. Ⓐ Ⓑ Ⓒ Ⓓ Ⓔ   18. Ⓐ Ⓑ Ⓒ Ⓓ Ⓔ
2. Ⓐ Ⓑ Ⓒ Ⓓ Ⓔ   11. Ⓐ Ⓑ Ⓒ Ⓓ Ⓔ   19. Ⓐ Ⓑ Ⓒ Ⓓ Ⓔ
3. Ⓐ Ⓑ Ⓒ Ⓓ Ⓔ   12. Ⓐ Ⓑ Ⓒ Ⓓ Ⓔ   20. Ⓐ Ⓑ Ⓒ Ⓓ Ⓔ
4. Ⓐ Ⓑ Ⓒ Ⓓ Ⓔ   13. Ⓐ Ⓑ Ⓒ Ⓓ Ⓔ   21. Ⓐ Ⓑ Ⓒ Ⓓ Ⓔ
5. Ⓐ Ⓑ Ⓒ Ⓓ Ⓔ   14. Ⓐ Ⓑ Ⓒ Ⓓ Ⓔ   22. Ⓐ Ⓑ Ⓒ Ⓓ Ⓔ
6. Ⓐ Ⓑ Ⓒ Ⓓ Ⓔ   15. Ⓐ Ⓑ Ⓒ Ⓓ Ⓔ   23. Ⓐ Ⓑ Ⓒ Ⓓ Ⓔ
7. Ⓐ Ⓑ Ⓒ Ⓓ Ⓔ   16. Ⓐ Ⓑ Ⓒ Ⓓ Ⓔ   24. Ⓐ Ⓑ Ⓒ Ⓓ Ⓔ
8. Ⓐ Ⓑ Ⓒ Ⓓ Ⓔ   17. Ⓐ Ⓑ Ⓒ Ⓓ Ⓔ   25. Ⓐ Ⓑ Ⓒ Ⓓ Ⓔ
9. Ⓐ Ⓑ Ⓒ Ⓓ Ⓔ

This transcript and word list for part of the dictation are similar to those each competitor will receive for the dictation test. Many words have been omitted from the transcript. Compare your notes with it. When you come to a blank space in the transcript, decide what word (or words) belongs there. Look for the missing word in the word list. Notice what letter (A), (B), (C), or (D) is printed beside the word. Write that letter in the blank. Choice (B) is written in blank 1 to show how you are to record your choice. Write (E) if the exact answer is not in the word list. You may also write the word (or words) or the shorthand for it, if you wish. The same choice may belong in more than one blank.

ALPHABETIC WORD LIST

a — (D)
attitudes — (C)
be — (B)
been — (C)
began — (D)
being — (A)
completely — (A)
examination — (A)
examine — (B)
examining — (D)
feat — (A)
feature — (C)
full — (B)
fully — (D)
greater — (D)
grow — (B)
growing — (C)
had — (D)
has — (C)
has been — (B)
has had — (A)
has made — (A)
in — (C)
in part — (B)
influence — (A)
labor — (C)
main — (B)

make — (A)
making — (B)
market — (B)
markets — (D)
marking — (D)
never — (B)
not — (D)
over — (C)
part — (C)
partly — (D)
pension — (C)
practical — (C)
practice — (B)
private — (D)
proper — (C)
section — (D)
so — (B)
still — (A)
structure — (D)
structured — (B)
to — (D)
to be — (C)
trial — (A)
turn — (D)
turnover — (B)
values — (A)
yet — (C)

TRANSCRIPT

I realize that this __B__ dictation is _____ a
                           1   2
_____ of the _____ _____ and is _____
 3   4   5   6
_____ scored.
 7

    When _____ a _____ of the _____
             8   9   10
_____ _____ and its _____ on _____, the
 11   12   13   14
most striking _____ is its youth. As _____
           15   16
shown, the time of _____ growth began just a
              17
few years ago. The _____ that this growth
              18
_____ on the labor _____ and worker _____
 19   20   21
is hard to assess, _____ because the effects
            22
have not yet _____ evolved and many are
           23
_____ in the _____ stage. . . .
 24   25

(For the next sentences, you would receive another word list in the actual test, if the entire sample dictation were transcribed.)

You will be given an answer sheet like the sample. This allows your answers to be scored by machine. Each number on the answer sheet stands for the blank with the same number in the transcript. Darken the space for the letter that is the same as the letter you wrote in the transcript. If you have not finished writing letters in the blanks in the transcript, or if you wish to make sure you have lettered them correctly, you may continue to use your notes after you begin marking the answer sheet.

ANSWER KEY

1. B	6. D	11. C	16. B	21. C
2. D	7. C	12. D	17. E	22. D
3. C	8. B	13. A	18. A	23. D
4. A	9. E	14. B	19. A	24. A
5. C	10. D	15. C	20. B	25. C

answers exercises

Exam 712—Sample Typing Test

A mastery of good typing skills is a basic prerequisite for working as a clerk-typist, clerk-stenographer, and mark-up clerk, automated. While the score on the written exam determines your position on the list, you must also demonstrate that your typing proficiency satisfies the speed and accuracy requirements mandated for the work position involved.

Assuming that you already know how to type, the best preparation for the Clerk-Typist and Clerk-Stenographer Typing Test—or indeed for any typing test—is typing. You may choose any material at all and practice copying it line for line, exactly as you see it. As on the actual typing test, spell, capitalize, punctuate, and begin and end lines exactly as they appear on the page being copied. The actual basic speed required on typing tests varies from 35 wpm to 50 wpm, depending on the job itself. Once you meet the minimum speed, accuracy counts even more than speed. Try to balance yourself to meet speed requirements while maintaining a very high level of accuracy.

The proctor will distribute a practice exercise. In any typing test situation, the proctor will give you five minutes to practice copying a paragraph. This give you the chance to limber up your fingers and to gain familiarity with the testing keyboard. The practice exercise will not count.

The following is a typical test exercise, though NOT the actual test exercise that you will be given. Follow instructions exactly—and practice, practice, practice. Words-per-minute points are marked on the test exercise for your guidance. Try to keep your typing error-free; if you make errors, try to increase your speed. Use an accurate signal timer or have a friend or relative time you.

Space, paragraph, spell, punctuate, capitalize, and begin and end each line precisely as shown in the exercise.

You will have exactly five minutes in which to make repeated copies of the test exercise itself. Each time you complete the exercise, simply double-space once and begin again. Keep on typing until told to stop.

Keep in mind that you must meet minimum standards in both speed and accuracy and that, above these standards, accuracy is twice as important as speed.

EXERCISE 5

Directions: In the examination you will have five minutes in which to make copies of the test exercise, keeping in mind that your eligibility will depend on accuracy as well as speed. When you complete the exercise, simply double space and begin again.

TEST EXERCISE

	1st typing of exercise	2nd typing of exercise
Because they have often learned to know types of archi-	_____	52 wpm
tecture by decoration, casual observers sometimes fail to	_____	54
realize that the significant part of a structure is not the	_____	56
ornamentation but the body itself. Architecture, because	_____	59
of its close contact with human lives, is peculiarly and	_____	61
intimately governed by climate. For instance, a home built	_____	64
for comfort in the cold and snow of the northern areas of	_____	66
this country would be unbearably warm in a country with	_____	68
weather such as that of Cuba. A Cuban house, with its open	_____	71
court, would prove impossible to heat in a northern winter.	_____	73
Since the purpose of architecture is the construction of	_____	76
shelters in which human beings may carry on their numerous	_____	78
activities, the designer must consider not only climatic con-	_____	80
ditions, but also the function of a building. Thus, although	_____	_____
the climate of a certain locality requires that an auditorium	_____	_____
and a hospital have several features in common, the purposes	_____	_____
for which they will be used demand some difference in struc-	40 wpm	
ture. For centuries builders have first complied with these	42	_____
two requirements and later added whatever ornamentation they	44	_____
wished. Logically, we should see as mere additions, not as	47	_____
basic parts, the details by which we identify architecture.	49	_____

Each time you reach this point, double-space once and begin again.

Exam 715—Sample Questions for Mark-up Clerk, Automated

The Postal Service does not issue official sample questions for Exam 715.

Exam 715, the typing test for Mark-up Clerk applicants, is quite different from an ordinary typing test. You will take this test by private appointment, and all interaction will be between you and a computer. Even if you have had no experience whatsoever with computers, this is not an intimidating test. The computer program is very specific in spelling out directions. And, unless you are a typing whiz, the typing test itself is probably easier than a plain paper copying test.

As Exam 715 begins, the computer screen explains to you which buttons you will be using and what each does. You need to use very few buttons—letters, numbers, "return," "delete," and "lock caps." You will get a chance to use these and to become familiar with their operation as you fill in basic name and social security number types of information. A test administrator remains in the room to answer questions.

The computer then explains the typing task of the exam itself. A letter-number code appears on the upper right screen; you are to copy it, then press the return button to bring the next code to the screen. That's it. The codes all consist of four letters and three numbers, such as TYHO346 or BZIP801. The faster you type, the more codes you have an opportunity to copy. In the explanation phase of the exam, you will have 15 seconds in which to copy five codes. The computer will tell you how many you copied correctly.

After the explanation phase comes a practice session. You will be allowed five minutes to copy as many codes as you can correctly, again one at a time. The five-minute practice session does not count. This is your chance to experiment with looking at your fingers or at the screen; with memorizing each code to be typed, or with staring at the code while typing; with typing as fast as you can, not even looking at the screen to see if you are typing correctly; or with checking to make sure you are copying correctly and repairing errors before continuing.

Be aware that an error that has been corrected on the computer is not counted as an error. Since accuracy is so important and since correction is so easy on the computer, it is worthwhile to correct errors. Unless you are extremely inaccurate, you will not lose much time correcting errors and will gain valuable points through accuracy.

Here is a suggested approach:

1. Look at the code and quickly memorize it; four letters and three numbers should pose no problem for such a short-term task.

2. Type in the code, looking at the center of the screen where the letters and numbers that you are typing appear.

3. Delete and retype if you spot an error.

4. Hit the return button and do the same for the next code.

The five-minute practice period should allow you to establish a rhythm for this process. When the five minutes are up, your score will flash on the screen. A score of 14 is required for passing. If you have scored 14 or higher, approach the actual test with confidence. If your score is lower than 14, be reassured that it will not be counted. Remember that you used the first few minutes of the practice period to perfect your system. You now have five minutes to use the system with which you have become comfortable. Your second score, the score that does count, will be higher.

The actual test session is exactly like the practice session—with different codes of course. At the end of the five-minute test, your final score will appear on the screen. You will know instantly whether you have passed or failed—whether you are eligible or ineligible. If you are eligible, you can expect to be called for an employment interview.

EXERCISE 6

Directions: Use the following letter-number codes to test your ability to record them accurately into a computer. Starting from the top left column, try to memorize each letter-number code, type it using your keyboard, and press return. Go on to the next code.

RJKF566	BVEI155	GKZP876
YTMN068	FUQS478	EDBJ582
FULD727	JMGE610	OLDE751
TTHU950	SQWP0I0	LEAP274
NORT707	BDEY851	PHYX593
FLIO015	CZDT874	BLDV592
OYJX055	FTTD123	KHTP805
GYKN094	RHVZ417	IFWK173
WEST301	TGIF629	YCWI142
DRHK967	PDQD157	OLZT809
AVNB893	EAST383	VMHW649
RKBY775	GSAP013	HTCQ858
LGBU919	UQFP180	JFTA862

STATE TESTING

The Clerical examination is made up of three parts: a written test, typing test and a stenographic test. All applicants must take a written and a typing test. The written test will be weighted 50 percent and the typing test will be weighted 50 percent. Applicants for Clerk Stenographer 1 and 2 must also pass a stenographic test. The stenographic test will not be weighted as part of the final score.

You must pass all parts of the test to be considered for employment. Any part of the test may be cancelled by the Commission and the weight added to the remaining part.

Written Test

The written test will consist of a twelve-minute Name and Number Checking speed test, and a 90-minute clerical abilities test that will cover the subject areas below.

Subject Matter Areas	Number of Questions
Name and Number Checking	65
Sorting File Material	10
Alphabetizing	15
Taking Telephone Messages	15
Capitalization/Punctuation/Grammar	15
Effective Expression	10
Spelling	25
Arithmetic Operations	15
TOTAL	170

Typing Test

The typing performance test will consist of a five-minute practice exercise followed by the actual test, which will have a five-minute time limit. You must achieve a score of 40 words per minute, after deduction for errors, to pass the typing performance test.

Stenographic Test

The stenographic test will consist of a practice exercise, followed by the actual test. You will take dictation at the rate of 80 words per minute. Applicants will have time to transcribe their notes. Applicants for Clerk Stenographer 1 must not have more than 10 percent wrong on the stenographic test. Applicants for Clerk Stenographer 2 must not have more than 5 percent wrong on the test. Any stenographic system, including the use of a shorthand machine, is acceptable.

Test Results

Employment and promotion lists will be established. You will be notified in writing of your test results.

If you take the test and want to take it again, you may be retested six months after the date of your last examination. You must retake all parts of the examination. A new application is required for a retest.

LOCAL TESTING

The examination for this title will consist of two parts: a written test and a qualifying typing performance test. The written test will cover knowledge, skills, and/or abilities in such areas as office practices, English usage, reading comprehension, arithmetic reasoning, and record keeping. The straight-copy typing test is rated for speed and accuracy at 35 words per minute on a personal computer.

There is so much variation in county clerical examinations that a sample exam might prove misleading. The best preparation for a county clerical examination—and indeed for any clerical examination—is thorough grounding in basic clerical skills and practice with many different kinds of exams.

Straight-copy typing tests, on the other hand, are all alike. Only the speed and error standards and requirements may vary. The section entitled "Sample Typing Test" specifically addresses this test for the Postal Clerk-Typist Exam. However, your own exam, for whatever typing-inclusive clerical position you seek, will be very similar to it.

CLERICAL EMPLOYMENT TESTS FOR COURT-RELATED AND PRIVATE-SECTOR POSITIONS

Testing for Court Positions

The following is a description of the types of questions you might be asked for court positions or in the private sector.

The written examination will be multiple-choice and will assess the following:

1. **Spelling:** These questions are designed to test a candidate's ability to spell words that office clerical employees encounter in their daily work.

2. **Knowledge of English grammar and usage, punctuation, and sentence structure:** These questions are designed to test a candidate's knowledge of the basic rules of English grammar, usage, punctuation, and sentence structure.

③ **Clerical checking:** These questions are designed to test a candidate's ability to identify differences among sets of written materials that are almost alike. Candidates are presented with sets of information containing names, numbers, codes, and so on, and must determine how the sets may differ.

④ **Office record-keeping:** These questions are designed to test a candidate's ability to read, combine, and manipulate written information culled from several different sources. Candidates are presented with different types of tables that contain names, numbers, and codes. They must combine and reorganize the information to answer questions. All of the information required to answer the questions is provided in the tables; candidates are not required to have any special knowledge relating to the information provided.

⑤ **Reading, understanding, and interpreting written material:** These questions are designed to test how well candidates understand what they have read. Candidates are provided with short written passages from which some words have been removed. They are required to select from four alternatives the word that best fits in each of the spaces.

KEYBOARDING TEST

Candidates will be notified when to appear for the performance examination. Only candidates who obtain a passing score on the written examination will be invited to participate in the performance examination(s).

All candidates who are successful on the above written exam will be called to take a qualifying performance test in keyboarding (typing) which will be held after the written examination date. Candidates will be required to type an exact copy of a selection at the rate of 45 words per minute. This is a five-minute test of accuracy and speed of keyboarding from straight copy.

The sample examination for senior office typist, New York Unified Court System, in this book is based upon recent administration of this exam. In some ways, it is similar to many other clerical examinations; in some ways, it is unique. This exam introduces some new question styles and formats. It will be very much worth your time to try these questions. You want to prepare yourself for whatever type of question appears on your exam. In a field of competent applicants, familiarity with question styles can give you the competitive edge, a higher score, and ultimately an offer of employment.

TESTING IN THE PRIVATE SECTOR

Since private-sector testing is not organized or regulated, there is no one battery of tests and no one format. However, common sense dictates that prospective clerical workers are likely to be tested for ability in some of the following areas:

reading comprehension	vocabulary
spelling	simple arithmetic calculations
ability to follow directions	grammar and English usage
clerical speed and accuracy	interpreting tables and charts
typing	computer literacy

Just as the subjects for examination may vary, so the means for testing may vary as well. Since use of the computer is central to so much clerical work—data entry, word processing, information retrieval, etc.—testing by computer is highly appropriate and is becoming more and more prevalent.

The most significant difference between public- and private-sector testing is the nature of the competition. In a public-sector Civil Service test, you compete against the entire population taking that test and strive for a high competitive rating. In a private-sector testing situation, you are proving your own skills as an individual. While you may well be competing against other applicants for the same opening, your test performance only proves your competence for the work at hand.

The best preparation for a private-sector exam, as for a civil service exam, is competence in the subject areas and practice in the skills areas. If you can gain experience with a number of computer programs, you are more likely to find yourself being tested on a familiar machine. Familiarity leads to self-confidence and better performance.

The private-sector clerical examination in this book is typical of that given by a number of large employment agencies that specialize in placement of clerical workers on both temporary and permanent bases. It is not an actual exam. Your exam may be quite different. Practice with this exam, however, will give you exposure to the non-multiple-choice exam style often favored by private-sector employers.

In this section, you have had a brief overview of the types of questions and tests that you might encounter when you take a clerical exam. One very important aspect of taking a test that we continue to stress is to be sure you understand the directions. Since most tests are timed, it is inportant to focus on the questions when taking the test. That is easier if you understand what the questions are asking and don't have to waste time trying to interpret what is being asked of you.

In Part III of this book, you will find dozens of different types of questions covering four major skill areas: verbal, mathematics, clerical, and coding. Take your time to work on the questions and check your answers carefully. Reread and learn the directions and instructions. You will find this practice extremely helpful when you are taking any exam.

SUMMING IT UP

- Most civil service exams include multiple-choice questions; some also test keyboarding and other secretarial skills. With the exception of keyboarding tests, most exams do not test speed. Usually tests are graded by computer, and passing grades range from 70–99.

- Applicants for civil service jobs must meet education and experience requirements posted in job announcements. Civil service exams are then administered to assess an applicant's level of training, experience, and skills. The exams usually include sections testing verbal and clerical skills; depending on the type of job desired, they may also include sections assessing keyboard skill, record-keeping skills, dictation, fact-checking ability, or stenography skill.

- Verbal test sections assess an applicant's ability to spell, understand word meaning and word relationships, and recognize grammar errors. They also assess the applicant's ability to read and understand written material and to apply that information to other tasks.

- Clerical test sections assess an applicant's speed and accuracy in performing specific clerical tasks. Points are deducted from the total test score for incorrect answers, so while it's important to complete these tests as quickly as possible, it's also important to be accurate.

- Private-sector testing is not organized or regulated—applicants may not be tested at all. However, when you are required to complete an exam for a private-sector job, you will likely encounter a broad array of test styles. The best way to prepare for such exams is to take as many different kinds of practice tests as possible, so you become familiar with a variety of test styles and formats.

Test-Taking Techniques

OVERVIEW

- Preparing for the test
- Taking the test
- Should you guess?
- Scoring
- Summing it up

PREPARING FOR THE TEST

Many factors are involved in earning a high test score. The most important one, of course, is your ability to understand and answer the questions. This in turn indicates your ability to learn and perform the duties of a job. Assuming you have this ability, finding out what to expect on the exam and becoming familiar with the techniques of effective test taking can give you the confidence you need to do your best.

There is no quick substitute for long-term study and for practicing your skills before you take the exam. However, you can take certain steps to boost your confidence before and during the exam. We'll review these steps in this chapter.

First, don't make the test harder than it has to be by not preparing yourself. You are taking a very important step by reading this book and taking the sample tests. This helps you become familiar with the tests and the types of questions you will have to answer on the actual exam.

As you use this book, read the sample questions and directions for taking the tests carefully. When you take the sample tests, time yourself the way you will be timed during the real exam.

As you are working on the sample questions, try not to look at the correct answers before you try to answer them on your own. Looking at them might fool you into thinking that you understand a question when you really don't. So try it on your own first, then compare your answer with the one provided.

chapter 4

Remember, in a sample test, you are your own grader, so you won't gain anything by pretending to understand something that you're not clear about.

On the exam day assigned to you, make the test itself the main "event" of the day. Try not to squeeze it in between other activities. Be sure to bring your admission card, identification, pencils, and anything else you are instructed to bring. Gather these things the night before the exam and have them in a convenient place where you won't forget to bring them with you or be flustered by a last-minute scramble to assemble them. Arrive at the exam center rested and relaxed. Plan to arrive at the exam center a bit early. This will leave plenty of time for unexpected delays such as traffic tie-ups that might upset or rush you and interfere with your test performance.

Once you are in the test room, the examiner will hand out forms for you to fill out. He or she will give you the instructions that you must follow when taking the exam. The examiner will also tell you how to fill in the grids on the answer forms. Fill in the grids on the forms carefully and accurately. Misgridding may lead to a miscalculation of test results, or, if you are a veteran, you may lose the credits to which you're entitled.

The examiner will also explain time limits and timing signals. If you do not understand any of the examiner's instructions, do not hesitate to *ask questions*. It would be a shame to risk a lower score on your exam because of a communication problem. Do not begin the exam until you are told to begin. Stop when the examiner tells you to stop. Do not turn pages until you are told to do so, and do not return to parts you have already completed. Any infraction of these rules is considered cheating; if you do so, your test paper will not be scored, and you will not be eligible for appointment.

TAKING THE TEST

The answer sheet for most multiple-choice exams is scored by machine, so no written explanations of your answers will be registered. This means you must fill out the answer sheet clearly and correctly. Here are some tips to follow:

- Blacken your answer space firmly and completely. ● is the only correct way to mark the answer sheet. ◑, ⊗, ⊘, and ∅ are all unacceptable. The machine might not read them at all.

- Mark only one answer for each question. If you mark more than one answer, the machine scoring will consider your response incorrect, even if one of the answers you mark is correct.

- If you change your mind, you must erase your mark. Attempting to cross out an incorrect answer like this ✸ will not work. You must erase any incorrect answer completely. An incomplete erasure might be read as a second answer.

ALERT!

The single greatest factor that determines whether you choose the right answer or the wrong one is to *read carefully*. Say the directions say to choose the word that means the *opposite* of the underlined word. You misread the directions and choose the word that means the *same* as the underlined word. You've then marked the wrong answers for a whole series of questions.

- The scoring machine does not read English, so all of your answers should be in the form of blackened spaces. Do not write notes in the margins.

- For the typing tests, type steadily and carefully, but don't rush—that's when you are most likely to make errors. Keep in mind that each error you make subtracts from your final score.

- MOST IMPORTANT: When you are answering multiple-choice questions for which you must darken circles, make sure you are answering each question in the right place. Question 1 must be answered in space 1 on your answer sheet; question 52 must be answered in space 52. If you skip an answer space and mark a series of answers in the wrong spaces, you must erase all of those answers and fill in the spaces all over again, marking your answers in the proper spaces. You cannot afford to use your limited time that way, so as you answer each question, look at its number and double-check that you are marking your answer in the appropriate space on the answer sheet.

Don't reduce your score by making careless mistakes. Always read the instructions for each test section carefully, even when you think you already know what they are. This is why we stress throughout this book the importance of fully understanding the directions for the different question types *before* you take the actual exam. It will not only reduce the likelihood that you'll make errors, but it will also save you time—the time you need for answering the questions.

For example, vocabulary questions can sometimes focus on synonyms (words that have similar meanings) and sometimes on antonyms (words that have opposite meanings). You can easily see how mistaking one for the other when reading the instructions can make a whole set of your answers incorrect.

If you have time, reread any complicated instructions after you answer the first few questions in that section to check that you really do understand them. Of course, whenever permitted, ask the examiner to clarify anything you don't clearly understand.

Other mistakes might affect only your response to particular questions. This often happens with arithmetic questions, but it can happen with other types as well. This kind of mistake, called a "response error," usually stems from a momentary lapse of concentration.

EXAMPLE

The question reads: "The capital of Massachusetts is . . . ." The answer is (D) Boston, but you mark (B) because "B" is the first letter of the word "Boston."

EXAMPLE

The question reads: "8 − 5 = ..." The answer is (A) 3, but you mark (C), thinking "third letter of the alphabet."

A common error in reading comprehension exam sections is bringing your own knowledge into answering the questions. For example, say you encounter a passage that discusses a subject you know something about. While this will likely make the passage easier to read, it might also tempt you to rely on your own knowledge instead of on the information presented in the reading sample. You must rely only on the information within that passage for your answers. In fact, sometimes the "wrong" answer for a question is based on true information about the subject that is not provided in the passage. Since the test is meant to assess your reading ability rather than your general knowledge of the subject, an answer based on information that isn't contained in the passage is considered incorrect.

Before you begin the exam, take a moment to plan your progress through the test. Although you are usually not expected to answer all of the questions on a test, you should at least get an idea of how much time you should spend on each question should you be able to answer them all. For example, if you have 60 questions to answer in 30 minutes, you have 30 seconds to spend on each one.

Keep track of the time using a watch or the room clock, but don't fixate on the time remaining. Your task is to answer questions. Do not spend too much time on any one question. If you find that you're stuck on one, don't take the puzzler as a personal challenge; you will only waste time you could be spending on other questions. Either guess and mark the answer on your answer sheet or skip the question entirely and go on to the next one. If you decide to skip it, be sure to mark the question as skipped and be careful to skip the answer space on the answer sheet as well. If you have time at the end of the exam or section, you can return to any skipped questions and give them a second try.

Almost all of the tests given on civil service exams are in multiple-choice format. This means that you normally have four or five answer choices. Don't let the choices overwhelm you. Here's a basic technique you can use to help you answer multiple-choice questions more easily.

First, keep in mind that only one answer is correct. This type of test has been administered countless times and the test developers have a good sense of which questions work well and which don't work—so it's rare when your choices are ambiguous. They may be complex and somewhat confusing, but there is still only one correct answer.

Next, look at the question for a moment without looking at the answer choices. Then select the correct answer. This may sound simplistic, but it's usually the case that your first answer choice is the correct one. If you go back and rethink it or redo a problem again and again, you are more likely to end up with an incorrect answer. Follow your first instinct. Once you have come up with the answer, look at the answer choices more carefully. If your original answer is one of the choices, you're probably correct. Although this method isn't 100 percent infallible, the chances of your choosing the correct answer are very strong.

When it comes to math questions, you should first solve the problem. If your answer is among the choices, you're probably correct. Be careful not to ignore proper function signs (adding, subtracting, multiplying, and dividing), negative and positive numbers, and so on.

What if you don't know the correct answer? In these cases, it's best to use what's called the process of elimination, a time-honored technique for test takers. Here's how it works: Say each of your questions has four answer choices. There is always one correct answer. There is also usually one answer choice that is totally incorrect—a "distracter." If one of the answer choices seems highly unlikely to be correct, eliminate it. You've just whittled down your choices to three. Now weigh the remaining choices. If any of them seem incorrect, eliminate them too. Using this process, you've increased your odds of choosing the correct answer.

In the end, you may still be left with two choices. At that point, it's a matter of guessing the correct one—but with only two answers left, you now have a 50 percent chance of guessing the right one, instead of the 25 percent chance you had when you started with four answer choices.

SHOULD YOU GUESS?

You've probably been wondering whether it is wise to guess when you are unsure of an answer (even if you've increased the odds of choosing the correct one) or whether it's better to skip the question when you're not certain. How wise it is to guess depends on the scoring method for the particular exam or section. If scoring is "rights only"—that is, you gain one point for each correct answer and no subtraction for incorrect answers—then by all means you should guess. Read the question and all of the answers very carefully. Eliminate the choices that you are sure are incorrect. Then guess from among the remaining choices. You cannot gain a point if you leave the answer space blank, and you may gain a point if you take an educated guess, or even if you take a lucky guess.

In fact, it would be foolish to leave any spaces blank on a test scored with the "rights only" method. If it appears that you are about to run out of time before completing such an exam, mark the same letter for all the remaining blank answer spaces. According to the law of averages, you should get some of those questions right.

If the scoring method is "rights minus wrongs," such as in the address-checking test of the Postal Clerk Exam 473, *do not guess.* In this type of test, a wrong answer counts against you. Do not rush to fill answer spaces randomly at the end of this kind of test. Work as quickly as you can while concentrating on being accurate. Keep working carefully until time is called. Then stop and leave the remaining answer spaces blank.

In guessing answers to multiple-choice questions, follow the process of elimination method as described above. Once you have decided to make a guess—whether it's an educated guess or a wild stab—do it quickly and move on. Don't keep thinking about it or you may waste valuable time. It's a good idea to mark the questions for which you guessed the answer; if you have time, you can return to them and take a second shot at them.

Some exams are scored by subtracting a fraction of a point for each incorrect answer from the total score. In these cases, whether or not you should guess is really up to you. A correct answer gives you one point; a skipped answer gives you nothing at all but costs you the chance to get the answer right. On the other hand, a wrong answer costs you 1/4 point. If you are uncomfortable with guessing, you should skip a question, but you must then remember to skip the corresponding answer space. The risk of losing your place if you skip questions is so great that we suggest you try to answer each question in order, even if you have to guess. It is better to lose a few 1/4 points on incorrect answers than to lose valuable time figuring out where you started marking answers in the wrong place, erasing them, and re-marking the answers in the correct spaces. On the other hand, when exams are scored this way, it's best not to mark random answers at the end of the answer sheet if time is up before you're finished. Instead, work steadily until time is called.

One of the questions you should ask the examiner before the exam beings is what scoring method will be used on your exam. You can then decide on a strategy for handling questions for which you're unsure of the correct answer.

SCORING

If your exam is a short-answer exam, such as those often used by private-sector companies, a personnel officer trained in grading test questions will grade your answers. If you blackened spaces on the separate answer sheet accompanying a multiple-choice exam, your answer sheet will be machine-graded or will be hand-scored using a punch card stencil. This raw score will then be calculated using a scoring formula that applies to that test or test portion. It may be rights only, rights minus wrongs, or rights minus a fraction of wrongs. Raw test scores are then added together for a total raw score.

A raw score is not a final exam score. The raw score is not the one that ends up on an eligibility list. The civil service testing authority, the Postal Service, or other testing body converts these scores to a scaled score according to an unpublished formula of its own. The scaling formula allows for slight differences in difficulty of questions from one form of the exam to another and allows for equating the scores of all candidates who took the exam. Regardless of the number of questions and possible different weights of different parts of the exam, most civil service clerical test scores are reported on a scale of 1 to 10.

The entire process of converting from raw to scaled score is confidential information. The score you receive is not the number of questions you answered correctly and it is not your raw score. In addition, despite being numbered on a scale of 1 to 100, it is not a percentage. If you are entitled to veterans' service points, these are added to your passing scaled score to boost your rank on the eligibility list. Veterans' points are added only to passing scores, however. A failing score cannot be brought up to passing level by adding veterans' points. The score earned plus veterans' service points, if any, is the score that ends up on the rank order eligibility list. Highest scores are at the top of the list.

SUMMING IT UP

- Prepare yourself for the exam. Reading this book and taking the practice tests is a step in the right direction. Be sure you get plenty of sleep the night before the exam and don't plan other activities on the day of the exam. Gather all the materials you need ahead of time, and allow yourself extra time to get to the exam center so you're relaxed and alert.

- Listen carefully to the examiner and read all instructions before beginning the exam. Don't hesitate to ask questions if you don't understand something.

- Fill in answer spaces carefully and completely. Do not to fill in more than one per question, and avoid making notes or stray marks on the answer sheet. If you're taking a keyboarding test, work steadily and quickly, but be as accurate as possible.

- Keep an eye on the time, but do not let it rush or panic you. Work at a steady pace.

- If a question is particularly difficult, you may decide to skip it or take an educated guess, but do not spend extra time on it.

- Find out the type of scoring method used to grade your exam. Armed with this knowledge, you can decide whether it's to your advantage to take educated guesses or skip questions for which you don't know the answer. This also helps if you run out of time: In some cases it's best to leave the rest of the answer spaces unmarked; in other cases you may want to randomly mark them before turning in your answer sheet.

PART II

DIAGNOSING STRENGTHS AND WEAKNESSES

CHAPTER 5   Practice Test 1: Diagnostic

ANSWER SHEET PRACTICE TEST 1: DIAGNOSTIC

VOCABULARY

1. Ⓐ Ⓑ Ⓒ Ⓓ	18. Ⓐ Ⓑ Ⓒ Ⓓ	35. Ⓐ Ⓑ Ⓒ Ⓓ
2. Ⓐ Ⓑ Ⓒ Ⓓ	19. Ⓐ Ⓑ Ⓒ Ⓓ	36. Ⓐ Ⓑ Ⓒ Ⓓ
3. Ⓐ Ⓑ Ⓒ Ⓓ	20. Ⓐ Ⓑ Ⓒ Ⓓ	37. Ⓐ Ⓑ Ⓒ Ⓓ
4. Ⓐ Ⓑ Ⓒ Ⓓ	21. Ⓐ Ⓑ Ⓒ Ⓓ	38. Ⓐ Ⓑ Ⓒ Ⓓ
5. Ⓐ Ⓑ Ⓒ Ⓓ	22. Ⓐ Ⓑ Ⓒ Ⓓ	39. Ⓐ Ⓑ Ⓒ Ⓓ
6. Ⓐ Ⓑ Ⓒ Ⓓ	23. Ⓐ Ⓑ Ⓒ Ⓓ	40. Ⓐ Ⓑ Ⓒ Ⓓ
7. Ⓐ Ⓑ Ⓒ Ⓓ	24. Ⓐ Ⓑ Ⓒ Ⓓ	41. Ⓐ Ⓑ Ⓒ Ⓓ
8. Ⓐ Ⓑ Ⓒ Ⓓ	25. Ⓐ Ⓑ Ⓒ Ⓓ	42. Ⓐ Ⓑ Ⓒ Ⓓ
9. Ⓐ Ⓑ Ⓒ Ⓓ	26. Ⓐ Ⓑ Ⓒ Ⓓ	43. Ⓐ Ⓑ Ⓒ Ⓓ
10. Ⓐ Ⓑ Ⓒ Ⓓ	27. Ⓐ Ⓑ Ⓒ Ⓓ	44. Ⓐ Ⓑ Ⓒ Ⓓ
11. Ⓐ Ⓑ Ⓒ Ⓓ	28. Ⓐ Ⓑ Ⓒ Ⓓ	45. Ⓐ Ⓑ Ⓒ Ⓓ
12. Ⓐ Ⓑ Ⓒ Ⓓ	29. Ⓐ Ⓑ Ⓒ Ⓓ	46. Ⓐ Ⓑ Ⓒ Ⓓ
13. Ⓐ Ⓑ Ⓒ Ⓓ	30. Ⓐ Ⓑ Ⓒ Ⓓ	47. Ⓐ Ⓑ Ⓒ Ⓓ
14. Ⓐ Ⓑ Ⓒ Ⓓ	31. Ⓐ Ⓑ Ⓒ Ⓓ	48. Ⓐ Ⓑ Ⓒ Ⓓ
15. Ⓐ Ⓑ Ⓒ Ⓓ	32. Ⓐ Ⓑ Ⓒ Ⓓ	49. Ⓐ Ⓑ Ⓒ Ⓓ
16. Ⓐ Ⓑ Ⓒ Ⓓ	33. Ⓐ Ⓑ Ⓒ Ⓓ	50. Ⓐ Ⓑ Ⓒ Ⓓ
17. Ⓐ Ⓑ Ⓒ Ⓓ	34. Ⓐ Ⓑ Ⓒ Ⓓ	

SPELLING

1. Ⓐ Ⓑ	18. Ⓐ Ⓑ	35. Ⓐ Ⓑ
2. Ⓐ Ⓑ	19. Ⓐ Ⓑ	36. Ⓐ Ⓑ
3. Ⓐ Ⓑ	20. Ⓐ Ⓑ	37. Ⓐ Ⓑ
4. Ⓐ Ⓑ	21. Ⓐ Ⓑ	38. Ⓐ Ⓑ
5. Ⓐ Ⓑ	22. Ⓐ Ⓑ	39. Ⓐ Ⓑ
6. Ⓐ Ⓑ	23. Ⓐ Ⓑ	40. Ⓐ Ⓑ
7. Ⓐ Ⓑ	24. Ⓐ Ⓑ	41. Ⓐ Ⓑ
8. Ⓐ Ⓑ	25. Ⓐ Ⓑ	42. Ⓐ Ⓑ
9. Ⓐ Ⓑ	26. Ⓐ Ⓑ	43. Ⓐ Ⓑ
10. Ⓐ Ⓑ	27. Ⓐ Ⓑ	44. Ⓐ Ⓑ
11. Ⓐ Ⓑ	28. Ⓐ Ⓑ	45. Ⓐ Ⓑ
12. Ⓐ Ⓑ	29. Ⓐ Ⓑ	46. Ⓐ Ⓑ
13. Ⓐ Ⓑ	30. Ⓐ Ⓑ	47. Ⓐ Ⓑ
14. Ⓐ Ⓑ	31. Ⓐ Ⓑ	48. Ⓐ Ⓑ
15. Ⓐ Ⓑ	32. Ⓐ Ⓑ	49. Ⓐ Ⓑ
16. Ⓐ Ⓑ	33. Ⓐ Ⓑ	50. Ⓐ Ⓑ
17. Ⓐ Ⓑ	34. Ⓐ Ⓑ	

CODING

1. Ⓐ Ⓑ Ⓒ Ⓓ
2. Ⓐ Ⓑ Ⓒ Ⓓ
3. Ⓐ Ⓑ Ⓒ Ⓓ
4. Ⓐ Ⓑ Ⓒ Ⓓ
5. Ⓐ Ⓑ Ⓒ Ⓓ
6. Ⓐ Ⓑ Ⓒ Ⓓ
7. Ⓐ Ⓑ Ⓒ Ⓓ
8. Ⓐ Ⓑ Ⓒ Ⓓ
9. Ⓐ Ⓑ Ⓒ Ⓓ
10. Ⓐ Ⓑ Ⓒ Ⓓ
11. Ⓐ Ⓑ Ⓒ Ⓓ
12. Ⓐ Ⓑ Ⓒ Ⓓ
13. Ⓐ Ⓑ Ⓒ Ⓓ
14. Ⓐ Ⓑ Ⓒ Ⓓ
15. Ⓐ Ⓑ Ⓒ Ⓓ
16. Ⓐ Ⓑ Ⓒ Ⓓ
17. Ⓐ Ⓑ Ⓒ Ⓓ
18. Ⓐ Ⓑ Ⓒ Ⓓ
19. Ⓐ Ⓑ Ⓒ Ⓓ
20. Ⓐ Ⓑ Ⓒ Ⓓ
21. Ⓐ Ⓑ Ⓒ Ⓓ
22. Ⓐ Ⓑ Ⓒ Ⓓ
23. Ⓐ Ⓑ Ⓒ Ⓓ
24. Ⓐ Ⓑ Ⓒ Ⓓ
25. Ⓐ Ⓑ Ⓒ Ⓓ
26. Ⓐ Ⓑ Ⓒ Ⓓ
27. Ⓐ Ⓑ Ⓒ Ⓓ
28. Ⓐ Ⓑ Ⓒ Ⓓ
29. Ⓐ Ⓑ Ⓒ Ⓓ
30. Ⓐ Ⓑ Ⓒ Ⓓ
31. Ⓐ Ⓑ Ⓒ Ⓓ
32. Ⓐ Ⓑ Ⓒ Ⓓ
33. Ⓐ Ⓑ Ⓒ Ⓓ
34. Ⓐ Ⓑ Ⓒ Ⓓ

35. Ⓐ Ⓑ Ⓒ Ⓓ
36. Ⓐ Ⓑ Ⓒ Ⓓ
37. Ⓐ Ⓑ Ⓒ Ⓓ
38. Ⓐ Ⓑ Ⓒ Ⓓ
39. Ⓐ Ⓑ Ⓒ Ⓓ
40. Ⓐ Ⓑ Ⓒ Ⓓ
41. Ⓐ Ⓑ Ⓒ Ⓓ
42. Ⓐ Ⓑ Ⓒ Ⓓ
43. Ⓐ Ⓑ Ⓒ Ⓓ
44. Ⓐ Ⓑ Ⓒ Ⓓ
45. Ⓐ Ⓑ Ⓒ Ⓓ
46. Ⓐ Ⓑ Ⓒ Ⓓ
47. Ⓐ Ⓑ Ⓒ Ⓓ
48. Ⓐ Ⓑ Ⓒ Ⓓ
49. Ⓐ Ⓑ Ⓒ Ⓓ
50. Ⓐ Ⓑ Ⓒ Ⓓ
51. Ⓐ Ⓑ Ⓒ Ⓓ
52. Ⓐ Ⓑ Ⓒ Ⓓ
53. Ⓐ Ⓑ Ⓒ Ⓓ
54. Ⓐ Ⓑ Ⓒ Ⓓ
55. Ⓐ Ⓑ Ⓒ Ⓓ
56. Ⓐ Ⓑ Ⓒ Ⓓ
57. Ⓐ Ⓑ Ⓒ Ⓓ
58. Ⓐ Ⓑ Ⓒ Ⓓ
59. Ⓐ Ⓑ Ⓒ Ⓓ
60. Ⓐ Ⓑ Ⓒ Ⓓ
61. Ⓐ Ⓑ Ⓒ Ⓓ
62. Ⓐ Ⓑ Ⓒ Ⓓ
63. Ⓐ Ⓑ Ⓒ Ⓓ
64. Ⓐ Ⓑ Ⓒ Ⓓ
65. Ⓐ Ⓑ Ⓒ Ⓓ
66. Ⓐ Ⓑ Ⓒ Ⓓ
67. Ⓐ Ⓑ Ⓒ Ⓓ

68. Ⓐ Ⓑ Ⓒ Ⓓ
69. Ⓐ Ⓑ Ⓒ Ⓓ
70. Ⓐ Ⓑ Ⓒ Ⓓ
71. Ⓐ Ⓑ Ⓒ Ⓓ
72. Ⓐ Ⓑ Ⓒ Ⓓ
73. Ⓐ Ⓑ Ⓒ Ⓓ
74. Ⓐ Ⓑ Ⓒ Ⓓ
75. Ⓐ Ⓑ Ⓒ Ⓓ
76. Ⓐ Ⓑ Ⓒ Ⓓ
77. Ⓐ Ⓑ Ⓒ Ⓓ
78. Ⓐ Ⓑ Ⓒ Ⓓ
79. Ⓐ Ⓑ Ⓒ Ⓓ
80. Ⓐ Ⓑ Ⓒ Ⓓ
81. Ⓐ Ⓑ Ⓒ Ⓓ
82. Ⓐ Ⓑ Ⓒ Ⓓ
83. Ⓐ Ⓑ Ⓒ Ⓓ
84. Ⓐ Ⓑ Ⓒ Ⓓ
85. Ⓐ Ⓑ Ⓒ Ⓓ
86. Ⓐ Ⓑ Ⓒ Ⓓ
87. Ⓐ Ⓑ Ⓒ Ⓓ
88. Ⓐ Ⓑ Ⓒ Ⓓ
89. Ⓐ Ⓑ Ⓒ Ⓓ
90. Ⓐ Ⓑ Ⓒ Ⓓ
91. Ⓐ Ⓑ Ⓒ Ⓓ
92. Ⓐ Ⓑ Ⓒ Ⓓ
93. Ⓐ Ⓑ Ⓒ Ⓓ
94. Ⓐ Ⓑ Ⓒ Ⓓ
95. Ⓐ Ⓑ Ⓒ Ⓓ
96. Ⓐ Ⓑ Ⓒ Ⓓ
97. Ⓐ Ⓑ Ⓒ Ⓓ
98. Ⓐ Ⓑ Ⓒ Ⓓ
99. Ⓐ Ⓑ Ⓒ Ⓓ
100. Ⓐ Ⓑ Ⓒ Ⓓ

MATH

1. Ⓐ Ⓑ Ⓒ Ⓓ
2. Ⓐ Ⓑ Ⓒ Ⓓ
3. Ⓐ Ⓑ Ⓒ Ⓓ
4. Ⓐ Ⓑ Ⓒ Ⓓ
5. Ⓐ Ⓑ Ⓒ Ⓓ
6. Ⓐ Ⓑ Ⓒ Ⓓ
7. Ⓐ Ⓑ Ⓒ Ⓓ
8. Ⓐ Ⓑ Ⓒ Ⓓ
9. Ⓐ Ⓑ Ⓒ Ⓓ
10. Ⓐ Ⓑ Ⓒ Ⓓ
11. Ⓐ Ⓑ Ⓒ Ⓓ
12. Ⓐ Ⓑ Ⓒ Ⓓ
13. Ⓐ Ⓑ Ⓒ Ⓓ
14. Ⓐ Ⓑ Ⓒ Ⓓ
15. Ⓐ Ⓑ Ⓒ Ⓓ
16. Ⓐ Ⓑ Ⓒ Ⓓ
17. Ⓐ Ⓑ Ⓒ Ⓓ
18. Ⓐ Ⓑ Ⓒ Ⓓ
19. Ⓐ Ⓑ Ⓒ Ⓓ
20. Ⓐ Ⓑ Ⓒ Ⓓ
21. Ⓐ Ⓑ Ⓒ Ⓓ
22. Ⓐ Ⓑ Ⓒ Ⓓ
23. Ⓐ Ⓑ Ⓒ Ⓓ
24. Ⓐ Ⓑ Ⓒ Ⓓ

25. Ⓐ Ⓑ Ⓒ Ⓓ
26. Ⓐ Ⓑ Ⓒ Ⓓ
27. Ⓐ Ⓑ Ⓒ Ⓓ
28. Ⓐ Ⓑ Ⓒ Ⓓ
29. Ⓐ Ⓑ Ⓒ Ⓓ
30. Ⓐ Ⓑ Ⓒ Ⓓ
31. Ⓐ Ⓑ Ⓒ Ⓓ
32. Ⓐ Ⓑ Ⓒ Ⓓ
33. Ⓐ Ⓑ Ⓒ Ⓓ
34. Ⓐ Ⓑ Ⓒ Ⓓ
35. Ⓐ Ⓑ Ⓒ Ⓓ
36. Ⓐ Ⓑ Ⓒ Ⓓ
37. Ⓐ Ⓑ Ⓒ Ⓓ
38. Ⓐ Ⓑ Ⓒ Ⓓ
39. Ⓐ Ⓑ Ⓒ Ⓓ
40. Ⓐ Ⓑ Ⓒ Ⓓ
41. Ⓐ Ⓑ Ⓒ Ⓓ
42. Ⓐ Ⓑ Ⓒ Ⓓ
43. Ⓐ Ⓑ Ⓒ Ⓓ
44. Ⓐ Ⓑ Ⓒ Ⓓ
45. Ⓐ Ⓑ Ⓒ Ⓓ
46. Ⓐ Ⓑ Ⓒ Ⓓ
47. Ⓐ Ⓑ Ⓒ Ⓓ

48. Ⓐ Ⓑ Ⓒ Ⓓ
49. Ⓐ Ⓑ Ⓒ Ⓓ
50. Ⓐ Ⓑ Ⓒ Ⓓ
51. Ⓐ Ⓑ Ⓒ Ⓓ
52. Ⓐ Ⓑ Ⓒ Ⓓ
53. Ⓐ Ⓑ Ⓒ Ⓓ
54. Ⓐ Ⓑ Ⓒ Ⓓ
55. Ⓐ Ⓑ Ⓒ Ⓓ
56. Ⓐ Ⓑ Ⓒ Ⓓ
57. Ⓐ Ⓑ Ⓒ Ⓓ
58. Ⓐ Ⓑ Ⓒ Ⓓ
59. Ⓐ Ⓑ Ⓒ Ⓓ
60. Ⓐ Ⓑ Ⓒ Ⓓ
61. Ⓐ Ⓑ Ⓒ Ⓓ
62. Ⓐ Ⓑ Ⓒ Ⓓ
63. Ⓐ Ⓑ Ⓒ Ⓓ
64. Ⓐ Ⓑ Ⓒ Ⓓ
65. Ⓐ Ⓑ Ⓒ Ⓓ
66. Ⓐ Ⓑ Ⓒ Ⓓ
67. Ⓐ Ⓑ Ⓒ Ⓓ
68. Ⓐ Ⓑ Ⓒ Ⓓ
69. Ⓐ Ⓑ Ⓒ Ⓓ
70. Ⓐ Ⓑ Ⓒ Ⓓ

answer sheet

Practice Test 1: Diagnostic

VOCABULARY

50 QUESTIONS • 20 MINUTES

Directions: Read each sentence carefully. Choose the letter of the word that best answers the question.

1. Which word means the same as PROMINENT?

   (A) apathetic
   (B) everything
   (C) sinuous
   (D) conspicuous

2. Which word means the same as SENILITY?

   (A) discern
   (B) ebullience
   (C) dotage
   (D) proficient

3. Which word means the opposite of ADEPT?

   (A) inept
   (B) skilled
   (C) niche
   (D) witticism

4. Which word means the same as TORSION?

   (A) breadth
   (B) twisting
   (C) indolent
   (D) tribulation

5. Which word means the same as FEINT?

   (A) cunning
   (B) lethargic
   (C) sham
   (D) oblique

6. Which word means the opposite of ABROGATE?

   (A) annul
   (B) question
   (C) accept
   (D) establish

7. Which word means the opposite of SKIMPY?

   (A) ample
   (B) emulate
   (C) apprehend
   (D) stealthy

8. Which word means the opposite of SOLICITOUS?

   (A) proficient
   (B) redundant
   (C) incoherent
   (D) remiss

9. Which word means the opposite of LACKLUSTER?

   (A) cold
   (B) trivial
   (C) forlorn
   (D) glowing

10. Which word means the same as SCHISM?

   (A) join
   (B) division
   (C) dynamic
   (D) absolve

11. Which word means the opposite of DURABLE?

   (A) lasting
   (B) fragile
   (C) forlorn
   (D) opulent

12. Which word means the same as CONCURRENT?

   (A) animosity
   (B) animation
   (C) simultaneous
   (D) abrogate

13. Which word means the opposite of GROSS?

   (A) petty
   (B) substantial
   (C) dilation
   (D) consolation

14. Which word means the opposite of LARGESSE?

   (A) gift
   (B) benefactor
   (C) nice
   (D) meanness

15. Which word means the opposite of RUSTIC?

   (A) urbane
   (B) delete
   (C) hostile
   (D) slash

16. Which word means the opposite of SCRUPULOUS?

   (A) dormant
   (B) elucidate
   (C) meager
   (D) deceitful

17. Which word means the same as ABATE?

   (A) malice
   (B) subside
   (C) opaque
   (D) apathetic

18. Which word means the opposite of ANTAGONIST?

   (A) colleague
   (B) sequester
   (C) brevity
   (D) discern

19. Which word means the opposite of PROPITIATE?

   (A) placate
   (B) censure
   (C) antagonize
   (D) glib

20. Which word means the same as PROMULGATE?

   (A) adopt
   (B) spread
   (C) revolt
   (D) abrogate

21. Which word means the opposite of ADOPT?

   (A) carry
   (B) pledge
   (C) discard
   (D) embrace

22. Which word means the same as EFFORT?

    (A) laxity
    (B) cautious
    (C) exertion
    (D) effectiveness

23. Which word means the opposite of HABITUAL?

    (A) usual
    (B) frequent
    (C) often
    (D) occasional

24. Which word means the same as ADMIRE?

    (A) love
    (B) refrain
    (C) watch
    (D) esteem

25. Which word means the same as INQUIRE?

    (A) probe
    (B) elaborate
    (C) oblivious
    (D) delete

26. Which word means the same as GRATUITOUS?

    (A) amicable
    (B) complimentary
    (C) large
    (D) elegant

27. Which word means the same as INFAMY?

    (A) disgrace
    (B) popularity
    (C) error
    (D) reality

28. Which word means the same as ANIMOSITY?

    (A) negligence
    (B) rivalry
    (C) enmity
    (D) skepticism

29. Which word means the opposite of FICKLE?

    (A) reliable
    (B) tedious
    (C) energetic
    (D) inconsistent

30. Which word means the opposite of CLANDESTINE?

    (A) secret
    (B) medical
    (C) open
    (D) complicated

31. Which word means the same as OSTRACIZE?

    (A) alter
    (B) feint
    (C) exile
    (D) beneath

32. Which word means the opposite of INSIPID?

    (A) conceited
    (B) tasty
    (C) affluent
    (D) decisive

33. Which word means the opposite of MALICE?

    (A) exile
    (B) benevolence
    (C) malign
    (D) effort

34. Which word means the opposite of PLACID?

    (A) inept
    (B) pleasant
    (C) furtive
    (D) choleric

35. Which word means the opposite of PLACATE?

    (A) pacify
    (B) confess
    (C) enrage
    (D) expedite

36. Which word means the same as SALIENT?

    (A) timid
    (B) reserved
    (C) conspicuous
    (D) omniscient

37. Which word means the same as ASTOUND?

    (A) ample
    (B) pardon
    (C) limit
    (D) astonish

38. Which word means the same as MEANDER?

    (A) curtail
    (B) sequester
    (C) bewilder
    (D) wander

39. Which word means the opposite of FUTILE?

    (A) effective
    (B) pristine
    (C) zealous
    (D) illicit

40. Which word means the same as TRIBULATION?

    (A) idea
    (B) trial
    (C) agreement
    (D) understanding

41. Which word means the opposite of VERBOSE?

    (A) valid
    (B) dull
    (C) concise
    (D) lavish

42. Which word means the opposite of LETHARGY?

    (A) energy
    (B) languor
    (C) anarchy
    (D) panacea

43. Which word means the same as ABATE?

    (A) ridicule
    (B) discern
    (C) subside
    (D) challenge

44. Which word means the opposite of VAGUE?

    (A) hazy
    (B) obscured
    (C) fashionable
    (D) clear

45. Which word means the opposite of ADEPT?

    (A) proficient
    (B) inept
    (C) skilled
    (D) compatible

46. Which word means the same as FORLORN?

    (A) desperate
    (B) fortunate
    (C) rustic
    (D) unique

47. Which word means the same as OBTRUDE?

    (A) slanted
    (B) obscure
    (C) obstruct
    (D) project

48. Which word means the same as CENSURE?

(A) separate
(B) reproach
(C) commend
(D) aspire

49. Which word means the opposite of TORPOR?

(A) lethargy
(B) activity
(C) tepid
(D) vision

50. Which word means the same as PERNICIOUS?

(A) liberal
(B) meticulous
(C) gaseous
(D) destructive

S T O P End of Vocabulary section. If you finish before time is up, check your work on this part only. Do not turn to the next part until the signal is given.

SPELLING

50 QUESTIONS • 9 MINUTES

Directions: Find the incorrectly spelled word in each question and darken your answer sheet indicating which answer is spelled incorrectly.

1. **(A)** prevail
   (B) prevale

2. **(A)** eccept
   (B) except

3. **(A)** blind
   (B) blinde

4. **(A)** anonymous
   (B) anoynomus

5. **(A)** county
   (B) countey

6. **(A)** admitted
   (B) admited

7. **(A)** Chicago
   (B) Chicagoe

8. **(A)** Connecticut
   (B) Connetecut

9. **(A)** Rhode Island
   (B) Rode Iland

10. **(A)** nephew
    (B) nefhew

11. **(A)** brotherly
    (B) brootherly

12. **(A)** their
    (B) thier

13. **(A)** setting
    (B) seting

14. **(A)** indcident
    (B) incident

15. **(A)** operastion
    (B) operation

16. **(A)** filing
    (B) fileing

17. **(A)** typewriter
    (B) typewritter

18. **(A)** computer
    (B) computter

19. **(A)** edittorial
    (B) editorial

20. **(A)** guilty
    (B) guiltey

21. **(A)** warriour
    (B) warrior

22. **(A)** stapler
    (B) stapeler

23. **(A)** carpett
    (B) carpet

24. **(A)** numeros
    (B) numerous

25. **(A)** assistant
    (B) assistent

26. **(A)** sailed
    (B) saild

27. **(A)** boring
    (B) boreing

28. **(A)** haunted
    (B) hauntted

29. **(A)** didn't
    (B) diddn't

30. **(A)** electted
    (B) elected

31. **(A)** componnent
    (B) component

32. **(A)** bacgage
    (B) baggage

33. (A) resignation
    (B) resegnation

34. (A) sevear
    (B) severe

35. (A) edition
    (B) eddition

36. (A) organist
    (B) oraganist

37. (A) coming
    (B) comming

38. (A) closet
    (B) closett

39. (A) skimppy
    (B) skimpy

40. (A) pressident
    (B) president

41. (A) profesional
    (B) professional

42. (A) swimer
    (B) swimmer

43. (A) tackle
    (B) tackel

44. (A) inventer
    (B) inventor

45. (A) cary
    (B) carry

46. (A) persentd
    (B) presented

47. (A) classified
    (B) clasified

48. (A) refridgerator
    (B) refrigerator

49. (A) maters
    (B) matters

50. (A) apear
    (B) appear

S T O P End of Spelling section. If you finish before time is up, check your work on this part only. Do not turn to the next part until the signal is given.

CODING

100 QUESTIONS • 9 MINUTES

Sample Answer Sheet

1. Ⓐ Ⓑ Ⓒ Ⓓ   3. Ⓐ Ⓑ Ⓒ Ⓓ   5. Ⓐ Ⓑ Ⓒ Ⓓ
2. Ⓐ Ⓑ Ⓒ Ⓓ   4. Ⓐ Ⓑ Ⓒ Ⓓ

Directions: Using the data bank supplied, match the letter in each question with its corresponding number from the data bank.

Example:

BIN	JJN	TOM	KCT
21	42	76	88

XET	OMJ	YUP	ECD
80	54	65	12

1. BIN   **(A)** 33   **(B)** 76   **(C)** 21   **(D)** 88
2. TOM   **(A)** 76   **(B)** 96   **(C)** 43   **(D)** 21
3. KCT   **(A)** 43   **(B)** 54   **(C)** 21   **(D)** 88
4. OMJ   **(A)** 24   **(B)** 42   **(C)** 88   **(D)** 54
5. ECD   **(A)** 73   **(B)** 12   **(C)** 80   **(D)** 42

Answer Key

1. C	2. A	3. D	4. D	5. B

TOR	JIN	TEY	DUD	WAT	QUN
34	64	72	23	73	60

GTE	BDT	CNT	MIK	OST	FPD
45	87	12	27	37	41

1. TOR   **(A)** 64   **(B)** 12   **(C)** 34   **(D)** 37
2. BDT   **(A)** 12   **(B)** 64   **(C)** 87   **(D)** 60
3. QUN   **(A)** 23   **(B)** 60   **(C)** 64   **(D)** 37
4. FPD   **(A)** 14   **(B)** 73   **(C)** 41   **(D)** 12
5. TEY   **(A)** 23   **(B)** 34   **(C)** 73   **(D)** 72
6. DUD   **(A)** 27   **(B)** 19   **(C)** 32   **(D)** 23
7. WAT   **(A)** 37   **(B)** 64   **(C)** 60   **(D)** 73
8. MIK   **(A)** 72   **(B)** 12   **(C)** 27   **(D)** 37
9. OST   **(A)** 34   **(B)** 37   **(C)** 60   **(D)** 45

TOR	JIN	TEY	DUD	WAT	QUN
34	64	72	23	73	60

GTE	BDT	CNT	MIK	OST	FPD
45	87	12	27	37	41

10. CNT   (A) 87   (B) 12   (C) 27   (D) 23
11. BDT   (A) 12   (B) 64   (C) 87   (D) 41
12. JIN   (A) 72   (B) 45   (C) 73   (D) 64
13. GTE   (A) 60   (B) 54   (C) 45   (D) 64
14. OST   (A) 43   (B) 37   (C) 19   (D) 89
15. MIK   (A) 27   (B) 85   (C) 72   (D) 51
16. DUD   (A) 51   (B) 29   (C) 43   (D) 23
17. OST   (A) 27   (B) 64   (C) 34   (D) 37
18. FPD   (A) 41   (B) 14   (C) 64   (D) 12
19. CNT   (A) 12   (B) 27   (C) 55   (D) 92
20. GTE   (A) 45   (B) 12   (C) 37   (D) 41
21. TOR   (A) 45   (B) 27   (C) 34   (D) 23
22. TEY   (A) 23   (B) 72   (C) 27   (D) 65
23. CNT   (A) 27   (B) 78   (C) 21   (D) 12
24. QUN   (A) 16   (B) 17   (C) 55   (D) 60
25. JIN   (A) 56   (B) 65   (C) 72   (D) 64
26. DUD   (A) 51   (B) 29   (C) 43   (D) 23
27. OST   (A) 27   (B) 64   (C) 34   (D) 37
28. FPD   (A) 41   (B) 14   (C) 64   (D) 12
29. CNT   (A) 12   (B) 27   (C) 55   (D) 92
30. GTE   (A) 45   (B) 12   (C) 37   (D) 41
31. TOR   (A) 45   (B) 27   (C) 34   (D) 23
32. TEY   (A) 23   (B) 72   (C) 27   (D) 65
33. CNT   (A) 27   (B) 78   (C) 21   (D) 12
34. QUN   (A) 16   (B) 17   (C) 55   (D) 60
35. JIN   (A) 56   (B) 65   (C) 72   (D) 64
36. TEY   (A) 12   (B) 81   (C) 27   (D) 72
37. TOR   (A) 23   (B) 34   (C) 43   (D) 63
38. MIK   (A) 37   (B) 74   (C) 41   (D) 27
39. BDT   (A) 87   (B) 78   (C) 23   (D) 13
40. QUN   (A) 60   (B) 52   (C) 78   (D) 73
41. WAT   (A) 60   (B) 12   (C) 72   (D) 73
42. FPD   (A) 14   (B) 41   (C) 89   (D) 77
43. DUD   (A) 32   (B) 23   (C) 41   (D) 37
44. GTE   (A) 87   (B) 27   (C) 98   (D) 45

TOR	JIN	TEY	DUD	WAT	QUN
34	64	72	23	73	60

GTE	BDT	CNT	MIK	OST	FPD
45	87	12	27	37	41

		(A)	**(B)**	**(C)**	**(D)**
45.	TOR	(A) 56	(B) 65	(C) 28	(D) 34
46.	BDT	(A) 12	(B) 56	(C) 98	(D) 87
47.	OST	(A) 51	(B) 37	(C) 89	(D) 72
48.	FPD	(A) 44	(B) 41	(C) 12	(D) 45
49.	WAT	(A) 73	(B) 37	(C) 17	(D) 96
50.	TEY	(A) 27	(B) 96	(C) 78	(D) 72
51.	OST	(A) 51	(B) 37	(C) 89	(D) 72
52.	FPD	(A) 44	(B) 41	(C) 12	(D) 45
53.	WAT	(A) 73	(B) 37	(C) 17	(D) 96
54.	TEY	(A) 27	(B) 96	(C) 78	(D) 72
55.	JIN	(A) 29	(B) 64	(C) 46	(D) 72
56.	BDT	(A) 12	(B) 56	(C) 98	(D) 87
57.	TOR	(A) 45	(B) 27	(C) 34	(D) 23
58.	TEY	(A) 23	(B) 72	(C) 27	(D) 65
59.	CNT	(A) 27	(B) 78	(C) 21	(D) 12
60.	FPD	(A) 14	(B) 41	(C) 89	(D) 77
61.	DUD	(A) 32	(B) 23	(C) 41	(D) 37
62.	GTE	(A) 87	(B) 27	(C) 98	(D) 45
63.	DUD	(A) 27	(B) 19	(C) 32	(D) 23
64.	WAT	(A) 37	(B) 64	(C) 60	(D) 73
65.	MIK	(A) 72	(B) 12	(C) 27	(D) 37
66.	OST	(A) 34	(B) 37	(C) 60	(D) 45
67.	TOR	(A) 64	(B) 12	(C) 34	(D) 37
68.	BDT	(A) 12	(B) 64	(C) 87	(D) 60
69.	QUN	(A) 23	(B) 60	(C) 64	(D) 37
70.	FPD	(A) 14	(B) 73	(C) 41	(D) 12
71.	TEY	(A) 23	(B) 34	(C) 73	(D) 72
72.	BDT	(A) 12	(B) 56	(C) 98	(D) 87
73.	OST	(A) 51	(B) 37	(C) 89	(D) 72
74.	FPD	(A) 44	(B) 41	(C) 12	(D) 45
75.	TOR	(A) 64	(B) 45	(C) 56	(D) 34
76.	DUD	(A) 60	(B) 64	(C) 19	(D) 23
77.	OST	(A) 37	(B) 60	(C) 34	(D) 55
78.	BDT	(A) 87	(B) 89	(C) 78	(D) 41
79.	CNT	(A) 58	(B) 72	(C) 27	(D) 12

TOR	JIN	TEY	DUD	WAT	QUN
34	64	72	23	73	60

GTE	BDT	CNT	MIK	OST	FPD
45	87	12	27	37	41

80. BDT   **(A)** 12   **(B)** 64   **(C)** 87   **(D)** 41
81. JIN   **(A)** 72   **(B)** 45   **(C)** 73   **(D)** 64
82. GTE   **(A)** 60   **(B)** 54   **(C)** 45   **(D)** 64
83. OST   **(A)** 43   **(B)** 37   **(C)** 19   **(D)** 89
84. MIK   **(A)** 27   **(B)** 85   **(C)** 72   **(D)** 51
85. JIN   **(A)** 29   **(B)** 64   **(C)** 46   **(D)** 72
86. DUD   **(A)** 51   **(B)** 29   **(C)** 43   **(D)** 23
87. OST   **(A)** 27   **(B)** 64   **(C)** 34   **(D)** 37
88. FPD   **(A)** 41   **(B)** 14   **(C)** 64   **(D)** 12
89. CNT   **(A)** 12   **(B)** 27   **(C)** 55   **(D)** 92
90. GTE   **(A)** 45   **(B)** 12   **(C)** 37   **(D)** 41
91. OST   **(A)** 51   **(B)** 37   **(C)** 89   **(D)** 72
92. FPD   **(A)** 44   **(B)** 41   **(C)** 12   **(D)** 45
93. WAT   **(A)** 73   **(B)** 37   **(C)** 17   **(D)** 96
94. TOR   **(A)** 45   **(B)** 27   **(C)** 34   **(D)** 23
95. TEY   **(A)** 23   **(B)** 72   **(C)** 27   **(D)** 65
96. CNT   **(A)** 27   **(B)** 78   **(C)** 21   **(D)** 12
97. DUD   **(A)** 60   **(B)** 64   **(C)** 19   **(D)** 23
98. OST   **(A)** 37   **(B)** 60   **(C)** 34   **(D)** 55
99. GTE   **(A)** 45   **(B)** 12   **(C)** 37   **(D)** 41
100. FPD   **(A)** 41   **(B)** 15   **(C)** 60   **(D)** 45

S T O P   End of Coding section. If you finish before time is up, check your work on this part only. Do not turn to the next part until the signal is given.

MATH

70 QUESTIONS • 50 MINUTES

Directions: Perform the operation as indicated in the question and find the answer among the list of responses. You may use scrap paper.

1. 895 − 237 =

   (A) 658
   (B) 1,358
   (C) 558
   (D) 1,132

2. 18 + 75 =

   (A) 93
   (B) 99
   (C) 57
   (D) 89

3. 40 + 20 + 1 =

   (A) 61
   (B) 66
   (C) 56
   (D) 60

4. 9,700 + 300 =

   (A) 10,000
   (B) 100,000
   (C) 9,400
   (D) 1,000

5. 456 + 456 =

   (A) 789
   (B) 912
   (C) 802
   (D) 1,324

6. 1,900 + 1,900 =

   (A) 2,100
   (B) 3,800
   (C) 38,000
   (D) 2,900

7. 180 + 180 =

   (A) 280
   (B) 380
   (C) 680
   (D) 360

8. 20 + 20 =

   (A) 40
   (B) 360
   (C) 0
   (D) 60

9. 6,790 + 6,799 =

   (A) 13,589
   (B) 15,892
   (C) 13,580
   (D) 17,853

10. Two offices competed in a sales contest. The Eastern Office exceeded the goal for sales by $1,862. The Southern Office exceeded the sales goal by $5,564. The Vice President promised the winning office a bonus on April 14th. The bonus would be $500.00 per person. The Eastern Office has a staff of 100 people, and the Southern Office has a staff of 432 people. On April 14th, which office received the bonus and how much was the total amount of the bonus for the winning office?

    (A) Eastern, $216,000
    (B) Southern, $100,000
    (C) Eastern, $100,000
    (D) Southern, $216,000

11. $2 + 8(3 \times 3) =$

    (A) 99
    (B) 19
    (C) 106
    (D) 74

12. 80 + 80 =
   (A) 180
   (B) 640
   (C) 190
   (D) 160

13. A legal file cabinet has 4 drawers, and a letter file cabinet has 5 drawers. In the Western Office, they have 66 letter file cabinets and 44 legal file cabinets. The Northern Office has 187 letter cabinets and 62 legal file cabinets. How many drawers does a Northern Office legal file cabinet have?

   (A) 106
   (B) 424
   (C) 1,265
   (D) 4

14. 4 × 3 =
   (A) 12
   (B) 32
   (C) 16
   (D) 13

15. The current price of a gallon of gasoline is $2.990. If gas prices rise 20 percent in the next 8 months, what will the price of two gallons of gas be?

   (A) not enough information
   (B) $3.588
   (C) $4.50
   (D) $7.176

16. If unleaded gasoline is $2.99 a gallon and super unleaded is 17 percent more expensive than unleaded, how much is a gallon of super unleaded gasoline?

   (A) $3.4983
   (B) $3.299
   (C) $34.983
   (D) not enough information

17. The stapler has a capacity of 500 staples. If, in an 8-hour day, Lucy uses 50 percent of the staples, Mary uses 30 percent of the staples, and Todd uses 25 percent of the staples, will there be enough staples, and if so how many staples will be left?

   (A) 0
   (B) not enough staples
   (C) 5
   (D) 25

18. Each new box of files contains 500 individual files. If Lauren was told to purchase 25,000 boxes of files, how many individual files would there be?

   (A) 12,500
   (B) 12,500,000
   (C) 125,000,000
   (D) 1,250,000

19. 1.5 + 1.5 + 1.5 + 1.5 =
   (A) 6.0
   (B) 5.5
   (C) 6.5
   (D) 10

20. The current sales tax in New Jersey is .07. How much tax will you pay on office supplies worth $97.00?

   (A) $6.79
   (B) $5.46
   (C) $9.87
   (D) $9.70

QUESTIONS 21–30 ARE BASED ON THE INFORMATION BELOW.

United States Data Bank

In 2005, the latest data bank on the population of the United States was completed. The population was compiled by 500 people in each of the 50 states. Puerto Rico, as a sovereign of the United States, had 50 people assigned to compile data. Data collection for all regions began in January 2003. The data collection in Puerto Rico ended on July 31, 2003. The United States data collectors were finished on December 31, 2004. Each worker gathered information on the population of each assigned state or sovereign. When the data was compiled, each worker had to send the information to Washington, D.C. Each worker was assigned to work 20 hours a month. Each worker generated 10 reports a month. After the data was completed, 75 people reviewed the data. The reviewers worked from January 2005 to December 2005.

21. How many reports were generated from January 2003 to March 2003 by the Sovereign of Puerto Rico?

    (A) 1,000
    (B) 15
    (C) 150
    (D) 1,500

22. How many workers in total were collecting data in July 2004?

    (A) 500
    (B) 50
    (C) 550
    (D) 0

23. How many reports were generated in March of 2004?

    (A) 500
    (B) 5,500
    (C) 5,000
    (D) 250

24. What was the total amount of hours worked in July 2003?

    (A) 10,000
    (B) 20,000
    (C) 11,000
    (D) 55,000

25. How many workers were there in January 2003?

    (A) 500
    (B) 450
    (C) 550
    (D) 50

26. How many hours were worked between January 2003 and March 2003?

    (A) 20,000
    (B) 30,000
    (C) 33,000
    (D) 55,000

27. How many reports were generated between January 2003 and July 2003?

    (A) 77,000
    (B) 38,500
    (C) 110,000
    (D) 350,000

28. In May 2003, how many workers were collecting data?

    (A) 550
    (B) 500
    (C) 450
    (D) 50

29. How many reports were submitted in month of December 2004?

    (A) 500
    (B) 50,000
    (C) 2,500
    (D) 5,000

30. How many reviewers worked in January 2005?

    (A) 75
    (B) 125
    (C) 0
    (D) 150

31. $13 + 17 + 7 =$
    (A) 37
    (B) 58
    (C) 100
    (D) 48

32. $5 \times 7 \times 4 =$
    (A) 144
    (B) 240
    (C) 380
    (D) 140

33. $60 + 40 + 30 =$
    (A) 120
    (B) 180
    (C) 160
    (D) 130

34. $1,050 + 3,760 =$
    (A) 4,908
    (B) 6,000
    (C) 4,810
    (D) 2,345

35. Which number represents seven tenths?
    (A) 0.07
    (B) 0.7
    (C) 7.0
    (D) .077

36. Which number represents one and three tenths?
    (A) 0.133
    (B) 1.30
    (C) 1.030
    (D) .0130

37. Which number represents twenty-one hundredths?
    (A) 0.21
    (B) 2.100
    (C) 21.100
    (D) .0210

38. Which number represents six tenths?
    (A) 0.006
    (B) 0.60
    (C) 6.0
    (D) .0610

39. Which number represents three and seven tenths?
    (A) 37.37
    (B) 0.37
    (C) 3.7
    (D) 3.370

40. Which number represents thirty-two and six tenths?
    (A) .3260
    (B) 3.260
    (C) 32.610
    (D) 32.60

41. Which number represents forty and sixteen hundredths?
    (A) 40.16
    (B) 416.100
    (C) 40.016
    (D) 0.416

42. Which number represents fifty-one and one hundredth?
    (A) 0.5110
    (B) 5.110
    (C) 51.01
    (D) 51.10

43. Which number represents six tenths?
    (A) 0.06
    (B) 0.6
    (C) 0.006
    (D) 6.0

44. Which number represents seven and five tenths?
    (A) 7.5
    (B) 0.75
    (C) 7.05
    (D) 0.705

45. Which number represents forty-one hundredths?
    (A) 0.41
    (B) 4.01
    (C) .0041
    (D) .041

46. $3 \times 3 + 9 =$

(A) 18
(B) 81
(C) 18
(D) 96

47. $4 \times 12 =$

(A) 48
(B) 36
(C) 54
(D) 44

48. $5 \times 20 =$

(A) 100
(B) 10
(C) 200
(D) 150

49. $100 \times 20 =$

(A) 2,000
(B) 200
(C) 20,000
(D) 2,200

50. $7 \times 100 + 7 =$

(A) 700
(B) 707
(C) 749
(D) 179

51. $4,000 \times 9 =$

(A) 3,600
(B) 360,000
(C) 36,000
(D) 38,000

52. Sam must place 10 files on each shelf. How many files does he need to fill up 35 shelves?

(A) 35
(B) 35.50
(C) 350
(D) 3,500

53. A bicycle trip across the United States is about 3,000 miles. On average, how many miles would you need to travel every day to complete a 2,660-mile trip in four weeks?

(A) 100
(B) 89
(C) 95
(D) 90

54. There were 16 computers and only 4 monitors. How many more monitors are needed to have an equal amount of computers and monitors?

(A) 11
(B) 13
(C) 12
(D) not enough information

55. At 8:00 a.m., 84 workers were present in the office. The office has a total number of 130 workers. At 9:00 a.m., 10 more workers were in the office. At 9:00 a.m., how many workers were not in the office?

(A) 132
(B) 36
(C) 94
(D) not enough information

56. Ginger had to purchase 40 hole punchers for the office. The hole punchers come in a package of 8 for $1.29. How many packages should Ginger buy?

(A) 5
(B) 8
(C) 40
(D) not enough information

57. There are 5 work days in a week. Employees work 40 hours a week. Since there are 52 weeks in a year, how many hours a year will an employee work?

(A) 2,080
(B) 2,120
(C) 2,210
(D) 14,840

58. Russell works 180 days a year. When Russell has finished 120 days of work, how many days are left to work?

  (A) 60
  (B) 90
  (C) 40
  (D) not enough information

59. Peter is transferred to a new office. The new office has 26 employees. There are only 17 present during a bad storm. How many were absent?

  (A) 19
  (B) 8
  (C) 13
  (D) 9

60. Blaine and 12 coworkers decide to have an office party. According to the caterer, they must have 18 people for a party. How many more office workers do they need to invite?

  (A) 18
  (B) 8
  (C) 13
  (D) 5

61. Blair and Nancy earned $240.00 for a local charity during an office fund-raiser. They decided to give the same amount to each of 4 charities. How much did they give to each charity?

  (A) $120
  (B) $70
  (C) $80
  (D) $60

62. $12 \times 12 =$

  (A) 142
  (B) 124
  (C) 144
  (D) 148

63. $15 \times 2 =$

  (A) 45
  (B) 35
  (C) 30
  (D) 50

64. $30 \times 3 =$

  (A) 90
  (B) 120
  (C) 33
  (D) 900

65. Roberto has 100 pens in his desk. Fifty percent of the pens are blue ink, 25 percent are red ink, and the remaining 25 percent are black ink. How many pens are in black and red ink?

  (A) 25
  (B) 50
  (C) 75
  (D) 35

66. $25 + 125 - 100 =$

  (A) 75
  (B) 100
  (C) 50
  (D) 25

67. The office is raising money for a new computer system. The goal is $7,500. So far, the office has saved $5,687. How much more is needed?

  (A) $1,873
  (B) $2,346
  (C) $1,313
  (D) $1,813

68. The supervisor at a local motor vehicle office estimates that they will have 1,200 customers on December 30th. On December 29th a meeting is held, and 50 employees are told that they each will see the same estimated number of customers on December 30th. What is the estimated number of customers that each employee will see?

  (A) 24
  (B) 240
  (C) 20
  (D) not enough information

69. At a local office complex, there were 27 businesses in building #1 and 35 businesses in building #2. How many businesses were in both buildings?

(A) 62
(B) 65
(C) 61
(D) not enough information

70. There are 70 employees working on a project. Fifty percent of the workers are engineers, and 10 workers are laborers. The remaining workers are clerical staff. How many clerical workers are there working on this project?

(A) 25
(B) 32
(C) 7
(D) not enough information

STOP End of Math section. If you finish before time is up, check your work on this part only.

ANSWER KEY AND EXPLANATIONS

Vocabulary

1. D	11. B	21. C	31. C	41. C
2. C	12. C	22. C	32. B	42. A
3. A	13. A	23. D	33. B	43. C
4. B	14. D	24. D	34. D	44. D
5. C	15. A	25. A	35. C	45. B
6. D	16. D	26. B	36. C	46. A
7. A	17. B	27. A	37. D	47. D
8. D	18. A	28. C	38. D	48. B
9. D	19. C	29. A	39. A	49. B
10. B	20. B	30. C	40. B	50. D

Spelling

1. B	11. B	21. A	31. A	41. A
2. A	12. B	22. B	32. A	42. A
3. B	13. B	23. A	33. B	43. B
4. B	14. A	24. A	34. A	44. A
5. B	15. A	25. B	35. B	45. A
6. B	16. B	26. B	36. B	46. A
7. B	17. B	27. B	37. B	47. B
8. B	18. B	28. B	38. B	48. A
9. B	19. A	29. B	39. A	49. A
10. B	20. B	30. A	40. A	50. A

answers diagnostic test

Coding

1.	C	21.	C	41.	D	61.	B	81.	D
2.	C	22.	B	42.	B	62.	D	82.	C
3.	B	23.	D	43.	B	63.	D	83.	B
4.	C	24.	D	44.	D	64.	D	84.	A
5.	D	25.	D	45.	D	65.	C	85.	B
6.	D	26.	D	46.	D	66.	B	86.	D
7.	D	27.	D	47.	B	67.	C	87.	D
8.	C	28.	A	48.	B	68.	C	88.	A
9.	B	29.	A	49.	A	69.	B	89.	A
10.	B	30.	A	50.	D	70.	C	90.	A
11.	C	31.	C	51.	B	71.	D	91.	B
12.	D	32.	B	52.	B	72.	D	92.	B
13.	C	33.	D	53.	A	73.	B	93.	A
14.	B	34.	D	54.	D	74.	B	94.	C
15.	A	35.	D	55.	B	75.	D	95.	B
16.	D	36.	D	56.	D	76.	D	96.	D
17.	D	37.	B	57.	C	77.	A	97.	D
18.	A	38.	D	58.	B	78.	A	98.	A
19.	A	39.	A	59.	D	79.	D	100.	A
20.	A	40.	A	60.	B	80.	C		

Math

1.	A	15.	D	29.	D	43.	B	57.	A
2.	A	16.	A	30.	A	44.	A	58.	A
3.	A	17.	B	31.	A	45.	A	59.	D
4.	A	18.	B	32.	D	46.	A	60.	D
5.	B	19.	A	33.	D	47.	A	61.	D
6.	B	20.	A	34.	C	48.	A	62.	C
7.	D	21.	D	35.	A	49.	A	63.	C
8.	A	22.	A	36.	B	50.	B	64.	A
9.	A	23.	C	37.	A	51.	C	65.	B
10.	D	24.	C	38.	B	52.	C	66.	C
11.	D	25.	C	39.	C	53.	C	67.	D
12.	D	26.	C	40.	D	54.	C	68.	A
13.	D	27.	B	41.	A	55.	B	69.	A
14.	A	28.	A	42.	C	56.	A	70.	A

1. **The correct answer is (A).**

$$
\begin{array}{r}
895 \\
-\ 237 \\
\hline
658
\end{array}
$$

2. **The correct answer is (A).**

$$
\begin{array}{r}
18 \\
+\ 75 \\
\hline
93
\end{array}
$$

3. **The correct answer is (A).**

$$
\begin{array}{r}
40 \\
20 \\
+\ \ 1 \\
\hline
61
\end{array}
$$

4. **The correct answer is (A).**

$$
\begin{array}{r}
9{,}700 \\
+\ \ \ \ 300 \\
\hline
10{,}000
\end{array}
$$

5. **The correct answer is (B).**

$$
\begin{array}{r}
456 \\
+\ 456 \\
\hline
912
\end{array}
$$

6. **The correct answer is (B).**

$$
\begin{array}{r}
1{,}900 \\
+\ 1{,}900 \\
\hline
3{,}800
\end{array}
$$

7. **The correct answer is (D).**

$$
\begin{array}{r}
180 \\
+\ 180 \\
\hline
360
\end{array}
$$

8. **The correct answer is (A).**

$$
\begin{array}{r}
20 \\
+\ 20 \\
\hline
40
\end{array}
$$

9. **The correct answer is (A).**

$$\begin{array}{r} 6{,}790 \\ +\ \ 6{,}799 \\ \hline 13{,}589 \end{array}$$

10. **The correct answer is (D).** The Southern Office wins the sales contest. Multiply the number of office staff members (432) by the amount of the bonus ($500.00):

$$\begin{array}{r} \$500 \\ \times\,432 \\ \hline \$216{,}00 \end{array}$$

11. **The correct answer is (D).** The order of operation is: multiplication within parentheses, then multiplication, then addition: $2 + 8(3 \times 3) = 2 + 8 \times 9 = 2 + 72 = 74$.

12. **The correct answer is (D)**

$$\begin{array}{r} 80 \\ +\ \ 80 \\ \hline 160 \end{array}$$

13. **The correct answer is (D).** No math is required to answer this question. The premise states that a legal file cabinet has 4 drawers.

14. **The correct answer is (A).**

$$\begin{array}{r} 4 \\ \times\,3 \\ \hline 12 \end{array}$$

15. **The correct answer is (D).** The price of a gallon of gas is $2.990. Multiply this by 20 percent, or .20:

$$\begin{array}{r} \$2.990 \\ \times\,.20 \\ \hline .598 \end{array}$$

Take this sum and add it to 2.990:

$$\begin{array}{r} \$2.990 \\ +\,.598 \\ \hline 3.588 \end{array}$$

This is the new price of one gallon of gas. Now multiply this by 2 to get the price of two gallons of gas:

$$\begin{array}{r} \$3.588 \\ \times\,2 \\ \hline \$7.176 \end{array}$$

16. **The correct answer is (A).** Multiply the price of a gallon of gas, $2.99, by 17 percent, or .17:

$2.99
× .17
.5083

Take this sum and add it to $2.99:

.5083
+ $2.99
$3.4983

17. **The correct answer is (B).** Add the percentages of staples used. As the percent used is greater than 100 percent, you will not have enough staples.

50
30
+ 25
105

18. **The correct answer is (B).**

25,000
× 500
12,500,000

There are 12,500,000 individual files.

19. **The correct answer is (A).**

1.5
1.5
1.5
+ 1.5
6.0

20. **The correct answer is (A).**

$97.00
× .07
$6.79

For questions 21–30, you must read and understand the information in the question. It may help you to use scrap paper and make a list like this one:

- 2005: Last data bank completed

- 500 people collected data in the United States: began January 2003/ended December 2004

- 50 people collected data in Puerto Rico: began January 2003/ended July 2003

- All workers: employed 20 hours per month

- All workers: generated 10 reports a month

- After collection ended: 75 people reviewed data/reviewers worked from January 2005– December 2005

21. **The correct answer is (D).** There are 50 data collectors in Puerto Rico, and each of them is required to write 10 reports a month. Multiply these two numbers to find out how many reports were done in one month:

$$\begin{array}{r} 50 \\ \times\,10 \\ \hline 500 \end{array}$$

Now multiply this by 3 to find how many reports were done in three months in Puerto Rico:

$$\begin{array}{r} 500 \\ \times\,3 \\ \hline 1{,}500 \end{array}$$

22. **The correct answer is (A).** Check your chart and you will find that only data collectors in the United States were working in July of 2004.

23. **The correct answer is (C).** Check you chart and you will find that only data collectors in the United States were working in March of 2004. Multiply the number of workers (500) by the number of reports (10 per month) to find how many reports were generated in March:

$$\begin{array}{r} 500 \\ \times\,10 \\ \hline 5{,}000 \end{array}$$

24. **The correct answer is (C).** In July of 2003, there were a total of 550 workers, and they each worked 20 hours. So,

$$\begin{array}{r} 550 \\ \times\,20 \\ \hline 11{,}000 \end{array}$$

The total number of hours worked is 11,000.

25. **The correct answer is (C).** Add together the number of United States and Puerto Rico employees:

$$\begin{array}{r} 500 \\ +50 \\ \hline 550 \end{array}$$

26. **The correct answer is (C).** Between January and March of 2003, there were 550 workers. Multiply this by 20 (the number of hours worked) to find how many hours were worked in one month:

$$\begin{array}{r} 550 \\ \times\,20 \\ \hline 11,000 \end{array}$$

Multiply this by 3 to find how many hours were worked in three months:

$$\begin{array}{r} 11,000 \\ \times\,3 \\ \hline 33,000 \end{array}$$

27. **The correct answer is (B).** Between January and July of 2003, there were 550 workers. Multiply this by 10 (the number of reports per month per worker) to find how many reports were generated in one month:

$$\begin{array}{r} 550 \\ \times\,10 \\ \hline 5,500 \end{array}$$

Multiply this by 7 to find how many reports were generated in the seven months from January to July:

$$\begin{array}{r} 5,500 \\ \times\,7 \\ \hline 38,500 \end{array}$$

28. **The correct answer is (A).** Add together the number of United States and Puerto Rico employees:

$$\begin{array}{r} 500 \\ +50 \\ \hline 500 \end{array}$$

29. **The correct answer is (D).** In December 2004, only 500 workers were employed, and they each completed 10 reports a month.

$$\begin{array}{r} 500 \\ \times\,10 \\ \hline 5,000 \end{array}$$

30. **The correct answer is (A).** There were 75 reviewers working from January 2005 to December 2005.

31. **The correct answer is (A).** Make this problem easy: $7 + 13 = 20$ and $20 + 17 = 37$. You can also solve it like this:

$$\begin{array}{r} 13 \\ 17 \\ +7 \\ \hline 30 \end{array}$$

32. **The correct answer is (D).** $5 \times 7 = 35$, and $35 \times 4 = 140$.

33. **The correct answer is (D).**

$$\begin{array}{r} 60 \\ +40 \\ \hline 100 \end{array}$$

$$\begin{array}{r} 100 \\ +30 \\ \hline 130 \end{array}$$

34. **The correct answer is (C).**

$$\begin{array}{r} 1{,}050 \\ +3{,}760 \\ \hline 4{,}810 \end{array}$$

Questions 35–45 deal with decimals and placements.

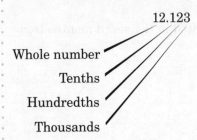

Whole number
Tenths
Hundredths
Thousands

35. **The correct answer is (A).**
36. **The correct answer is (B).**
37. **The correct answer is (A).**
38. **The correct answer is (B).**
39. **The correct answer is (C).**
40. **The correct answer is (D).**
41. **The correct answer is (A).**
42. **The correct answer is (C).**
43. **The correct answer is (B).**
44. **The correct answer is (A).**
45. **The correct answer is (A).**

46. **The correct answer is (A).** The order of operation is: multiplication first, then addition:

    $3 \times 3 = 9$

    $9 + 9 = 18$

47. **The correct answer is (A).**

    $$\begin{array}{r} 12 \\ \times\ 4 \\ \hline 48 \end{array}$$

48. **The correct answer is (A).**

    $$\begin{array}{r} 20 \\ \times\ 5 \\ \hline 100 \end{array}$$

49. **The correct answer is (A).**

    $$\begin{array}{r} 100 \\ \times\ 20 \\ \hline 2,000 \end{array}$$

50. **The correct answer is (B).** Order of operation: multiplication first, then addition.

    $7 \times 100 = 700$

    $700 + 7 = 707$

51. **The correct answer is (C).**

    $$\begin{array}{r} 4,000 \\ \times\ 9 \\ \hline 36,000 \end{array}$$

52. **The correct answer is (C).** There are 35 shelves, and 10 files per shelf. So,

    $$\begin{array}{r} 35 \\ \times\ 10 \\ \hline 350 \end{array}$$

    Sam needs a total of 350 files.

53. **The correct answer is (C).** The first sentence presents information that is not needed. Implied is the fact that there are 7 days in a week. Thus, multiply $7 \times 4 = 28$ days in four weeks. Divide the 2,660-mile trip by the 28 days: $2,660 \div 28 = 95$.

54. **The correct answer is (C).**

    $$\begin{array}{r} 16 \\ -\ 4 \\ \hline 12 \end{array}$$

55. The correct answer is (B). Create a quick list:

8:00 a.m.: 84 workers present

9:00 a.m.: 10 more workers present

Total by 9 a.m.: 84 + 10 = 94 workers present

$$\begin{array}{r} 130 \\ -94 \\ \hline 36 \end{array}$$

At 9 a.m., 36 workers were not yet at the office.

56. The correct answer is (A). The price is not needed and the problem can be solved by simply dividing 40 by 8: $40 \div 8 = 5$.

57. The correct answer is (A). There are 40 work hours in a week and 52 weeks in a year. Multiply these two numbers to find the work hours in a year:

$$\begin{array}{r} 40 \\ \times\,52 \\ \hline 2{,}080 \end{array}$$

58. The correct answer is (A). Russell works 180 days a year, and he has already worked 120 days. Subtract 120 from 180 to find how many days he has left to work:

$$\begin{array}{r} 180 \\ -\,120 \\ \hline 60 \end{array}$$

59. The correct answer is (D). Subtract the number of employees present (17) from the number of total employees (26) to find how many employees are absent:

$$\begin{array}{r} 26 \\ -\,17 \\ \hline 9 \end{array}$$

60. The correct answer is (D). Subtract the number of coworkers ready for the party (13-don't forget to add in Blaine) from the minimum number of coworkers needed for a party (18) to find how many more coworkers they need to invite:

$$\begin{array}{r} 18 \\ -\,13 \\ \hline 5 \end{array}$$

61. The correct answer is (D). Divide $240 by 4 to find how much they give to each charity:

$240 \div 4 = \$60$.

62. **The correct answer is (C).**

$$
\begin{array}{r}
12 \\
\times\ 12 \\
\hline
144
\end{array}
$$

63. **The correct answer is (C).**

$$
\begin{array}{r}
15 \\
\times\ 2 \\
\hline
30
\end{array}
$$

64. **The correct answer is (A).**

$$
\begin{array}{r}
30 \\
\times\ 3 \\
\hline
90
\end{array}
$$

65. **The correct answer is (B).** Fifty percent of 100 = 50 blue ink pens. The remaining pens are red and black ink pens.

66. **The correct answer is (C).**

$$
\begin{array}{r}
25 \\
+\ 125 \\
\hline
150
\end{array}
$$

$$
\begin{array}{r}
150 \\
-\ 100 \\
\hline
50
\end{array}
$$

67. **The correct answer is (D).** Subtract the amount of money already saved ($5,687) from the total amount of money needed ($7,500) to find how much money is still needed to achieve the goal:

$$
\begin{array}{r}
\$7,500 \\
-\ \$5,687 \\
\hline
\$1,813
\end{array}
$$

68. **The correct answer is (A).** Ignore the dates, since you don't need this information to solve the problem. Simply divide 1200 customers by 50 employees: $1,200 \div 50 = 24$.

69. **The correct answer is (A).** You don't need to know the building numbers to solve the problem. Simply add the number of businesses:

$$
\begin{array}{r}
27 \\
+\ 35 \\
\hline
62
\end{array}
$$

70. **The correct answer is (A).** To find the number of engineers, multiply the total number of workers (70) by 50 percent, or .50:

$$\begin{array}{r} 70 \\ \times\ .50 \\ \hline 35 \end{array}$$

So, 35 workers are engineers. Add to this the number of laborers (10):

$$\begin{array}{r} 35 \\ +\ 10 \\ \hline 45 \end{array}$$

Now, subtract this number from the total number of workers to find how many clerical workers there are:

$$\begin{array}{r} 70 \\ -\ 45 \\ \hline 25 \end{array}$$

PART III

EIGHT PRACTICE TESTS

ANSWER SHEET PRACTICE TEST 2

VOCABULARY

1. Ⓐ Ⓑ Ⓒ Ⓓ
2. Ⓐ Ⓑ Ⓒ Ⓓ
3. Ⓐ Ⓑ Ⓒ Ⓓ
4. Ⓐ Ⓑ Ⓒ Ⓓ
5. Ⓐ Ⓑ Ⓒ Ⓓ
6. Ⓐ Ⓑ Ⓒ Ⓓ
7. Ⓐ Ⓑ Ⓒ Ⓓ
8. Ⓐ Ⓑ Ⓒ Ⓓ
9. Ⓐ Ⓑ Ⓒ Ⓓ
10. Ⓐ Ⓑ Ⓒ Ⓓ
11. Ⓐ Ⓑ Ⓒ Ⓓ
12. Ⓐ Ⓑ Ⓒ Ⓓ
13. Ⓐ Ⓑ Ⓒ Ⓓ
14. Ⓐ Ⓑ Ⓒ Ⓓ
15. Ⓐ Ⓑ Ⓒ Ⓓ
16. Ⓐ Ⓑ Ⓒ Ⓓ
17. Ⓐ Ⓑ Ⓒ Ⓓ

18. Ⓐ Ⓑ Ⓒ Ⓓ
19. Ⓐ Ⓑ Ⓒ Ⓓ
20. Ⓐ Ⓑ Ⓒ Ⓓ
21. Ⓐ Ⓑ Ⓒ Ⓓ
22. Ⓐ Ⓑ Ⓒ Ⓓ
23. Ⓐ Ⓑ Ⓒ Ⓓ
24. Ⓐ Ⓑ Ⓒ Ⓓ
25. Ⓐ Ⓑ Ⓒ Ⓓ
26. Ⓐ Ⓑ Ⓒ Ⓓ
27. Ⓐ Ⓑ Ⓒ Ⓓ
28. Ⓐ Ⓑ Ⓒ Ⓓ
29. Ⓐ Ⓑ Ⓒ Ⓓ
30. Ⓐ Ⓑ Ⓒ Ⓓ
31. Ⓐ Ⓑ Ⓒ Ⓓ
32. Ⓐ Ⓑ Ⓒ Ⓓ
33. Ⓐ Ⓑ Ⓒ Ⓓ
34. Ⓐ Ⓑ Ⓒ Ⓓ

35. Ⓐ Ⓑ Ⓒ Ⓓ
36. Ⓐ Ⓑ Ⓒ Ⓓ
37. Ⓐ Ⓑ Ⓒ Ⓓ
38. Ⓐ Ⓑ Ⓒ Ⓓ
39. Ⓐ Ⓑ Ⓒ Ⓓ
40. Ⓐ Ⓑ Ⓒ Ⓓ
41. Ⓐ Ⓑ Ⓒ Ⓓ
42. Ⓐ Ⓑ Ⓒ Ⓓ
43. Ⓐ Ⓑ Ⓒ Ⓓ
44. Ⓐ Ⓑ Ⓒ Ⓓ
45. Ⓐ Ⓑ Ⓒ Ⓓ
46. Ⓐ Ⓑ Ⓒ Ⓓ
47. Ⓐ Ⓑ Ⓒ Ⓓ
48. Ⓐ Ⓑ Ⓒ Ⓓ
49. Ⓐ Ⓑ Ⓒ Ⓓ
50. Ⓐ Ⓑ Ⓒ Ⓓ

MATH

1. Ⓐ Ⓑ Ⓒ Ⓓ
2. Ⓐ Ⓑ Ⓒ Ⓓ
3. Ⓐ Ⓑ Ⓒ Ⓓ
4. Ⓐ Ⓑ Ⓒ Ⓓ
5. Ⓐ Ⓑ Ⓒ Ⓓ
6. Ⓐ Ⓑ Ⓒ Ⓓ
7. Ⓐ Ⓑ Ⓒ Ⓓ
8. Ⓐ Ⓑ Ⓒ Ⓓ
9. Ⓐ Ⓑ Ⓒ Ⓓ
10. Ⓐ Ⓑ Ⓒ Ⓓ
11. Ⓐ Ⓑ Ⓒ Ⓓ
12. Ⓐ Ⓑ Ⓒ Ⓓ
13. Ⓐ Ⓑ Ⓒ Ⓓ
14. Ⓐ Ⓑ Ⓒ Ⓓ
15. Ⓐ Ⓑ Ⓒ Ⓓ
16. Ⓐ Ⓑ Ⓒ Ⓓ
17. Ⓐ Ⓑ Ⓒ Ⓓ

18. Ⓐ Ⓑ Ⓒ Ⓓ
19. Ⓐ Ⓑ Ⓒ Ⓓ
20. Ⓐ Ⓑ Ⓒ Ⓓ
21. Ⓐ Ⓑ Ⓒ Ⓓ
22. Ⓐ Ⓑ Ⓒ Ⓓ
23. Ⓐ Ⓑ Ⓒ Ⓓ
24. Ⓐ Ⓑ Ⓒ Ⓓ
25. Ⓐ Ⓑ Ⓒ Ⓓ
26. Ⓐ Ⓑ Ⓒ Ⓓ
27. Ⓐ Ⓑ Ⓒ Ⓓ
28. Ⓐ Ⓑ Ⓒ Ⓓ
29. Ⓐ Ⓑ Ⓒ Ⓓ
30. Ⓐ Ⓑ Ⓒ Ⓓ
31. Ⓐ Ⓑ Ⓒ Ⓓ
32. Ⓐ Ⓑ Ⓒ Ⓓ
33. Ⓐ Ⓑ Ⓒ Ⓓ
34. Ⓐ Ⓑ Ⓒ Ⓓ

35. Ⓐ Ⓑ Ⓒ Ⓓ
36. Ⓐ Ⓑ Ⓒ Ⓓ
37. Ⓐ Ⓑ Ⓒ Ⓓ
38. Ⓐ Ⓑ Ⓒ Ⓓ
39. Ⓐ Ⓑ Ⓒ Ⓓ
40. Ⓐ Ⓑ Ⓒ Ⓓ
41. Ⓐ Ⓑ Ⓒ Ⓓ
42. Ⓐ Ⓑ Ⓒ Ⓓ
43. Ⓐ Ⓑ Ⓒ Ⓓ
44. Ⓐ Ⓑ Ⓒ Ⓓ
45. Ⓐ Ⓑ Ⓒ Ⓓ
46. Ⓐ Ⓑ Ⓒ Ⓓ
47. Ⓐ Ⓑ Ⓒ Ⓓ
48. Ⓐ Ⓑ Ⓒ Ⓓ
49. Ⓐ Ⓑ Ⓒ Ⓓ
50. Ⓐ Ⓑ Ⓒ Ⓓ

answer sheet

PERCEPTUAL SKILLS

1. Ⓢ Ⓓ
2. Ⓢ Ⓓ
3. Ⓢ Ⓓ
4. Ⓢ Ⓓ
5. Ⓢ Ⓓ
6. Ⓢ Ⓓ
7. Ⓢ Ⓓ
8. Ⓢ Ⓓ
9. Ⓢ Ⓓ
10. Ⓢ Ⓓ
11. Ⓢ Ⓓ
12. Ⓢ Ⓓ
13. Ⓢ Ⓓ
14. Ⓢ Ⓓ
15. Ⓢ Ⓓ
16. Ⓢ Ⓓ
17. Ⓢ Ⓓ

18. Ⓢ Ⓓ
19. Ⓢ Ⓓ
20. Ⓢ Ⓓ
21. Ⓢ Ⓓ
22. Ⓢ Ⓓ
23. Ⓢ Ⓓ
24. Ⓢ Ⓓ
25. Ⓢ Ⓓ
26. Ⓢ Ⓓ
27. Ⓢ Ⓓ
28. Ⓢ Ⓓ
29. Ⓢ Ⓓ
30. Ⓢ Ⓓ
31. Ⓢ Ⓓ
32. Ⓢ Ⓓ
33. Ⓢ Ⓓ
34. Ⓢ Ⓓ

35. Ⓢ Ⓓ
36. Ⓢ Ⓓ
37. Ⓢ Ⓓ
38. Ⓢ Ⓓ
39. Ⓢ Ⓓ
40. Ⓢ Ⓓ
41. Ⓢ Ⓓ
42. Ⓢ Ⓓ
43. Ⓢ Ⓓ
44. Ⓢ Ⓓ
45. Ⓢ Ⓓ
46. Ⓢ Ⓓ
47. Ⓢ Ⓓ
48. Ⓢ Ⓓ
49. Ⓢ Ⓓ
50. Ⓢ Ⓓ

SPELLING

1. Ⓐ Ⓑ
2. Ⓐ Ⓑ
3. Ⓐ Ⓑ
4. Ⓐ Ⓑ
5. Ⓐ Ⓑ
6. Ⓐ Ⓑ
7. Ⓐ Ⓑ
8. Ⓐ Ⓑ
9. Ⓐ Ⓑ
10. Ⓐ Ⓑ
11. Ⓐ Ⓑ
12. Ⓐ Ⓑ
13. Ⓐ Ⓑ
14. Ⓐ Ⓑ
15. Ⓐ Ⓑ
16. Ⓐ Ⓑ
17. Ⓐ Ⓑ

18. Ⓐ Ⓑ
19. Ⓐ Ⓑ
20. Ⓐ Ⓑ
21. Ⓐ Ⓑ
22. Ⓐ Ⓑ
23. Ⓐ Ⓑ
24. Ⓐ Ⓑ
25. Ⓢ Ⓑ
26. Ⓐ Ⓑ
27. Ⓐ Ⓑ
28. Ⓐ Ⓑ
29. Ⓐ Ⓑ
30. Ⓐ Ⓑ
31. Ⓐ Ⓑ
32. Ⓐ Ⓑ
33. Ⓐ Ⓑ
34. Ⓐ Ⓑ

35. Ⓐ Ⓑ
36. Ⓐ Ⓑ
37. Ⓐ Ⓑ
38. Ⓐ Ⓑ
39. Ⓐ Ⓑ
40. Ⓐ Ⓑ
41. Ⓐ Ⓑ
42. Ⓐ Ⓑ
43. Ⓐ Ⓑ
44. Ⓐ Ⓑ
45. Ⓐ Ⓑ
46. Ⓐ Ⓑ
47. Ⓐ Ⓑ
48. Ⓐ Ⓑ
49. Ⓐ Ⓑ
50. Ⓐ Ⓑ

CODING

1. Ⓐ Ⓑ Ⓒ Ⓓ	35. Ⓐ Ⓑ Ⓒ Ⓓ	68. Ⓐ Ⓑ Ⓒ Ⓓ
2. Ⓐ Ⓑ Ⓒ Ⓓ	36. Ⓐ Ⓑ Ⓒ Ⓓ	69. Ⓐ Ⓑ Ⓒ Ⓓ
3. Ⓐ Ⓑ Ⓒ Ⓓ	37. Ⓐ Ⓑ Ⓒ Ⓓ	70. Ⓐ Ⓑ Ⓒ Ⓓ
4. Ⓐ Ⓑ Ⓒ Ⓓ	38. Ⓐ Ⓑ Ⓒ Ⓓ	71. Ⓐ Ⓑ Ⓒ Ⓓ
5. Ⓐ Ⓑ Ⓒ Ⓓ	39. Ⓐ Ⓑ Ⓒ Ⓓ	72. Ⓐ Ⓑ Ⓒ Ⓓ
6. Ⓐ Ⓑ Ⓒ Ⓓ	40. Ⓐ Ⓑ Ⓒ Ⓓ	73. Ⓐ Ⓑ Ⓒ Ⓓ
7. Ⓐ Ⓑ Ⓒ Ⓓ	41. Ⓐ Ⓑ Ⓒ Ⓓ	74. Ⓐ Ⓑ Ⓒ Ⓓ
8. Ⓐ Ⓑ Ⓒ Ⓓ	42. Ⓐ Ⓑ Ⓒ Ⓓ	75. Ⓐ Ⓑ Ⓒ Ⓓ
9. Ⓐ Ⓑ Ⓒ Ⓓ	43. Ⓐ Ⓑ Ⓒ Ⓓ	76. Ⓐ Ⓑ Ⓒ Ⓓ
10. Ⓐ Ⓑ Ⓒ Ⓓ	44. Ⓐ Ⓑ Ⓒ Ⓓ	77. Ⓐ Ⓑ Ⓒ Ⓓ
11. Ⓐ Ⓑ Ⓒ Ⓓ	45. Ⓐ Ⓑ Ⓒ Ⓓ	78. Ⓐ Ⓑ Ⓒ Ⓓ
12. Ⓐ Ⓑ Ⓒ Ⓓ	46. Ⓐ Ⓑ Ⓒ Ⓓ	79. Ⓐ Ⓑ Ⓒ Ⓓ
13. Ⓐ Ⓑ Ⓒ Ⓓ	47. Ⓐ Ⓑ Ⓒ Ⓓ	80. Ⓐ Ⓑ Ⓒ Ⓓ
14. Ⓐ Ⓑ Ⓒ Ⓓ	48. Ⓐ Ⓑ Ⓒ Ⓓ	81. Ⓐ Ⓑ Ⓒ Ⓓ
15. Ⓐ Ⓑ Ⓒ Ⓓ	49. Ⓐ Ⓑ Ⓒ Ⓓ	82. Ⓐ Ⓑ Ⓒ Ⓓ
16. Ⓐ Ⓑ Ⓒ Ⓓ	50. Ⓐ Ⓑ Ⓒ Ⓓ	83. Ⓐ Ⓑ Ⓒ Ⓓ
17. Ⓐ Ⓑ Ⓒ Ⓓ	51. Ⓐ Ⓑ Ⓒ Ⓓ	84. Ⓐ Ⓑ Ⓒ Ⓓ
18. Ⓐ Ⓑ Ⓒ Ⓓ	52. Ⓐ Ⓑ Ⓒ Ⓓ	85. Ⓐ Ⓑ Ⓒ Ⓓ
19. Ⓐ Ⓑ Ⓒ Ⓓ	53. Ⓐ Ⓑ Ⓒ Ⓓ	86. Ⓐ Ⓑ Ⓒ Ⓓ
20. Ⓐ Ⓑ Ⓒ Ⓓ	54. Ⓐ Ⓑ Ⓒ Ⓓ	87. Ⓐ Ⓑ Ⓒ Ⓓ
21. Ⓐ Ⓑ Ⓒ Ⓓ	55. Ⓐ Ⓑ Ⓒ Ⓓ	88. Ⓐ Ⓑ Ⓒ Ⓓ
22. Ⓐ Ⓑ Ⓒ Ⓓ	56. Ⓐ Ⓑ Ⓒ Ⓓ	89. Ⓐ Ⓑ Ⓒ Ⓓ
23. Ⓐ Ⓑ Ⓒ Ⓓ	57. Ⓐ Ⓑ Ⓒ Ⓓ	90. Ⓐ Ⓑ Ⓒ Ⓓ
24. Ⓐ Ⓑ Ⓒ Ⓓ	58. Ⓐ Ⓑ Ⓒ Ⓓ	91. Ⓐ Ⓑ Ⓒ Ⓓ
25. Ⓐ Ⓑ Ⓒ Ⓓ	59. Ⓐ Ⓑ Ⓒ Ⓓ	92. Ⓐ Ⓑ Ⓒ Ⓓ
26. Ⓐ Ⓑ Ⓒ Ⓓ	60. Ⓐ Ⓑ Ⓒ Ⓓ	93. Ⓐ Ⓑ Ⓒ Ⓓ
27. Ⓐ Ⓑ Ⓒ Ⓓ	61. Ⓐ Ⓑ Ⓒ Ⓓ	94. Ⓐ Ⓑ Ⓒ Ⓓ
28. Ⓐ Ⓑ Ⓒ Ⓓ	62. Ⓐ Ⓑ Ⓒ Ⓓ	95. Ⓐ Ⓑ Ⓒ Ⓓ
29. Ⓐ Ⓑ Ⓒ Ⓓ	63. Ⓐ Ⓑ Ⓒ Ⓓ	96. Ⓐ Ⓑ Ⓒ Ⓓ
30. Ⓐ Ⓑ Ⓒ Ⓓ	64. Ⓐ Ⓑ Ⓒ Ⓓ	97. Ⓐ Ⓑ Ⓒ Ⓓ
31. Ⓐ Ⓑ Ⓒ Ⓓ	65. Ⓐ Ⓑ Ⓒ Ⓓ	98. Ⓐ Ⓑ Ⓒ Ⓓ
32. Ⓐ Ⓑ Ⓒ Ⓓ	66. Ⓐ Ⓑ Ⓒ Ⓓ	99. Ⓐ Ⓑ Ⓒ Ⓓ
33. Ⓐ Ⓑ Ⓒ Ⓓ	67. Ⓐ Ⓑ Ⓒ Ⓓ	100. Ⓐ Ⓑ Ⓒ Ⓓ
34. Ⓐ Ⓑ Ⓒ Ⓓ		

answer sheet

Practice Test 2

VOCABULARY

50 QUESTIONS • 20 MINUTES

Directions: Read each sentence carefully. Choose the letter of the word that best answers the question.

1. Which word means the same as MALADROIT?

   (A) evil
   (B) arrogant
   (C) clumsy
   (D) annex

2. Which word means the same as ANNUAL?

   (A) yearly
   (B) timely
   (C) period
   (D) occurrence

3. Which word means the opposite of PUSILLANI-MOUS?

   (A) cowardly
   (B) hesitant
   (C) vicious
   (D) brave

4. Which word means the opposite of NEFARIOUS?

   (A) moral
   (B) heinous
   (C) near
   (D) certain

5. Which word means the same as FECKLESS?

   (A) ineffective
   (B) worthy
   (C) copious
   (D) exempt

6. Which word means the same as EPHEMERAL?

   (A) temporary
   (B) disparage
   (C) illuminate
   (D) alter

7. Which word means the opposite of PLETHORA?

   (A) abundance
   (B) flora
   (C) shortage
   (D) censure

8. Which word means the same as CENSURE?

   (A) lethargy
   (B) criticize
   (C) candid
   (D) shortage

9. Which word means the same as TORPOR?

   (A) lethargy
   (B) decrease
   (C) subside
   (D) meander

10. Which word means the same as ELUCIDATE?

   (A) detest
   (B) reproach
   (C) obscure
   (D) clarify

11. Which word means the opposite of FORLORN?

   (A) optimistic
   (B) curtail
   (C) dormant
   (D) sedate

12. Which word means the opposite of ABROGATE?

   (A) cease
   (B) indolent
   (C) commence
   (D) establish

13. Which word means the same as TEMERITY?

   (A) rashness
   (B) caution
   (C) futile
   (D) wander

14. Which word means the same as ACIDULOUS?

   (A) aesthetic
   (B) bitter
   (C) nullify
   (D) niche

15. Which word means the same as INSIPID?

   (A) insulting
   (B) liberal
   (C) commend
   (D) bland

16. Which word means the opposite of DESPONDENT?

   (A) happy
   (B) depressed
   (C) upset
   (D) brave

17. Which word means the same as ASTOUND?

   (A) zealous
   (B) rancor
   (C) ephemeral
   (D) astonish

18. Which word means the same as CONDUCT?

   (A) risk
   (B) lead
   (C) myth
   (D) enigma

19. Which word means the opposite of OBSCURE?

   (A) extensive
   (B) tedious
   (C) obvious
   (D) devious

20. Which word means the opposite of ABHOR?

   (A) offensive
   (B) cherish
   (C) trivial
   (D) equate

21. Which word means the same as EFFORT?

   (A) exertion
   (B) indolence
   (C) site
   (D) reality

22. Which word means the same as OBTRUDE?

    (A) pacify
    (B) procure
    (C) brevity
    (D) intrude

23. Which word means the opposite of LASSITUDE?

    (A) argument
    (B) vigor
    (C) nourish
    (D) fickle

24. Which word means the same as EXTROVERT?

    (A) introvert
    (B) enhance
    (C) society
    (D) outgoing

25. Which word means the opposite of PROTRACT?

    (A) extend
    (B) hesitant
    (C) curtail
    (D) plethora

26. Which word means the opposite of CONSERVE?

    (A) relinquish
    (B) waste
    (C) proficient
    (D) rigid

27. Which word means the same as CONFINE?

    (A) limit
    (B) languor
    (C) discern
    (D) paucity

28. Which word means the same as RISK?

    (A) exceed
    (B) admire
    (C) alter
    (D) hazard

29. Which word means the same as APATHETIC?

    (A) protract
    (B) quiet
    (C) effective
    (D) dull

30. Which word means the opposite of FICKLE?

    (A) reliable
    (B) abrogate
    (C) oblique
    (D) frigid

31. Which word means the same as INDOLENT?

    (A) insipid
    (B) meager
    (C) lazy
    (D) reserved

32. Which word means the same as TRANSLUCENT?

    (A) forlorn
    (B) transparent
    (C) prominent
    (D) debilitate

33. Which word means the same as SINUOUS?

    (A) firm
    (B) winding
    (C) pathetic
    (D) lavish

34. Which word means the opposite of DISSIPATE?

    (A) scatter
    (B) emancipate
    (C) engage
    (D) accumulate

practice test

35. Which word means the opposite of
PROFANE?

   (A) secular
   (B) sacred
   (C) clandestine
   (D) concur

36. Which word means the same as
OBLIQUE?

   (A) obscure
   (B) diverse
   (C) identical
   (D) slanted

37. Which word means the opposite of
HABITUAL?

   (A) occasional
   (B) negligent
   (C) breadth
   (D) truculent

38. Which word means the same as
SEDATE?

   (A) malicious
   (B) faltering
   (C) hinder
   (D) quiet

39. Which word means the same as
DISCERN?

   (A) protest
   (B) observe
   (C) obtrude
   (D) impotent

40. Which word means the opposite of
INTREPID?

   (A) oblique
   (B) lucrative
   (C) fearful
   (D) verbose

41. Which word means the same as
CONNIVE?

   (A) conspire
   (B) abate
   (C) deliberate
   (D) assimilate

42. Which word means the same as
TRUCULENT?

   (A) permanent
   (B) barbarous
   (C) reluctant
   (D) tedious

43. Which word means the opposite of
DEXTROUS?

   (A) adroit
   (B) defend
   (C) clumsy
   (D) sumptuous

44. Which word means the same as
ANIMATED?

   (A) alive
   (B) affluent
   (C) urbane
   (D) fortuitous

45. Which word means the opposite of
ADOPT?

   (A) discard
   (B) fickle
   (C) lassitude
   (D) seldom

46. Which word means the same as
PANACEA?

   (A) cure
   (B) vow
   (C) rancor
   (D) desolate

47. Which word means the opposite of
LETHARGY?

   (A) energy
   (B) indigenous
   (C) reciprocal
   (D) apathy

48. Which word means the same as JUDICIOUS?

(A) hostile
(B) dissension
(C) sapient
(D) illicit

49. Which word means the same as LEGEND?

(A) map
(B) myth
(C) ratification
(D) torsion

50. Which word means the opposite of OBSTRUCT?

(A) facilitate
(B) elucidate
(C) nefarious
(D) disseminate

STOP End of Vocabulary section. If you finish before time is up, check your work on this part only. Do not turn to the next part until the signal is given.

MATH

50 QUESTIONS • 35 MINUTES

Directions: Perform the operation as indicated in the question and find the answer among the list of responses. You may use scrap paper.

1. 470 + 330 =
   - **(A)** 900
   - **(B)** 800
   - **(C)** 140
   - **(D)** 730

2. 550 + 550 =
   - **(A)** 1,000
   - **(B)** 1,200
   - **(C)** 1,100
   - **(D)** 950

3. 1.5 + 1.5 + 6 =
   - **(A)** 7.10
   - **(B)** 9.5
   - **(C)** 9
   - **(D)** 0

4. 990 + 1 =
   - **(A)** 1,000
   - **(B)** 9,910
   - **(C)** 890
   - **(D)** 991

5. 700 × 5 =
   - **(A)** 705
   - **(B)** 3,500
   - **(C)** 2,800
   - **(D)** 4,000

6. 435 − 222 =
   - **(A)** 215
   - **(B)** 213
   - **(C)** 312
   - **(D)** 123

7. 213 − 87 + 19 =
   - **(A)** 319
   - **(B)** 278
   - **(C)** 154
   - **(D)** 145

8. 145 × 19 =
   - **(A)** 2,755
   - **(B)** 164
   - **(C)** 1,775
   - **(D)** 3,275

9. 472(10 × 59) =
   - **(A)** 4,779
   - **(B)** 1,062
   - **(C)** 278,480
   - **(D)** 288,590

10. 791(578 + 12) =
    - **(A)** 457,210
    - **(B)** 466,690
    - **(C)** 466,960
    - **(D)** 452,710

11. Jim had 19 file cabinets in his office. All of the file cabinets had 6 drawers. How many drawers were there in total?
    - **(A)** 142
    - **(B)** 411
    - **(C)** 114
    - **(D)** 133

12. Jane and Paul are clerks for the Federal Government. They each are paid an hourly wage of $13.47. Jane works 32 hours a week and Paul works 38 hours a week. What is the difference in weekly pay between Jane and Paul?
    - **(A)** $800.82
    - **(B)** $80.82
    - **(C)** $26.94
    - **(D)** $13.47

13. Michael earns $864.34 a week working for the Tempos Company as an office assistant. Each week, 6 percent of his paycheck is invested in the company 401K plan. How much does Michael invest each week in his 401K rounded to the nearest penny?

    (A) $519.86
    (B) $5.18
    (C) $86.64
    (D) $51.86

14. The office just purchased 32 telephones. Each phone cost $13.99 each. How much did the 32 phones cost?

    (A) $447.68
    (B) $475.00
    (C) $181.87
    (D) $497.68

15. What would be the total cost with 7 percent sales tax added to the total purchase price of the phones in question 14?

    (A) $514.78
    (B) $479.02
    (C) $512.03
    (D) $31.34

16. Jeffrey and Lauren work for a landscaping company as office staff. They are given five days off a month. How many days off are they given in a year?

    (A) 25
    (B) 60
    (C) 84
    (D) 45

17. Nancy and John each earn $500 a week. If Nancy receives a 25 percent raise how much more will she make than John?

    (A) $625
    (B) $75.00
    (C) $225
    (D) $125

18. Russell received a pay raise of 7 percent. What will his yearly salary be if he was earning $25,700 before his raise?

    (A) $1,799
    (B) $27,499
    (C) $32,400
    (D) $27,500

19. Ginger received a pay raise of 10 percent. Her yearly salary was $40,000. How much more money did she receive after her raise?

    (A) $44,000
    (B) $4,400
    (C) $400
    (D) $4,000

20. Peter received a pay raise of 20 percent. His yearly salary is $50,000. How much more money did he receive after his raise?

    (A) $60,000
    (B) $15,000
    (C) $10,000
    (D) $5,000

21. $100 + 200 - 50 + 10 =$

    (A) 240
    (B) 260
    (C) 360
    (D) 160

22. $600 \times 2 =$

  (A) 1,800
  (B) 1,600
  (C) 1,200
  (D) 12,000

23. $899 + 199 =$

  (A) 999
  (B) 1,098
  (C) 1,200
  (D) 1,198

24. Which is greater: $\frac{1}{2}$ or $\frac{1}{3}$?

  (A) $\frac{1}{2}$

  (B) $\frac{1}{3}$

25. Which is greater: $\frac{1}{3}$ or $\frac{3}{4}$?

  (A) $\frac{1}{3}$

  (B) $\frac{3}{4}$

26. Which is greater: $\frac{7}{8}$ or $\frac{1}{3}$?

  (A) $\frac{1}{3}$

  (B) $\frac{7}{8}$

27. Which is greater: $\frac{4}{5}$ or $\frac{3}{8}$?

  (A) $\frac{4}{5}$

  (B) $\frac{3}{8}$

28. Which is greater: $\frac{1}{8}$ or $\frac{1}{4}$?

  (A) $\frac{1}{8}$

  (B) $\frac{1}{4}$

29. Which is greater: $\frac{1}{2}$ or $\frac{3}{4}$?

  (A) $\frac{1}{2}$

  (B) $\frac{3}{4}$

30. Which is greater: .25 or .75?

  (A) .25
  (B) .75

31. How many quarters are there in $100.00?

  (A) 40
  (B) 400
  (C) 40.5
  (D) 100

32. How many dimes are there in $220.00?

  (A) 22,200
  (B) 22
  (C) 2,200
  (D) 20,200

33. 50% of 1,000 =

  (A) 150
  (B) 500
  (C) 1,100
  (D) 250

34. 75% of 8,000 =

  (A) 2,000
  (B) 4,000
  (C) 6,000
  (D) 14,000

35. 25% of 10,000 =

  (A) 2,500
  (B) 7,500
  (C) 5,000
  (D) 12,500

36. 50% of 7,000 =

  (A) 4,000
  (B) 3,500
  (C) 1,500
  (D) 5,000

37. 80% of 100 =

  (A) 8,000
  (B) 20
  (C) 80
  (D) 800

38. 23% of 1,000 =

(A) 320
(B) 2,300
(C) 230
(D) 770

39. 67% of 200 =

(A) 125
(B) 321
(C) 134
(D) 431

40. 90% of 10,000 =

(A) 8,000
(B) 9,000
(C) 1,000
(D) 900

41. Marge works in the office of a shipping company. Her annual rate of pay is $52,000. What does she earn an hour if she works 40 hours a week for 52 weeks a year?

(A) $50
(B) $52
(C) $25
(D) $47

42. If Edward is twice as old as Jack and Jack is 13, how old is Edward?

(A) 32
(B) 26
(C) 38
(D) unknown

43. Carole purchased gasoline for her vehicle. She needed 20 gallons of gas and she paid a total of $51.00. How much did Carole pay per gallon of gasoline?

(A) $2.55
(B) $3.00
(C) $2.50
(D) unknown

44. Roger is purchasing the following items: 3 staplers, 4 phones, and 20 coffee mugs. He has a budget of $45.00. The coffee mugs are on sale for 10 for $2.00, the staplers are 3 for $5.00, and the phones are $20.00 apiece. How much more money will Roger need to purchase all of the items?

(A) $45
(B) $44
(C) $19
(D) unknown

QUESTIONS 45–50 ARE BASED ON THE INFORMATION BELOW.

Office City	Sales Rank	Production Material Produced	Rank for Production	Damaged Materials	Employees	Percent of Profit	Sales Points	Weeks without Injuries
Chicago	12.6	281	11	2	24	41	36	7
Pittsburgh	16	284	3	4	15	47	20	4
Indianapolis	15	270	9	6	24	40	21	3
Denver	4	20	5	10	28	21	20	8
Tampa Bay	80	2	80	78	123	10	2	0
Dallas	1	380	1	0	85	72	100	16
Minnesota	7	300	8	12	32	33	90	12
Detroit	81	1	81	82	81	19	9	2
Buffalo	3	299	3	6	69	32	70	4

This graph is a small section of a much larger production graph of the Urbana International Paper and Plastic Company.

45. What was the total number of Damaged Materials for the Dallas and Buffalo offices?

(A) 23
(B) 6
(C) 12
(D) 10

46. How many offices have had 10 or more weeks without an injury?

(A) 2
(B) 8
(C) 6
(D) 0

47. What was the total number of Damaged Materials for the Buffalo, Chicago, Pittsburgh, and Denver offices?

(A) 22
(B) 16
(C) 78
(D) 32

48. What were the total sales points of Dallas, Minnesota, and Detroit?

(A) 198
(B) 298
(C) 197
(D) 199

49. Which office had the lowest number of weeks without an injury?

(A) Dallas
(B) Tampa Bay
(C) Detroit
(D) Minnesota

50. Tampa Bay has 123 employees. What is the total number of employees of Dallas, Detroit, and Pittsburgh?

(A) 304
(B) 181
(C) 323
(D) 201

S T O P End of Math section. If you finish before time is up, check your work on this part only. Do not turn to the next part until the signal is given.

PERCEPTUAL SKILLS

50 QUESTIONS • 7 MINUTES

Sample Answer Sheet

1. Ⓢ Ⓓ   2. Ⓢ Ⓓ   3. Ⓢ Ⓓ

Directions: Compare the two choices if they are the same or different. Darken your answer sheets **S**—Indicating Same or **D**—Indicating Different.

Example:

	S—Indicates Same	**D**—Indicates Different		
1.	2345	2345	**(S)**	**(D)**
2.	HNU8	HNU8	**(S)**	**(D)**
3.	UJO90	UJ009	**(S)**	**(D)**

Answers:

1. ● Ⓓ (Same)

2. ● Ⓓ (Same)

3. Ⓢ ● (Different)

	S—Indicates Same	**D**—Indicates Different		
1.	8U8U	8UH8	**(S)**	**(D)**
2.	9LOP	9LOP	**(S)**	**(D)**
3.	1Q21	1Q21	**(S)**	**(D)**
4.	9823	9823	**(S)**	**(D)**
5.	1WS3	1W3S	**(S)**	**(D)**
6.	9MJ8	9MJ8	**(S)**	**(D)**
7.	B89112	B89112	**(S)**	**(D)**
8.	PO99P99	PO99P9	**(S)**	**(D)**
9.	77LL77	77LL77	**(S)**	**(D)**
10.	12332HN	12332NH	**(S)**	**(D)**
11.	NNMNN33	NNNMNN33	**(S)**	**(D)**
12.	JJK09922	JJKK09922	**(S)**	**(D)**
13.	8890POPP	8890POPP	**(S)**	**(D)**
14.	TTY677890	TTY67908	**(S)**	**(D)**
15.	9PO2345	9PO2345	**(S)**	**(D)**
16.	XFXXXE3	XFXXEX3	**(S)**	**(D)**
17.	1595651	159951	**(S)**	**(D)**

S—Indicates Same   **D**—Indicates Different

18.	3697895	3697895	**(S)**	**(D)**
19.	8998	8998	**(S)**	**(D)**
20.	90912	90912	**(S)**	**(D)**
21.	TUN90	TON90	**(S)**	**(D)**
22.	12344321	1234321	**(S)**	**(D)**
23.	L92387	L98234	**(S)**	**(D)**
24.	J980O	JP98O	**(S)**	**(D)**
25.	4587	4587	**(S)**	**(D)**
26.	B896321	896369871	**(S)**	**(D)**
27.	8BPLM	B8PLM	**(S)**	**(D)**
28.	98789	98789	**(S)**	**(D)**
29.	ED873	ED87E	**(S)**	**(D)**
30.	147852	147852	**(S)**	**(D)**
31.	K9852	K9258	**(S)**	**(D)**
32.	95147	95174	**(S)**	**(D)**
33.	J9870	J9870	**(S)**	**(D)**
34.	NJU7	NJU7	**(S)**	**(D)**
35.	543345	543345	**(S)**	**(D)**
36.	L7L78M	L7L78M	**(S)**	**(D)**
37.	357753	357753	**(S)**	**(D)**
38.	3WSZSW	3WZSWS	**(S)**	**(D)**
39.	878987	8788987	**(S)**	**(D)**
40.	QQ112	QQ1122	**(S)**	**(D)**
41.	8766YHGV	8766YHGW	**(S)**	**(D)**
42.	VGY7	VGY7	**(S)**	**(D)**
43.	8BC2L7	B8C2L7	**(S)**	**(D)**
44.	HGT6	HGT6	**(S)**	**(D)**
45.	4587	4587	**(S)**	**(D)**
46.	33SS33	(S)S33SS33	**(S)**	**(D)**
47.	TG56765	TG56765	**(S)**	**(D)**
48.	1Q2W3	1Q2W3	**(S)**	**(D)**
49.	HU8899	HU9988	**(S)**	**(D)**
50.	963369	93669	**(S)**	**(D)**

S T O P   End of Perceptual Skills section. If you finish before time is up, check your work on this part only. Do not turn to the next part until the signal is given.

SPELLING

50 QUESTIONS • 9 MINUTES

Directions: Find the correctly spelled word in each question and darken your answer sheet indicating which answer is spelled correctly.

1. (A) spindal
    (B) spindle

2. (A) university
    (B) universety

3. (A) handle
    (B) handel

4. (A) cellular
    (B) celular

5. (A) clearence
    (B) clearance

6. (A) inintial
    (B) initial

7. (A) Januarry
    (B) January

8. (A) importent
    (B) important

9. (A) confine
    (B) comfine

10. (A) telephown
    (B) telephone

11. (A) financiel
    (B) financial

12. (A) serviecs
    (B) services

13. (A) tuiton
    (B) tuition

14. (A) diplomaetic
    (B) diplomatic

15. (A) durable
    (B) dureable

16. (A) signel
    (B) signal

17. (A) yesterday
    (B) yestarday

18. (A) thirilled
    (B) thrilled

19. (A) situation
    (B) sitution

20. (A) negotiator
    (B) negociator

21. (A) steretch
    (B) stretch

22. (A) spokesman
    (B) spokeman

23. (A) speaker
    (B) speakar

24. (A) proposal
    (B) proposel

25. (A) embraces
    (B) embrases

26. (A) arrivel
    (B) arrival

27. (A) express
    (B) expres

28. (A) calcuelate
    (B) calculate

29. (A) compleatley
    (B) completely

30. (A) comunters
    (B) commuters

31. (A) buera
    (B) bureau

32. (A) marshall
    (B) marshal

33. (A) inheritance
    (B) inherritance

34. (A) obituary
    (B) obetuary

35. (A) sieze
    (B) seize

36. (A) yesterday
    (B) yestarday

37. (A) horrible
    (B) horible

38. (A) edditorial
    (B) editorial

39. (A) cheif
    (B) chief

40. (A) elaments
    (B) elements

41. (A) interperate
    (B) interpret

42. (A) scaner
    (B) scanner

43. (A) civilen
    (B) civilian

44. (A) responsibility
    (B) responsibillity

45. (A) individuel
    (B) individual

46. (A) diddn't
    (B) didn't

47. (A) observerd
    (B) observed

48. (A) respond
    (B) repond

49. (A) morror
    (B) mirror

50. (A) reflection
    (B) reflaction

STOP   End of Spelling section. If you finish before time is up, check your work on this part only. Do not turn to the next part until the signal is given.

CODING

100 QUESTIONS • 9 MINUTES

Sample Answer Sheet

1. Ⓐ Ⓑ Ⓒ Ⓓ   3. Ⓐ Ⓑ Ⓒ Ⓓ   5. Ⓐ Ⓑ Ⓒ Ⓓ
2. Ⓐ Ⓑ Ⓒ Ⓓ   4. Ⓐ Ⓑ Ⓒ Ⓓ

Directions: Using the data bank supplied, match the letter in each question with its corresponding number from the data bank.

Example:

JPV	HID	GMT	NRK	DLP	TUT
66	34	63	67	12	19

LEN	JVH	ASI	MVM	NIT	LOQ
92	20	44	50	72	75

1. LEN   **(A)** 20   **(B)** 92   **(C)** 50   **(D)** 66
2. TOM   **(A)** 76   **(B)** 96   **(C)** 43   **(D)** 21
3. KCT   **(A)** 43   **(B)** 54   **(C)** 21   **(D)** 88
4. OMJ   **(A)** 24   **(B)** 42   **(C)** 88   **(D)** 54
5. ECD   **(A)** 73   **(B)** 12   **(C)** 80   **(D)** 42

Answer Key

1. C   2. A   3. D   4. D   5. B

JPV	HID	GMT	NRK	DLP	TUT
66	34	63	67	12	19

LEN	JVH	ASI	MVM	NIT	LOQ
92	20	44	50	72	75

1. LEN   **(A)** 20   **(B)** 92   **(C)** 50   **(D)** 66
2. JVH   **(A)** 44   **(B)** 19   **(C)** 20   **(D)** 75
3. ASI   **(A)** 67   **(B)** 92   **(C)** 44   **(D)** 12
4. JPV   **(A)** 34   **(B)** 76   **(C)** 92   **(D)** 66
5. TUT   **(A)** 19   **(B)** 91   **(C)** 34   **(D)** 20
6. MVM   **(A)** 55   **(B)** 67   **(C)** 44   **(D)** 50
7. ASI   **(A)** 12   **(B)** 44   **(C)** 72   **(D)** 75
8. LOQ   **(A)** 75   **(B)** 96   **(C)** 92   **(D)** 59
9. HID   **(A)** 34   **(B)** 43   **(C)** 99   **(D)** 66

JPV	HID	GMT	NRK	DLP	TUT
66	34	63	67	12	19

LEN	JVH	ASI	MVM	NIT	LOQ
92	20	44	50	72	75

10. GMT (A) 36 (B) 77 (C) 63 (D) 19
11. NRK (A) 76 (B) 67 (C) 12 (D) 44
12. LOQ (A) 19 (B) 66 (C) 92 (D) 75
13. NIT (A) 12 (B) 72 (C) 45 (D) 65
14. JPV (A) 34 (B) 63 (C) 66 (D) 50
15. LEN (A) 92 (B) 20 (C) 34 (D) 98
16. ASI (A) 50 (B) 45 (C) 85 (D) 44
17. JPV (A) 66 (B) 34 (C) 63 (D) 20
18. MVM (A) 77 (B) 54 (C) 66 (D) 50
19. GMT (A) 67 (B) 72 (C) 63 (D) 98
20. JVH (A) 44 (B) 20 (C) 27 (D) 77
21. HID (A) 34 (B) 19 (C) 51 (D) 50
22. ASI (A) 20 (B) 44 (C) 27 (D) 45
23. TUT (A) 19 (B) 63 (C) 51 (D) 98
24. DLP (A) 72 (B) 12 (C) 13 (D) 87
25. LOQ (A) 75 (B) 19 (C) 20 (D) 51
26. NRK (A) 76 (B) 67 (C) 12 (D) 44
27. LOQ (A) 19 (B) 66 (C) 92 (D) 75
28. NIT (A) 12 (B) 72 (C) 45 (D) 65
29. ASI (A) 50 (B) 45 (C) 85 (D) 44
30. JPV (A) 66 (B) 34 (C) 63 (D) 20
31. MVM (A) 77 (B) 54 (C) 66 (D) 50
32. NRK (A) 67 (B) 12 (C) 72 (D) 66
33. DLP (A) 12 (B) 72 (C) 44 (D) 51
34. LOQ (A) 19 (B) 75 (C) 34 (D) 92
35. LEN (A) 92 (B) 78 (C) 63 (D) 67
36. ASI (A) 34 (B) 66 (C) 20 (D) 44
37. NIT (A) 27 (B) 72 (C) 50 (D) 96
38. JVH (A) 19 (B) 69 (C) 72 (D) 20
39. DLP (A) 54 (B) 12 (C) 41 (D) 26
40. TUT (A) 91 (B) 68 (C) 19 (D) 48
41. LEN (A) 92 (B) 95 (C) 72 (D) 62
42. JPV (A) 66 (B) 34 (C) 63 (D) 20
43. MVM (A) 77 (B) 54 (C) 66 (D) 50
44. GMT (A) 67 (B) 72 (C) 63 (D) 98

JPV	HID	GMT	NRK	DLP	TUT
66	34	63	67	12	19
LEN	JVH	ASI	MVM	NIT	LOQ
92	20	44	50	72	75

45. NRK **(A)** 67 **(B)** 12 **(C)** 72 **(D)** 66
46. DLP **(A)** 12 **(B)** 72 **(C)** 44 **(D)** 51
47. LOQ **(A)** 19 **(B)** 75 **(C)** 34 **(D)** 92
48. ASI **(A)** 20 **(B)** 44 **(C)** 27 **(D)** 45
49. TUT **(A)** 19 **(B)** 63 **(C)** 51 **(D)** 98
50. DLP **(A)** 72 **(B)** 12 **(C)** 13 **(D)** 87
51. LOQ **(A)** 75 **(B)** 19 **(C)** 20 **(D)** 51
52. NIT **(A)** 27 **(B)** 50 **(C)** 72 **(D)** 19
53. ASI **(A)** 15 **(B)** 44 **(C)** 66 **(D)** 91
54. TUT **(A)** 91 **(B)** 19 **(C)** 34 **(D)** 66
55. GMT **(A)** 36 **(B)** 63 **(C)** 15 **(D)** 66
56. JVH **(A)** 20 **(B)** 64 **(C)** 85 **(D)** 37
57. LEN **(A)** 91 **(B)** 32 **(C)** 92 **(D)** 41
58. ASI **(A)** 44 **(B)** 54 **(C)** 36 **(D)** 74
59. LOQ **(A)** 57 **(B)** 75 **(C)** 14 **(D)** 96
60. TUT **(A)** 91 **(B)** 36 **(C)** 19 **(D)** 53
61. LEN **(A)** 92 **(B)** 95 **(C)** 72 **(D)** 62
62. JPV **(A)** 66 **(B)** 34 **(C)** 63 **(D)** 20
63. MVM **(A)** 97 **(B)** 54 **(C)** 26 **(D)** 50
64. GMT **(A)** 67 **(B)** 72 **(C)** 63 **(D)** 98
65. LOQ **(A)** 19 **(B)** 75 **(C)** 34 **(D)** 92
66. ASI **(A)** 20 **(B)** 44 **(C)** 27 **(D)** 45
67. NIT **(A)** 12 **(B)** 72 **(C)** 45 **(D)** 65
68. ASI **(A)** 50 **(B)** 45 **(C)** 85 **(D)** 44
69. JPV **(A)** 66 **(B)** 34 **(C)** 63 **(D)** 20
70. MVM **(A)** 77 **(B)** 54 **(C)** 66 **(D)** 50
71. NRK **(A)** 67 **(B)** 12 **(C)** 72 **(D)** 66
72. DLP **(A)** 12 **(B)** 72 **(C)** 44 **(D)** 51
73. LOQ **(A)** 19 **(B)** 75 **(C)** 34 **(D)** 92
74. LEN **(A)** 92 **(B)** 78 **(C)** 63 **(D)** 67
75. DLP **(A)** 12 **(B)** 85 **(C)** 67 **(D)** 72
76. DLP **(A)** 21 **(B)** 12 **(C)** 17 **(D)** 63
77. TUT **(A)** 91 **(B)** 26 **(C)** 54 **(D)** 19
78. LEN **(A)** 52 **(B)** 74 **(C)** 92 **(D)** 63
79. HID **(A)** 43 **(B)** 34 **(C)** 67 **(D)** 44

JPV	HID	GMT	NRK	DLP	TUT
66	34	63	67	12	19

LEN	JVH	ASI	MVM	NIT	LOQ
92	20	44	50	72	75

80. MVM   **(A)** 89   **(B)** 19   **(C)** 51   **(D)** 50
81. GMT   **(A)** 36   **(B)** 74   **(C)** 99   **(D)** 63
82. LOQ   **(A)** 57   **(B)** 75   **(C)** 63   **(D)** 25
83. NRK   **(A)** 75   **(B)** 14   **(C)** 67   **(D)** 23
84. TUT   **(A)** 58   **(B)** 19   **(C)** 91   **(D)** 50
85. JVH   **(A)** 19   **(B)** 91   **(C)** 20   **(D)** 66
86. JPV   **(A)** 57   **(B)** 19   **(C)** 91   **(D)** 66
87. ASI   **(A)** 34   **(B)** 66   **(C)** 20   **(D)** 44
88. NIT   **(A)** 27   **(B)** 72   **(C)** 50   **(D)** 96
89. JVH   **(A)** 19   **(B)** 69   **(C)** 72   **(D)** 20
90. ASI   **(A)** 20   **(B)** 44   **(C)** 27   **(D)** 45
91. NIT   **(A)** 12   **(B)** 72   **(C)** 45   **(D)** 65
92. DLP   **(A)** 12   **(B)** 72   **(C)** 44   **(D)** 51
93. LOQ   **(A)** 19   **(B)** 75   **(C)** 34   **(D)** 92
94. TUT   **(A)** 91   **(B)** 19   **(C)** 34   **(D)** 66
95. GMT   **(A)** 36   **(B)** 63   **(C)** 15   **(D)** 66
96. JVH   **(A)** 20   **(B)** 64   **(C)** 85   **(D)** 37
97. MVM   **(A)** 97   **(B)** 54   **(C)** 26   **(D)** 50
98. GMT   **(A)** 67   **(B)** 72   **(C)** 63   **(D)** 98
99. LEN   **(A)** 92   **(B)** 56   **(C)** 74   **(D)** 24
100. DLP   **(A)** 21   **(B)** 92   **(C)** 27   **(D)** 12

STOP   End of Coding section. If you finish before time is up, check your work on this part only.

ANSWER KEY AND EXPLANATIONS

Vocabulary

1. C	11. A	21. A	31. C	41. A
2. A	12. D	22. D	32. B	42. B
3. D	13. A	23. B	33. B	43. C
4. A	14. B	24. D	34. D	44. A
5. A	15. D	25. C	35. B	45. A
6. A	16. A	26. B	36. D	46. A
7. C	17. D	27. A	37. A	47. A
8. B	18. B	28. D	38. D	48. C
9. A	19. C	29. D	39. B	49. B
10. D	20. B	30. A	40. C	50. A

Math

1. B	11. C	21. B	31. B	41. C
2. C	12. B	22. C	32. C	42. B
3. C	13. D	23. B	33. B	43. A
4. D	14. A	24. A	34. C	44. B
5. B	15. B	25. B	35. A	45. B
6. B	16. B	26. B	36. B	46. A
7. D	17. D	27. A	37. A	47. A
8. A	18. B	28. B	38. C	48. D
9. C	19. D	29. B	39. C	49. B
10. B	20. C	30. B	40. B	50. B

1. **The correct answer is (B).**

    $$470$$
    $$+\ 330$$
    $$\overline{\quad 800}$$

2. **The correct answer is (C).**

    $$550$$
    $$+\ 550$$
    $$\overline{1{,}100}$$

3. **The correct answer is (C).**

    $1.5 + 1.5 = 3$

    $3 + 6 = 9$

4. **The correct answer is (D).** This is quick math you can do in your head.

5. The correct answer is (B).

$$
\begin{array}{r}
700 \\
\times\ 5 \\
\hline
3{,}500
\end{array}
$$

6. The correct answer is (B).

$$
\begin{array}{r}
435 \\
-\ 222 \\
\hline
213
\end{array}
$$

7. The correct answer is (D).

$$
\begin{array}{r}
213 \\
-\ \ 87 \\
\hline
126 \\
+\ \ 19 \\
\hline
145
\end{array}
$$

8. The correct answer is (A).

$$
\begin{array}{r}
145 \\
\times\ 19 \\
\hline
2{,}755
\end{array}
$$

9. The correct answer is (C). Order of operation: multiplication within parentheses first.

$$
\begin{array}{r}
10 \\
\times\ 59 \\
\hline
590 \\
\times\ 472 \\
\hline
278{,}580
\end{array}
$$

10. The correct answer is (B). Order of operation: addition within parentheses first, then multiplication.

$$
\begin{array}{r}
578 \\
+\ \ 12 \\
\hline
590 \\
\times\ 791 \\
\hline
466{,}690
\end{array}
$$

11. The correct answer is (C).

$$
\begin{array}{r}
19 \\
\times\ 6 \\
\hline
144
\end{array}
$$

12. **The correct answer is (B).** Work this out by subtracting Jane's weekly pay from Paul's weekly pay to find the difference.

Paul $13.47 pay rate × 38 hours $511.86 weekly pay
Jane $13.47 pay rate × 32 hours − $431.04 weekly pay
                                    $80.82

13. **The correct answer is (D).**

$864.34
× .06
$51.8604

14. **The correct answer is (A).**

$13.99
× 32
$447.68

15. **The correct answer is (B).** Take your answer to question 14 and multiply by 7 percent.

447.68
× .07
31.3376

447.68
+ 31.34
479.02

16. **The correct answer is (B).**

12
× 5
60

17. **The correct answer is (D).** Watch the wording of the question: How much more will Nancy earn than John, rather than what Nancy's total earnings will be.

$500
× .25
$125

18. **The correct answer is (B).**

$25,700
× .07
$1,799

$25,700
+ $1,799
$27,499

19. **The correct answer is (D).**

$40,000
× .10
$4,000

20. **The correct answer is (C).**

$50,000
× .20
$10,000

21. **The correct answer is (B).**

$$\begin{array}{r} 100 \\ + \ 200 \\ \hline 300 \\ - \ \ 50 \\ \hline 250 \\ + \ \ 10 \\ \hline 260 \end{array}$$

22. **The correct answer is (C).** This is quick math you can do in your head.

23. **The correct answer is (B).**

$$\begin{array}{r} 899 \\ + \ 199 \\ \hline 1,098 \end{array}$$

24. **The correct answer is (A).**

25. **The correct answer is (B).**

26. **The correct answer is (B).**

27. **The correct answer is (A).**

28. **The correct answer is (B).**

29. **The correct answer is (B).**

30. **The correct answer is (B).**

31. **The correct answer is (B).** Divide $100.00 by .25 (which is 25 cents).

32. **The correct answer is (C).** Divide $200.00 by .10 (which is 10 cents).

33. **The correct answer is (B).** Multiply .50 (which is 50 percent) × 1,000.

34. **The correct answer is (C).** Multiply .75 (which is 75 percent) × 8,000.

35. **The correct answer is (A).** Multiply .25 (which is 25 percent) × 10,000.

36. **The correct answer is (B).** Multiply .50 (which is 50 percent) × 7,000.

37. **The correct answer is (A).** Multiply .80 (which is 80 percent) × 100.

38. **The correct answer is (C).** Multiply .23 (which is 23 percent) ×100.

39. **The correct answer is (C).** Multiply .67 (which is 67 percent) × 200.

40. **The correct answer is (B).** Multiply .90 (which is 90 percent) × 10,000.

41. **The correct answer is (C).** Divide $52,000 by 52 weeks a year to find the amount of pay for one week of work: $52,000 ÷ 52 = $1,000 = $1,000. One week of work equals 40 hours. Divide 1,000 by 40 to get the hourly rate of pay: $1,000 ÷ 40 = $25.00.

42. **The correct answer is (B).**

$$\begin{array}{r} 13 \\ \times\ 2 \\ \hline 26 \end{array}$$

43. **The correct answer is (A).** Divide the amount she paid ($51.00) by the number of gallons of gas (20) to find the price of one gallon: $51.00 ÷ 20 = $2.55.

44. **The correct answer is (B).** Make a chart.

Item	Quantity	Cost
Mugs	20	$ 4.00
Staplers	3	$ 5.00
Phones	4	+ $ 80.00
TOTAL COST		$ 89.00

Now subtract the budgeted amount ($45.00) from the total cost to find how much extra money Roger needs to purchase all of the items:

$$\begin{array}{r} \$89.00 \\ -\ \$45.00 \\ \hline \$44.00 \end{array}$$

For questions 45–50 you must read and understand the information in the chart below.

Office City	Sales Rank	Production Material Produced	Rank for Production	Damaged Materials	Employees	Percent of Profit	Sales Points	Weeks without Injuries
Chicago	12.6	281	11	2	24	41	36	7
Pittsburgh	16	284	3	4	15	47	20	4
Indianapolis	15	270	9	6	24	40	21	3
Denver	4	20	5	10	28	21	20	8
Tampa Bay	80	2	80	78	123	10	2	0
Dallas	1	380	1	0	85	72	100	16
Minnesota	7	300	8	12	32	33	90	12
Detroit	81	1	81	82	81	19	9	2
Buffalo	3	299	3	6	69	32	70	4

45. **The correct answer is (B).**

46. **The correct answer is (A).**

47. **The correct answer is (A).**

48. **The correct answer is (D).**

49. **The correct answer is (B).**

50. **The correct answer is (B).**

$15 + 85 + 81 = 181$

Be careful. In this question you were given a factor of 123 for Tampa Bay. The examiners were trying to persuade you to add 123 to your equation. If you did that, your answer would have been 304.

Perceptual Skills

1. D	11. D	21. D	31. D	41. D
2. S	12. D	22. D	32. D	42. S
3. S	13. S	23. D	33. S	43. D
4. S	14. D	24. D	34. S	44. S
5. D	15. D	25. S	35. S	45. S
6. S	16. D	26. D	36. S	46. D
7. S	17. D	27. D	37. S	47. S
8. D	18. S	28. S	38. D	48. S
9. S	19. S	29. D	39. D	49. D
10. D	20. S	30. S	40. D	50. D

Spelling

1. B	11. B	21. B	31. B	41. B
2. A	12. B	22. A	32. B	42. B
3. A	13. B	23. A	33. A	43. B
4. A	14. B	24. A	34. A	44. A
5. B	15. A	25. A	35. B	45. B
6. B	16. B	26. B	36. A	46. B
7. B	17. A	27. B	37. A	47. B
8. B	18. B	28. A	38. B	48. A
9. A	19. A	29. B	39. B	49. B
10. B	20. A	30. B	40. B	50. A

Coding

1.	B	21.	A	41.	A	61.	A	81.	D
2.	C	22.	B	42.	A	62.	A	82.	B
3.	C	23.	A	43.	D	63.	D	83.	C
4.	D	24.	B	44.	C	64.	C	84.	B
5.	A	25.	A	45.	A	65.	B	85.	C
6.	D	26.	B	46.	A	66.	B	86.	D
7.	B	27.	D	47.	B	67.	B	87.	D
8.	A	28.	B	48.	B	68.	D	88.	B
9.	A	29.	D	49.	A	69.	A	89.	D
10.	C	30.	A	50.	B	70.	D	90.	B
11.	B	31.	D	51.	A	71.	A	91.	B
12.	D	32.	A	52.	C	72.	A	92.	A
13.	B	33.	A	53.	B	73.	B	93.	B
14.	C	34.	B	54.	B	74.	A	94.	B
15.	A	35.	A	55.	B	75.	A	95.	B
16.	D	36.	D	56.	A	76.	B	96.	A
17.	A	37.	B	57.	C	77.	D	97.	D
18.	D	38.	D	58.	A	78.	C	98.	C
19.	C	39.	B	59.	B	79.	B	99.	A
20.	B	40.	C	60.	C	80.	D	100.	D

answers practice test 2

ANSWER SHEET PRACTICE TEST 3

VOCABULARY

1. Ⓐ Ⓑ Ⓒ Ⓓ
2. Ⓐ Ⓑ Ⓒ Ⓓ
3. Ⓐ Ⓑ Ⓒ Ⓓ
4. Ⓐ Ⓑ Ⓒ Ⓓ
5. Ⓐ Ⓑ Ⓒ Ⓓ
6. Ⓐ Ⓑ Ⓒ Ⓓ
7. Ⓐ Ⓑ Ⓒ Ⓓ
8. Ⓐ Ⓑ Ⓒ Ⓓ
9. Ⓐ Ⓑ Ⓒ Ⓓ
10. Ⓐ Ⓑ Ⓒ Ⓓ
11. Ⓐ Ⓑ Ⓒ Ⓓ
12. Ⓐ Ⓑ Ⓒ Ⓓ
13. Ⓐ Ⓑ Ⓒ Ⓓ
14. Ⓐ Ⓑ Ⓒ Ⓓ
15. Ⓐ Ⓑ Ⓒ Ⓓ
16. Ⓐ Ⓑ Ⓒ Ⓓ
17. Ⓐ Ⓑ Ⓒ Ⓓ

18. Ⓐ Ⓑ Ⓒ Ⓓ
19. Ⓐ Ⓑ Ⓒ Ⓓ
20. Ⓐ Ⓑ Ⓒ Ⓓ
21. Ⓐ Ⓑ Ⓒ Ⓓ
22. Ⓐ Ⓑ Ⓒ Ⓓ
23. Ⓐ Ⓑ Ⓒ Ⓓ
24. Ⓐ Ⓑ Ⓒ Ⓓ
25. Ⓐ Ⓑ Ⓒ Ⓓ
26. Ⓐ Ⓑ Ⓒ Ⓓ
27. Ⓐ Ⓑ Ⓒ Ⓓ
28. Ⓐ Ⓑ Ⓒ Ⓓ
29. Ⓐ Ⓑ Ⓒ Ⓓ
30. Ⓐ Ⓑ Ⓒ Ⓓ
31. Ⓐ Ⓑ Ⓒ Ⓓ
32. Ⓐ Ⓑ Ⓒ Ⓓ
33. Ⓐ Ⓑ Ⓒ Ⓓ
34. Ⓐ Ⓑ Ⓒ Ⓓ

35. Ⓐ Ⓑ Ⓒ Ⓓ
36. Ⓐ Ⓑ Ⓒ Ⓓ
37. Ⓐ Ⓑ Ⓒ Ⓓ
38. Ⓐ Ⓑ Ⓒ Ⓓ
39. Ⓐ Ⓑ Ⓒ Ⓓ
40. Ⓐ Ⓑ Ⓒ Ⓓ
41. Ⓐ Ⓑ Ⓒ Ⓓ
42. Ⓐ Ⓑ Ⓒ Ⓓ
43. Ⓐ Ⓑ Ⓒ Ⓓ
44. Ⓐ Ⓑ Ⓒ Ⓓ
45. Ⓐ Ⓑ Ⓒ Ⓓ
46. Ⓐ Ⓑ Ⓒ Ⓓ
47. Ⓐ Ⓑ Ⓒ Ⓓ
48. Ⓐ Ⓑ Ⓒ Ⓓ
49. Ⓐ Ⓑ Ⓒ Ⓓ
50. Ⓐ Ⓑ Ⓒ Ⓓ

answer sheet

CODING

1. Ⓐ Ⓑ Ⓒ Ⓓ
2. Ⓐ Ⓑ Ⓒ Ⓓ
3. Ⓐ Ⓑ Ⓒ Ⓓ
4. Ⓐ Ⓑ Ⓒ Ⓓ
5. Ⓐ Ⓑ Ⓒ Ⓓ
6. Ⓐ Ⓑ Ⓒ Ⓓ
7. Ⓐ Ⓑ Ⓒ Ⓓ
8. Ⓐ Ⓑ Ⓒ Ⓓ
9. Ⓐ Ⓑ Ⓒ Ⓓ
10. Ⓐ Ⓑ Ⓒ Ⓓ
11. Ⓐ Ⓑ Ⓒ Ⓓ
12. Ⓐ Ⓑ Ⓒ Ⓓ
13. Ⓐ Ⓑ Ⓒ Ⓓ
14. Ⓐ Ⓑ Ⓒ Ⓓ
15. Ⓐ Ⓑ Ⓒ Ⓓ
16. Ⓐ Ⓑ Ⓒ Ⓓ
17. Ⓐ Ⓑ Ⓒ Ⓓ
18. Ⓐ Ⓑ Ⓒ Ⓓ
19. Ⓐ Ⓑ Ⓒ Ⓓ
20. Ⓐ Ⓑ Ⓒ Ⓓ
21. Ⓐ Ⓑ Ⓒ Ⓓ
22. Ⓐ Ⓑ Ⓒ Ⓓ
23. Ⓐ Ⓑ Ⓒ Ⓓ
24. Ⓐ Ⓑ Ⓒ Ⓓ
25. Ⓐ Ⓑ Ⓒ Ⓓ
26. Ⓐ Ⓑ Ⓒ Ⓓ
27. Ⓐ Ⓑ Ⓒ Ⓓ
28. Ⓐ Ⓑ Ⓒ Ⓓ
29. Ⓐ Ⓑ Ⓒ Ⓓ
30. Ⓐ Ⓑ Ⓒ Ⓓ
31. Ⓐ Ⓑ Ⓒ Ⓓ
32. Ⓐ Ⓑ Ⓒ Ⓓ
33. Ⓐ Ⓑ Ⓒ Ⓓ
34. Ⓐ Ⓑ Ⓒ Ⓓ

35. Ⓐ Ⓑ Ⓒ Ⓓ
36. Ⓐ Ⓑ Ⓒ Ⓓ
37. Ⓐ Ⓑ Ⓒ Ⓓ
38. Ⓐ Ⓑ Ⓒ Ⓓ
39. Ⓐ Ⓑ Ⓒ Ⓓ
40. Ⓐ Ⓑ Ⓒ Ⓓ
41. Ⓐ Ⓑ Ⓒ Ⓓ
42. Ⓐ Ⓑ Ⓒ Ⓓ
43. Ⓐ Ⓑ Ⓒ Ⓓ
44. Ⓐ Ⓑ Ⓒ Ⓓ
45. Ⓐ Ⓑ Ⓒ Ⓓ
46. Ⓐ Ⓑ Ⓒ Ⓓ
47. Ⓐ Ⓑ Ⓒ Ⓓ
48. Ⓐ Ⓑ Ⓒ Ⓓ
49. Ⓐ Ⓑ Ⓒ Ⓓ
50. Ⓐ Ⓑ Ⓒ Ⓓ
51. Ⓐ Ⓑ Ⓒ Ⓓ
52. Ⓐ Ⓑ Ⓒ Ⓓ
53. Ⓐ Ⓑ Ⓒ Ⓓ
54. Ⓐ Ⓑ Ⓒ Ⓓ
55. Ⓐ Ⓑ Ⓒ Ⓓ
56. Ⓐ Ⓑ Ⓒ Ⓓ
57. Ⓐ Ⓑ Ⓒ Ⓓ
58. Ⓐ Ⓑ Ⓒ Ⓓ
59. Ⓐ Ⓑ Ⓒ Ⓓ
60. Ⓐ Ⓑ Ⓒ Ⓓ
61. Ⓐ Ⓑ Ⓒ Ⓓ
62. Ⓐ Ⓑ Ⓒ Ⓓ
63. Ⓐ Ⓑ Ⓒ Ⓓ
64. Ⓐ Ⓑ Ⓒ Ⓓ
65. Ⓐ Ⓑ Ⓒ Ⓓ
66. Ⓐ Ⓑ Ⓒ Ⓓ
67. Ⓐ Ⓑ Ⓒ Ⓓ

68. Ⓐ Ⓑ Ⓒ Ⓓ
69. Ⓐ Ⓑ Ⓒ Ⓓ
70. Ⓐ Ⓑ Ⓒ Ⓓ
71. Ⓐ Ⓑ Ⓒ Ⓓ
72. Ⓐ Ⓑ Ⓒ Ⓓ
73. Ⓐ Ⓑ Ⓒ Ⓓ
74. Ⓐ Ⓑ Ⓒ Ⓓ
75. Ⓐ Ⓑ Ⓒ Ⓓ
76. Ⓐ Ⓑ Ⓒ Ⓓ
77. Ⓐ Ⓑ Ⓒ Ⓓ
78. Ⓐ Ⓑ Ⓒ Ⓓ
79. Ⓐ Ⓑ Ⓒ Ⓓ
80. Ⓐ Ⓑ Ⓒ Ⓓ
81. Ⓐ Ⓑ Ⓒ Ⓓ
82. Ⓐ Ⓑ Ⓒ Ⓓ
83. Ⓐ Ⓑ Ⓒ Ⓓ
84. Ⓐ Ⓑ Ⓒ Ⓓ
85. Ⓐ Ⓑ Ⓒ Ⓓ
86. Ⓐ Ⓑ Ⓒ Ⓓ
87. Ⓐ Ⓑ Ⓒ Ⓓ
88. Ⓐ Ⓑ Ⓒ Ⓓ
89. Ⓐ Ⓑ Ⓒ Ⓓ
90. Ⓐ Ⓑ Ⓒ Ⓓ
91. Ⓐ Ⓑ Ⓒ Ⓓ
92. Ⓐ Ⓑ Ⓒ Ⓓ
93. Ⓐ Ⓑ Ⓒ Ⓓ
94. Ⓐ Ⓑ Ⓒ Ⓓ
95. Ⓐ Ⓑ Ⓒ Ⓓ
96. Ⓐ Ⓑ Ⓒ Ⓓ
97. Ⓐ Ⓑ Ⓒ Ⓓ
98. Ⓐ Ⓑ Ⓒ Ⓓ
99. Ⓐ Ⓑ Ⓒ Ⓓ
100. Ⓐ Ⓑ Ⓒ Ⓓ

MATH

1. Ⓐ Ⓑ Ⓒ Ⓓ	11. Ⓐ Ⓑ Ⓒ Ⓓ	21. Ⓐ Ⓑ Ⓒ Ⓓ
2. Ⓐ Ⓑ Ⓒ Ⓓ	12. Ⓐ Ⓑ Ⓒ Ⓓ	22. Ⓐ Ⓑ Ⓒ Ⓓ
3. Ⓐ Ⓑ Ⓒ Ⓓ	13. Ⓐ Ⓑ Ⓒ Ⓓ	23. Ⓐ Ⓑ Ⓒ Ⓓ
4. Ⓐ Ⓑ Ⓒ Ⓓ	14. Ⓐ Ⓑ Ⓒ Ⓓ	24. Ⓐ Ⓑ Ⓒ Ⓓ
5. Ⓐ Ⓑ Ⓒ Ⓓ	15. Ⓐ Ⓑ Ⓒ Ⓓ	25. Ⓐ Ⓑ Ⓒ Ⓓ
6. Ⓐ Ⓑ Ⓒ Ⓓ	16. Ⓐ Ⓑ Ⓒ Ⓓ	26. Ⓐ Ⓑ Ⓒ Ⓓ
7. Ⓐ Ⓑ Ⓒ Ⓓ	17. Ⓐ Ⓑ Ⓒ Ⓓ	27. Ⓐ Ⓑ Ⓒ Ⓓ
8. Ⓐ Ⓑ Ⓒ Ⓓ	18. Ⓐ Ⓑ Ⓒ Ⓓ	28. Ⓐ Ⓑ Ⓒ Ⓓ
9. Ⓐ Ⓑ Ⓒ Ⓓ	19. Ⓐ Ⓑ Ⓒ Ⓓ	29. Ⓐ Ⓑ Ⓒ Ⓓ
10. Ⓐ Ⓑ Ⓒ Ⓓ	20. Ⓐ Ⓑ Ⓒ Ⓓ	30. Ⓐ Ⓑ Ⓒ Ⓓ

answer sheet

PERCEPTUAL SKILLS

1. Ⓢ Ⓓ
2. Ⓢ Ⓓ
3. Ⓢ Ⓓ
4. Ⓢ Ⓓ
5. Ⓢ Ⓓ
6. Ⓢ Ⓓ
7. Ⓢ Ⓓ
8. Ⓢ Ⓓ
9. Ⓢ Ⓓ
10. Ⓢ Ⓓ
11. Ⓢ Ⓓ
12. Ⓢ Ⓓ
13. Ⓢ Ⓓ
14. Ⓢ Ⓓ
15. Ⓢ Ⓓ
16. Ⓢ Ⓓ
17. Ⓢ Ⓓ
18. Ⓢ Ⓓ
19. Ⓢ Ⓓ
20. Ⓢ Ⓓ
21. Ⓢ Ⓓ
22. Ⓢ Ⓓ
23. Ⓢ Ⓓ
24. Ⓢ Ⓓ
25. Ⓢ Ⓓ
26. Ⓢ Ⓓ
27. Ⓢ Ⓓ
28. Ⓢ Ⓓ
29. Ⓢ Ⓓ
30. Ⓢ Ⓓ
31. Ⓢ Ⓓ
32. Ⓢ Ⓓ
33. Ⓢ Ⓓ
34. Ⓢ Ⓓ

35. Ⓢ Ⓓ
36. Ⓢ Ⓓ
37. Ⓢ Ⓓ
38. Ⓢ Ⓓ
39. Ⓢ Ⓓ
40. Ⓢ Ⓓ
41. Ⓢ Ⓓ
42. Ⓢ Ⓓ
43. Ⓢ Ⓓ
44. Ⓢ Ⓓ
45. Ⓢ Ⓓ
46. Ⓢ Ⓓ
47. Ⓢ Ⓓ
48. Ⓢ Ⓓ
49. Ⓢ Ⓓ
50. Ⓢ Ⓓ
51. Ⓢ Ⓓ
52. Ⓢ Ⓓ
53. Ⓢ Ⓓ
54. Ⓢ Ⓓ
55. Ⓢ Ⓓ
56. Ⓢ Ⓓ
57. Ⓢ Ⓓ
58. Ⓢ Ⓓ
59. Ⓢ Ⓓ
60. Ⓢ Ⓓ
61. Ⓢ Ⓓ
62. Ⓢ Ⓓ
63. Ⓢ Ⓓ
64. Ⓢ Ⓓ
65. Ⓢ Ⓓ
66. Ⓢ Ⓓ
67. Ⓢ Ⓓ

68. Ⓢ Ⓓ
69. Ⓢ Ⓓ
70. Ⓢ Ⓓ
71. Ⓢ Ⓓ
72. Ⓢ Ⓓ
73. Ⓢ Ⓓ
74. Ⓢ Ⓓ
75. Ⓢ Ⓓ
76. Ⓢ Ⓓ
77. Ⓢ Ⓓ
78. Ⓢ Ⓓ
79. Ⓢ Ⓓ
80. Ⓢ Ⓓ
81. Ⓢ Ⓓ
82. Ⓢ Ⓓ
83. Ⓢ Ⓓ
84. Ⓢ Ⓓ
85. Ⓢ Ⓓ
86. Ⓢ Ⓓ
87. Ⓢ Ⓓ
88. Ⓢ Ⓓ
89. Ⓢ Ⓓ
90. Ⓢ Ⓓ
91. Ⓢ Ⓓ
92. Ⓢ Ⓓ
93. Ⓢ Ⓓ
94. Ⓢ Ⓓ
95. Ⓢ Ⓓ
96. Ⓢ Ⓓ
97. Ⓢ Ⓓ
98. Ⓢ Ⓓ
99. Ⓢ Ⓓ
100. Ⓢ Ⓓ

Practice Test 3

VOCABULARY

50 QUESTIONS • 20 MINUTES

Directions: Read each sentence carefully. Choose the letter of the word which best answers the question.

1. Which word means the same as EQUATE?

   (A) ordinary
   (B) vow
   (C) firm
   (D) compare

2. Which word means the same as REVOLT?

   (A) anger
   (B) rebel
   (C) comply
   (D) diffuse

3. Which word means the opposite of FRIGID?

   (A) hot
   (B) gross
   (C) fertile
   (D) valid

4. Which word means the same as VAGUE?

   (A) polite
   (B) detain
   (C) frugal
   (D) cloudy

5. Which word means the opposite of IDENTICAL?

   (A) twin
   (B) diverse
   (C) similar
   (D) equivalent

6. Which word means the opposite of OBSCURE?

   (A) dim
   (B) obscene
   (C) shining
   (D) obvious

7. Which word means the same as ENIGMA?

   (A) poem
   (B) mystery
   (C) anarchy
   (D) panacea

8. Which word means the same as PREVAIL?

   (A) confess
   (B) alter
   (C) triumph
   (D) expand

9. Which word means the same as ILLICIT?

(A) illegal
(B) defer
(C) verbose
(D) extract

10. Which word means the opposite of CONCUR?

(A) assemble
(B) disagree
(C) alter
(D) strong

11. Which word means the opposite of ACCEPT?

(A) obtain
(B) send
(C) fail
(D) refuse

12. Which word means the same as DISSENSION?

(A) reconstruction
(B) praise
(C) controversy
(D) risk

13. Which word means the opposite of EFFICIENT?

(A) incompetent
(B) accidental
(C) exceed
(D) worthy

14. Which word means the opposite of DELETE?

(A) gaudy
(B) pristine
(C) annex
(D) invest

15. Which word means the same as CONFINE?

(A) liberate
(B) boarder
(C) limit
(D) compel

16. Which word means the same as ABOLISH?

(A) annul
(B) criticize
(C) curtail
(D) acclaim

17. Which word means the opposite of SKIMPY?

(A) sketchy
(B) overbearing
(C) tiny
(D) ample

18. Which word means the same as ACTIVE?

(A) energetic
(B) idle
(C) hurried
(D) athletic

19. Which word means the opposite of CONFUSE?

(A) clarify
(B) bewilder
(C) dictate
(D) discuss

20. Which word means the same as TEDIOUS?

(A) daring
(B) simple
(C) copious
(D) drudging

21. Which word means the opposite of ABHOR?

(A) despise
(B) stealthy
(C) zealous
(D) adore

22. Which word means the same as PROVOKE?

    (A) refuse
    (B) defer
    (C) risk
    (D) incite

23. Which word means the same as ALTER?

    (A) nullify
    (B) delete
    (C) adjust
    (D) impede

24. Which word means the opposite of FICKLE?

    (A) changeable
    (B) reliable
    (C) straight
    (D) strong

25. Which word means the opposite of LETHARGY?

    (A) torpor
    (B) languor
    (C) vigor
    (D) strong

26. Which word means the same as FRUGAL?

    (A) conserving
    (B) sequester
    (C) daring
    (D) seldom

27. Which word means the same as VIGILANT?

    (A) jealous
    (B) alert
    (C) insane
    (D) flexible

28. Which word means the opposite of RUSTIC?

    (A) urbane
    (B) pristine
    (C) smooth
    (D) transparent

29. Which word means the opposite of COMPLACENT?

    (A) consenting
    (B) argue
    (C) strive
    (D) anxious

30. Which word means the same as OPULENT?

    (A) large
    (B) affluent
    (C) conceited
    (D) difficult

31. Which word means the opposite of PROTRACT?

    (A) calculate
    (B) obstruct
    (C) protest
    (D) curtail

32. Which word means the opposite of DYNAMIC?

    (A) explosive
    (B) abundant
    (C) apathetic
    (D) consistent

33. Which word means the same as COPIOUS?

    (A) meticulous
    (B) abundant
    (C) aesthetic
    (D) consistent

34. Which word means the opposite of INANE?

    (A) profound
    (B) silly
    (C) suspect
    (D) ordinary

35. Which word means the same as UNIFORM?

(A) consistent
(B) affixed
(C) furtive
(D) dormant

36. Which word means the opposite of OBLIQUE?

(A) obscured
(B) defensive
(C) corrosive
(D) upright

37. Which word means the opposite of INDOLENT?

(A) condescending
(B) industrious
(C) lazy
(D) thoughtful

38. Which word means the opposite of LARGESSE?

(A) primary
(B) heavy
(C) considerate
(D) pittance

39. Which word means the same as MEAGER?

(A) paltry
(B) daunting
(C) frigid
(D) temporary

40. Which word means the same as LASSITUDE?

(A) lethargy
(B) flexibility
(C) tenacity
(D) infamy

41. Which word means the opposite of PERUSE?

(A) examine
(B) read
(C) cleat
(D) scan

42. Which word means the opposite of DEVIOUS?

(A) maniacal
(B) straightforward
(C) learned
(D) polite

43. Which word means the same as IMPEDE?

(A) empty
(B) plethora
(C) obstruct
(D) neglect

44. Which word means the same as PROCURE?

(A) acquire
(B) prevent
(C) expunge
(D) abhor

45. Which word means the opposite of ADEPT?

(A) astute
(B) envious
(C) serene
(D) inept

46. Which word means the opposite of TEMERITY?

(A) exhaustion
(B) vitality
(C) caution
(D) paucity

47. Which word means the same as WITTICISM?

(A) plethora
(B) jest
(C) senility
(D) sanction

48. Which word means the same as
SEDATE?

    (A) calm
    (B) gross
    (C) scoured
    (D) earnest

49. Which word means the opposite of
CONCEDE?

    (A) dispute
    (B) sermon
    (C) academic
    (D) similar

50. Which word means the same as
PLETHORA?

    (A) laxity
    (B) scarcity
    (C) surplus
    (D) aptitude

S T O P End of Vocabulary section. If you finish before time is up, check your
work on this part only. Do not turn to the next part until the signal
is given.

CODING

100 QUESTIONS • 9 MINUTES

Sample Answer Sheet

1. Ⓐ Ⓑ Ⓒ Ⓓ   3. Ⓐ Ⓑ Ⓒ Ⓓ   5. Ⓐ Ⓑ Ⓒ Ⓓ
2. Ⓐ Ⓑ Ⓒ Ⓓ   4. Ⓐ Ⓑ Ⓒ Ⓓ

Directions: Using the data bank supplied, match the letter in each question with its corresponding number from the data bank.

Example:

JPV	HID	GMT	NRK	DLP	TUT
66	34	63	67	12	19

LEN	JVH	ASI	MVM	NIT	LOQ
92	20	44	50	72	75

1. LEN   **(A)** 20   **(B)** 92   **(C)** 50   **(D)** 66
2. TOM   **(A)** 76   **(B)** 96   **(C)** 43   **(D)** 21
3. KCT   **(A)** 43   **(B)** 54   **(C)** 21   **(D)** 88
4. OMJ   **(A)** 24   **(B)** 42   **(C)** 88   **(D)** 54
5. ECD   **(A)** 73   **(B)** 12   **(C)** 80   **(D)** 42

Answer Key

1. C   2. A   3. D   4. D   5. B

RDX	RID	WMT	NEK	TEP	BST
68	38	61	17	52	19

YOP	KLM	GUD	LOM	BIT	EMN
22	41	77	37	98	83

1. EMN   **(A)** 38   **(B)** 91   **(C)** 83   **(D)** 22
2. YOP   **(A)** 41   **(B)** 22   **(C)** 61   **(D)** 19
3. RDX   **(A)** 38   **(B)** 17   **(C)** 44   **(D)** 68
4. WMT   **(A)** 16   **(B)** 22   **(C)** 61   **(D)** 83
5. KLM   **(A)** 37   **(B)** 41   **(C)** 77   **(D)** 17
6. TEP   **(A)** 25   **(B)** 52   **(C)** 68   **(D)** 83
7. GUD   **(A)** 85   **(B)** 41   **(C)** 98   **(D)** 77
8. BIT   **(A)** 98   **(B)** 61   **(C)** 38   **(D)** 22
9. NEK   **(A)** 25   **(B)** 17   **(C)** 89   **(D)** 52

RDX	RID	WMT	NEK	TEP	BST
68	38	61	17	52	19

YOP	KLM	GUD	LOM	BIT	EMN
22	41	77	37	98	83

10. RID   (A) 83   (B) 52   (C) 92   (D) 38
11. LOM   (A) 57   (B) 37   (C) 22   (D) 92
12. KLM   (A) 11   (B) 96   (C) 74   (D) 41
13. BST   (A) 19   (B) 58   (C) 63   (D) 74
14. BIT   (A) 17   (B) 98   (C) 74   (D) 35
15. WMT   (A) 66   (B) 74   (C) 61   (D) 38
16. YOP   (A) 58   (B) 95   (C) 22   (D) 83
17. EMN   (A) 38   (B) 83   (C) 16   (D) 71
18. GUD   (A) 89   (B) 77   (C) 28   (D) 35
19. NEK   (A) 34   (B) 61   (C) 17   (D) 63
20. TEP   (A) 55   (B) 52   (C) 64   (D) 42
21. RDX   (A) 82   (B) 68   (C) 41   (D) 77
22. KLM   (A) 22   (B) 41   (C) 77   (D) 68
23. BIT   (A) 91   (B) 19   (C) 98   (D) 22
24. WMT   (A) 61   (B) 22   (C) 35   (D) 71
25. EMN   (A) 83   (B) 61   (C) 17   (D) 95
26. KLM   (A) 11   (B) 96   (C) 74   (D) 41
27. LOM   (A) 57   (B) 37   (C) 22   (D) 92
28. NEK   (A) 11   (B) 96   (C) 74   (D) 17
29. BIT   (A) 17   (B) 98   (C) 74   (D) 35
30. WMT   (A) 66   (B) 74   (C) 61   (D) 38
31. RDX   (A) 82   (B) 68   (C) 41   (D) 77
32. KLM   (A) 22   (B) 41   (C) 77   (D) 68
33. TEP   (A) 55   (B) 52   (C) 64   (D) 42
34. LOM   (A) 75   (B) 37   (C) 65   (D) 95
35. RDX   (A) 82   (B) 68   (C) 41   (D) 77
36. GUD   (A) 88   (B) 31   (C) 78   (D) 77
37. KLM   (A) 22   (B) 41   (C) 77   (D) 68
38. BIT   (A) 91   (B) 19   (C) 98   (D) 22
39. WMT   (A) 61   (B) 22   (C) 35   (D) 71
40. EMN   (A) 83   (B) 61   (C) 17   (D) 95
41. NEK   (A) 71   (B) 17   (C) 95   (D) 68
42. YOP   (A) 22   (B) 65   (C) 32   (D) 68
43. BST   (A) 83   (B) 19   (C) 74   (D) 15
44. RID   (A) 38   (B) 96   (C) 74   (D) 11

RDX	RID	WMT	NEK	TEP	BST
68	38	61	17	52	19

YOP	KLM	GUD	LOM	BIT	EMN
22	41	77	37	98	83

45. RDX   **(A)** 22   **(B)** 68   **(C)** 41   **(D)** 83
46. LOM   **(A)** 73   **(B)** 37   **(C)** 85   **(D)** 65
47. TEP   **(A)** 52   **(B)** 74   **(C)** 98   **(D)** 41
48. YOP   **(A)** 68   **(B)** 22   **(C)** 41   **(D)** 52
49. BIT   **(A)** 89   **(B)** 98   **(C)** 66   **(D)** 14
50. NEK   **(A)** 17   **(B)** 71   **(C)** 37   **(D)** 81
51. EMN   **(A)** 83   **(B)** 61   **(C)** 17   **(D)** 95
52. NEK   **(A)** 71   **(B)** 17   **(C)** 95   **(D)** 68
53. YOP   **(A)** 22   **(B)** 65   **(C)** 29   **(D)** 78
54. LOM   **(A)** 73   **(B)** 37   **(C)** 85   **(D)** 65
55. TEP   **(A)** 52   **(B)** 74   **(C)** 98   **(D)** 41
56. YOP   **(A)** 68   **(B)** 22   **(C)** 41   **(D)** 52
57. KLM   **(A)** 11   **(B)** 96   **(C)** 74   **(D)** 41
58. BIT   **(A)** 17   **(B)** 98   **(C)** 74   **(D)** 35
59. WMT   **(A)** 66   **(B)** 74   **(C)** 61   **(D)** 38
60. NEK   **(A)** 71   **(B)** 17   **(C)** 95   **(D)** 88
61. YOP   **(A)** 22   **(B)** 65   **(C)** 32   **(D)** 78
62. BST   **(A)** 83   **(B)** 19   **(C)** 74   **(D)** 15
63. RDX   **(A)** 82   **(B)** 68   **(C)** 41   **(D)** 77
64. KLM   **(A)** 22   **(B)** 41   **(C)** 77   **(D)** 58
65. NEK   **(A)** 71   **(B)** 17   **(C)** 95   **(D)** 99
66. YOP   **(A)** 22   **(B)** 65   **(C)** 32   **(D)** 93
67. WMT   **(A)** 52   **(B)** 61   **(C)** 78   **(D)** 85
68. GUD   **(A)** 41   **(B)** 77   **(C)** 22   **(D)** 68
69. RDX   **(A)** 38   **(B)** 16   **(C)** 86   **(D)** 68
70. BIT   **(A)** 98   **(B)** 75   **(C)** 81   **(D)** 33
71. RID   **(A)** 61   **(B)** 68   **(C)** 41   **(D)** 38
72. NEK   **(A)** 17   **(B)** 61   **(C)** 38   **(D)** 55
73. EMN   **(A)** 17   **(B)** 83   **(C)** 61   **(D)** 68
74. KLM   **(A)** 38   **(B)** 41   **(C)** 33   **(D)** 22
75. BST   **(A)** 19   **(B)** 14   **(C)** 38   **(D)** 17
76. RDX   **(A)** 86   **(B)** 68   **(C)** 45   **(D)** 54
77. LOM   **(A)** 37   **(B)** 73   **(C)** 98   **(D)** 77
78. BST   **(A)** 91   **(B)** 62   **(C)** 19   **(D)** 63
79. GUD   **(A)** 77   **(B)** 68   **(C)** 15   **(D)** 26

RDX	RID	WMT	NEK	TEP	BST
68	38	61	17	52	19
YOP	KLM	GUD	LOM	BIT	EMN
22	41	77	37	98	83

80.	YOP	**(A)** 65	**(B)** 22	**(C)** 83	**(D)** 96
81.	WMT	**(A)** 41	**(B)** 38	**(C)** 17	**(D)** 61
82.	BIT	**(A)** 98	**(B)** 74	**(C)** 83	**(D)** 20
83.	RID	**(A)** 50	**(B)** 79	**(C)** 38	**(D)** 22
84.	BST	**(A)** 91	**(B)** 19	**(C)** 40	**(D)** 77
85.	EMN	**(A)** 98	**(B)** 83	**(C)** 38	**(D)** 70
86.	NEK	**(A)** 90	**(B)** 17	**(C)** 58	**(D)** 56
87.	YOP	**(A)** 23	**(B)** 22	**(C)** 78	**(D)** 68
88.	WMT	**(A)** 16	**(B)** 61	**(C)** 17	**(D)** 83
89.	TEP	**(A)** 25	**(B)** 52	**(C)** 11	**(D)** 10
90.	RID	**(A)** 29	**(B)** 38	**(C)** 41	**(D)** 15
91.	KLM	**(A)** 41	**(B)** 80	**(C)** 13	**(D)** 68
92.	WMT	**(A)** 16	**(B)** 61	**(C)** 22	**(D)** 83
93.	TEP	**(A)** 25	**(B)** 52	**(C)** 16	**(D)** 82
94.	GUD	**(A)** 22	**(B)** 77	**(C)** 19	**(D)** 40
95.	LOM	**(A)** 52	**(B)** 98	**(C)** 37	**(D)** 12
96.	RDX	**(A)** 22	**(B)** 68	**(C)** 16	**(D)** 74
97.	EMN	**(A)** 85	**(B)** 45	**(C)** 83	**(D)** 60
98.	BIT	**(A)** 56	**(B)** 98	**(C)** 87	**(D)** 17
99.	NEK	**(A)** 17	**(B)** 11	**(C)** 80	**(D)** 37
100.	RID	**(A)** 39	**(B)** 38	**(C)** 60	**(D)** 22

STOP **End of Coding section. If you finish before time is up, check your work on this part only. Do not turn to the next part until the signal is given.**

practice test

MATH

30 QUESTIONS • 35 MINUTES

Directions: Perform the operation as indicated in the question and find the answer among the list of responses. You may use scrap paper.

1. James and six friends went to the movies. Tickets cost $7.00 each. How much did they pay for the tickets?

    (A) $49.00
    (B) $42.00
    (C) $56.00
    (D) $36.00

2. There are 15 office workers. If every computer is shared by 3 people, how many computers are there?

    (A) 12
    (B) 9
    (C) 5
    (D) not enough information

3. Nancy bought a ticket for $7.00, a hat for $2.50 and spent $4.00 on food. How much did she spend in all?

    (A) $16.80
    (B) $13.50
    (C) $30.00
    (D) not enough information

4. Twenty file cabinets were in each of three rows. How many file cabinets were there?

    (A) 60
    (B) 20
    (C) 3
    (D) not enough information

5. Jeffrey spent $5.00 more than Lauren. Lauren spent $138.50. How much did Jeffrey spend?

    (A) $127.00
    (B) $133.50
    (C) $143.50
    (D) not enough information

6. Juan earned $54.00 for three days of work. He worked 3 hours a day. What was his hourly rate of pay?

    (A) $15.00
    (B) $6.00
    (C) $7.50
    (D) not enough information

7. Joyce estimates it will take her 30 hours do complete her filing. If she works 4 hours a day for 6 days, how many hours of work will remain?

    (A) 6
    (B) 7
    (C) 26
    (D) not enough information

8. Carole earned $80.00. To do so she worked 7 hours a day on Thursday, 4 hours on Friday, and 5 hours on Saturday. How much did she earn an hour?

    (A) $5.00
    (B) $6.00
    (C) $4.95
    (D) not enough information

9. Three office workers answered phones. If they received 21 calls in an hour, how many calls would each answer to divide the work equally?

    (A) 3
    (B) 8
    (C) 7
    (D) not enough information

10. Jimmy is an office clerk. He is paid $16.00 per hour. He works 40 hours per week, of which 8 hours are unpaid. How much money will he earn per week?

    (A) $512.00
    (B) $640.00
    (C) $384.00
    (D) $480.00

11. 18 + 5 + 15 =

    (A) 38
    (B) 45
    (C) 48
    (D) 18

12. 20 + 47 + 80 =

    (A) 47
    (B) 100
    (C) 147
    (D) 152

13. 25 + 45 + 25 =

    (A) 45
    (B) 145
    (C) 105
    (D) 95

14. 120 + 170 + 180 =

    (A) 570
    (B) 380
    (C) 470
    (D) 160

15. 60 + 50 + 40 =

    (A) 140
    (B) 150
    (C) 210
    (D) 170

16. 225 + 157 + 175 =

    (A) 557
    (B) 610
    (C) 475
    (D) 625

17. 3 × 15 =

    (A) 45
    (B) 39
    (C) 50
    (D) 5

18. 83 × 2 =

    (A) 210
    (B) 160
    (C) 166
    (D) 266

19. 53 × 5 =

    (A) 265
    (B) 365
    (C) 225
    (D) 235

20. 6 × 63 =

    (A) 278
    (B) 379
    (C) 266
    (D) 378

21. 403 × 403 =

    (A) 187,234
    (B) 164,980
    (C) 162,409
    (D) 187,909

22. 25 × 3 =

    (A) 100
    (B) 65
    (C) 85
    (D) 75

23. 8 × 30 =

    (A) 24
    (B) 240
    (C) 320
    (D) 200

24. 22 + 14 + 6 =

    (A) 52
    (B) 64
    (C) 24
    (D) 42

25. 325 × 2 =

    (A) 650
    (B) 720
    (C) 625
    (D) 725

practice test

QUESTIONS 26–30 ARE BASED ON THE INFORMATION BELOW.

State	Miles of Highway
Connecticut	989
New Jersey	2,867
New York	2,980
Delaware	500
Maryland	5,104
Rhode Island	614
Virginia	5,304

26. How many states have less than 700 miles of highway?

(A) 3
(B) 5
(C) 2
(D) 7

27. What is the total distance for the highways of New Jersey and New York?

(A) 5,847 miles
(B) 5,857 kilometers
(C) 5,847 kilometers
(D) 5,847 decameters

28. Which state has the greatest number of highway miles?

(A) Virginia
(B) Maryland
(C) New Jersey
(D) California

29. Which state has the lowest number of highway miles on the chart?

(A) Rhode Island
(B) New Jersey
(C) Kansas
(D) Delaware

30. What are the combined highway miles of Delaware and Rhode Island?

(A) 114
(B) 945
(C) 1,114
(D) 1,014

STOP End of Math section. If you finish before time is up, check your work on this part only. Do not turn to the next part until the signal is given.

PERCEPTUAL SKILLS

100 QUESTIONS • 7 MINUTES

Sample Answer Sheet

1. Ⓢ Ⓓ   3. Ⓢ Ⓓ   4. Ⓢ Ⓓ
2. Ⓢ Ⓓ

Directions: Compare the two choices if they are the same or different. Darken your answer sheets **S**—Indicating Same or **D**—Indicating Different.

Example:

   S—Indicates Same   **D**—Indicates Different

1. 123   132   **(S)** **(D)**
2. 467   467   **(S)** **(D)**
3. 8988   8898   **(S)** **(D)**
4. 777353   777353   **(S)** **(D)**

Answers:

1. Ⓢ   ●   (Different)
2. ●   Ⓓ   (Same)
3. Ⓢ   ●   (Different)
4. ●   Ⓓ   (Same)

   S—Indicates Same   **D**—Indicates Different

1. 9KOP   9KOP   **(S)** **(D)**
2. HB789   HB798   **(S)** **(D)**
3. 7YHB   7YHB   **(S)** **(D)**
4. 23432   23433   **(S)** **(D)**
5. 98766   98766   **(S)** **(D)**
6. NJ541   JN541   **(S)** **(D)**
7. AW34   AW34   **(S)** **(D)**
8. BHU8   8HU8   **(S)** **(D)**
9. 5RDXDR   5RDXDR   **(S)** **(D)**
10. 9IJNJI9   9IJNJI9   **(S)** **(D)**
11. AW34ES   AW34ES   **(S)** **(D)**
12. 8765   8765   **(S)** **(D)**
13. 009I   009I   **(S)** **(D)**
14. CFT6   CFT6   **(S)** **(D)**

S—Indicates Same   D—Indicates Different

15.	654R	654R	(S)	(D)
16.	765	765	(S)	(D)
17.	BHU09	BHU09	(S)	(D)
18.	XDR55	XDR55	(S)	(D)
19.	NBV711	NBY711	(S)	(D)
20.	890POL	890POL	(S)	(D)
21.	IJN9	IJN9	(S)	(D)
22.	876IJNH	876HNJH	(S)	(D)
23.	54567	54675	(S)	(D)
24.	8U889	88U99	(S)	(D)
25.	98765	98756	(S)	(D)
26.	6767	7676	(S)	(D)
27.	67566	65766	(S)	(D)
28.	324ED	324ED	(S)	(D)
29.	0OLP	0OLP	(S)	(D)
30.	5T6Y7	5T6Y7	(S)	(D)
31.	3131	3131	(S)	(D)
32.	76543456	654567	(S)	(D)
33.	7657657	7657657	(S)	(D)
34.	9KM90	9KM9L	(S)	(D)
35.	E5678	E5678	(S)	(D)
36.	6TGY7	6TGY7	(S)	(D)
37.	67890987	6780987	(S)	(D)
38.	4434565778	4434565778	(S)	(D)
39.	877665RF5TFR	877665RF5TFR	(S)	(D)
40.	8UHBHU89995	8UHBHU89995	(S)	(D)
41.	6TFVDSOFOIH	6TFVDSOFOIH	(S)	(D)
42.	7UJHN78UI9I8	7UJHN78UI9I8	(S)	(D)
43.	56TGGHBH00	56TGGHBH00	(S)	(D)
44.	7UJHN78UI9I8	7UJH7N8IU9I8	(S)	(D)
45.	6TFVDSOFOIH	6TFDVSOFOIH	(S)	(D)
46.	67YHDH000P	67YDH000P	(S)	(D)
47.	7U893	7U893	(S)	(D)
48.	39876	39876	(S)	(D)
49.	789021	789021	(S)	(D)
50.	665544	665544	(S)	(D)
51.	NJUHB88	JNUHB88	(S)	(D)
52.	87657889123	876578889123	(S)	(D)
53.	CX45678	CX456789	(S)	(D)

S—Indicates Same   **D**—Indicates Different

54.	9872341F5	9872341F5	(S)	(D)
55.	5T6711P	5T7611P	(S)	(D)
56.	123321	1233211	(S)	(D)
57.	98M7Y6	98M7Y6	(S)	(D)
58.	87678BV77	8767B8V77	(S)	(D)
59.	N778631	N778613	(S)	(D)
60.	K04538B	K0453B8	(S)	(D)
61.	77H51TDT	77H15TDT	(S)	(D)
62.	697174	697174	(S)	(D)
63.	6363663	6363363	(S)	(D)
64.	31J89K0	31J98K0	(S)	(D)
65.	G6754	G6754J	(S)	(D)
66.	6TFVDSOFOIH	6TFVDSOFOIH	(S)	(D)
67.	7U3JHN78UI9I8	7UJHN78UI9I8	(S)	(D)
68.	56TGGHBH00	56TGGHBH00	(S)	(D)
69.	7UJHN78UI9I8	7UJHND78FI9I8	(S)	(D)
70.	6TFVDSOFOIH	6TEVDSOFOIH	(S)	(D)
71.	6HBG	6HGB	(S)	(D)
72.	8I9N	819N	(S)	(D)
73.	8UJ9	9UJ9	(S)	(D)
74.	4554H	4554H	(S)	(D)
75.	60911	60991	(S)	(D)
76.	46789011X	46789011X	(S)	(D)
77.	88BB	88BB	(S)	(D)
78.	BB88BB	BB88BB	(S)	(D)
79.	B88BB88BB	B8BB88BB	(S)	(D)
80.	88998899	88998899	(S)	(D)
81.	4B77M	4B77M	(S)	(D)
82.	47CC48998	47CC48998	(S)	(D)
83.	7NB023M	7NB023W	(S)	(D)
84.	667B999	67B999	(S)	(D)
85.	85588B	855888	(S)	(D)
86.	45GB99123	45BG99123	(S)	(D)
87.	OK721119	QK721119	(S)	(D)
88.	7LQO3212	7LQO2321	(S)	(D)
89.	T590123NN	T5901234N	(S)	(D)
90.	89BB84H	89BB84H	(S)	(D)
91.	MKO999	MKO999	(S)	(D)
92.	9M33ED	9M33DE	(S)	(D)

S—Indicates Same   **D**—Indicates Different

93.	782345N00	782345NQO	**(S)**	**(D)**
94.	7888777	788777	**(S)**	**(D)**
95.	9KII10	9KII110	**(S)**	**(D)**
96.	34HNJU	34NHHU	**(S)**	**(D)**
97.	789	789	**(S)**	**(D)**
98.	985	985	**(S)**	**(D)**
99.	U884466	U884466	**(S)**	**(D)**
100.	B84F67	B84E67	**(S)**	**(D)**

S T O P End of Perceptual Skills section. If you finish before time is up, check your work on this part only.

ANSWER KEY AND EXPLANATIONS

Vocabulary

1.	D	11.	D	21.	D	31.	D	41.	D
2.	B	12.	C	22.	D	32.	C	42.	B
3.	A	13.	A	23.	C	33.	B	43.	C
4.	D	14.	C	24.	B	34.	A	44.	A
5.	B	15.	C	25.	C	35.	A	45.	D
6.	D	16.	A	26.	A	36.	D	46.	C
7.	B	17.	D	27.	B	37.	B	47.	B
8.	C	18.	A	28.	A	38.	D	48.	A
9.	A	19.	A	29.	D	39.	A	49.	A
10.	B	20.	D	30.	B	40.	A	50.	C

Coding

1.	C	21.	B	41.	B	61.	A	81.	D
2.	B	22.	B	42.	A	62.	B	82.	A
3.	D	23.	C	43.	B	63.	B	83.	C
4.	C	24.	A	44.	A	64.	B	84.	B
5.	B	25.	A	45.	B	65.	B	85.	B
6.	B	26.	D	46.	B	66.	A	86.	B
7.	D	27.	B	47.	A	67.	B	87.	B
8.	A	28.	D	48.	B	68.	B	88.	B
9.	B	29.	B	49.	B	69.	D	89.	B
10.	D	30.	C	50.	A	70.	A	90.	B
11.	B	31.	B	51.	A	71.	D	91.	A
12.	D	32.	B	52.	B	72.	A	92.	B
13.	A	33.	B	53.	A	73.	B	93.	B
14.	B	34.	B	54.	B	74.	B	94.	B
15.	C	35.	B	55.	A	75.	A	95.	C
16.	C	36.	D	56.	B	76.	B	96.	B
17.	B	37.	B	57.	D	77.	A	97.	C
18.	B	38.	C	58.	B	78.	C	98.	B
19.	C	39.	A	59.	C	79.	A	99.	A
20.	B	40.	A	60.	B	80.	B	100.	B

Math

1. A	7. A	13. D	19. A	25. A
2. C	8. A	14. C	20. D	26. C
3. B	9. C	15. B	21. C	27. A
4. A	10. A	16. A	22. D	28. A
5. C	11. A	17. A	23. B	29. D
6. B	12. C	18. C	24. D	30. C

1. **The correct answer is (A).** 7 people (don't forget to include James) × $7.00 = $49.00

2. **The correct answer is (C).** Divide 15 by 3.

3. **The correct answer is (B).**

$$\begin{aligned} \$7.00 \\ \$2.50 \\ + \quad \$4.00 \\ \hline \$13.50 \end{aligned}$$

4. **The correct answer is (A).**

$20 \times 3 = 60$

5. **The correct answer is (C).**

$$\begin{aligned} \$138.50 \\ + \quad 5.00 \\ \hline \$143.50 \end{aligned}$$

6. **The correct answer is (B).**

3 hours × 3 days = 9 hours worked
$54.00 ÷ 9 hours = $6.00 per hour

7. **The correct answer is (A).**

4 hours a day × 6 days = 24 hours

Subtract this from the estimated 30 hours needed to find how many hours of work remain:

$$\begin{aligned} 30 \\ - \quad 24 \\ \hline 6 \end{aligned}$$

8. **The correct answer is (A).**

7 hours + 4 hours + 5 hours = 16 hours
$80.00 ÷ 16 hours = $5.00 per hour

9. **The correct answer is (C).**

21 calls ÷ 3 workers = 7 calls per worker

10. **The correct answer is (A).** Subtract the hours that are unpaid (8) from his total weekly hours (40) to get the hours that are paid each week:

$$\begin{array}{r} 40 \\ -8 \\ \hline 32 \end{array}$$

Multiply this by his hourly pay rate to find how much he earns a week:

$$\begin{array}{r} 32 \\ \times\ \$16.00 \\ \hline \$512.00 \end{array}$$

11. **The correct answer is (A).**

$$\begin{array}{r} 18 \\ 5 \\ +\ 15 \\ \hline 38 \end{array}$$

12. **The correct answer is (C).**

$$\begin{array}{r} 20 \\ 47 \\ +\ 80 \\ \hline 147 \end{array}$$

13. **The correct answer is (D).**

$$\begin{array}{r} 25 \\ 45 \\ +\ 25 \\ \hline 95 \end{array}$$

14. **The correct answer is (C).**

$$\begin{array}{r} 120 \\ 170 \\ +\ 180 \\ \hline 470 \end{array}$$

15. **The correct answer is (B).**

$$\begin{array}{r} 60 \\ 50 \\ +\ 40 \\ \hline 150 \end{array}$$

16. **The correct answer is (A).**

$$\begin{array}{r} 225 \\ 157 \\ +\ 175 \\ \hline 557 \end{array}$$

17. **The correct answer is (A).**

$$\begin{array}{r} 15 \\ \times\ 3 \\ \hline 45 \end{array}$$

18. **The correct answer is (C).**

$$\begin{array}{r} 83 \\ \times\ 2 \\ \hline 166 \end{array}$$

19. **The correct answer is (A).**

$$\begin{array}{r} 53 \\ \times\ 5 \\ \hline 265 \end{array}$$

20. **The correct answer is (D).**

$$\begin{array}{r} 63 \\ \times\ 6 \\ \hline 378 \end{array}$$

21. **The correct answer is (C).**

$$\begin{array}{r} 403 \\ \times\ 403 \\ \hline 1,209 \\ 000 \\ +\ 1,612 \\ \hline 162,409 \end{array}$$

22. **The correct answer is (D).**

$$\begin{array}{r} 25 \\ \times\ 3 \\ \hline 75 \end{array}$$

23. **The correct answer is (B).**

$$\begin{array}{r} 30 \\ \times\ 8 \\ \hline 240 \end{array}$$

24. **The correct answer is (D).**

$$\begin{array}{r} 22 \\ 14 \\ +\ 6 \\ \hline 42 \end{array}$$

25. The correct answer is (A).

$$\begin{array}{r} 325 \\ \times\ 2 \\ \hline 650 \end{array}$$

26. The correct answer is (C). Two states have fewer than 700 miles of highway: Delaware and Rhode Island.

27. The correct answer is (A). Add the distance given for New Jersey (2,867) to the distance given for New York (2,980). Be careful to understand that the chart provides the measurements in miles.

$$\begin{array}{r} 2{,}867 \\ +\ 2{,}980 \\ \hline 5{,}847 \end{array}$$

28. The correct answer is (A). Virginia has 5,304 miles of highway.

29. The correct answer is (D). Delaware has 500 miles of highway.

30. The correct answer is (C). Add the highway miles of Delaware (500) to the highway miles of Rhode Island (614).

$$\begin{array}{r} 500 \\ +\ 614 \\ \hline 1{,}114 \end{array}$$

Perceptual Skills

1.	S	21.	S	41.	S	61.	D	81.	S
2.	D	22.	D	42.	S	62.	S	82.	S
3.	S	23.	D	43.	S	63.	D	83.	D
4.	D	24.	D	44.	D	64.	D	84.	D
5.	S	25.	D	45.	D	65.	D	85.	D
6.	D	26.	D	46.	D	66.	S	86.	D
7.	S	27.	D	47.	S	67.	D	87.	D
8.	D	28.	S	48.	S	68.	S	88.	D
9.	S	29.	S	49.	S	69.	D	89.	D
10.	S	30.	S	50.	S	70.	D	90.	S
11.	S	31.	S	51.	D	71.	D	91.	S
12.	S	32.	D	52.	D	72.	D	92.	D
13.	S	33.	S	53.	D	73.	D	93.	D
14.	S	34.	D	54.	S	74.	S	94.	D
15.	S	35.	S	55.	D	75.	D	95.	D
16.	S	36.	S	56.	D	76.	S	96.	D
17.	S	37.	D	57.	S	77.	S	97.	S
18.	S	38.	S	58.	D	78.	S	98.	S
19.	D	39.	S	59.	D	79.	D	99.	S
20.	S	40.	S	60.	D	80.	S	100.	D

ANSWER SHEET PRACTICE TEST 4: FEDERAL CLERICAL EXAMINATION

VOCABULARY

1. Ⓐ Ⓑ Ⓒ Ⓓ Ⓔ
2. Ⓐ Ⓑ Ⓒ Ⓓ Ⓔ
3. Ⓐ Ⓑ Ⓒ Ⓓ Ⓔ
4. Ⓐ Ⓑ Ⓒ Ⓓ Ⓔ
5. Ⓐ Ⓑ Ⓒ Ⓓ Ⓔ
6. Ⓐ Ⓑ Ⓒ Ⓓ Ⓔ
7. Ⓐ Ⓑ Ⓒ Ⓓ Ⓔ
8. Ⓐ Ⓑ Ⓒ Ⓓ Ⓔ
9. Ⓐ Ⓑ Ⓒ Ⓓ Ⓔ
10. Ⓐ Ⓑ Ⓒ Ⓓ Ⓔ
11. Ⓐ Ⓑ Ⓒ Ⓓ Ⓔ
12. Ⓐ Ⓑ Ⓒ Ⓓ Ⓔ
13. Ⓐ Ⓑ Ⓒ Ⓓ Ⓔ
14. Ⓐ Ⓑ Ⓒ Ⓓ Ⓔ
15. Ⓐ Ⓑ Ⓒ Ⓓ Ⓔ
16. Ⓐ Ⓑ Ⓒ Ⓓ Ⓔ
17. Ⓐ Ⓑ Ⓒ Ⓓ Ⓔ
18. Ⓐ Ⓑ Ⓒ Ⓓ Ⓔ
19. Ⓐ Ⓑ Ⓒ Ⓓ Ⓔ
20. Ⓐ Ⓑ Ⓒ Ⓓ Ⓔ
21. Ⓐ Ⓑ Ⓒ Ⓓ Ⓔ
22. Ⓐ Ⓑ Ⓒ Ⓓ Ⓔ
23. Ⓐ Ⓑ Ⓒ Ⓓ Ⓔ
24. Ⓐ Ⓑ Ⓒ Ⓓ Ⓔ
25. Ⓐ Ⓑ Ⓒ Ⓓ Ⓔ
26. Ⓐ Ⓑ Ⓒ Ⓓ Ⓔ
27. Ⓐ Ⓑ Ⓒ Ⓓ Ⓔ
28. Ⓐ Ⓑ Ⓒ Ⓓ Ⓔ
29. Ⓐ Ⓑ Ⓒ Ⓓ Ⓔ

30. Ⓐ Ⓑ Ⓒ Ⓓ Ⓔ
31. Ⓐ Ⓑ Ⓒ Ⓓ Ⓔ
32. Ⓐ Ⓑ Ⓒ Ⓓ Ⓔ
33. Ⓐ Ⓑ Ⓒ Ⓓ Ⓔ
34. Ⓐ Ⓑ Ⓒ Ⓓ Ⓔ
35. Ⓐ Ⓑ Ⓒ Ⓓ Ⓔ
36. Ⓐ Ⓑ Ⓒ Ⓓ Ⓔ
37. Ⓐ Ⓑ Ⓒ Ⓓ Ⓔ
38. Ⓐ Ⓑ Ⓒ Ⓓ Ⓔ
39. Ⓐ Ⓑ Ⓒ Ⓓ Ⓔ
40. Ⓐ Ⓑ Ⓒ Ⓓ Ⓔ
41. Ⓐ Ⓑ Ⓒ Ⓓ Ⓔ
42. Ⓐ Ⓑ Ⓒ Ⓓ Ⓔ
43. Ⓐ Ⓑ Ⓒ Ⓓ Ⓔ
44. Ⓐ Ⓑ Ⓒ Ⓓ Ⓔ
45. Ⓐ Ⓑ Ⓒ Ⓓ Ⓔ
46. Ⓐ Ⓑ Ⓒ Ⓓ Ⓔ
47. Ⓐ Ⓑ Ⓒ Ⓓ Ⓔ
48. Ⓐ Ⓑ Ⓒ Ⓓ Ⓔ
49. Ⓐ Ⓑ Ⓒ Ⓓ Ⓔ
50. Ⓐ Ⓑ Ⓒ Ⓓ Ⓔ
51. Ⓐ Ⓑ Ⓒ Ⓓ Ⓔ
52. Ⓐ Ⓑ Ⓒ Ⓓ Ⓔ
53. Ⓐ Ⓑ Ⓒ Ⓓ Ⓔ
54. Ⓐ Ⓑ Ⓒ Ⓓ Ⓔ
55. Ⓐ Ⓑ Ⓒ Ⓓ Ⓔ
56. Ⓐ Ⓑ Ⓒ Ⓓ Ⓔ
57. Ⓐ Ⓑ Ⓒ Ⓓ Ⓔ

58. Ⓐ Ⓑ Ⓒ Ⓓ Ⓔ
59. Ⓐ Ⓑ Ⓒ Ⓓ Ⓔ
60. Ⓐ Ⓑ Ⓒ Ⓓ Ⓔ
61. Ⓐ Ⓑ Ⓒ Ⓓ Ⓔ
62. Ⓐ Ⓑ Ⓒ Ⓓ Ⓔ
63. Ⓐ Ⓑ Ⓒ Ⓓ Ⓔ
64. Ⓐ Ⓑ Ⓒ Ⓓ Ⓔ
65. Ⓐ Ⓑ Ⓒ Ⓓ Ⓔ
66. Ⓐ Ⓑ Ⓒ Ⓓ Ⓔ
67. Ⓐ Ⓑ Ⓒ Ⓓ Ⓔ
68. Ⓐ Ⓑ Ⓒ Ⓓ Ⓔ
69. Ⓐ Ⓑ Ⓒ Ⓓ Ⓔ
70. Ⓐ Ⓑ Ⓒ Ⓓ Ⓔ
71. Ⓐ Ⓑ Ⓒ Ⓓ Ⓔ
72. Ⓐ Ⓑ Ⓒ Ⓓ Ⓔ
73. Ⓐ Ⓑ Ⓒ Ⓓ Ⓔ
74. Ⓐ Ⓑ Ⓒ Ⓓ Ⓔ
75. Ⓐ Ⓑ Ⓒ Ⓓ Ⓔ
76. Ⓐ Ⓑ Ⓒ Ⓓ Ⓔ
77. Ⓐ Ⓑ Ⓒ Ⓓ Ⓔ
78. Ⓐ Ⓑ Ⓒ Ⓓ Ⓔ
79. Ⓐ Ⓑ Ⓒ Ⓓ Ⓔ
80. Ⓐ Ⓑ Ⓒ Ⓓ Ⓔ
81. Ⓐ Ⓑ Ⓒ Ⓓ Ⓔ
82. Ⓐ Ⓑ Ⓒ Ⓓ Ⓔ
83. Ⓐ Ⓑ Ⓒ Ⓓ Ⓔ
84. Ⓐ Ⓑ Ⓒ Ⓓ Ⓔ
85. Ⓐ Ⓑ Ⓒ Ⓓ Ⓔ

CLERICAL SKILLS

1. Ⓐ Ⓑ Ⓒ Ⓓ Ⓔ
2. Ⓐ Ⓑ Ⓒ Ⓓ Ⓔ
3. Ⓐ Ⓑ Ⓒ Ⓓ Ⓔ
4. Ⓐ Ⓑ Ⓒ Ⓓ Ⓔ
5. Ⓐ Ⓑ Ⓒ Ⓓ Ⓔ
6. Ⓐ Ⓑ Ⓒ Ⓓ Ⓔ
7. Ⓐ Ⓑ Ⓒ Ⓓ Ⓔ
8. Ⓐ Ⓑ Ⓒ Ⓓ Ⓔ
9. Ⓐ Ⓑ Ⓒ Ⓓ Ⓔ
10. Ⓐ Ⓑ Ⓒ Ⓓ Ⓔ
11. Ⓐ Ⓑ Ⓒ Ⓓ Ⓔ
12. Ⓐ Ⓑ Ⓒ Ⓓ Ⓔ
13. Ⓐ Ⓑ Ⓒ Ⓓ Ⓔ
14. Ⓐ Ⓑ Ⓒ Ⓓ Ⓔ
15. Ⓐ Ⓑ Ⓒ Ⓓ Ⓔ
16. Ⓐ Ⓑ Ⓒ Ⓓ Ⓔ
17. Ⓐ Ⓑ Ⓒ Ⓓ Ⓔ
18. Ⓐ Ⓑ Ⓒ Ⓓ Ⓔ
19. Ⓐ Ⓑ Ⓒ Ⓓ Ⓔ
20. Ⓐ Ⓑ Ⓒ Ⓓ Ⓔ
21. Ⓐ Ⓑ Ⓒ Ⓓ Ⓔ
22. Ⓐ Ⓑ Ⓒ Ⓓ Ⓔ
23. Ⓐ Ⓑ Ⓒ Ⓓ Ⓔ
24. Ⓐ Ⓑ Ⓒ Ⓓ Ⓔ
25. Ⓐ Ⓑ Ⓒ Ⓓ Ⓔ
26. Ⓐ Ⓑ Ⓒ Ⓓ Ⓔ
27. Ⓐ Ⓑ Ⓒ Ⓓ Ⓔ
28. Ⓐ Ⓑ Ⓒ Ⓓ Ⓔ
29. Ⓐ Ⓑ Ⓒ Ⓓ Ⓔ
30. Ⓐ Ⓑ Ⓒ Ⓓ Ⓔ
31. Ⓐ Ⓑ Ⓒ Ⓓ Ⓔ
32. Ⓐ Ⓑ Ⓒ Ⓓ Ⓔ
33. Ⓐ Ⓑ Ⓒ Ⓓ Ⓔ
34. Ⓐ Ⓑ Ⓒ Ⓓ Ⓔ
35. Ⓐ Ⓑ Ⓒ Ⓓ Ⓔ
36. Ⓐ Ⓑ Ⓒ Ⓓ Ⓔ
37. Ⓐ Ⓑ Ⓒ Ⓓ Ⓔ
38. Ⓐ Ⓑ Ⓒ Ⓓ Ⓔ
39. Ⓐ Ⓑ Ⓒ Ⓓ Ⓔ
40. Ⓐ Ⓑ Ⓒ Ⓓ Ⓔ

41. Ⓐ Ⓑ Ⓒ Ⓓ Ⓔ
42. Ⓐ Ⓑ Ⓒ Ⓓ Ⓔ
43. Ⓐ Ⓑ Ⓒ Ⓓ Ⓔ
44. Ⓐ Ⓑ Ⓒ Ⓓ Ⓔ
45. Ⓐ Ⓑ Ⓒ Ⓓ Ⓔ
46. Ⓐ Ⓑ Ⓒ Ⓓ Ⓔ
47. Ⓐ Ⓑ Ⓒ Ⓓ Ⓔ
48. Ⓐ Ⓑ Ⓒ Ⓓ Ⓔ
49. Ⓐ Ⓑ Ⓒ Ⓓ Ⓔ
50. Ⓐ Ⓑ Ⓒ Ⓓ Ⓔ
51. Ⓐ Ⓑ Ⓒ Ⓓ Ⓔ
52. Ⓐ Ⓑ Ⓒ Ⓓ Ⓔ
53. Ⓐ Ⓑ Ⓒ Ⓓ Ⓔ
54. Ⓐ Ⓑ Ⓒ Ⓓ Ⓔ
55. Ⓐ Ⓑ Ⓒ Ⓓ Ⓔ
56. Ⓐ Ⓑ Ⓒ Ⓓ Ⓔ
57. Ⓐ Ⓑ Ⓒ Ⓓ Ⓔ
58. Ⓐ Ⓑ Ⓒ Ⓓ Ⓔ
59. Ⓐ Ⓑ Ⓒ Ⓓ Ⓔ
60. Ⓐ Ⓑ Ⓒ Ⓓ Ⓔ
61. Ⓐ Ⓑ Ⓒ Ⓓ Ⓔ
62. Ⓐ Ⓑ Ⓒ Ⓓ Ⓔ
63. Ⓐ Ⓑ Ⓒ Ⓓ Ⓔ
64. Ⓐ Ⓑ Ⓒ Ⓓ Ⓔ
65. Ⓐ Ⓑ Ⓒ Ⓓ Ⓔ
66. Ⓐ Ⓑ Ⓒ Ⓓ Ⓔ
67. Ⓐ Ⓑ Ⓒ Ⓓ Ⓔ
68. Ⓐ Ⓑ Ⓒ Ⓓ Ⓔ
69. Ⓐ Ⓑ Ⓒ Ⓓ Ⓔ
70. Ⓐ Ⓑ Ⓒ Ⓓ Ⓔ
71. Ⓐ Ⓑ Ⓒ Ⓓ Ⓔ
72. Ⓐ Ⓑ Ⓒ Ⓓ Ⓔ
73. Ⓐ Ⓑ Ⓒ Ⓓ Ⓔ
74. Ⓐ Ⓑ Ⓒ Ⓓ Ⓔ
75. Ⓐ Ⓑ Ⓒ Ⓓ Ⓔ
76. Ⓐ Ⓑ Ⓒ Ⓓ Ⓔ
77. Ⓐ Ⓑ Ⓒ Ⓓ Ⓔ
78. Ⓐ Ⓑ Ⓒ Ⓓ Ⓔ
79. Ⓐ Ⓑ Ⓒ Ⓓ Ⓔ
80. Ⓐ Ⓑ Ⓒ Ⓓ Ⓔ

81. Ⓐ Ⓑ Ⓒ Ⓓ Ⓔ
82. Ⓐ Ⓑ Ⓒ Ⓓ Ⓔ
83. Ⓐ Ⓑ Ⓒ Ⓓ Ⓔ
84. Ⓐ Ⓑ Ⓒ Ⓓ Ⓔ
85. Ⓐ Ⓑ Ⓒ Ⓓ Ⓔ
86. Ⓐ Ⓑ Ⓒ Ⓓ Ⓔ
87. Ⓐ Ⓑ Ⓒ Ⓓ Ⓔ
88. Ⓐ Ⓑ Ⓒ Ⓓ Ⓔ
89. Ⓐ Ⓑ Ⓒ Ⓓ Ⓔ
90. Ⓐ Ⓑ Ⓒ Ⓓ Ⓔ
91. Ⓐ Ⓑ Ⓒ Ⓓ Ⓔ
92. Ⓐ Ⓑ Ⓒ Ⓓ Ⓔ
93. Ⓐ Ⓑ Ⓒ Ⓓ Ⓔ
94. Ⓐ Ⓑ Ⓒ Ⓓ Ⓔ
95. Ⓐ Ⓑ Ⓒ Ⓓ Ⓔ
96. Ⓐ Ⓑ Ⓒ Ⓓ Ⓔ
97. Ⓐ Ⓑ Ⓒ Ⓓ Ⓔ
98. Ⓐ Ⓑ Ⓒ Ⓓ Ⓔ
99. Ⓐ Ⓑ Ⓒ Ⓓ Ⓔ
100. Ⓐ Ⓑ Ⓒ Ⓓ Ⓔ
101. Ⓐ Ⓑ Ⓒ Ⓓ Ⓔ
102. Ⓐ Ⓑ Ⓒ Ⓓ Ⓔ
103. Ⓐ Ⓑ Ⓒ Ⓓ Ⓔ
104. Ⓐ Ⓑ Ⓒ Ⓓ Ⓔ
105. Ⓐ Ⓑ Ⓒ Ⓓ Ⓔ
106. Ⓐ Ⓑ Ⓒ Ⓓ Ⓔ
107. Ⓐ Ⓑ Ⓒ Ⓓ Ⓔ
108. Ⓐ Ⓑ Ⓒ Ⓓ Ⓔ
109. Ⓐ Ⓑ Ⓒ Ⓓ Ⓔ
110. Ⓐ Ⓑ Ⓒ Ⓓ Ⓔ
111. Ⓐ Ⓑ Ⓒ Ⓓ Ⓔ
112. Ⓐ Ⓑ Ⓒ Ⓓ Ⓔ
113. Ⓐ Ⓑ Ⓒ Ⓓ Ⓔ
114. Ⓐ Ⓑ Ⓒ Ⓓ Ⓔ
115. Ⓐ Ⓑ Ⓒ Ⓓ Ⓔ
116. Ⓐ Ⓑ Ⓒ Ⓓ Ⓔ
117. Ⓐ Ⓑ Ⓒ Ⓓ Ⓔ
118. Ⓐ Ⓑ Ⓒ Ⓓ Ⓔ
119. Ⓐ Ⓑ Ⓒ Ⓓ Ⓔ
120. Ⓐ Ⓑ Ⓒ Ⓓ Ⓔ

Practice Test 4: Federal Clerical Examination

VOCABULARY

85 QUESTIONS • 35 MINUTES

Directions: Read each question carefully. Select the best answer and darken the answer space of your choice on the answer sheet.

1. *Flexible* means most nearly

   (A) breakable
   (B) flammable
   (C) pliable
   (D) weak

2. *Option* means most nearly

   (A) use
   (B) choice
   (C) value
   (D) blame

3. To *verify* means most nearly to

   (A) examine
   (B) explain
   (C) confirm
   (D) guarantee

4. *Indolent* means most nearly

   (A) moderate
   (B) hopeless
   (C) selfish
   (D) lazy

5. *Respiration* means most nearly

   (A) recovery
   (B) breathing
   (C) pulsation
   (D) sweating

6. PLUMBER is related to WRENCH as PAINTER is related to

   (A) brush
   (B) pipe
   (C) shop
   (D) hammer

7. LETTER is related to MESSAGE as PACKAGE is related to

   (A) sender
   (B) merchandise
   (C) insurance
   (D) business

8. FOOD is related to HUNGER as SLEEP is related to

   (A) night
   (B) dream
   (C) weariness
   (D) rest

9. KEY is related to TYPEWRITER as DIAL is related to

   (A) sun
   (B) number
   (C) circle
   (D) telephone

10. **(A)** I think that they will promote whoever has the best record.
    (B) The firm would have liked to have promoted all employees with good records.
    (C) Such of them that have the best records have excellent prospects of promotion.
    (D) I feel sure they will give the promotion to whomever has the best record.

11. **(A)** The receptionist must answer courteously the questions of all them callers.
    (B) The receptionist must answer courteously the question what are asked by the callers.
    (C) There would have been no trouble if the receptionist had have always answered courteously.
    (D) The receptionist should answer courteously the questions of all callers.

12. **(A)** collapsible
    (B) collapseable
    (C) collapseble
    (D) none of these

13. **(A)** ambigeuous
    (B) ambigeous
    (C) ambiguous
    (D) none of these

14. **(A)** predesessor
    (B) predecesar
    (C) predecesser
    (D) none of these

15. **(A)** sanctioned
    (B) sancktioned
    (C) sanctionned
    (D) none of these

16. "Some fire-resistant buildings, although wholly constructed of materials that will not burn, may be completely gutted by the spread of fire through their contents by way of hallways and other openings. They may even suffer serious structural damage by the collapse of metal beams and columns."

The quotation best supports the statement that some fire-resistant buildings

    (A) can be damaged seriously by fire.
    (B) have specially constructed halls and doors.
    (C) afford less protection to their contents than would ordinary buildings.
    (D) will burn readily.

17. Civilization started to move ahead more rapidly when people freed themselves of the shackles that restricted their search for the truth.

The paragraph best supports the statement that the progress of civilization

    (A) came as a result of people's dislike for obstacles
    (B) did not begin until restrictions on learning were removed
    (C) has been aided by people's efforts to find the truth
    (D) is based on continually increasing efforts

18. *Vigilant* means most nearly

    (A) sensible
    (B) watchful
    (C) suspicious
    (D) restless

19. *Incidental* means most nearly

    (A) independent
    (B) needless
    (C) infrequent
    (D) casual

20. *Conciliatory* means most nearly

    (A) pacific
    (B) contentious
    (C) obligatory
    (D) offensive

21. *Altercation* means most nearly

    (A) defeat
    (B) concurrence
    (C) controversy
    (D) vexation

22. *Irresolute* means most nearly

    (A) wavering
    (B) insubordinate
    (C) impudent
    (D) unobservant

23. DARKNESS is related to SUNLIGHT as STILLNESS is related to

    (A) quiet
    (B) moonlight
    (C) sound
    (D) dark

24. DESIGNED is related to INTENTION as ACCIDENTAL is related to

    (A) purpose
    (B) caution
    (C) damage
    (D) chance

25. ERROR is related to PRACTICE as SOUND is related to

    (A) deafness
    (B) noise
    (C) muffler
    (D) horn

26. RESEARCH is related to FINDINGS as TRAINING is related to

    (A) skill
    (B) tests
    (C) supervision
    (D) teaching

27. (A) If properly addressed, the letter will reach my mother and I.
    (B) The letter had been addressed to myself and my mother.
    (C) I believe the letter was addressed to either my mother or 1.
    (D) My mother's name, as well as mine, was on the letter.

28. (A) The supervisors reprimanded the typists, whom she believed I had made careless errors.
    (B) The typists would have corrected the errors had they of known that the supervisor would see the report.
    (C) The errors in the typed reports were so numerous that they could hardly be overlooked.
    (D) Many errors were found in the reports which they typed and could not disregard them.

29. (A) minieture
    (B) minneature
    (C) mineature
    (D) none of these

30. (A) extemporaneous
    (B) extempuraneus
    (C) extemperaneous
    (D) none of these

31. (A) problemmatical
    (B) problematical
    (C) problematicle
    (D) none of these

32. (A) descendant
    (B) decendant
    (C) desendant
    (D) none of these

33. The likelihood of America's exhausting its natural resources seems to be growing less. All kinds of waste are being reworked and new uses are constantly being found for almost everything. We are getting more use out of our goods and are making many new byproducts out of what was formerly thrown away.

The paragraph best supports the statement that we seem to be in less danger of exhausting our resources because

- **(A)** economy is found to lie in the use of substitutes.
- **(B)** more service is obtained from a given amount of material.
- **(C)** we are allowing time for nature to restore them.
- **(D)** supply and demand are better controlled.

34. Telegrams should be clear, concise, and brief. Omit all unnecessary words. The parts of speech most often used in telegrams are nouns, verbs, adjectives, and adverbs. If possible, do without pronouns, prepositions, articles, and copulative verbs. Use simple sentences, rather than complex or compound ones.

The paragraph best supports the statement that in writing telegrams one should always use

- **(A)** common and simple words.
- **(B)** only nouns, verbs, adjectives, and adverbs.
- **(C)** incomplete sentences.
- **(D)** only the words essential to the meaning.

35. To *counteract* means most nearly to

- **(A)** undermine
- **(B)** censure
- **(C)** preserve
- **(D)** neutralize

36. *Deferred* means most nearly

- **(A)** reversed
- **(B)** delayed
- **(C)** considered
- **(D)** forbidden

37. *Feasible* means most nearly

- **(A)** capable
- **(B)** justifiable
- **(C)** practicable
- **(D)** beneficial

38. To *encounter* means most nearly to

- **(A)** meet
- **(B)** recall
- **(C)** overcome
- **(D)** retreat

39. *Innate* means most nearly

- **(A)** eternal
- **(B)** well-developed
- **(C)** native
- **(D)** prospective

40. STUDENT is related to TEACHER as DISCIPLE is related to

- **(A)** follower
- **(B)** master
- **(C)** principal
- **(D)** pupil

41. LECTURE is related to AUDITORIUM as EXPERIMENT is related to

- **(A)** scientist
- **(B)** chemistry
- **(C)** laboratory
- **(D)** discovery

42. BODY is related to FOOD as ENGINE is related to

- **(A)** wheels
- **(B)** fuel
- **(C)** motion
- **(D)** smoke

43. SCHOOL is related to EDUCATION as THEATER is related to

- **(A)** management
- **(B)** stage
- **(C)** recreation
- **(D)** preparation

44. **(A)** Most all these statements have been supported by persons who are reliable and can be depended upon.
    (B) The persons which have guaranteed these statements are reliable.
    (C) Reliable persons guarantee the facts with regards to the truth of these statements.
    (D) These statements can be depended on, for their truth has been guaranteed by reliable persons.

45. **(A)** The success of the book pleased both the publisher and authors.
    (B) Both the publisher and they was pleased with the success of the book.
    (C) Neither they or their publisher was disappointed with the success of the book.
    (D) Their publisher was as pleased as they with the success of the book.

46. **(A)** extercate
    (B) extracate
    (C) extricate
    (D) none of these

47. **(A)** hereditory
    (B) hereditary
    (C) hereditairy
    (D) none of these

48. **(A)** auspiceous
    (B) auspiseous
    (C) auspicious
    (D) none of these

49. **(A)** sequance
    (B) sequence
    (C) sequense
    (D) none of these

50. The prevention of accidents makes it necessary not only that safety devices be used to guard exposed machinery but also that mechanics be instructed in safety rules which they must follow for their own protection, and that the lighting in the plant be adequate.

The paragraph best supports the statement that industrial accidents

(A) may be due to ignorance.
(B) are always avoidable.
(C) usually result from inadequate machinery.
(D) cannot be entirely overcome.

51. The English language is peculiarly rich in synonyms, and there is scarcely a language spoken that has not some representative in English speech. The spirit of the Anglo-Saxon people has subjugated these various elements to one idiom, making not a patchwork, but a composite language.

The paragraph best supports the statement that the English language

(A) has few idiomatic expressions.
(B) is difficult to translate.
(C) is used universally.
(D) has absorbed words from other languages.

52. *To acquiesce* means most nearly to

(A) assent
(B) acquire
(C) complete
(D) participate

53. *Unanimity* means most nearly

(A) emphasis
(B) namelessness
(C) harmony
(D) impartiality

54. *Precedent* means most nearly

(A) example
(B) theory
(C) law
(D) conformity

55. *Versatile* means most nearly

(A) broad-minded
(B) well-known
(C) up-to-date
(D) many-sided

56. *Authentic* means most nearly

(A) detailed
(B) reliable
(C) valuable
(D) practical

57. BIOGRAPHY is related to FACT as NOVEL is related to

(A) fiction
(B) literature
(C) narration
(D) book

58. COPY is related to CARBON PAPER as MOTION PICTURE is related to

(A) theater
(B) film
(C) duplicate
(D) television

59. EFFICIENCY is related to REWARD as CARELESSNESS is related to

(A) improvement
(B) disobedience
(C) reprimand
(D) repetition

60. ABUNDANT is related to CHEAP as SCARCE is related to

(A) ample
(B) costly
(C) inexpensive
(D) unobtainable

61. (A) Brown's & Company employees have recently received increases in salary.
(B) Brown & Company recently increased the salaries of all its employees.
(C) Recently Brown & Company has increased their employees' salaries.
(D) Brown & Company have recently increased the salaries of all its employees.

62. (A) In reviewing the typists' work reports, the job analyst found records of unusual typing speeds.
(B) It says in the job analyst's report that some employees type with great speed.
(C) The job analyst found that, in reviewing the typists' work reports, that some unusual typing speeds had been made.
(D) In the reports of typists' speeds, the job analyst found some records that are kind of unusual.

63. (A) oblitorate
(B) oblitterat
(C) obbliterate
(D) none of these

64. (A) diagnoesis
(B) diagnossis
(C) diagnosis
(D) none of these

65. (A) contenance
(B) countenance
(C) countinance
(D) none of these

66. (A) conceivably
(B) concieveably
(C) conceiveably
(D) none of these

67. Through advertising, manufacturers exercise a high degree of control over consumers' desires. However, the manufacturer assumes enormous risks in attempting to predict what consumers will want and in producing goods in quantity and distributing them in advance of final selection by the consumers.

The paragraph best supports the statement that manufacturers

(A) can eliminate the risk of overproduction by advertising.

(B) distribute goods directly to the consumers.

(C) must depend upon the final consumers for the success of their undertakings.

(D) can predict with great accuracy the success of any product they put on the market.

68. In the relations of humans to nature, the procuring of food and shelter is fundamental. With the migration of humans to various climates, ever new adjustments to the food supply and to the climate became necessary.

The paragraph best supports the statement that the means by which humans supply their material needs are

(A) accidental.

(B) varied.

(C) limited.

(D) inadequate.

69. *Strident* means most nearly

(A) swaggering

(B) domineering

(C) angry

(D) harsh

70. To *confine* means most nearly to

(A) hide

(B) restrict

(C) eliminate

(D) punish

71. To *accentuate* means most nearly to

(A) modify

(B) hasten

(C) sustain

(D) intensify

72. *Banal* means most nearly

(A) commonplace

(B) reliable

(C) tranquil

(D) indifferent

73. *Incorrigible* means most nearly

(A) intolerable

(B) retarded

(C) irreformable

(D) brazen

74. POLICEMAN is related to ORDER as DOCTOR is related to

(A) physician

(B) hospital

(C) sickness

(D) health

75. ARTIST is related to EASEL as WEAVER is related to

(A) loom

(B) cloth

(C) threads

(D) spinner

76. CROWD is related to PERSONS as FLEET is related to

(A) expedition

(B) officers

(C) navy

(D) ships

77. CALENDAR is related to DATE as MAP is related to

(A) geography

(B) trip

(C) mileage

(D) vacation

78. **(A)** Since the report lacked the needed information, it was of no use to them.
    (B) This report was useless to them because there were no needed information in the shortest time.
    (C) Since the report did not contain the needed information, it was not real useful to them.
    (D) Being that the report lacked the needed information, they could not use it.

79. **(A)** The company had hardly declared the dividend till the notices were prepared for mailing.
    (B) They had no sooner declared the dividend when they sent the notices to the stockholders.
    (C) No sooner had the dividend been declared than the notices were prepared for mailing.
    (D) Scarcely had the dividend been declared than the notices were sent out.

80. **(A)** compitition
    (B) competition
    (C) competetion
    (D) none of these

81. **(A)** occassion
    (B) occasion
    (C) ocassion
    (D) none of these

82. **(A)** knowlege
    (B) knolledge
    (C) knowledge
    (D) none of these

83. **(A)** deliborate
    (B) deliberate
    (C) delibrate
    (D) none of these

84. What constitutes skill in any line of work is not always easy to determine; economy of time must be carefully distinguished from economy of energy as the quickest method may require the greatest expenditure of muscular effort, and may not be essential or at all desirable.

The paragraph best supports the statement that

(A) the most efficiently executed task is not always the one done in the shortest time.
(B) energy and time cannot both be conserved in performing a single task.
(C) a task is well done when it is performed in the shortest time.
(D) skill in performing a task should not be acquired at the expense of time.

85. It is difficult to distinguish between bookkeeping and accounting. In attempts to do so, bookkeeping is called the art, and accounting the science of recording business transactions. Bookkeeping gives the history of the business in a systematic manner; and accounting classifies, analyzes, and interprets the facts thus recorded.

The paragraph best supports the statement that

(A) accounting is less systematic than bookkeeping.
(B) accounting and bookkeeping are closely related.
(C) bookkeeping and accounting cannot be distinguished from one another.
(D) bookkeeping has been superseded by accounting.

STOP   End of Vocabulary section. If you finish before time is up, check your work on this part only. Do not go to the next section until the signal is given.

CLERICAL SKILLS

120 QUESTIONS • 15 MINUTES

Directions: In each line across the page there are three names, addresses, or codes that are very much alike. Compare the three and decide which ones are EXACTLY alike. On your answer sheet, mark:

(A) if **ALL THREE** names, addresses, or codes are exactly **ALIKE**
(B) if only the **FIRST** and **SECOND** names, addresses, or codes are exactly **ALIKE**
(C) if only the **FIRST** and **THIRD** names, addresses, or codes are exactly **ALIKE**
(D) if only the **SECOND** and **THIRD** names, addresses, or codes are exactly **ALIKE**
(E) if **ALL THREE** names, addresses, or codes are **DIFFERENT**

1. 5261383   5261383   5261338
2. 8125690   8126690   8125609
3. W. E. Johnston   W. E. Johnson   W. E. Johnson
4. Vergil L. Muller   Vergil L. Muller   Vergil L. Muller
5. Atherton R. Warde   Asheton R. Warde   Atherton P. Warde

Directions: For each question there is a name, number, or code in a box at the left and four other names, numbers, or codes in alphabetical or numerical order at the right. Find the correct space for the boxed name or number so that it will be in alphabetical and/or numerical order with the others and darken the answer space of your choice on your answer sheet.

6. | Hackett, Gerald |

(A) →
Habert, James
(B) →
Hachett, J. J.
(C) →
Hachetts, K. Larson
(D) →
Hachettson, Leroy
(E) →

7. | Margenroth, Alvin |

(A) →
Margeroth, Albert
(B) →
Margestein, Dan
(C) →
Margestein, David
(D) →
Margue, Edgar
(E) →

8.   Bobbitt, Olivier E.

   (A) →
   Bobbitt, D. Olivier
   (B) →
   Bobbitt, Olive B.
   (C) →
   Bobbitt, Olivia H.
   (D) →
   Bobbitt, R. Olivia
   (E) →

9.   Mosely, Werner

   (A) →
   Mosely, Albert
   (B) →
   Mosley, Alvin
   (C) →
   Mosley, S. M.
   (D) →
   Mosley, Vinson, N.
   (E) →

10. Youmuns, Frank L.

   (A) →
   Youmons, Frank G.
   (B) →
   Youmons, Frank H.
   (C) →
   Youmons, Frank K.
   (D) →
   Youmons, Frank M.
   (E) →

Directions: In the following questions, solve each problem and find your answer among the list of suggested answers for that question. Choose (A), (B), (C), or (D) for the answer you obtained, or if your answer is not among these, darken (E) for that question.

11. Add: 43
         + 32

   (A) 55
   (B) 65
   (C) 66
   (D) 75
   (E) none of these

12. Subtract: 83
              − 4

   (A) 73
   (B) 79
   (C) 80
   (D) 89
   (E) none of these

13. Multiply: 41
              × 7

   (A) 281
   (B) 287
   (C) 291
   (D) 297
   (E) none of these

14. Divide: 6)306

   (A) 44
   (B) 51
   (C) 52
   (D) 60
   (E) none of these

15. Add: 37
         + 15

   (A) 42
   (B) 52
   (C) 53
   (D) 62
   (E) none of these

Directions: Find which suggested answer contains numbers and letters all of which appear in the question. If no suggested answer fits, darken (E) for that question.

16. 6 2 5 K 4 P T G
17. L 4 7 2 T 6 V K
18. 3 5 4 L 9 V T G
19. G 4 K 7 L 3 5 Z
20. 4 K 2 9 N 5 T G

Suggested Answers

(A) = 4, 5, K, T
(B) = 4, 7, G, K
(C) = 2, 5, G, L
(D) = 2, 7, L, T
(E) = none of these

Directions: In each line across the page there are three names, addresses, or codes that are very much alike. Compare the three and decide which ones are EXACTLY alike. On your answer sheet, mark:

(A) if **ALL THREE** names, addresses, or codes are exactly **ALIKE**
(B) if only the **FIRST** and **SECOND** names, addresses, or codes are exactly **ALIKE**
(C) if only the **FIRST** and **THIRD** names, addresses, or codes are exactly **ALIKE**
(D) if only the **SECOND** and **THIRD** names, addresses, or codes are exactly **ALIKE**
(E) if **ALL THREE** names, addresses, or codes are **DIFFERENT**

21.	2395890	2395890	2395890
22.	1926341	1926347	1926314
23.	E. Owens McVey	E. Owen McVey	E. Owen McVay
24.	Emily Neal Rouse	Emily Neal Rowse	Emily Neal Rowse
25.	H. Merritt Audubon	H. Merriott Audubon	H. Merritt Audubon

Directions: For each question there is a name, number, or code in a box at the left and four other names, numbers, or codes in alphabetical or numerical order at the right. Find the correct space for the boxed name or number so that it will be in alphabetical and/or numerical order with the others and darken the answer space of your choice on your answer sheet.

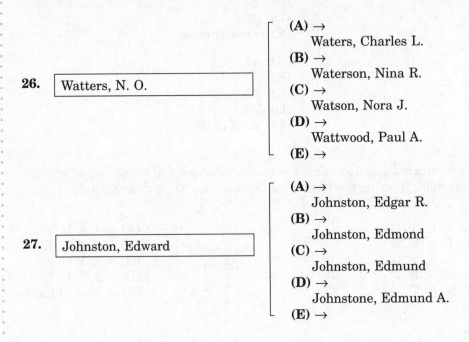

26. | Watters, N. O. |

(A) →
　　Waters, Charles L.
(B) →
　　Waterson, Nina R.
(C) →
　　Watson, Nora J.
(D) →
　　Wattwood, Paul A.
(E) →

27. | Johnston, Edward |

(A) →
　　Johnston, Edgar R.
(B) →
　　Johnston, Edmond
(C) →
　　Johnston, Edmund
(D) →
　　Johnstone, Edmund A.
(E) →

28. | Rensch, Adeline |

(A) →
Ramsay, Amos
(B) →
Remschel, Augusta
(C) →
Renshaw, Austin
(D) →
Rentzel, Becky
(E) →

29. | Schnyder, Maurice |

(A) →
Schneider, Martin
(B) →
Schneider, Mertens
(C) →
Schnyder, Newman
(D) →
Schreibner, Norman
(E) →

30. | Freedenburg, C. Erma |

(A) →
Freedenberg, Emerson
(B) →
Freedenberg, Erma
(C) →
Freedenberg, Erma E.
(D) →
Freedinberg, Erma F.
(E) →

Directions: In the following questions, solve each problem and find your answer among the list of suggested answers for that question. Choose (A), (B), (C), or (D) for the answer you obtained, or if your answer is not among these, darken (E) for that question.

31. Subtract: 68
    − 47

    (A) 10
    (B) 11
    (C) 20
    (D) 22
    (E) none of these

32. Multiply: 50
    × 8

    (A) 400
    (B) 408
    (C) 450
    (D) 458
    (E) none of these

33. Divide: 9)180

    (A) 20
    (B) 29
    (C) 30
    (D) 39
    (E) none of these

34. Add: 78
    + 63

    (A) 131
    (B) 140
    (C) 141
    (D) 151
    (E) none of these

35. Subtract: 89
    − 70

    (A) 9
    (B) 18
    (C) 19
    (D) 29
    (E) none of these

Directions: Find which suggested answer contains numbers and letters all of which appear in the question. If no suggested answer fits, darken (E) for that question.

36. 9 G Z 3 L 4 6 N
37. L 5 N K 4 3 9 V
38. 8 2 V P 9 L Z 5
39. V P 9 Z 5 L 8 7
40. 5 T 8 N 2 9 V L

Suggested Answers

(A) = 4, 9, L, V
(B) = 4, 5, N, Z
(C) = 5, 8, L, Z
(D) = 8, 9, N, V
(E) = none of these

Directions: In each line across the page there are three names, addresses, or codes that are very much alike. Compare the three and decide which ones are EXACTLY alike. On your answer sheet, mark:

(A) if **ALL THREE** names, addresses, or codes are exactly **ALIKE**
(B) if only the **FIRST** and **SECOND** names, addresses, or codes are exactly **ALIKE**
(C) if only the **FIRST** and **THIRD** names, addresses, or codes are exactly **ALIKE**
(D) if only the **SECOND** and **THIRD** names, addresses, or codes are exactly **ALIKE**
(E) if **ALL THREE** names, addresses, or codes are **DIFFERENT**

41.	6219354	6219354	6219354
42.	2312793	2312793	2312793
43.	1065407	1065407	1065047
44.	Francis Ransdell	Frances Ramsdell	Francis Ramsdell
45.	Cornelius Detwiler	Cornelius Detwiler	Cornelius Detwiler

Directions: For each question there is a name, number, or code in a box at the left and four other names, numbers, or codes in alphabetical or numerical order at the right. Find the correct space for the boxed name or number so that it will be in alphabetical and/or numerical order with the others and darken the answer space of your choice on your answer sheet.

46. | DeMattia, Jessica |

(A) →
    DeLong, Jesse
(B) →
    DeMatteo, Jessie
(C) →
    Derby, Jessie S.
(D) →
    DeShazo, L. M.
(E) →

47. | Theriault, Louis |

(A) →
    Therien, Annette
(B) →
    Therien, Elaine
(C) →
    Thibeault, Gerald
(D) →
    Thiebeault, Pierre
(E) →

48. | Gaston, M. Hubert |

(A) →
Gaston, Dorothy M.
(B) →
Gaston, Henry N.
(C) →
Gaston, Isabel
(D) →
Gaston, M. Melvin
(E) →

49. | SanMiguel, Carlos |

(A) →
SanLuis, Juana
(B) →
Santilli, Laura
(C) →
Stinnett, Nellie
(D) →
Stoddard, Victor
(E) →

50. | DeLaTour, Hall F. |

(A) →
Delargy, Harold
(B) →
DeLathouder, Hilda
(C) →
Lathrop, Hillary
(D) →
LaTour, Hulbert E.
(E) →

Directions: In the following questions, solve each problem and find your answer among the list of suggested answers for that question. Choose (A), (B), (C), or (D) for the answer you obtained, or if your answer is not among these, darken (E) for that question.

51. Multiply: 62
    × 5

    (A) 300
    (B) 310
    (C) 315
    (D) 360
    (E) none of these

52. Divide: 3)153

    (A) 41
    (B) 43
    (C) 51
    (D) 53
    (E) none of these

53. Add: 47
    + 21

    (A) 58
    (B) 59
    (C) 67
    (D) 68
    (E) none of these

54. Subtract: 87
    − 42

    (A) 34
    (B) 35
    (C) 44
    (D) 45
    (E) none of these

55. Multiply: 37
    × 3

    (A) 91
    (B) 101
    (C) 104
    (D) 114
    (E) none of these

Directions: Find which suggested answer contains numbers and letters all of which appear in the question. If no suggested answer fits, darken (E) for that question.

56. N 5 4 7 T K 3 Z
57. 8 5 3 V L 2 Z N
58. 7 2 5 N 9 K L V
59. 9 8 L 2 5 Z K V
60. Z 6 5 V 9 3 P N

Suggested Answers

(A) = 3, 8, K, N
(B) = 5, 8, N, V
(C) = 3, 9, V, Z
(D) = 5, 9, K, Z
(E) = none of these

Directions: In each line across the page there are three names, addresses, or codes that are very much alike. Compare the three and decide which ones are EXACTLY alike. On your answer sheet, mark:

    (A) if **ALL THREE** names, addresses, or codes are exactly **ALIKE**
    (B) if only the **FIRST** and **SECOND** names, addresses, or codes are exactly **ALIKE**
    (C) if only the **FIRST** and **THIRD** names, addresses, or codes are exactly **ALIKE**
    (D) if only the **SECOND** and **THIRD** names, addresses, or codes are exactly **ALIKE**
    (E) if **ALL THREE** names, addresses, or codes are **DIFFERENT**

61.	6452054	6452654	6452054
62.	8501268	8501268	8501286
63.	Ella Burk Newham	Ella Burk Newnham	Elena Burk Newnham
64.	Jno. K. Ravencroft	Jno. H. Ravencroft	Jno. H. Ravencraft
65.	Martin Wills Pullen	Martin Wills Pulen	Martin Wills Pullen

Directions: For each question there is a name, number, or code in a box at the left and four other names, numbers, or codes in alphabetical or numerical order at the right. Find the correct space for the boxed name or number so that it will be in alphabetical and/or numerical order with the others and darken the answer space of your choice on your answer sheet.

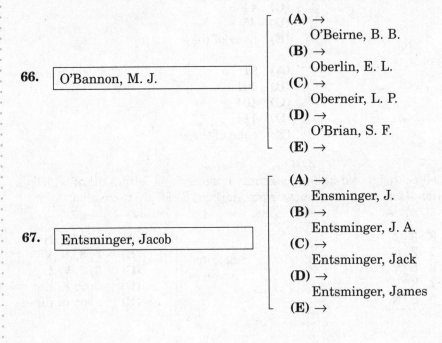

66.   O'Bannon, M. J.

    (A) →
         O'Beirne, B. B.
    (B) →
         Oberlin, E. L.
    (C) →
         Oberneir, L. P.
    (D) →
         O'Brian, S. F.
    (E) →

67.   Entsminger, Jacob

    (A) →
         Ensminger, J.
    (B) →
         Entsminger, J. A.
    (C) →
         Entsminger, Jack
    (D) →
         Entsminger, James
    (E) →

68. | Iacone, Pete R. |

(A) →
Iacone, Pedro
(B) →
Iacone, Pedro M.
(C) →
Iacone, Peter F.
(D) →
Iascone, Peter W.
(E) →

69. | Sheppard, Gladys |

(A) →
Shepard, Dwight
(B) →
Shepard, F. H.
(C) →
Shephard, Louise
(D) →
Shepperd, Stella
(E) →

70. | Thackton, Melvin T. |

(A) →
Thackston, Milton G.
(B) →
Thackston, Milton W.
(C) →
Thackston, Theodore
(D) →
Thackston, Thomas G.
(E) →

Directions: In the following questions, solve each problem and find your answer among the list of suggested answers for that question. Choose (A), (B), (C), or (D) for the answer you obtained, or if your answer is not among these, darken (E) for that question.

71. Divide: 7)357

(A) 51
(B) 52
(C) 53
(D) 54
(E) none of these

72. Add: 58
       + 27

(A) 75
(B) 84
(C) 85
(D) 95
(E) none of these

73. Subtract: 86
           − 57

(A) 18
(B) 29
(C) 38
(D) 39
(E) none of these

74. Multiply: 68
            × 4

(A) 242
(B) 264
(C) 272
(D) 274
(E) none of these

75. Divide: 9)639

(A) 71
(B) 73
(C) 81
(D) 83
(E) none of these

Directions: Find which suggested answer contains numbers and letters all of which appear in the question. If no suggested answer fits, darken (E) for that question.

76.   6 Z T N 8 7 4 V
77.   V 7 8 6 N 5 P L
78.   N 7 P V 8 4 2 L
79.   7 8 G 4 3 V L T
80.   4 8 G 2 T N 6 L

Suggested
Answers

(A) = 2, 7, L, N
(B) = 2, 8, T, V
(C) = 6, 8, L, T
(D) = 6, 7, N, V
(E) = none of these

Directions: In each line across the page there are three names, addresses, or codes that are very much alike. Compare the three and decide which ones are EXACTLY alike. On your answer sheet, mark:

- **(A)** if **ALL THREE** names, addresses, or codes are exactly **ALIKE**
- **(B)** if only the **FIRST** and **SECOND** names, addresses, or codes are exactly **ALIKE**
- **(C)** if only the **FIRST** and **THIRD** names, addresses, or codes are exactly **ALIKE**
- **(D)** if only the **SECOND** and **THIRD** names, addresses, or codes are exactly **ALIKE**
- **(E)** if **ALL THREE** names, addresses, or codes are **DIFFERENT**

81.	3457988	3457986	3457986
82.	4695682	4695862	4695682
83.	Stricklund Kanedy	Stricklund Kanedy	Stricklund Kanedy
84.	Joy Harlor Witner	Joy Harloe Witner	Joy Harloe Witner
85.	R. M. O. Uberroth	R. M. O. Uberroth	R. N. O. Uberroth

Directions: For each question there is a name, number, or code in a box at the left and four other names, numbers, or codes in alphabetical or numerical order at the right. Find the correct space for the boxed name or number so that it will be in alphabetical and/or numerical order with the others and darken the answer space of your choice on your answer sheet.

86. | Dunlavey, M. Hilary |

    (A) →
    Dunleavy, Hilary G.
    (B) →
    Dunleavy, Hilary K.
    (C) →
    Dunleavy, Hilary S.
    (D) →
    Dunleavy, Hilery W.
    (E) →

87. | Yarbrough, Maria |

    (A) →
    Yabroudy, Margy
    (B) →
    Yarboro, Marie
    (C) →
    Yarborough, Marina
    (D) →
    Yarborough, Mary
    (E) →

88. | Prouty, Martha |

(A) →
Proutey, Margaret
(B) →
Proutey, Maude
(C) →
Prouty, Myra
(D) →
Prouty, Naomi
(E) →

89. | Pawlowicz, Ruth M. |

(A) →
Pawalek, Edward
(B) →
Pawelek, Flora G.
(C) →
Pawlowski, Joan M.
(D) →
Pawtowski, Wanda
(E) →

90. | Vanstory, George |

(A) →
Vanover, Eva
(B) →
VanSwinderen, Floyd
(C) →
VanSyckle, Harry
(D) →
Vanture, Laurence
(E) →

Directions: In the following questions, solve each problem and find your answer among the list of suggested answers for that question. Choose (A), (B), (C), or (D) for the answer you obtained, or if your answer is not among these, darken (E) for that question.

91. Add: 28
         + 35

    (A) 53
    (B) 62
    (C) 64
    (D) 73
    (E) none of these

92. Subtract: 78
             − 69

    (A) 7
    (B) 8
    (C) 18
    (D) 19
    (E) none of these

93. Multiply: 86
             × 6

    (A) 492
    (B) 506
    (C) 516
    (D) 526
    (E) none of these

94. Divide: $8\overline{)648}$

    (A) 71
    (B) 76
    (C) 81
    (D) 89
    (E) none of these

95. Add: 97
        + 34

    (A) 131
    (B) 132
    (C) 140
    (D) 141
    (E) none of these

Directions: Find which suggested answer contains numbers and letters all of which appear in the question. If no suggested answer fits, darken (E) for that question.

96.	V	5	7	Z	N	9	4	T
97.	4	6	P	T	2	N	K	9
98.	6	4	N	2	P	8	Z	K
99.	7	P	5	2	4	N	K	T
100.	K	T	8	5	4	N	2	P

Suggested Answers

    (A) = 2, 5, N, Z
    (B) = 4, 5, N, P
    (C) = 2, 9, P, T
    (D) = 4, 9, T, Z
    (E) = none of these

Directions: In each line across the page there are three names, addresses, or codes that are very much alike. Compare the three and decide which ones are EXACTLY alike. On your answer sheet, mark:

(A) if **ALL THREE** names, addresses, or codes are exactly **ALIKE**
(B) if only the **FIRST** and **SECOND** names, addresses, or codes are exactly **ALIKE**
(C) if only the **FIRST** and **THIRD** names, addresses, or codes are exactly **ALIKE**
(D) if only the **SECOND** and **THIRD** names, addresses, or codes are exactly **ALIKE**
(E) if **ALL THREE** names, addresses, or codes are **DIFFERENT**

101.	1592514	159257	41592574
102.	2010202	2010202	2010220
103.	6177396	6177936	6177396
104.	Drusilla S. Ridgeley	Drusilla S. Ridgeley	Drusilla S. Ridgeley
105.	Andrei I. Toumantzev	Andrei I. Tourmantzev	Andrei I. Toumantzov

Directions: For each question there is a name, number, or code in a box at the left and four other names, numbers, or codes in alphabetical or numerical order at the right. Find the correct space for the boxed name or number so that it will be in alphabetical and/or numerical order with the others and darken the answer space of your choice on your answer sheet.

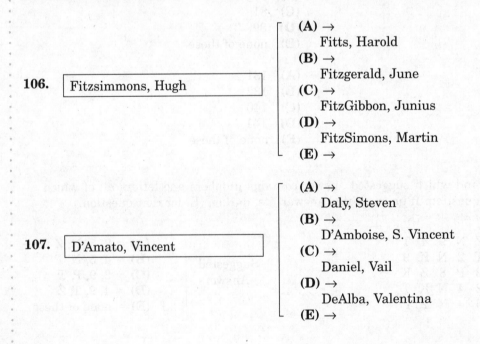

106.   Fitzsimmons, Hugh

(A) →
    Fitts, Harold
(B) →
    Fitzgerald, June
(C) →
    FitzGibbon, Junius
(D) →
    FitzSimons, Martin
(E) →

107.   D'Amato, Vincent

(A) →
    Daly, Steven
(B) →
    D'Amboise, S. Vincent
(C) →
    Daniel, Vail
(D) →
    DeAlba, Valentina
(E) →

108.

| Schaeffer, Roger D. |

(A) →
Schaffert, Evelyn M.
(B) →
Schaffner, Margaret M.
(C) →
Schafhirt, Milton G.
(D) →
Shafer, Richard E.
(E) →

109.

| White-Lewis, Cecil |

(A) →
Whitelaw, Cordelia
(B) →
White-Leigh, Nancy
(C) →
Whitely, Rodney
(D) →
Whitlock, Warren
(E) →

110.

| VanDerHeggen, Don |

(A) →
VanDemark, Doris
(B) →
Vandenberg, H. E.
(C) →
VanDercook, Marie
(D) →
vanderLinden, Robert
(E) →

practice test

Directions: In the following questions, solve each problem and find your answer among the list of suggested answers for that question. Choose (A), (B), (C), or (D) for the answer you obtained, or if your answer is not among these, darken (E) for that question.

111. Add: 75
         + 49

   (A) 124
   (B) 125
   (C) 134
   (D) 225
   (E) none of these

112. Subtract: 69
             − 45

   (A) 14
   (B) 23
   (C) 24
   (D) 26
   (E) none of these

113. Multiply: 36
             × 8

   (A) 246
   (B) 262
   (C) 288
   (D) 368
   (E) none of these

114. Divide: 8)$\overline{328}$

   (A) 31
   (B) 41
   (C) 42
   (D) 48
   (E) none of these

115. Multiply: 58
             × 9

   (A) 472
   (B) 513
   (C) 521
   (D) 522
   (E) none of these

Directions: Find which suggested answer contains numbers and letters all of which appear in the question. If no suggested answer fits, darken (E) for that question.

116. Z 3 N P G 5 4 2
117. 6 N 2 8 G 4 P T
118. 6 N 4 T V G 8 2
119. T 3 P 4 N 8 G 2
120. 6 7 K G N 2 L 5

Suggested Answers

(A) = 2, 3, G, N
(B) = 2, 6, N, T
(C) = 3, 4, G, K
(D) = 4, 6, K, T
(E) = none of these

S T O P   End of Clerical Skills section. If you finish before time is up, check your work on this section only. Do not go to the next section until the signal is given.

ANSWER KEY AND EXPLANATIONS

Vocabulary

1.	C	18.	B	35.	D	52.	A	69.	D
2.	B	19.	D	36.	B	53.	C	70.	B
3.	C	20.	A	37.	C	54.	A	71.	D
4.	D	21.	C	38.	A	55.	D	72.	A
5.	B	22.	A	39.	C	56.	B	73.	C
6.	A	23.	C	40.	B	57.	A	74.	D
7.	B	24.	D	41.	C	58.	B	75.	A
8.	C	25.	C	42.	B	59.	C	76.	D
9.	D	26.	A	43.	C	60.	B	77.	C
10.	A	27.	D	44.	D	61.	B	78.	A
11.	D	28.	C	45.	D	62.	A	79.	C
12.	A	29.	D	46.	C	63.	D	80.	B
13.	C	30.	A	47.	B	64.	C	81.	B
14.	D	31.	B	48.	C	65.	B	82.	B
15.	A	32.	A	49.	B	66.	A	83.	B
16.	A	33.	B	50.	A	67.	C	84.	A
17.	C	34.	D	51.	D	68.	B	85.	B

1. **The correct answer is (C).** FLEXIBLE means *adjustable* or *pliable*. An office which offers flexible hours may operate from 6 a.m. to 10 p.m.

2. **The correct answer is (B).** An OPTION is a *choice*. When you cast your vote, you are exercising your option.

3. **The correct answer is (C).** To VERIFY is to *check the accuracy of* or to *confirm*. A notary stamp verifies that the signature on the document is the signature of the person named.

4. **The correct answer is (D).** INDOLENT means *idle* or *lazy*. An indolent person is not likely to become a productive employee.

5. **The correct answer is (B).** RESPIRATION is *breathing*. Respiration is the process by which animals inhale and exhale air.

6. **The correct answer is (A).** A BRUSH is a tool of the PAINTER's trade as a WRENCH is a tool of the PLUMBER's trade.

7. **The correct answer is (B).** A PACKAGE transports MERCHANDISE just as a LETTER transmits a MESSAGE.

8. **The correct answer is (C).** SLEEP alleviates WEARINESS just as FOOD alleviates HUNGER.

9. **The correct answer is (D).** The DIAL is an input device of a TELEPHONE just as a KEY is an input device of a TYPEWRITER.

10. **The correct answer is (A).** *Whoever* is the subject of the phrase "whoever has the best record." Choices (B) and (C) are wordy and awkward.

11. **The correct answer is (D).** All the other choices contain obvious errors.

12. **The correct answer is (A).** The correct spelling is: collapsible.

13. **The correct answer is (C).** The correct spelling is: ambiguous.

14. **The correct answer is (D).** The correct spelling is: predecessor.

15. **The correct answer is (A).** The correct spelling is: sanctioned.

16. **The correct answer is (A).** The paragraph presents the problems of fire in fire-resistant buildings. It suggests that the contents of the buildings may burn even though the structural materials themselves do not, and the ensuing fire may even cause the collapse of the buildings. The paragraph does not compare the problem of fire in fire-resistant buildings with that of fire in ordinary buildings.

17. **The correct answer is (C).** The search for truth has speeded the progress of civilization. Choice B is incorrect in its statement that "civilization did not begin until. . . ." Civilization moved ahead slowly even before restrictions on learning were removed.

18. **The correct answer is (B).** VIGILANT means *alert* or *watchful*. A worker must remain vigilant to avoid accidents on the job.

19. **The correct answer is (D).** INCIDENTAL means *happening in connection with something else* or *casual*. Having the windshield washed is incidental to filling the gas tank and checking the oil.

20. **The correct answer is (A).** CONCILIATORY means *tending to reconcile* or *to make peace*. The apology was offered as a conciliatory gesture.

21. **The correct answer is (C).** An ALTERCATION is a *quarrel* or a *controversy*. The two drivers had an angry altercation as to who was at fault in the accident.

22. **The correct answer is (A).** IRRESOLUTE means *indecisive* or *wavering*. The couple was irresolute as to the choice of next summer's vacation.

23. **The correct answer is (C).** STILLNESS and SOUND are opposites, as are DARKNESS and SUNLIGHT.

24. **The correct answer is (D).** That which is ACCIDENTAL happens by CHANCE as that which is DESIGNED happens by INTENTION.

25. **The correct answer is (C).** A MUFFLER reduces SOUND as PRACTICE reduces ERRORs.

26. **The correct answer is (A).** The desired result of TRAINING is the development of SKILL as the desired result of RESEARCH is scientific FINDINGS.

27. **The correct answer is (D).** Choices A and C are incorrect in use of the subject form "I" instead of the object of the preposition "me." Choice B incorrectly uses the reflexive "myself." Only I can address a letter to myself.

28. **The correct answer is (C).** All the other choices are quite obviously incorrect.

29. **The correct answer is (D).** The correct spelling is: miniature.

30. **The correct answer is (A).** The correct spelling is: extemporaneous.

31. **The correct answer is (B).** The correct spelling is: problematical.

32. **The correct answer is (A).** The correct spelling of first choice is: descendant. An alternative spelling which is also correct is descendent. A correct spelling is offered among the choices, so choice (A) is the correct answer.

33. **The correct answer is (B).** In a word, we are preserving our natural resources through recycling.

34. **The correct answer is (D).** If you omit all unnecessary words, you use only the words essential to the meaning.

35. **The correct answer is (D).** To COUNTERACT is to *act directly against* or to *neutralize*. My father's vote for the Republican candidate always counteracts my mother's vote for the Democrat.

36. **The correct answer is (B).** DEFERRED means *postponed* or *delayed*. Because I had no money in the bank, I deferred paying my taxes until the due date.

37. **The correct answer is (C).** FEASIBLE means *possible* or *practicable*. It is not feasible for the 92-year-old woman to travel abroad.

38. **The correct answer is (A).** To ENCOUNTER is to *come upon* or to *meet*. If you encounter my brother at the ball game, please give my regards.

39. **The correct answer is (C).** INNATE means *existing naturally* or *native*. Some people argue that the maternal instinct is learned rather than innate.

40. **The correct answer is (B).** The DISCIPLE learns from a MASTER as a STUDENT learns from a TEACHER.

41. **The correct answer is (C).** In this analogy of place, an EXPERIMENT occurs in a LABORATORY as a LECTURE occurs in an AUDITORIUM.

42. **The correct answer is (B).** FUEL powers the ENGINE as FOOD powers the BODY

43. **The correct answer is (C).** RECREATION occurs in the THEATER as EDUCATION occurs in a SCHOOL.

44. **The correct answer is (D).** Choice A might state either "most" or "all" but not both; choice B should read "persons who"; choice C should read "with regard to. . . ."

45. **The correct answer is (D).** Choice (A) is incorrect because *both* can refer to only two, but the publisher and authors implies at least three; choice B requires the plural verb "were"; choice C requires the correlative construction "neither . . . nor."

46. **The correct answer is (C).** The correct spelling is: extricate.

47. **The correct answer is (B).** The correct spelling is: hereditary.

48. **The correct answer is (C).** The correct spelling is: auspicious.

49. **The correct answer is (B).** The correct spelling is: sequence.

50. **The correct answer is (A).** If instruction in safety rules will help to prevent accidents, some accidents must occur because of ignorance.

51. **The correct answer is (D).** The language that has some representative in English speech has had some of its words absorbed into English.

52. **The correct answer is (A).** To ACQUIESCE is to *give in* or to *assent*. I reluctantly will acquiesce to your request to stay out late with your friends.

53. **The correct answer is (C).** UNANIMITY is *complete agreement* or *harmony*. The plan had such widespread acceptance that the vote resulted in unanimity.

54. **The correct answer is (A).** A PRECEDENT is *an example that sets a standard*. After one employee was permitted to wear jeans in the office, a precedent had been set and soon others also dressed casually.

55. **The correct answer is (D).** VERSATILE means *adaptable* or *many-sided*. This versatile vacuum cleaner can be used indoors or out under both dry and wet conditions.

56. **The correct answer is (B).** AUTHENTIC means *genuine* or *reliable*. The painting attributed to Rembrandt was guaranteed to be authentic.

57. **The correct answer is (A).** The information and substance of a NOVEL is FICTION while the information and substance of BIOGRAPHY is FACT.

58. **The correct answer is (B).** FILM is the medium through which the action of a MOTION PICTURE is projected onto a screen; CARBON PAPER is the medium through which a COPY of words or drawings is transmitted from one piece of paper to another.

59. **The correct answer is (C).** CARELESSNESS earns a REPRIMAND as EFFICIENCY merits a REWARD.

60. **The correct answer is (B).** This analogy refers to the marketplace and the law of supply and demand. That which is SCARCE is likely to be COSTLY while that which is ABUNDANT will be CHEAP.

61. **The correct answer is (B).** In choice A the placement of the apostrophe is inappropriate; choices C and D use the plural, but there is only one company.

62. **The correct answer is (A).** Choices C and D are glaringly poor. Choice B is not incorrect, but choice A is far better.

63. **The correct answer is (D).** The correct spelling is: obliterate.

64. **The correct answer is (C).** The correct spelling is: diagnosis.

65. **The correct answer is (B).** The correct spelling is: countenance.

66. **The correct answer is (A).** The correct spelling is: conceivably.

67. **The correct answer is (C).** Since manufacturers are assuming risks in attempting to predict what consumers will want, their success depends on the ultimate purchases made by the consumers.

68. **The correct answer is (B).** Humans migrate to various climates and make adjustments to the food supply in each climate; obviously the means by which they supply their needs are varied.

69. **The correct answer is (D).** STRIDENT means *grating* or *harsh-sounding*. The sergeant barked out the orders in strident tones.

70. **The correct answer is (B).** To CONFINE is to *limit* or to *restrict*. If the child's illness is contagious, we must confine him to his home.

71. **The correct answer is (D).** To ACCENTUATE is to *stress, emphasize,* or *intensify*. Life is more pleasant when those we deal with accentuate the positive.

72. **The correct answer is (A).** BANAL means *insipid* or *commonplace*. His commentary was so banal that I had to stifle many yawns.

73. **The correct answer is (C).** One who is INCORRIGIBLE *cannot be changed or corrected;* the person is *irreformable.* Incorrigible offenders should be sentenced to prison for life.

74. **The correct answer is (D).** A DOCTOR promotes HEALTH as a POLICEMAN promotes ORDER.

75. **The correct answer is (A).** A WEAVER creates on a LOOM as an ARTIST creates on an EASEL.

76. **The correct answer is (D).** Many SHIPS make up the FLEET as many PERSONS make up a CROWD.

77. **The correct answer is (C).** MILEAGE is read from a MAP as the DATE is read from a CALENDAR.

78. **The correct answer is (A).** The other choices are quite clearly incorrect.

79. **The correct answer is (C).** Choices A and B use adverbs incorrectly; choice D is awkward and unidiomatic.

80. **The correct answer is (B).** The correct spelling is: competition.

81. **The correct answer is (B).** The correct spelling is: occasion.

82. **The correct answer is (C).** The correct spelling is: knowledge.

83. **The correct answer is (B).** The correct spelling is: deliberate.

84. **The correct answer is (A).** Time and effort cannot be equated. Efficiency must be measured in terms of results.

85. **The correct answer is (B).** The first sentence of the paragraph makes this statement.

COMPUTING YOUR SCORE

The total raw score on this test consists of the total number of questions that are answered correctly. There is no penalty for wrong answers or correction made for guessing. However, no credit is given for any question with more than one answer marked.

My raw score _____

Clerical Skills

1. B	25. C	49. B	73. B	97. C
2. E	26. D	50. C	74. C	98. E
3. D	27. D	51. B	75. A	99. B
4. A	28. C	52. C	76. D	100. B
5. E	29. C	53. D	77. D	101. D
6. E	30. D	54. D	78. A	102. B
7. A	31. E	55. E	79. E	103. C
8. D	32. A	56. E	80. C	104. A
9. B	33. A	57. B	81. D	105. E
10. E	34. C	58. E	82. C	106. D
11. D	35. C	59. D	83. A	107. B
12. B	36. E	60. C	84. D	108. A
13. B	37. A	61. C	85. B	109. C
14. B	38. C	62. B	86. A	110. D
15. B	39. C	63. E	87. E	111. A
16. A	40. D	64. E	88. C	112. C
17. D	41. A	65. C	89. C	113. C
18. E	42. A	66. A	90. B	114. B
19. B	43. B	67. D	91. E	115. D
20. A	44. E	68. C	92. E	116. A
21. A	45. A	69. D	93. C	117. B
22. E	46. C	70. E	94. C	118. B
23. E	47. A	71. A	95. A	119. A
24. D	48. D	72. C	96. D	120. E

1. **The correct answer is (B).** The last two digits of the third number are reversed.

2. **The correct answer is (E).** The middle digit of the second number is "6" while that of the first and third numbers is "5." The last two digits of the third number are reversed.

3. **The correct answer is (D).** The surname of the second and third names is "Johnson"; the surname of the first name is "Johnston."

4. **The correct answer is (A).** All three names are exactly alike.

5. **The correct answer is (E).** The middle initial of the third name differs from the other two. "Asheton" of the second name differs from "Atherton" of the other two.

6. **The correct answer is (E).** Hachettson; Hackett

7. **The correct answer is (A).** Margenroth; Margeroth

8. **The correct answer is (D).** Bobbitt, Olivia H.; Bobbitt, Olivier E.; Bobbitt, R. Olivia

9. **The correct answer is (B).** Mosely, Albert J.; Mosely, Werner; Mosley, Alvin

10. **The correct answer is (E).** Youmons; Youmuns

11. **The correct answer is (D).**

$$\begin{array}{r} 43 \\ + 32 \\ \hline 75 \end{array}$$

12. **The correct answer is (B).**

$$\begin{array}{r} 83 \\ - 4 \\ \hline 79 \end{array}$$

13. **The correct answer is (B).**

$$\begin{array}{r} 41 \\ \times 7 \\ \hline 287 \end{array}$$

14. **The correct answer is (B).**

$$\begin{array}{r} 51 \\ 6\overline{)306} \end{array}$$

15. **The correct answer is (B).**

$$\begin{array}{r} 37 \\ + 15 \\ \hline 52 \end{array}$$

16. **The correct answer is (A).** 6 2 5 K 4 P T G.

17. **The correct answer is (D).** L 4 7 2 T 6 V K. The answer cannot be choice (A) because question 17 contains no **5**; it cannot be choice (B) or choice (C) because question 17 contains no **G**.

18. **The correct answer is (E).** The answer cannot be choice (A) or choice (B) because question 18 contains no **K**; it cannot be choice (C) or choice (D) because question 18 contains no **2**.

19. **The correct answer is (B).** G 4 K 7 L 3 5 Z. The answer cannot be choice (A) because question 19 contains no **T**.

20. **The correct answer is (A).** 4 K 2 9 N 5 T G.

21. **The correct answer is (A).** All three numbers are exactly alike.

22. **The correct answer is (E).** The last two digits are, respectively, "41," "47," and "14."

23. **The correct answer is (E).** In the first name, the given name is "Owens" while in the other two it is "Owen." The surname of the second name is "McVey" while in the third name it is "McVay."

24. **The correct answer is (D).** In the second and third names, the surname is "Rowse"; in the first name it is "Rouse."

25. **The correct answer is (C).** In the second name the given name is "Merriott"; in the first and third it is "Merritt."

26. **The correct answer is (D).** Watson; Watters; Wattwood

27. **The correct answer is (D).** Johnston, Edmund; Johnston, Edward; Johnstone, Edmund A.

28. **The correct answer is (C).** Remschel; Rensch; Renshaw

29. **The correct answer is (C).** Schneider, Mertens; Schnyder, Maurice; Schnyder, Newman

30. **The correct answer is (D).** Freedenberg; Freedenburg; Freedinberg

31. **The correct answer is (E).**

$$
\begin{array}{r}
68 \\
-47 \\
\hline
21
\end{array}
$$

32. **The correct answer is (A).**

$$
\begin{array}{r}
50 \\
\times\ 8 \\
\hline
400
\end{array}
$$

33. **The correct answer is (A).**

$$
9\overline{)180}
$$
quotient 9

34. **The correct answer is (C).**

$$
\begin{array}{r}
78 \\
+\ 63 \\
\hline
141
\end{array}
$$

35. **The correct answer is (C).**

$$
\begin{array}{r}
89 \\
-70 \\
\hline
19
\end{array}
$$

36. **The correct answer is (E).** The answer cannot be choice (A) because question 36 contains no **V**; it cannot be choice (B) or choice (C) because question 36 contains no **5**; it cannot be choice (D) because question 36 contains no **8** or **V**.

37. **The correct answer is (A).** L 5 N K 4 3 9 V.

38. **The correct answer is (C).** 8 2 V P 9 L Z 5. The answer cannot be choice (A) or choice (B) because question 38 contains no **4**.

39. **The correct answer is (C).** V P 9 Z 5 L 8 7. The answer cannot be choice (A) or choice (B) because question 39 contains no **4**.

40. **The correct answer is (D).** 5 T 8 N 2 9 V L. The answer cannot be choice (A) or choice (B) because question 40 contains no **4**; it cannot be choice (C) because question 40 contains no **Z**.

41. **The correct answer is (A).** All three numbers are exactly alike.

42. **The correct answer is (A).** All three numbers are exactly alike.

43. **The correct answer is (B).** In the third number, the digits "40" are reversed to read "04."

44. **The correct answer is (E).** The first and third names have the same given name but different surnames. The second name has the same surname as the third, but the given name is different.

45. **The correct answer is (A).** All three names are exactly alike.

46. **The correct answer is (C).** DeMatteo; DeMattia; Derby

47. **The correct answer is (A).** Theriault; Therien

48. **The correct answer is (D).** Gaston, Isabel; Gaston, M. Hubert; Gaston, M. Melvin

49. **The correct answer is (B).** SanLuis; SanMiguel; Santilli

50. **The correct answer is (C).** DeLathouder; DeLaTour; Lathrop

51. **The correct answer is (B).**

$$\begin{array}{r} 62 \\ \times\ 5 \\ \hline 310 \end{array}$$

52. **The correct answer is (C).**

$$\begin{array}{r} 51 \\ 3\overline{)153} \end{array}$$

53. **The correct answer is (D).**

$$\begin{array}{r} 47 \\ +\ 21 \\ \hline 68 \end{array}$$

54. **The correct answer is (D).**

$$\begin{array}{r} 87 \\ -\ 42 \\ \hline 45 \end{array}$$

55. **The correct answer is (E).**

$$\begin{array}{r} 37 \\ \times\ 3 \\ \hline 111 \end{array}$$

56. **The correct answer is (E).** The answer cannot be choice (A) or choice (B) because question 56 contains no **8**; it cannot be choice (C) or choice (D) because question 56 contains no **9**.

57. **The correct answer is (B).** 8 5 3 V L 2 Z N. The answer cannot be choice (A) because question 57 contains no **K**.

58. **The correct answer is (E).** The answer cannot be choice (A) or choice (B) because question 58 contains no **8**; it cannot be choice (C) or choice (D) because question 58 contains no **Z**.

59. **The correct answer is (D).** 9 8 L 2 5 Z K V. The answer cannot be choice (A) or choice (C) because question 59 contains no **3**; it cannot be choice (B) because question 59 contains no **N**.

60. **The correct answer is (C).** Z 6 5 **V 9 3** P N. The answer cannot be choice (A) or choice (B) because question 60 contains no **8**.

61. **The correct answer is (C).** In the second number, the fifth digit differs from that in the other numbers.

62. **The correct answer is (B).** In the third number, the last two digits are reversed.

63. **The correct answer is (E).** The given name of the third name differs from that of the first two names; the surname of the first name is different from that of the second and third names.

64. **The correct answer is (E).** The middle initial of the first name differs from the middle initials of the other two; the surname of the third name differs from that of the first and second names.

65. **The correct answer is (C).** The surname of the second name is different from the surname of the first and third.

66. **The correct answer is (A).** O'Bannon; O'Beirne

67. **The correct answer is (D).** Entsminger, Jack; Entsminger, Jacob; Entsminger, James

68. **The correct answer is (C).** Iacone, Pedro M.; Iacone, Pete R.; Iacone, Peter F

69. **The correct answer is (D).** Shephard; Sheppard; Shepperd

70. **The correct answer is (E).** Thackston; Mackton

71. **The correct answer is (A).**

$$7)\overline{357} = 51$$

72. **The correct answer is (C).**

$$58 + 27 = 85$$

73. **The correct answer is (B).**

$$86 - 57 = 29$$

74. **The correct answer is (C).**

$$68 \times 4 = 272$$

75. **The correct answer is (A).**

$$9)\overline{639} = 71$$

76. **The correct answer is (D).** 6 Z T N 8 7 4 **V**. The answer cannot be choice (A) or choice (B) because question 76 contains no **2**; it cannot be choice (C) because question 76 contains no **L**.

77. **The correct answer is (D).** V 7 8 6 N 5 P L. The answer cannot be choice (A) or choice (B) because question 77 contains no **2**; it cannot be choice (C) because question 77 contains no **T**.

78. **The correct answer is (A).** N 7 P V 8 4 2 L.

79. **The correct answer is (E).** The answer cannot be choice (A) or choice (B) because question 79 contains no **2**; it cannot be choice (C) or choice (D) because question 79 contains no **6**.

80. **The correct answer is (C).** 4 8 G 2 T N 6 L. The answer cannot be choice (A) because question 80 contains no **7**; it cannot be choice (B) because question 80 contains no **V**.

81. **The correct answer is (D).** The last digit of the first number differs from the last digit of the second and third numbers.

82. **The correct answer is (C).** The fifth and sixth digits of the middle number are the reverse of the fifth and sixth digits of the first and third numbers.

83. **The correct answer is (A).** All three names are exactly alike.

84. **The correct answer is (D).** In the second and third names, the middle name is "Harloe"; in the first name, it is "Harlor."

85. **The correct answer is (B).** The central initial in the third name differs from the central initial in the first and second names.

86. **The correct answer is (A).** Dunlavey; Dunleavy

87. **The correct answer is (E).** Yarborough; Yarbrough

88. **The correct answer is (C).** Proutey, Maude; Prouty, Martha; Prouty, Myra

89. **The correct answer is (C).** Pawalek; Pawlowicz; Pawlowski

90. **The correct answer is (B).** Vanover; Vanstory; VanSwinderen

91. **The correct answer is (E).**

$$\begin{array}{r} 28 \\ + 35 \\ \hline 63 \end{array}$$

92. **The correct answer is (E).**

$$\begin{array}{r} 76 \\ - 69 \\ \hline 9 \end{array}$$

93. **The correct answer is (C).**

$$\begin{array}{r} 86 \\ \times 6 \\ \hline 516 \end{array}$$

94. **The correct answer is (C).**

$$\begin{array}{r} 81 \\ 8\overline{)648} \end{array}$$

95. **The correct answer is (A).**

$$\begin{array}{r} 97 \\ +\ 34 \\ \hline 131 \end{array}$$

96. **The correct answer is (D).** V 5 7 Z N 9 4 T. The answer cannot be choice (A) or choice (C) because question 96 contains no **2**; it cannot be choice (B) because question 96 contains no **P**.

97. **The correct answer is (C).** 4 6 P T 2 N K 9. The answer cannot be choice (A) or choice (B) because question 97 contains no **5**.

98. **The correct answer is (E).** The answer cannot be choice (A) or choice (B) because question 98 contains no **5**; it cannot be choice (C) or choice (D) because question 98 contains no **9**.

99. **The correct answer is (B).** 7 P 5 2 4 N K T. The answer cannot be choice (A) because question 99 contains no **Z**.

100. **The correct answer is (B).** K T 8 5 4 N 2 P. The answer cannot be choice (A) because question 100 contains no Z.

101. **The correct answer is (D).** The next to the last digit of the first number differs from that of the other two numbers.

102. **The correct answer is (B).** The last two digits of the third number are reversed.

103. **The correct answer is (C).** The fifth and sixth digits of the second number are reversed.

104. **The correct answer is (A).** All three names are exactly alike.

105. **The correct answer is (E).** All three surnames are different.

106. **The correct answer is (D).** FitzGibbon; Fitzsimmons; FitzSimons

107. **The correct answer is (B).** Daly; D'Amato; D'Amboise

108. **The correct answer is (A).** Schaeffer; Schaffert

109. **The correct answer is (C).** White-Leigh; White-Lewis; Whitely

110. **The correct answer is (D).** VanDercook; VanDerHeggen; vanderLinden

111. **The correct answer is (A).**

$$\begin{array}{r} 75 \\ +\ 49 \\ \hline 124 \end{array}$$

112. **The correct answer is (C).**

$$\begin{array}{r} 69 \\ -\ 45 \\ \hline 24 \end{array}$$

113. **The correct answer is (C).**

$$\begin{array}{r} 36 \\ \times\ 8 \\ \hline 288 \end{array}$$

114. **The correct answer is (B).**

$$\begin{array}{r} 41 \\ 8\overline{)328} \end{array}$$

115. **The correct answer is (D).**

$$\begin{array}{r} 58 \\ \times9 \\ \hline 522 \end{array}$$

116. **The correct answer is (A).** Z 3 N P G 5 4 2.

117. **The correct answer is (B).** 6 N 2 8 G 4 P T. The answer cannot be choice (A) because question 117 contains no **3**.

118. **The correct answer is (B).** 6 N 4 T V G 8 2. The answer cannot be choice (A) because question 118 contains no **3**.

119. **The correct answer is (A).** T 3 P 4 N 8 G 2.

120. **The correct answer is (E).** The answer cannot be choice (A) or choice (C) because question 120 contains no **3**; it cannot be choice (B) or choice (D) because question 120 contains no **T**.

COMPUTING YOUR SCORE

On this test there is a penalty for wrong answers. The total raw score on the test is the number of right answers minus one-fourth of the number of wrong answers. (Fractions of one-half or less are dropped.) First count the number of correct answers you have made. Do not count as correct any questions with more than one answer marked. Then count the number of incorrect answers. Omissions are not counted as wrong answers, but double responses do count as wrong. Multiply the total number of incorrect answers by one-fourth. Subtract this number from the total number correct to get the test total score. For example, if you were to answer 89 questions correctly and 10 questions incorrectly, and you omitted 21 questions, your total score would be 87 (89 minus one-fourth of 10 equals 87).

89 questions correct, 10 questions incorrect

$$\begin{array}{r} 89 \\ -3 \quad (10 \div 4 = 2.5 = 3) \\ \hline 87 \ \text{Raw Score} \end{array}$$

Number Right	minus	Number Wrong	equals	Raw Score
_____	–	(___ ÷ 4)	=	_____

ANSWER SHEET PRACTICE TEST 5: U.S. POSTAL SERVICE CLERK, DISTRIBUTION CLERK, AND MARK-UP CLERK EXAM

ADDRESS CHECKING

1. Ⓐ Ⓓ	33. Ⓐ Ⓓ	65. Ⓐ Ⓓ
2. Ⓐ Ⓓ	34. Ⓐ Ⓓ	66. Ⓐ Ⓓ
3. Ⓐ Ⓓ	35. Ⓐ Ⓓ	67. Ⓐ Ⓓ
4. Ⓐ Ⓓ	36. Ⓐ Ⓓ	68. Ⓐ Ⓓ
5. Ⓐ Ⓓ	37. Ⓐ Ⓓ	69. Ⓐ Ⓓ
6. Ⓐ Ⓓ	38. Ⓐ Ⓓ	70. Ⓐ Ⓓ
7. Ⓐ Ⓓ	39. Ⓐ Ⓓ	71. Ⓐ Ⓓ
8. Ⓐ Ⓓ	40. Ⓐ Ⓓ	72. Ⓐ Ⓓ
9. Ⓐ Ⓓ	41. Ⓐ Ⓓ	73. Ⓐ Ⓓ
10. Ⓐ Ⓓ	42. Ⓐ Ⓓ	74. Ⓐ Ⓓ
11. Ⓐ Ⓓ	43. Ⓐ Ⓓ	75. Ⓐ Ⓓ
12. Ⓐ Ⓓ	44. Ⓐ Ⓓ	76. Ⓐ Ⓓ
13. Ⓐ Ⓓ	45. Ⓐ Ⓓ	77. Ⓐ Ⓓ
14. Ⓐ Ⓓ	46. Ⓐ Ⓓ	78. Ⓐ Ⓓ
15. Ⓐ Ⓓ	47. Ⓐ Ⓓ	79. Ⓐ Ⓓ
16. Ⓐ Ⓓ	48. Ⓐ Ⓓ	80. Ⓐ Ⓓ
17. Ⓐ Ⓓ	49. Ⓐ Ⓓ	81. Ⓐ Ⓓ
18. Ⓐ Ⓓ	50. Ⓐ Ⓓ	82. Ⓐ Ⓓ
19. Ⓐ Ⓓ	51. Ⓐ Ⓓ	83. Ⓐ Ⓓ
20. Ⓐ Ⓓ	52. Ⓐ Ⓓ	84. Ⓐ Ⓓ
21. Ⓐ Ⓓ	53. Ⓐ Ⓓ	85. Ⓐ Ⓓ
22. Ⓐ Ⓓ	54. Ⓐ Ⓓ	86. Ⓐ Ⓓ
23. Ⓐ Ⓓ	55. Ⓐ Ⓓ	87. Ⓐ Ⓓ
24. Ⓐ Ⓓ	56. Ⓐ Ⓓ	88. Ⓐ Ⓓ
25. Ⓐ Ⓓ	57. Ⓐ Ⓓ	89. Ⓐ Ⓓ
26. Ⓐ Ⓓ	58. Ⓐ Ⓓ	90. Ⓐ Ⓓ
27. Ⓐ Ⓓ	59. Ⓐ Ⓓ	91. Ⓐ Ⓓ
28. Ⓐ Ⓓ	60. Ⓐ Ⓓ	92. Ⓐ Ⓓ
29. Ⓐ Ⓓ	61. Ⓐ Ⓓ	93. Ⓐ Ⓓ
30. Ⓐ Ⓓ	62. Ⓐ Ⓓ	94. Ⓐ Ⓓ
31. Ⓐ Ⓓ	63. Ⓐ Ⓓ	95. Ⓐ Ⓓ
32. Ⓐ Ⓓ	64. Ⓐ Ⓓ	

answer sheet

MEMORY FOR ADDRESSES

Practice I

1. Ⓐ Ⓑ Ⓒ Ⓓ Ⓔ	31. Ⓐ Ⓑ Ⓒ Ⓓ Ⓔ	60. Ⓐ Ⓑ Ⓒ Ⓓ Ⓔ
2. Ⓐ Ⓑ Ⓒ Ⓓ Ⓔ	32. Ⓐ Ⓑ Ⓒ Ⓓ Ⓔ	61. Ⓐ Ⓑ Ⓒ Ⓓ Ⓔ
3. Ⓐ Ⓑ Ⓒ Ⓓ Ⓔ	33. Ⓐ Ⓑ Ⓒ Ⓓ Ⓔ	62. Ⓐ Ⓑ Ⓒ Ⓓ Ⓔ
4. Ⓐ Ⓑ Ⓒ Ⓓ Ⓔ	34. Ⓐ Ⓑ Ⓒ Ⓓ Ⓔ	63. Ⓐ Ⓑ Ⓒ Ⓓ Ⓔ
5. Ⓐ Ⓑ Ⓒ Ⓓ Ⓔ	35. Ⓐ Ⓑ Ⓒ Ⓓ Ⓔ	64. Ⓐ Ⓑ Ⓒ Ⓓ Ⓔ
6. Ⓐ Ⓑ Ⓒ Ⓓ Ⓔ	36. Ⓐ Ⓑ Ⓒ Ⓓ Ⓔ	65. Ⓐ Ⓑ Ⓒ Ⓓ Ⓔ
7. Ⓐ Ⓑ Ⓒ Ⓓ Ⓔ	37. Ⓐ Ⓑ Ⓒ Ⓓ Ⓔ	66. Ⓐ Ⓑ Ⓒ Ⓓ Ⓔ
8. Ⓐ Ⓑ Ⓒ Ⓓ Ⓔ	38. Ⓐ Ⓑ Ⓒ Ⓓ Ⓔ	67. Ⓐ Ⓑ Ⓒ Ⓓ Ⓔ
9. Ⓐ Ⓑ Ⓒ Ⓓ Ⓔ	39. Ⓐ Ⓑ Ⓒ Ⓓ Ⓔ	68. Ⓐ Ⓑ Ⓒ Ⓓ Ⓔ
10. Ⓐ Ⓑ Ⓒ Ⓓ Ⓔ	40. Ⓐ Ⓑ Ⓒ Ⓓ Ⓔ	69. Ⓐ Ⓑ Ⓒ Ⓓ Ⓔ
11. Ⓐ Ⓑ Ⓒ Ⓓ Ⓔ	41. Ⓐ Ⓑ Ⓒ Ⓓ Ⓔ	70. Ⓐ Ⓑ Ⓒ Ⓓ Ⓔ
12. Ⓐ Ⓑ Ⓒ Ⓓ Ⓔ	42. Ⓐ Ⓑ Ⓒ Ⓓ Ⓔ	71. Ⓐ Ⓑ Ⓒ Ⓓ Ⓔ
13. Ⓐ Ⓑ Ⓒ Ⓓ Ⓔ	43. Ⓐ Ⓑ Ⓒ Ⓓ Ⓔ	72. Ⓐ Ⓑ Ⓒ Ⓓ Ⓔ
14. Ⓐ Ⓑ Ⓒ Ⓓ Ⓔ	44. Ⓐ Ⓑ Ⓒ Ⓓ Ⓔ	73. Ⓐ Ⓑ Ⓒ Ⓓ Ⓔ
15. Ⓐ Ⓑ Ⓒ Ⓓ Ⓔ	45. Ⓐ Ⓑ Ⓒ Ⓓ Ⓔ	74. Ⓐ Ⓑ Ⓒ Ⓓ Ⓔ
16. Ⓐ Ⓑ Ⓒ Ⓓ Ⓔ	46. Ⓐ Ⓑ Ⓒ Ⓓ Ⓔ	75. Ⓐ Ⓑ Ⓒ Ⓓ Ⓔ
17. Ⓐ Ⓑ Ⓒ Ⓓ Ⓔ	47. Ⓐ Ⓑ Ⓒ Ⓓ Ⓔ	76. Ⓐ Ⓑ Ⓒ Ⓓ Ⓔ
18. Ⓐ Ⓑ Ⓒ Ⓓ Ⓔ	48. Ⓐ Ⓑ Ⓒ Ⓓ Ⓔ	77. Ⓐ Ⓑ Ⓒ Ⓓ Ⓔ
19. Ⓐ Ⓑ Ⓒ Ⓓ Ⓔ	49. Ⓐ Ⓑ Ⓒ Ⓓ Ⓔ	78. Ⓐ Ⓑ Ⓒ Ⓓ Ⓔ
20. Ⓐ Ⓑ Ⓒ Ⓓ Ⓔ	50. Ⓐ Ⓑ Ⓒ Ⓓ Ⓔ	79. Ⓐ Ⓑ Ⓒ Ⓓ Ⓔ
21. Ⓐ Ⓑ Ⓒ Ⓓ Ⓔ	51. Ⓐ Ⓑ Ⓒ Ⓓ Ⓔ	80. Ⓐ Ⓑ Ⓒ Ⓓ Ⓔ
22. Ⓐ Ⓑ Ⓒ Ⓓ Ⓔ	52. Ⓐ Ⓑ Ⓒ Ⓓ Ⓔ	81. Ⓐ Ⓑ Ⓒ Ⓓ Ⓔ
23. Ⓐ Ⓑ Ⓒ Ⓓ Ⓔ	53. Ⓐ Ⓑ Ⓒ Ⓓ Ⓔ	82. Ⓐ Ⓑ Ⓒ Ⓓ Ⓔ
24. Ⓐ Ⓑ Ⓒ Ⓓ Ⓔ	54. Ⓐ Ⓑ Ⓒ Ⓓ Ⓔ	83. Ⓐ Ⓑ Ⓒ Ⓓ Ⓔ
25. Ⓐ Ⓑ Ⓒ Ⓓ Ⓔ	55. Ⓐ Ⓑ Ⓒ Ⓓ Ⓔ	84. Ⓐ Ⓑ Ⓒ Ⓓ Ⓔ
26. Ⓐ Ⓑ Ⓒ Ⓓ Ⓔ	56. Ⓐ Ⓑ Ⓒ Ⓓ Ⓔ	85. Ⓐ Ⓑ Ⓒ Ⓓ Ⓔ
27. Ⓐ Ⓑ Ⓒ Ⓓ Ⓔ	57. Ⓐ Ⓑ Ⓒ Ⓓ Ⓔ	86. Ⓐ Ⓑ Ⓒ Ⓓ Ⓔ
28. Ⓐ Ⓑ Ⓒ Ⓓ Ⓔ	58. Ⓐ Ⓑ Ⓒ Ⓓ Ⓔ	87. Ⓐ Ⓑ Ⓒ Ⓓ Ⓔ
29. Ⓐ Ⓑ Ⓒ Ⓓ Ⓔ	59. Ⓐ Ⓑ Ⓒ Ⓓ Ⓔ	88. Ⓐ Ⓑ Ⓒ Ⓓ Ⓔ
30. Ⓐ Ⓑ Ⓒ Ⓓ Ⓔ		

Practice II

1. Ⓐ Ⓑ Ⓒ Ⓓ Ⓔ	31. Ⓐ Ⓑ Ⓒ Ⓓ Ⓔ	60. Ⓐ Ⓑ Ⓒ Ⓓ Ⓔ
2. Ⓐ Ⓑ Ⓒ Ⓓ Ⓔ	32. Ⓐ Ⓑ Ⓒ Ⓓ Ⓔ	61. Ⓐ Ⓑ Ⓒ Ⓓ Ⓔ
3. Ⓐ Ⓑ Ⓒ Ⓓ Ⓔ	33. Ⓐ Ⓑ Ⓒ Ⓓ Ⓔ	62. Ⓐ Ⓑ Ⓒ Ⓓ Ⓔ
4. Ⓐ Ⓑ Ⓒ Ⓓ Ⓔ	34. Ⓐ Ⓑ Ⓒ Ⓓ Ⓔ	63. Ⓐ Ⓑ Ⓒ Ⓓ Ⓔ
5. Ⓐ Ⓑ Ⓒ Ⓓ Ⓔ	35. Ⓐ Ⓑ Ⓒ Ⓓ Ⓔ	64. Ⓐ Ⓑ Ⓒ Ⓓ Ⓔ
6. Ⓐ Ⓑ Ⓒ Ⓓ Ⓔ	36. Ⓐ Ⓑ Ⓒ Ⓓ Ⓔ	65. Ⓐ Ⓑ Ⓒ Ⓓ Ⓔ
7. Ⓐ Ⓑ Ⓒ Ⓓ Ⓔ	37. Ⓐ Ⓑ Ⓒ Ⓓ Ⓔ	66. Ⓐ Ⓑ Ⓒ Ⓓ Ⓔ
8. Ⓐ Ⓑ Ⓒ Ⓓ Ⓔ	38. Ⓐ Ⓑ Ⓒ Ⓓ Ⓔ	67. Ⓐ Ⓑ Ⓒ Ⓓ Ⓔ
9. Ⓐ Ⓑ Ⓒ Ⓓ Ⓔ	39. Ⓐ Ⓑ Ⓒ Ⓓ Ⓔ	68. Ⓐ Ⓑ Ⓒ Ⓓ Ⓔ
10. Ⓐ Ⓑ Ⓒ Ⓓ Ⓔ	40. Ⓐ Ⓑ Ⓒ Ⓓ Ⓔ	69. Ⓐ Ⓑ Ⓒ Ⓓ Ⓔ
11. Ⓐ Ⓑ Ⓒ Ⓓ Ⓔ	41. Ⓐ Ⓑ Ⓒ Ⓓ Ⓔ	70. Ⓐ Ⓑ Ⓒ Ⓓ Ⓔ
12. Ⓐ Ⓑ Ⓒ Ⓓ Ⓔ	42. Ⓐ Ⓑ Ⓒ Ⓓ Ⓔ	71. Ⓐ Ⓑ Ⓒ Ⓓ Ⓔ
13. Ⓐ Ⓑ Ⓒ Ⓓ Ⓔ	43. Ⓐ Ⓑ Ⓒ Ⓓ Ⓔ	72. Ⓐ Ⓑ Ⓒ Ⓓ Ⓔ
14. Ⓐ Ⓑ Ⓒ Ⓓ Ⓔ	44. Ⓐ Ⓑ Ⓒ Ⓓ Ⓔ	73. Ⓐ Ⓑ Ⓒ Ⓓ Ⓔ
15. Ⓐ Ⓑ Ⓒ Ⓓ Ⓔ	45. Ⓐ Ⓑ Ⓒ Ⓓ Ⓔ	74. Ⓐ Ⓑ Ⓒ Ⓓ Ⓔ
16. Ⓐ Ⓑ Ⓒ Ⓓ Ⓔ	46. Ⓐ Ⓑ Ⓒ Ⓓ Ⓔ	75. Ⓐ Ⓑ Ⓒ Ⓓ Ⓔ
17. Ⓐ Ⓑ Ⓒ Ⓓ Ⓔ	47. Ⓐ Ⓑ Ⓒ Ⓓ Ⓔ	76. Ⓐ Ⓑ Ⓒ Ⓓ Ⓔ
18. Ⓐ Ⓑ Ⓒ Ⓓ Ⓔ	48. Ⓐ Ⓑ Ⓒ Ⓓ Ⓔ	77. Ⓐ Ⓑ Ⓒ Ⓓ Ⓔ
19. Ⓐ Ⓑ Ⓒ Ⓓ Ⓔ	49. Ⓐ Ⓑ Ⓒ Ⓓ Ⓔ	78. Ⓐ Ⓑ Ⓒ Ⓓ Ⓔ
20. Ⓐ Ⓑ Ⓒ Ⓓ Ⓔ	50. Ⓐ Ⓑ Ⓒ Ⓓ Ⓔ	79. Ⓐ Ⓑ Ⓒ Ⓓ Ⓔ
21. Ⓐ Ⓑ Ⓒ Ⓓ Ⓔ	51. Ⓐ Ⓑ Ⓒ Ⓓ Ⓔ	80. Ⓐ Ⓑ Ⓒ Ⓓ Ⓔ
22. Ⓐ Ⓑ Ⓒ Ⓓ Ⓔ	52. Ⓐ Ⓑ Ⓒ Ⓓ Ⓔ	81. Ⓐ Ⓑ Ⓒ Ⓓ Ⓔ
23. Ⓐ Ⓑ Ⓒ Ⓓ Ⓔ	53. Ⓐ Ⓑ Ⓒ Ⓓ Ⓔ	82. Ⓐ Ⓑ Ⓒ Ⓓ Ⓔ
24. Ⓐ Ⓑ Ⓒ Ⓓ Ⓔ	54. Ⓐ Ⓑ Ⓒ Ⓓ Ⓔ	83. Ⓐ Ⓑ Ⓒ Ⓓ Ⓔ
25. Ⓐ Ⓑ Ⓒ Ⓓ Ⓔ	55. Ⓐ Ⓑ Ⓒ Ⓓ Ⓔ	84. Ⓐ Ⓑ Ⓒ Ⓓ Ⓔ
26. Ⓐ Ⓑ Ⓒ Ⓓ Ⓔ	56. Ⓐ Ⓑ Ⓒ Ⓓ Ⓔ	85. Ⓐ Ⓑ Ⓒ Ⓓ Ⓔ
27. Ⓐ Ⓑ Ⓒ Ⓓ Ⓔ	57. Ⓐ Ⓑ Ⓒ Ⓓ Ⓔ	86. Ⓐ Ⓑ Ⓒ Ⓓ Ⓔ
28. Ⓐ Ⓑ Ⓒ Ⓓ Ⓔ	58. Ⓐ Ⓑ Ⓒ Ⓓ Ⓔ	87. Ⓐ Ⓑ Ⓒ Ⓓ Ⓔ
29. Ⓐ Ⓑ Ⓒ Ⓓ Ⓔ	59. Ⓐ Ⓑ Ⓒ Ⓓ Ⓔ	88. Ⓐ Ⓑ Ⓒ Ⓓ Ⓔ
30. Ⓐ Ⓑ Ⓒ Ⓓ Ⓔ		

answer sheet

Practice III

1. Ⓐ Ⓑ Ⓒ Ⓓ Ⓔ
2. Ⓐ Ⓑ Ⓒ Ⓓ Ⓔ
3. Ⓐ Ⓑ Ⓒ Ⓓ Ⓔ
4. Ⓐ Ⓑ Ⓒ Ⓓ Ⓔ
5. Ⓐ Ⓑ Ⓒ Ⓓ Ⓔ
6. Ⓐ Ⓑ Ⓒ Ⓓ Ⓔ
7. Ⓐ Ⓑ Ⓒ Ⓓ Ⓔ
8. Ⓐ Ⓑ Ⓒ Ⓓ Ⓔ
9. Ⓐ Ⓑ Ⓒ Ⓓ Ⓔ
10. Ⓐ Ⓑ Ⓒ Ⓓ Ⓔ
11. Ⓐ Ⓑ Ⓒ Ⓓ Ⓔ
12. Ⓐ Ⓑ Ⓒ Ⓓ Ⓔ
13. Ⓐ Ⓑ Ⓒ Ⓓ Ⓔ
14. Ⓐ Ⓑ Ⓒ Ⓓ Ⓔ
15. Ⓐ Ⓑ Ⓒ Ⓓ Ⓔ
16. Ⓐ Ⓑ Ⓒ Ⓓ Ⓔ
17. Ⓐ Ⓑ Ⓒ Ⓓ Ⓔ
18. Ⓐ Ⓑ Ⓒ Ⓓ Ⓔ
19. Ⓐ Ⓑ Ⓒ Ⓓ Ⓔ
20. Ⓐ Ⓑ Ⓒ Ⓓ Ⓔ
21. Ⓐ Ⓑ Ⓒ Ⓓ Ⓔ
22. Ⓐ Ⓑ Ⓒ Ⓓ Ⓔ
23. Ⓐ Ⓑ Ⓒ Ⓓ Ⓔ
24. Ⓐ Ⓑ Ⓒ Ⓓ Ⓔ
25. Ⓐ Ⓑ Ⓒ Ⓓ Ⓔ
26. Ⓐ Ⓑ Ⓒ Ⓓ Ⓔ
27. Ⓐ Ⓑ Ⓒ Ⓓ Ⓔ
28. Ⓐ Ⓑ Ⓒ Ⓓ Ⓔ
29. Ⓐ Ⓑ Ⓒ Ⓓ Ⓔ
30. Ⓐ Ⓑ Ⓒ Ⓓ Ⓔ

31. Ⓐ Ⓑ Ⓒ Ⓓ Ⓔ
32. Ⓐ Ⓑ Ⓒ Ⓓ Ⓔ
33. Ⓐ Ⓑ Ⓒ Ⓓ Ⓔ
34. Ⓐ Ⓑ Ⓒ Ⓓ Ⓔ
35. Ⓐ Ⓑ Ⓒ Ⓓ Ⓔ
36. Ⓐ Ⓑ Ⓒ Ⓓ Ⓔ
37. Ⓐ Ⓑ Ⓒ Ⓓ Ⓔ
38. Ⓐ Ⓑ Ⓒ Ⓓ Ⓔ
39. Ⓐ Ⓑ Ⓒ Ⓓ Ⓔ
40. Ⓐ Ⓑ Ⓒ Ⓓ Ⓔ
41. Ⓐ Ⓑ Ⓒ Ⓓ Ⓔ
42. Ⓐ Ⓑ Ⓒ Ⓓ Ⓔ
43. Ⓐ Ⓑ Ⓒ Ⓓ Ⓔ
44. Ⓐ Ⓑ Ⓒ Ⓓ Ⓔ
45. Ⓐ Ⓑ Ⓒ Ⓓ Ⓔ
46. Ⓐ Ⓑ Ⓒ Ⓓ Ⓔ
47. Ⓐ Ⓑ Ⓒ Ⓓ Ⓔ
48. Ⓐ Ⓑ Ⓒ Ⓓ Ⓔ
49. Ⓐ Ⓑ Ⓒ Ⓓ Ⓔ
50. Ⓐ Ⓑ Ⓒ Ⓓ Ⓔ
51. Ⓐ Ⓑ Ⓒ Ⓓ Ⓔ
52. Ⓐ Ⓑ Ⓒ Ⓓ Ⓔ
53. Ⓐ Ⓑ Ⓒ Ⓓ Ⓔ
54. Ⓐ Ⓑ Ⓒ Ⓓ Ⓔ
55. Ⓐ Ⓑ Ⓒ Ⓓ Ⓔ
56. Ⓐ Ⓑ Ⓒ Ⓓ Ⓔ
57. Ⓐ Ⓑ Ⓒ Ⓓ Ⓔ
58. Ⓐ Ⓑ Ⓒ Ⓓ Ⓔ
59. Ⓐ Ⓑ Ⓒ Ⓓ Ⓔ

60. Ⓐ Ⓑ Ⓒ Ⓓ Ⓔ
61. Ⓐ Ⓑ Ⓒ Ⓓ Ⓔ
62. Ⓐ Ⓑ Ⓒ Ⓓ Ⓔ
63. Ⓐ Ⓑ Ⓒ Ⓓ Ⓔ
64. Ⓐ Ⓑ Ⓒ Ⓓ Ⓔ
65. Ⓐ Ⓑ Ⓒ Ⓓ Ⓔ
66. Ⓐ Ⓑ Ⓒ Ⓓ Ⓔ
67. Ⓐ Ⓑ Ⓒ Ⓓ Ⓔ
68. Ⓐ Ⓑ Ⓒ Ⓓ Ⓔ
69. Ⓐ Ⓑ Ⓒ Ⓓ Ⓔ
70. Ⓐ Ⓑ Ⓒ Ⓓ Ⓔ
71. Ⓐ Ⓑ Ⓒ Ⓓ Ⓔ
72. Ⓐ Ⓑ Ⓒ Ⓓ Ⓔ
73. Ⓐ Ⓑ Ⓒ Ⓓ Ⓔ
74. Ⓐ Ⓑ Ⓒ Ⓓ Ⓔ
75. Ⓐ Ⓑ Ⓒ Ⓓ Ⓔ
76. Ⓐ Ⓑ Ⓒ Ⓓ Ⓔ
77. Ⓐ Ⓑ Ⓒ Ⓓ Ⓔ
78. Ⓐ Ⓑ Ⓒ Ⓓ Ⓔ
79. Ⓐ Ⓑ Ⓒ Ⓓ Ⓔ
80. Ⓐ Ⓑ Ⓒ Ⓓ Ⓔ
81. Ⓐ Ⓑ Ⓒ Ⓓ Ⓔ
82. Ⓐ Ⓑ Ⓒ Ⓓ Ⓔ
83. Ⓐ Ⓑ Ⓒ Ⓓ Ⓔ
84. Ⓐ Ⓑ Ⓒ Ⓓ Ⓔ
85. Ⓐ Ⓑ Ⓒ Ⓓ Ⓔ
86. Ⓐ Ⓑ Ⓒ Ⓓ Ⓔ
87. Ⓐ Ⓑ Ⓒ Ⓓ Ⓔ
88. Ⓐ Ⓑ Ⓒ Ⓓ Ⓔ

Actual Test

1. Ⓐ Ⓑ Ⓒ Ⓓ Ⓔ
2. Ⓐ Ⓑ Ⓒ Ⓓ Ⓔ
3. Ⓐ Ⓑ Ⓒ Ⓓ Ⓔ
4. Ⓐ Ⓑ Ⓒ Ⓓ Ⓔ
5. Ⓐ Ⓑ Ⓒ Ⓓ Ⓔ
6. Ⓐ Ⓑ Ⓒ Ⓓ Ⓔ
7. Ⓐ Ⓑ Ⓒ Ⓓ Ⓔ
8. Ⓐ Ⓑ Ⓒ Ⓓ Ⓔ
9. Ⓐ Ⓑ Ⓒ Ⓓ Ⓔ
10. Ⓐ Ⓑ Ⓒ Ⓓ Ⓔ
11. Ⓐ Ⓑ Ⓒ Ⓓ Ⓔ
12. Ⓐ Ⓑ Ⓒ Ⓓ Ⓔ
13. Ⓐ Ⓑ Ⓒ Ⓓ Ⓔ
14. Ⓐ Ⓑ Ⓒ Ⓓ Ⓔ
15. Ⓐ Ⓑ Ⓒ Ⓓ Ⓔ
16. Ⓐ Ⓑ Ⓒ Ⓓ Ⓔ
17. Ⓐ Ⓑ Ⓒ Ⓓ Ⓔ
18. Ⓐ Ⓑ Ⓒ Ⓓ Ⓔ
19. Ⓐ Ⓑ Ⓒ Ⓓ Ⓔ
20. Ⓐ Ⓑ Ⓒ Ⓓ Ⓔ
21. Ⓐ Ⓑ Ⓒ Ⓓ Ⓔ
22. Ⓐ Ⓑ Ⓒ Ⓓ Ⓔ
23. Ⓐ Ⓑ Ⓒ Ⓓ Ⓔ
24. Ⓐ Ⓑ Ⓒ Ⓓ Ⓔ
25. Ⓐ Ⓑ Ⓒ Ⓓ Ⓔ
26. Ⓐ Ⓑ Ⓒ Ⓓ Ⓔ
27. Ⓐ Ⓑ Ⓒ Ⓓ Ⓔ
28. Ⓐ Ⓑ Ⓒ Ⓓ Ⓔ
29. Ⓐ Ⓑ Ⓒ Ⓓ Ⓔ
30. Ⓐ Ⓑ Ⓒ Ⓓ Ⓔ

31. Ⓐ Ⓑ Ⓒ Ⓓ Ⓔ
32. Ⓐ Ⓑ Ⓒ Ⓓ Ⓔ
33. Ⓐ Ⓑ Ⓒ Ⓓ Ⓔ
34. Ⓐ Ⓑ Ⓒ Ⓓ Ⓔ
35. Ⓐ Ⓑ Ⓒ Ⓓ Ⓔ
36. Ⓐ Ⓑ Ⓒ Ⓓ Ⓔ
37. Ⓐ Ⓑ Ⓒ Ⓓ Ⓔ
38. Ⓐ Ⓑ Ⓒ Ⓓ Ⓔ
39. Ⓐ Ⓑ Ⓒ Ⓓ Ⓔ
40. Ⓐ Ⓑ Ⓒ Ⓓ Ⓔ
41. Ⓐ Ⓑ Ⓒ Ⓓ Ⓔ
42. Ⓐ Ⓑ Ⓒ Ⓓ Ⓔ
43. Ⓐ Ⓑ Ⓒ Ⓓ Ⓔ
44. Ⓐ Ⓑ Ⓒ Ⓓ Ⓔ
45. Ⓐ Ⓑ Ⓒ Ⓓ Ⓔ
46. Ⓐ Ⓑ Ⓒ Ⓓ Ⓔ
47. Ⓐ Ⓑ Ⓒ Ⓓ Ⓔ
48. Ⓐ Ⓑ Ⓒ Ⓓ Ⓔ
49. Ⓐ Ⓑ Ⓒ Ⓓ Ⓔ
50. Ⓐ Ⓑ Ⓒ Ⓓ Ⓔ
51. Ⓐ Ⓑ Ⓒ Ⓓ Ⓔ
52. Ⓐ Ⓑ Ⓒ Ⓓ Ⓔ
53. Ⓐ Ⓑ Ⓒ Ⓓ Ⓔ
54. Ⓐ Ⓑ Ⓒ Ⓓ Ⓔ
55. Ⓐ Ⓑ Ⓒ Ⓓ Ⓔ
56. Ⓐ Ⓑ Ⓒ Ⓓ Ⓔ
57. Ⓐ Ⓑ Ⓒ Ⓓ Ⓔ
58. Ⓐ Ⓑ Ⓒ Ⓓ Ⓔ
59. Ⓐ Ⓑ Ⓒ Ⓓ Ⓔ

60. Ⓐ Ⓑ Ⓒ Ⓓ Ⓔ
61. Ⓐ Ⓑ Ⓒ Ⓓ Ⓔ
62. Ⓐ Ⓑ Ⓒ Ⓓ Ⓔ
63. Ⓐ Ⓑ Ⓒ Ⓓ Ⓔ
64. Ⓐ Ⓑ Ⓒ Ⓓ Ⓔ
65. Ⓐ Ⓑ Ⓒ Ⓓ Ⓔ
66. Ⓐ Ⓑ Ⓒ Ⓓ Ⓔ
67. Ⓐ Ⓑ Ⓒ Ⓓ Ⓔ
68. Ⓐ Ⓑ Ⓒ Ⓓ Ⓔ
69. Ⓐ Ⓑ Ⓒ Ⓓ Ⓔ
70. Ⓐ Ⓑ Ⓒ Ⓓ Ⓔ
71. Ⓐ Ⓑ Ⓒ Ⓓ Ⓔ
72. Ⓐ Ⓑ Ⓒ Ⓓ Ⓔ
73. Ⓐ Ⓑ Ⓒ Ⓓ Ⓔ
74. Ⓐ Ⓑ Ⓒ Ⓓ Ⓔ
75. Ⓐ Ⓑ Ⓒ Ⓓ Ⓔ
76. Ⓐ Ⓑ Ⓒ Ⓓ Ⓔ
77. Ⓐ Ⓑ Ⓒ Ⓓ Ⓔ
78. Ⓐ Ⓑ Ⓒ Ⓓ Ⓔ
79. Ⓐ Ⓑ Ⓒ Ⓓ Ⓔ
80. Ⓐ Ⓑ Ⓒ Ⓓ Ⓔ
81. Ⓐ Ⓑ Ⓒ Ⓓ Ⓔ
82. Ⓐ Ⓑ Ⓒ Ⓓ Ⓔ
83. Ⓐ Ⓑ Ⓒ Ⓓ Ⓔ
84. Ⓐ Ⓑ Ⓒ Ⓓ Ⓔ
85. Ⓐ Ⓑ Ⓒ Ⓓ Ⓔ
86. Ⓐ Ⓑ Ⓒ Ⓓ Ⓔ
87. Ⓐ Ⓑ Ⓒ Ⓓ Ⓔ
88. Ⓐ Ⓑ Ⓒ Ⓓ Ⓔ

answer sheet

NUMBER SERIES

1. Ⓐ Ⓑ Ⓒ Ⓓ Ⓔ   9. Ⓐ Ⓑ Ⓒ Ⓓ Ⓔ   17. Ⓐ Ⓑ Ⓒ Ⓓ Ⓔ
2. Ⓐ Ⓑ Ⓒ Ⓓ Ⓔ   10. Ⓐ Ⓑ Ⓒ Ⓓ Ⓔ   18. Ⓐ Ⓑ Ⓒ Ⓓ Ⓔ
3. Ⓐ Ⓑ Ⓒ Ⓓ Ⓔ   11. Ⓐ Ⓑ Ⓒ Ⓓ Ⓔ   19. Ⓐ Ⓑ Ⓒ Ⓓ Ⓔ
4. Ⓐ Ⓑ Ⓒ Ⓓ Ⓔ   12. Ⓐ Ⓑ Ⓒ Ⓓ Ⓔ   20. Ⓐ Ⓑ Ⓒ Ⓓ Ⓔ
5. Ⓐ Ⓑ Ⓒ Ⓓ Ⓔ   13. Ⓐ Ⓑ Ⓒ Ⓓ Ⓔ   21. Ⓐ Ⓑ Ⓒ Ⓓ Ⓔ
6. Ⓐ Ⓑ Ⓒ Ⓓ Ⓔ   14. Ⓐ Ⓑ Ⓒ Ⓓ Ⓔ   22. Ⓐ Ⓑ Ⓒ Ⓓ Ⓔ
7. Ⓐ Ⓑ Ⓒ Ⓓ Ⓔ   15. Ⓐ Ⓑ Ⓒ Ⓓ Ⓔ   23. Ⓐ Ⓑ Ⓒ Ⓓ Ⓔ
8. Ⓐ Ⓑ Ⓒ Ⓓ Ⓔ   16. Ⓐ Ⓑ Ⓒ Ⓓ Ⓔ   24. Ⓐ Ⓑ Ⓒ Ⓓ Ⓔ

FORMS COMPLETION

1. Ⓐ Ⓑ Ⓒ Ⓓ   11. Ⓐ Ⓑ Ⓒ Ⓓ   21. Ⓐ Ⓑ Ⓒ Ⓓ
2. Ⓐ Ⓑ Ⓒ Ⓓ   12. Ⓐ Ⓑ Ⓒ Ⓓ   22. Ⓐ Ⓑ Ⓒ Ⓓ
3. Ⓐ Ⓑ Ⓒ Ⓓ   13. Ⓐ Ⓑ Ⓒ Ⓓ   23. Ⓐ Ⓑ Ⓒ Ⓓ
4. Ⓐ Ⓑ Ⓒ Ⓓ   14. Ⓐ Ⓑ Ⓒ Ⓓ   24. Ⓐ Ⓑ Ⓒ Ⓓ
5. Ⓐ Ⓑ Ⓒ Ⓓ   15. Ⓐ Ⓑ Ⓒ Ⓓ   25. Ⓐ Ⓑ Ⓒ Ⓓ
6. Ⓐ Ⓑ Ⓒ Ⓓ   16. Ⓐ Ⓑ Ⓒ Ⓓ   26. Ⓐ Ⓑ Ⓒ Ⓓ
7. Ⓐ Ⓑ Ⓒ Ⓓ   17. Ⓐ Ⓑ Ⓒ Ⓓ   27. Ⓐ Ⓑ Ⓒ Ⓓ
8. Ⓐ Ⓑ Ⓒ Ⓓ   18. Ⓐ Ⓑ Ⓒ Ⓓ   28. Ⓐ Ⓑ Ⓒ Ⓓ
9. Ⓐ Ⓑ Ⓒ Ⓓ   19. Ⓐ Ⓑ Ⓒ Ⓓ   29. Ⓐ Ⓑ Ⓒ Ⓓ
10. Ⓐ Ⓑ Ⓒ Ⓓ   20. Ⓐ Ⓑ Ⓒ Ⓓ   30. Ⓐ Ⓑ Ⓒ Ⓓ

CODING

1. Ⓐ Ⓑ Ⓒ Ⓓ   13. Ⓐ Ⓑ Ⓒ Ⓓ   25. Ⓐ Ⓑ Ⓒ Ⓓ
2. Ⓐ Ⓑ Ⓒ Ⓓ   14. Ⓐ Ⓑ Ⓒ Ⓓ   26. Ⓐ Ⓑ Ⓒ Ⓓ
3. Ⓐ Ⓑ Ⓒ Ⓓ   15. Ⓐ Ⓑ Ⓒ Ⓓ   27. Ⓐ Ⓑ Ⓒ Ⓓ
4. Ⓐ Ⓑ Ⓒ Ⓓ   16. Ⓐ Ⓑ Ⓒ Ⓓ   28. Ⓐ Ⓑ Ⓒ Ⓓ
5. Ⓐ Ⓑ Ⓒ Ⓓ   17. Ⓐ Ⓑ Ⓒ Ⓓ   29. Ⓐ Ⓑ Ⓒ Ⓓ
6. Ⓐ Ⓑ Ⓒ Ⓓ   18. Ⓐ Ⓑ Ⓒ Ⓓ   30. Ⓐ Ⓑ Ⓒ Ⓓ
7. Ⓐ Ⓑ Ⓒ Ⓓ   19. Ⓐ Ⓑ Ⓒ Ⓓ   31. Ⓐ Ⓑ Ⓒ Ⓓ
8. Ⓐ Ⓑ Ⓒ Ⓓ   20. Ⓐ Ⓑ Ⓒ Ⓓ   32. Ⓐ Ⓑ Ⓒ Ⓓ
9. Ⓐ Ⓑ Ⓒ Ⓓ   21. Ⓐ Ⓑ Ⓒ Ⓓ   33. Ⓐ Ⓑ Ⓒ Ⓓ
10. Ⓐ Ⓑ Ⓒ Ⓓ   22. Ⓐ Ⓑ Ⓒ Ⓓ   34. Ⓐ Ⓑ Ⓒ Ⓓ
11. Ⓐ Ⓑ Ⓒ Ⓓ   23. Ⓐ Ⓑ Ⓒ Ⓓ   35. Ⓐ Ⓑ Ⓒ Ⓓ
12. Ⓐ Ⓑ Ⓒ Ⓓ   24. Ⓐ Ⓑ Ⓒ Ⓓ   36. Ⓐ Ⓑ Ⓒ Ⓓ

FOLLOWING ORAL INSTRUCTIONS

1. Ⓐ Ⓑ Ⓒ Ⓓ Ⓔ
2. Ⓐ Ⓑ Ⓒ Ⓓ Ⓔ
3. Ⓐ Ⓑ Ⓒ Ⓓ Ⓔ
4. Ⓐ Ⓑ Ⓒ Ⓓ Ⓔ
5. Ⓐ Ⓑ Ⓒ Ⓓ Ⓔ
6. Ⓐ Ⓑ Ⓒ Ⓓ Ⓔ
7. Ⓐ Ⓑ Ⓒ Ⓓ Ⓔ
8. Ⓐ Ⓑ Ⓒ Ⓓ Ⓔ
9. Ⓐ Ⓑ Ⓒ Ⓓ Ⓔ
10. Ⓐ Ⓑ Ⓒ Ⓓ Ⓔ
11. Ⓐ Ⓑ Ⓒ Ⓓ Ⓔ
12. Ⓐ Ⓑ Ⓒ Ⓓ Ⓔ
13. Ⓐ Ⓑ Ⓒ Ⓓ Ⓔ
14. Ⓐ Ⓑ Ⓒ Ⓓ Ⓔ
15. Ⓐ Ⓑ Ⓒ Ⓓ Ⓔ
16. Ⓐ Ⓑ Ⓒ Ⓓ Ⓔ
17. Ⓐ Ⓑ Ⓒ Ⓓ Ⓔ
18. Ⓐ Ⓑ Ⓒ Ⓓ Ⓔ
19. Ⓐ Ⓑ Ⓒ Ⓓ Ⓔ
20. Ⓐ Ⓑ Ⓒ Ⓓ Ⓔ
21. Ⓐ Ⓑ Ⓒ Ⓓ Ⓔ
22. Ⓐ Ⓑ Ⓒ Ⓓ Ⓔ
23. Ⓐ Ⓑ Ⓒ Ⓓ Ⓔ
24. Ⓐ Ⓑ Ⓒ Ⓓ Ⓔ
25. Ⓐ Ⓑ Ⓒ Ⓓ Ⓔ
26. Ⓐ Ⓑ Ⓒ Ⓓ Ⓔ
27. Ⓐ Ⓑ Ⓒ Ⓓ Ⓔ
28. Ⓐ Ⓑ Ⓒ Ⓓ Ⓔ
29. Ⓐ Ⓑ Ⓒ Ⓓ Ⓔ
30. Ⓐ Ⓑ Ⓒ Ⓓ Ⓔ

31. Ⓐ Ⓑ Ⓒ Ⓓ Ⓔ
32. Ⓐ Ⓑ Ⓒ Ⓓ Ⓔ
33. Ⓐ Ⓑ Ⓒ Ⓓ Ⓔ
34. Ⓐ Ⓑ Ⓒ Ⓓ Ⓔ
35. Ⓐ Ⓑ Ⓒ Ⓓ Ⓔ
36. Ⓐ Ⓑ Ⓒ Ⓓ Ⓔ
37. Ⓐ Ⓑ Ⓒ Ⓓ Ⓔ
38. Ⓐ Ⓑ Ⓒ Ⓓ Ⓔ
39. Ⓐ Ⓑ Ⓒ Ⓓ Ⓔ
40. Ⓐ Ⓑ Ⓒ Ⓓ Ⓔ
41. Ⓐ Ⓑ Ⓒ Ⓓ Ⓔ
42. Ⓐ Ⓑ Ⓒ Ⓓ Ⓔ
43. Ⓐ Ⓑ Ⓒ Ⓓ Ⓔ
44. Ⓐ Ⓑ Ⓒ Ⓓ Ⓔ
45. Ⓐ Ⓑ Ⓒ Ⓓ Ⓔ
46. Ⓐ Ⓑ Ⓒ Ⓓ Ⓔ
47. Ⓐ Ⓑ Ⓒ Ⓓ Ⓔ
48. Ⓐ Ⓑ Ⓒ Ⓓ Ⓔ
49. Ⓐ Ⓑ Ⓒ Ⓓ Ⓔ
50. Ⓐ Ⓑ Ⓒ Ⓓ Ⓔ
51. Ⓐ Ⓑ Ⓒ Ⓓ Ⓔ
52. Ⓐ Ⓑ Ⓒ Ⓓ Ⓔ
53. Ⓐ Ⓑ Ⓒ Ⓓ Ⓔ
54. Ⓐ Ⓑ Ⓒ Ⓓ Ⓔ
55. Ⓐ Ⓑ Ⓒ Ⓓ Ⓔ
56. Ⓐ Ⓑ Ⓒ Ⓓ Ⓔ
57. Ⓐ Ⓑ Ⓒ Ⓓ Ⓔ
58. Ⓐ Ⓑ Ⓒ Ⓓ Ⓔ
59. Ⓐ Ⓑ Ⓒ Ⓓ Ⓔ

60. Ⓐ Ⓑ Ⓒ Ⓓ Ⓔ
61. Ⓐ Ⓑ Ⓒ Ⓓ Ⓔ
62. Ⓐ Ⓑ Ⓒ Ⓓ Ⓔ
63. Ⓐ Ⓑ Ⓒ Ⓓ Ⓔ
64. Ⓐ Ⓑ Ⓒ Ⓓ Ⓔ
65. Ⓐ Ⓑ Ⓒ Ⓓ Ⓔ
66. Ⓐ Ⓑ Ⓒ Ⓓ Ⓔ
67. Ⓐ Ⓑ Ⓒ Ⓓ Ⓔ
68. Ⓐ Ⓑ Ⓒ Ⓓ Ⓔ
69. Ⓐ Ⓑ Ⓒ Ⓓ Ⓔ
70. Ⓐ Ⓑ Ⓒ Ⓓ Ⓔ
71. Ⓐ Ⓑ Ⓒ Ⓓ Ⓔ
72. Ⓐ Ⓑ Ⓒ Ⓓ Ⓔ
73. Ⓐ Ⓑ Ⓒ Ⓓ Ⓔ
74. Ⓐ Ⓑ Ⓒ Ⓓ Ⓔ
75. Ⓐ Ⓑ Ⓒ Ⓓ Ⓔ
76. Ⓐ Ⓑ Ⓒ Ⓓ Ⓔ
77. Ⓐ Ⓑ Ⓒ Ⓓ Ⓔ
78. Ⓐ Ⓑ Ⓒ Ⓓ Ⓔ
79. Ⓐ Ⓑ Ⓒ Ⓓ Ⓔ
80. Ⓐ Ⓑ Ⓒ Ⓓ Ⓔ
81. Ⓐ Ⓑ Ⓒ Ⓓ Ⓔ
82. Ⓐ Ⓑ Ⓒ Ⓓ Ⓔ
83. Ⓐ Ⓑ Ⓒ Ⓓ Ⓔ
84. Ⓐ Ⓑ Ⓒ Ⓓ Ⓔ
85. Ⓐ Ⓑ Ⓒ Ⓓ Ⓔ
86. Ⓐ Ⓑ Ⓒ Ⓓ Ⓔ
87. Ⓐ Ⓑ Ⓒ Ⓓ Ⓔ
88. Ⓐ Ⓑ Ⓒ Ⓓ Ⓔ

answer sheet

PERSONAL CHARACTERISTICS AND EXPERIENCE INVENTORY

1. Ⓐ Ⓑ Ⓒ Ⓓ Ⓔ Ⓕ Ⓖ Ⓗ Ⓘ		40. Ⓐ Ⓑ Ⓒ Ⓓ Ⓔ Ⓕ Ⓖ Ⓗ Ⓘ
2. Ⓐ Ⓑ Ⓒ Ⓓ Ⓔ Ⓕ Ⓖ Ⓗ Ⓘ		41. Ⓐ Ⓑ Ⓒ Ⓓ Ⓔ Ⓕ Ⓖ Ⓗ Ⓘ
3. Ⓐ Ⓑ Ⓒ Ⓓ Ⓔ Ⓕ Ⓖ Ⓗ Ⓘ		42. Ⓐ Ⓑ Ⓒ Ⓓ Ⓔ Ⓕ Ⓖ Ⓗ Ⓘ
4. Ⓐ Ⓑ Ⓒ Ⓓ Ⓔ Ⓕ Ⓖ Ⓗ Ⓘ		43. Ⓐ Ⓑ Ⓒ Ⓓ Ⓔ Ⓕ Ⓖ Ⓗ Ⓘ
5. Ⓐ Ⓑ Ⓒ Ⓓ Ⓔ Ⓕ Ⓖ Ⓗ Ⓘ		44. Ⓐ Ⓑ Ⓒ Ⓓ Ⓔ Ⓕ Ⓖ Ⓗ Ⓘ
6. Ⓐ Ⓑ Ⓒ Ⓓ Ⓔ Ⓕ Ⓖ Ⓗ Ⓘ		45. Ⓐ Ⓑ Ⓒ Ⓓ Ⓔ Ⓕ Ⓖ Ⓗ Ⓘ
7. Ⓐ Ⓑ Ⓒ Ⓓ Ⓔ Ⓕ Ⓖ Ⓗ Ⓘ		46. Ⓐ Ⓑ Ⓒ Ⓓ Ⓔ Ⓕ Ⓖ Ⓗ Ⓘ
8. Ⓐ Ⓑ Ⓒ Ⓓ Ⓔ Ⓕ Ⓖ Ⓗ Ⓘ		47. Ⓐ Ⓑ Ⓒ Ⓓ Ⓔ Ⓕ Ⓖ Ⓗ Ⓘ
9. Ⓐ Ⓑ Ⓒ Ⓓ Ⓔ Ⓕ Ⓖ Ⓗ Ⓘ		48. Ⓐ Ⓑ Ⓒ Ⓓ Ⓔ Ⓕ Ⓖ Ⓗ Ⓘ
10. Ⓐ Ⓑ Ⓒ Ⓓ Ⓔ Ⓕ Ⓖ Ⓗ Ⓘ		49. Ⓐ Ⓑ Ⓒ Ⓓ Ⓔ Ⓕ Ⓖ Ⓗ Ⓘ
11. Ⓐ Ⓑ Ⓒ Ⓓ Ⓔ Ⓕ Ⓖ Ⓗ Ⓘ		50. Ⓐ Ⓑ Ⓒ Ⓓ Ⓔ Ⓕ Ⓖ Ⓗ Ⓘ
12. Ⓐ Ⓑ Ⓒ Ⓓ Ⓔ Ⓕ Ⓖ Ⓗ Ⓘ		51. Ⓐ Ⓑ Ⓒ Ⓓ Ⓔ Ⓕ Ⓖ Ⓗ Ⓘ
13. Ⓐ Ⓑ Ⓒ Ⓓ Ⓔ Ⓕ Ⓖ Ⓗ Ⓘ		52. Ⓐ Ⓑ Ⓒ Ⓓ Ⓔ Ⓕ Ⓖ Ⓗ Ⓘ
14. Ⓐ Ⓑ Ⓒ Ⓓ Ⓔ Ⓕ Ⓖ Ⓗ Ⓘ		53. Ⓐ Ⓑ Ⓒ Ⓓ Ⓔ Ⓕ Ⓖ Ⓗ Ⓘ
15. Ⓐ Ⓑ Ⓒ Ⓓ Ⓔ Ⓕ Ⓖ Ⓗ Ⓘ		54. Ⓐ Ⓑ Ⓒ Ⓓ Ⓔ Ⓕ Ⓖ Ⓗ Ⓘ
16. Ⓐ Ⓑ Ⓒ Ⓓ Ⓔ Ⓕ Ⓖ Ⓗ Ⓘ		55. Ⓐ Ⓑ Ⓒ Ⓓ Ⓔ Ⓕ Ⓖ Ⓗ Ⓘ
17. Ⓐ Ⓑ Ⓒ Ⓓ Ⓔ Ⓕ Ⓖ Ⓗ Ⓘ		56. Ⓐ Ⓑ Ⓒ Ⓓ Ⓔ Ⓕ Ⓖ Ⓗ Ⓘ
18. Ⓐ Ⓑ Ⓒ Ⓓ Ⓔ Ⓕ Ⓖ Ⓗ Ⓘ		57. Ⓐ Ⓑ Ⓒ Ⓓ Ⓔ Ⓕ Ⓖ Ⓗ Ⓘ
19. Ⓐ Ⓑ Ⓒ Ⓓ Ⓔ Ⓕ Ⓖ Ⓗ Ⓘ		58. Ⓐ Ⓑ Ⓒ Ⓓ Ⓔ Ⓕ Ⓖ Ⓗ Ⓘ
20. Ⓐ Ⓑ Ⓒ Ⓓ Ⓔ Ⓕ Ⓖ Ⓗ Ⓘ		59. Ⓐ Ⓑ Ⓒ Ⓓ Ⓔ Ⓕ Ⓖ Ⓗ Ⓘ
21. Ⓐ Ⓑ Ⓒ Ⓓ Ⓔ Ⓕ Ⓖ Ⓗ Ⓘ		60. Ⓐ Ⓑ Ⓒ Ⓓ Ⓔ Ⓕ Ⓖ Ⓗ Ⓘ
22. Ⓐ Ⓑ Ⓒ Ⓓ Ⓔ Ⓕ Ⓖ Ⓗ Ⓘ		61. Ⓐ Ⓑ Ⓒ Ⓓ Ⓔ Ⓕ Ⓖ Ⓗ Ⓘ
23. Ⓐ Ⓑ Ⓒ Ⓓ Ⓔ Ⓕ Ⓖ Ⓗ Ⓘ		62. Ⓐ Ⓑ Ⓒ Ⓓ Ⓔ Ⓕ Ⓖ Ⓗ Ⓘ
24. Ⓐ Ⓑ Ⓒ Ⓓ Ⓔ Ⓕ Ⓖ Ⓗ Ⓘ		63. Ⓐ Ⓑ Ⓒ Ⓓ Ⓔ Ⓕ Ⓖ Ⓗ Ⓘ
25. Ⓐ Ⓑ Ⓒ Ⓓ Ⓔ Ⓕ Ⓖ Ⓗ Ⓘ		64. Ⓐ Ⓑ Ⓒ Ⓓ Ⓔ Ⓕ Ⓖ Ⓗ Ⓘ
26. Ⓐ Ⓑ Ⓒ Ⓓ Ⓔ Ⓕ Ⓖ Ⓗ Ⓘ		65. Ⓐ Ⓑ Ⓒ Ⓓ Ⓔ Ⓕ Ⓖ Ⓗ Ⓘ
27. Ⓐ Ⓑ Ⓒ Ⓓ Ⓔ Ⓕ Ⓖ Ⓗ Ⓘ		66. Ⓐ Ⓑ Ⓒ Ⓓ Ⓔ Ⓕ Ⓖ Ⓗ Ⓘ
28. Ⓐ Ⓑ Ⓒ Ⓓ Ⓔ Ⓕ Ⓖ Ⓗ Ⓘ		67. Ⓐ Ⓑ Ⓒ Ⓓ Ⓔ Ⓕ Ⓖ Ⓗ Ⓘ
29. Ⓐ Ⓑ Ⓒ Ⓓ Ⓔ Ⓕ Ⓖ Ⓗ Ⓘ		68. Ⓐ Ⓑ Ⓒ Ⓓ Ⓔ Ⓕ Ⓖ Ⓗ Ⓘ
30. Ⓐ Ⓑ Ⓒ Ⓓ Ⓔ Ⓕ Ⓖ Ⓗ Ⓘ		69. Ⓐ Ⓑ Ⓒ Ⓓ Ⓔ Ⓕ Ⓖ Ⓗ Ⓘ
31. Ⓐ Ⓑ Ⓒ Ⓓ Ⓔ Ⓕ Ⓖ Ⓗ Ⓘ		70. Ⓐ Ⓑ Ⓒ Ⓓ Ⓔ Ⓕ Ⓖ Ⓗ Ⓘ
32. Ⓐ Ⓑ Ⓒ Ⓓ Ⓔ Ⓕ Ⓖ Ⓗ Ⓘ		71. Ⓐ Ⓑ Ⓒ Ⓓ Ⓔ Ⓕ Ⓖ Ⓗ Ⓘ
33. Ⓐ Ⓑ Ⓒ Ⓓ Ⓔ Ⓕ Ⓖ Ⓗ Ⓘ		72. Ⓐ Ⓑ Ⓒ Ⓓ Ⓔ Ⓕ Ⓖ Ⓗ Ⓘ
34. Ⓐ Ⓑ Ⓒ Ⓓ Ⓔ Ⓕ Ⓖ Ⓗ Ⓘ		73. Ⓐ Ⓑ Ⓒ Ⓓ Ⓔ Ⓕ Ⓖ Ⓗ Ⓘ
35. Ⓐ Ⓑ Ⓒ Ⓓ Ⓔ Ⓕ Ⓖ Ⓗ Ⓘ		74. Ⓐ Ⓑ Ⓒ Ⓓ Ⓔ Ⓕ Ⓖ Ⓗ Ⓘ
36. Ⓐ Ⓑ Ⓒ Ⓓ Ⓔ Ⓕ Ⓖ Ⓗ Ⓘ		75. Ⓐ Ⓑ Ⓒ Ⓓ Ⓔ Ⓕ Ⓖ Ⓗ Ⓘ
37. Ⓐ Ⓑ Ⓒ Ⓓ Ⓔ Ⓕ Ⓖ Ⓗ Ⓘ		76. Ⓐ Ⓑ Ⓒ Ⓓ Ⓔ Ⓕ Ⓖ Ⓗ Ⓘ
38. Ⓐ Ⓑ Ⓒ Ⓓ Ⓔ Ⓕ Ⓖ Ⓗ Ⓘ		77. Ⓐ Ⓑ Ⓒ Ⓓ Ⓔ Ⓕ Ⓖ Ⓗ Ⓘ
39. Ⓐ Ⓑ Ⓒ Ⓓ Ⓔ Ⓕ Ⓖ Ⓗ Ⓘ		78. Ⓐ Ⓑ Ⓒ Ⓓ Ⓔ Ⓕ Ⓖ Ⓗ Ⓘ

79. Ⓐ Ⓑ Ⓒ Ⓓ Ⓔ Ⓕ Ⓖ Ⓗ Ⓘ
80. Ⓐ Ⓑ Ⓒ Ⓓ Ⓔ Ⓕ Ⓖ Ⓗ Ⓘ
81. Ⓐ Ⓑ Ⓒ Ⓓ Ⓔ Ⓕ Ⓖ Ⓗ Ⓘ
82. Ⓐ Ⓑ Ⓒ Ⓓ Ⓔ Ⓕ Ⓖ Ⓗ Ⓘ
83. Ⓐ Ⓑ Ⓒ Ⓓ Ⓔ Ⓕ Ⓖ Ⓗ Ⓘ
84. Ⓐ Ⓑ Ⓒ Ⓓ Ⓔ Ⓕ Ⓖ Ⓗ Ⓘ
85. Ⓐ Ⓑ Ⓒ Ⓓ Ⓔ Ⓕ Ⓖ Ⓗ Ⓘ
86. Ⓐ Ⓑ Ⓒ Ⓓ Ⓔ Ⓕ Ⓖ Ⓗ Ⓘ
87. Ⓐ Ⓑ Ⓒ Ⓓ Ⓔ Ⓕ Ⓖ Ⓗ Ⓘ
88. Ⓐ Ⓑ Ⓒ Ⓓ Ⓔ Ⓕ Ⓖ Ⓗ Ⓘ
89. Ⓐ Ⓑ Ⓒ Ⓓ Ⓔ Ⓕ Ⓖ Ⓗ Ⓘ
90. Ⓐ Ⓑ Ⓒ Ⓓ Ⓔ Ⓕ Ⓖ Ⓗ Ⓘ
91. Ⓐ Ⓑ Ⓒ Ⓓ Ⓔ Ⓕ Ⓖ Ⓗ Ⓘ
92. Ⓐ Ⓑ Ⓒ Ⓓ Ⓔ Ⓕ Ⓖ Ⓗ Ⓘ
93. Ⓐ Ⓑ Ⓒ Ⓓ Ⓔ Ⓕ Ⓖ Ⓗ Ⓘ
94. Ⓐ Ⓑ Ⓒ Ⓓ Ⓔ Ⓕ Ⓖ Ⓗ Ⓘ
95. Ⓐ Ⓑ Ⓒ Ⓓ Ⓔ Ⓕ Ⓖ Ⓗ Ⓘ
96. Ⓐ Ⓑ Ⓒ Ⓓ Ⓔ Ⓕ Ⓖ Ⓗ Ⓘ
97. Ⓐ Ⓑ Ⓒ Ⓓ Ⓔ Ⓕ Ⓖ Ⓗ Ⓘ
98. Ⓐ Ⓑ Ⓒ Ⓓ Ⓔ Ⓕ Ⓖ Ⓗ Ⓘ
99. Ⓐ Ⓑ Ⓒ Ⓓ Ⓔ Ⓕ Ⓖ Ⓗ Ⓘ
100. Ⓐ Ⓑ Ⓒ Ⓓ Ⓔ Ⓕ Ⓖ Ⓗ Ⓘ
101. Ⓐ Ⓑ Ⓒ Ⓓ Ⓔ Ⓕ Ⓖ Ⓗ Ⓘ
102. Ⓐ Ⓑ Ⓒ Ⓓ Ⓔ Ⓕ Ⓖ Ⓗ Ⓘ
103. Ⓐ Ⓑ Ⓒ Ⓓ Ⓔ Ⓕ Ⓖ Ⓗ Ⓘ
104. Ⓐ Ⓑ Ⓒ Ⓓ Ⓔ Ⓕ Ⓖ Ⓗ Ⓘ
105. Ⓐ Ⓑ Ⓒ Ⓓ Ⓔ Ⓕ Ⓖ Ⓗ Ⓘ
106. Ⓐ Ⓑ Ⓒ Ⓓ Ⓔ Ⓕ Ⓖ Ⓗ Ⓘ
107. Ⓐ Ⓑ Ⓒ Ⓓ Ⓔ Ⓕ Ⓖ Ⓗ Ⓘ
108. Ⓐ Ⓑ Ⓒ Ⓓ Ⓔ Ⓕ Ⓖ Ⓗ Ⓘ
109. Ⓐ Ⓑ Ⓒ Ⓓ Ⓔ Ⓕ Ⓖ Ⓗ Ⓘ
110. Ⓐ Ⓑ Ⓒ Ⓓ Ⓔ Ⓕ Ⓖ Ⓗ Ⓘ
111. Ⓐ Ⓑ Ⓒ Ⓓ Ⓔ Ⓕ Ⓖ Ⓗ Ⓘ
112. Ⓐ Ⓑ Ⓒ Ⓓ Ⓔ Ⓕ Ⓖ Ⓗ Ⓘ
113. Ⓐ Ⓑ Ⓒ Ⓓ Ⓔ Ⓕ Ⓖ Ⓗ Ⓘ
114. Ⓐ Ⓑ Ⓒ Ⓓ Ⓔ Ⓕ Ⓖ Ⓗ Ⓘ
115. Ⓐ Ⓑ Ⓒ Ⓓ Ⓔ Ⓕ Ⓖ Ⓗ Ⓘ
116. Ⓐ Ⓑ Ⓒ Ⓓ Ⓔ Ⓕ Ⓖ Ⓗ Ⓘ
117. Ⓐ Ⓑ Ⓒ Ⓓ Ⓔ Ⓕ Ⓖ Ⓗ Ⓘ
118. Ⓐ Ⓑ Ⓒ Ⓓ Ⓔ Ⓕ Ⓖ Ⓗ Ⓘ

119. Ⓐ Ⓑ Ⓒ Ⓓ Ⓔ Ⓕ Ⓖ Ⓗ Ⓘ
120. Ⓐ Ⓑ Ⓒ Ⓓ Ⓔ Ⓕ Ⓖ Ⓗ Ⓘ
121. Ⓐ Ⓑ Ⓒ Ⓓ Ⓔ Ⓕ Ⓖ Ⓗ Ⓘ
122. Ⓐ Ⓑ Ⓒ Ⓓ Ⓔ Ⓕ Ⓖ Ⓗ Ⓘ
123. Ⓐ Ⓑ Ⓒ Ⓓ Ⓔ Ⓕ Ⓖ Ⓗ Ⓘ
124. Ⓐ Ⓑ Ⓒ Ⓓ Ⓔ Ⓕ Ⓖ Ⓗ Ⓘ
125. Ⓐ Ⓑ Ⓒ Ⓓ Ⓔ Ⓕ Ⓖ Ⓗ Ⓘ
126. Ⓐ Ⓑ Ⓒ Ⓓ Ⓔ Ⓕ Ⓖ Ⓗ Ⓘ
127. Ⓐ Ⓑ Ⓒ Ⓓ Ⓔ Ⓕ Ⓖ Ⓗ Ⓘ
128. Ⓐ Ⓑ Ⓒ Ⓓ Ⓔ Ⓕ Ⓖ Ⓗ Ⓘ
129. Ⓐ Ⓑ Ⓒ Ⓓ Ⓔ Ⓕ Ⓖ Ⓗ Ⓘ
130. Ⓐ Ⓑ Ⓒ Ⓓ Ⓔ Ⓕ Ⓖ Ⓗ Ⓘ
131. Ⓐ Ⓑ Ⓒ Ⓓ Ⓔ Ⓕ Ⓖ Ⓗ Ⓘ
132. Ⓐ Ⓑ Ⓒ Ⓓ Ⓔ Ⓕ Ⓖ Ⓗ Ⓘ
133. Ⓐ Ⓑ Ⓒ Ⓓ Ⓔ Ⓕ Ⓖ Ⓗ Ⓘ
134. Ⓐ Ⓑ Ⓒ Ⓓ Ⓔ Ⓕ Ⓖ Ⓗ Ⓘ
135. Ⓐ Ⓑ Ⓒ Ⓓ Ⓔ Ⓕ Ⓖ Ⓗ Ⓘ
136. Ⓐ Ⓑ Ⓒ Ⓓ Ⓔ Ⓕ Ⓖ Ⓗ Ⓘ
137. Ⓐ Ⓑ Ⓒ Ⓓ Ⓔ Ⓕ Ⓖ Ⓗ Ⓘ
138. Ⓐ Ⓑ Ⓒ Ⓓ Ⓔ Ⓕ Ⓖ Ⓗ Ⓘ
139. Ⓐ Ⓑ Ⓒ Ⓓ Ⓔ Ⓕ Ⓖ Ⓗ Ⓘ
140. Ⓐ Ⓑ Ⓒ Ⓓ Ⓔ Ⓕ Ⓖ Ⓗ Ⓘ
141. Ⓐ Ⓑ Ⓒ Ⓓ Ⓔ Ⓕ Ⓖ Ⓗ Ⓘ
142. Ⓐ Ⓑ Ⓒ Ⓓ Ⓔ Ⓕ Ⓖ Ⓗ Ⓘ
143. Ⓐ Ⓑ Ⓒ Ⓓ Ⓔ Ⓕ Ⓖ Ⓗ Ⓘ
144. Ⓐ Ⓑ Ⓒ Ⓓ Ⓔ Ⓕ Ⓖ Ⓗ Ⓘ
145. Ⓐ Ⓑ Ⓒ Ⓓ Ⓔ Ⓕ Ⓖ Ⓗ Ⓘ
146. Ⓐ Ⓑ Ⓒ Ⓓ Ⓔ Ⓕ Ⓖ Ⓗ Ⓘ
147. Ⓐ Ⓑ Ⓒ Ⓓ Ⓔ Ⓕ Ⓖ Ⓗ Ⓘ
148. Ⓐ Ⓑ Ⓒ Ⓓ Ⓔ Ⓕ Ⓖ Ⓗ Ⓘ
149. Ⓐ Ⓑ Ⓒ Ⓓ Ⓔ Ⓕ Ⓖ Ⓗ Ⓘ
150. Ⓐ Ⓑ Ⓒ Ⓓ Ⓔ Ⓕ Ⓖ Ⓗ Ⓘ
151. Ⓐ Ⓑ Ⓒ Ⓓ Ⓔ Ⓕ Ⓖ Ⓗ Ⓘ
152. Ⓐ Ⓑ Ⓒ Ⓓ Ⓔ Ⓕ Ⓖ Ⓗ Ⓘ
153. Ⓐ Ⓑ Ⓒ Ⓓ Ⓔ Ⓕ Ⓖ Ⓗ Ⓘ
154. Ⓐ Ⓑ Ⓒ Ⓓ Ⓔ Ⓕ Ⓖ Ⓗ Ⓘ
155. Ⓐ Ⓑ Ⓒ Ⓓ Ⓔ Ⓕ Ⓖ Ⓗ Ⓘ
156. Ⓐ Ⓑ Ⓒ Ⓓ Ⓔ Ⓕ Ⓖ Ⓗ Ⓘ
157. Ⓐ Ⓑ Ⓒ Ⓓ Ⓔ Ⓕ Ⓖ Ⓗ Ⓘ
158. Ⓐ Ⓑ Ⓒ Ⓓ Ⓔ Ⓕ Ⓖ Ⓗ Ⓘ

answer sheet

159. Ⓐ Ⓑ Ⓒ Ⓓ Ⓔ Ⓕ Ⓖ Ⓗ Ⓘ
160. Ⓐ Ⓑ Ⓒ Ⓓ Ⓔ Ⓕ Ⓖ Ⓗ Ⓘ
161. Ⓐ Ⓑ Ⓒ Ⓓ Ⓔ Ⓕ Ⓖ Ⓗ Ⓘ
162. Ⓐ Ⓑ Ⓒ Ⓓ Ⓔ Ⓕ Ⓖ Ⓗ Ⓘ
163. Ⓐ Ⓑ Ⓒ Ⓓ Ⓔ Ⓕ Ⓖ Ⓗ Ⓘ
164. Ⓐ Ⓑ Ⓒ Ⓓ Ⓔ Ⓕ Ⓖ Ⓗ Ⓘ
165. Ⓐ Ⓑ Ⓒ Ⓓ Ⓔ Ⓕ Ⓖ Ⓗ Ⓘ
166. Ⓐ Ⓑ Ⓒ Ⓓ Ⓔ Ⓕ Ⓖ Ⓗ Ⓘ
167. Ⓐ Ⓑ Ⓒ Ⓓ Ⓔ Ⓕ Ⓖ Ⓗ Ⓘ
168. Ⓐ Ⓑ Ⓒ Ⓓ Ⓔ Ⓕ Ⓖ Ⓗ Ⓘ
169. Ⓐ Ⓑ Ⓒ Ⓓ Ⓔ Ⓕ Ⓖ Ⓗ Ⓘ
170. Ⓐ Ⓑ Ⓒ Ⓓ Ⓔ Ⓕ Ⓖ Ⓗ Ⓘ
171. Ⓐ Ⓑ Ⓒ Ⓓ Ⓔ Ⓕ Ⓖ Ⓗ Ⓘ
172. Ⓐ Ⓑ Ⓒ Ⓓ Ⓔ Ⓕ Ⓖ Ⓗ Ⓘ
173. Ⓐ Ⓑ Ⓒ Ⓓ Ⓔ Ⓕ Ⓖ Ⓗ Ⓘ
174. Ⓐ Ⓑ Ⓒ Ⓓ Ⓔ Ⓕ Ⓖ Ⓗ Ⓘ
175. Ⓐ Ⓑ Ⓒ Ⓓ Ⓔ Ⓕ Ⓖ Ⓗ Ⓘ
176. Ⓐ Ⓑ Ⓒ Ⓓ Ⓔ Ⓕ Ⓖ Ⓗ Ⓘ
177. Ⓐ Ⓑ Ⓒ Ⓓ Ⓔ Ⓕ Ⓖ Ⓗ Ⓘ
178. Ⓐ Ⓑ Ⓒ Ⓓ Ⓔ Ⓕ Ⓖ Ⓗ Ⓘ
179. Ⓐ Ⓑ Ⓒ Ⓓ Ⓔ Ⓕ Ⓖ Ⓗ Ⓘ
180. Ⓐ Ⓑ Ⓒ Ⓓ Ⓔ Ⓕ Ⓖ Ⓗ Ⓘ
181. Ⓐ Ⓑ Ⓒ Ⓓ Ⓔ Ⓕ Ⓖ Ⓗ Ⓘ
182. Ⓐ Ⓑ Ⓒ Ⓓ Ⓔ Ⓕ Ⓖ Ⓗ Ⓘ
183. Ⓐ Ⓑ Ⓒ Ⓓ Ⓔ Ⓕ Ⓖ Ⓗ Ⓘ
184. Ⓐ Ⓑ Ⓒ Ⓓ Ⓔ Ⓕ Ⓖ Ⓗ Ⓘ
185. Ⓐ Ⓑ Ⓒ Ⓓ Ⓔ Ⓕ Ⓖ Ⓗ Ⓘ
186. Ⓐ Ⓑ Ⓒ Ⓓ Ⓔ Ⓕ Ⓖ Ⓗ Ⓘ
187. Ⓐ Ⓑ Ⓒ Ⓓ Ⓔ Ⓕ Ⓖ Ⓗ Ⓘ
188. Ⓐ Ⓑ Ⓒ Ⓓ Ⓔ Ⓕ Ⓖ Ⓗ Ⓘ
189. Ⓐ Ⓑ Ⓒ Ⓓ Ⓔ Ⓕ Ⓖ Ⓗ Ⓘ
190. Ⓐ Ⓑ Ⓒ Ⓓ Ⓔ Ⓕ Ⓖ Ⓗ Ⓘ
191. Ⓐ Ⓑ Ⓒ Ⓓ Ⓔ Ⓕ Ⓖ Ⓗ Ⓘ
192. Ⓐ Ⓑ Ⓒ Ⓓ Ⓔ Ⓕ Ⓖ Ⓗ Ⓘ
193. Ⓐ Ⓑ Ⓒ Ⓓ Ⓔ Ⓕ Ⓖ Ⓗ Ⓘ
194. Ⓐ Ⓑ Ⓒ Ⓓ Ⓔ Ⓕ Ⓖ Ⓗ Ⓘ
195. Ⓐ Ⓑ Ⓒ Ⓓ Ⓔ Ⓕ Ⓖ Ⓗ Ⓘ
196. Ⓐ Ⓑ Ⓒ Ⓓ Ⓔ Ⓕ Ⓖ Ⓗ Ⓘ
197. Ⓐ Ⓑ Ⓒ Ⓓ Ⓔ Ⓕ Ⓖ Ⓗ Ⓘ

198. Ⓐ Ⓑ Ⓒ Ⓓ Ⓔ Ⓕ Ⓖ Ⓗ Ⓘ
199. Ⓐ Ⓑ Ⓒ Ⓓ Ⓔ Ⓕ Ⓖ Ⓗ Ⓘ
200. Ⓐ Ⓑ Ⓒ Ⓓ Ⓔ Ⓕ Ⓖ Ⓗ Ⓘ
201. Ⓐ Ⓑ Ⓒ Ⓓ Ⓔ Ⓕ Ⓖ Ⓗ Ⓘ
202. Ⓐ Ⓑ Ⓒ Ⓓ Ⓔ Ⓕ Ⓖ Ⓗ Ⓘ
203. Ⓐ Ⓑ Ⓒ Ⓓ Ⓔ Ⓕ Ⓖ Ⓗ Ⓘ
204. Ⓐ Ⓑ Ⓒ Ⓓ Ⓔ Ⓕ Ⓖ Ⓗ Ⓘ
205. Ⓐ Ⓑ Ⓒ Ⓓ Ⓔ Ⓕ Ⓖ Ⓗ Ⓘ
206. Ⓐ Ⓑ Ⓒ Ⓓ Ⓔ Ⓕ Ⓖ Ⓗ Ⓘ
207. Ⓐ Ⓑ Ⓒ Ⓓ Ⓔ Ⓕ Ⓖ Ⓗ Ⓘ
208. Ⓐ Ⓑ Ⓒ Ⓓ Ⓔ Ⓕ Ⓖ Ⓗ Ⓘ
209. Ⓐ Ⓑ Ⓒ Ⓓ Ⓔ Ⓕ Ⓖ Ⓗ Ⓘ
210. Ⓐ Ⓑ Ⓒ Ⓓ Ⓔ Ⓕ Ⓖ Ⓗ Ⓘ
211. Ⓐ Ⓑ Ⓒ Ⓓ Ⓔ Ⓕ Ⓖ Ⓗ Ⓘ
212. Ⓐ Ⓑ Ⓒ Ⓓ Ⓔ Ⓕ Ⓖ Ⓗ Ⓘ
213. Ⓐ Ⓑ Ⓒ Ⓓ Ⓔ Ⓕ Ⓖ Ⓗ Ⓘ
214. Ⓐ Ⓑ Ⓒ Ⓓ Ⓔ Ⓕ Ⓖ Ⓗ Ⓘ
215. Ⓐ Ⓑ Ⓒ Ⓓ Ⓔ Ⓕ Ⓖ Ⓗ Ⓘ
216. Ⓐ Ⓑ Ⓒ Ⓓ Ⓔ Ⓕ Ⓖ Ⓗ Ⓘ
217. Ⓐ Ⓑ Ⓒ Ⓓ Ⓔ Ⓕ Ⓖ Ⓗ Ⓘ
218. Ⓐ Ⓑ Ⓒ Ⓓ Ⓔ Ⓕ Ⓖ Ⓗ Ⓘ
219. Ⓐ Ⓑ Ⓒ Ⓓ Ⓔ Ⓕ Ⓖ Ⓗ Ⓘ
220. Ⓐ Ⓑ Ⓒ Ⓓ Ⓔ Ⓕ Ⓖ Ⓗ Ⓘ
221. Ⓐ Ⓑ Ⓒ Ⓓ Ⓔ Ⓕ Ⓖ Ⓗ Ⓘ
222. Ⓐ Ⓑ Ⓒ Ⓓ Ⓔ Ⓕ Ⓖ Ⓗ Ⓘ
223. Ⓐ Ⓑ Ⓒ Ⓓ Ⓔ Ⓕ Ⓖ Ⓗ Ⓘ
224. Ⓐ Ⓑ Ⓒ Ⓓ Ⓔ Ⓕ Ⓖ Ⓗ Ⓘ
225. Ⓐ Ⓑ Ⓒ Ⓓ Ⓔ Ⓕ Ⓖ Ⓗ Ⓘ
226. Ⓐ Ⓑ Ⓒ Ⓓ Ⓔ Ⓕ Ⓖ Ⓗ Ⓘ
227. Ⓐ Ⓑ Ⓒ Ⓓ Ⓔ Ⓕ Ⓖ Ⓗ Ⓘ
228. Ⓐ Ⓑ Ⓒ Ⓓ Ⓔ Ⓕ Ⓖ Ⓗ Ⓘ
229. Ⓐ Ⓑ Ⓒ Ⓓ Ⓔ Ⓕ Ⓖ Ⓗ Ⓘ
230. Ⓐ Ⓑ Ⓒ Ⓓ Ⓔ Ⓕ Ⓖ Ⓗ Ⓘ
231. Ⓐ Ⓑ Ⓒ Ⓓ Ⓔ Ⓕ Ⓖ Ⓗ Ⓘ
232. Ⓐ Ⓑ Ⓒ Ⓓ Ⓔ Ⓕ Ⓖ Ⓗ Ⓘ
233. Ⓐ Ⓑ Ⓒ Ⓓ Ⓔ Ⓕ Ⓖ Ⓗ Ⓘ
234. Ⓐ Ⓑ Ⓒ Ⓓ Ⓔ Ⓕ Ⓖ Ⓗ Ⓘ
235. Ⓐ Ⓑ Ⓒ Ⓓ Ⓔ Ⓕ Ⓖ Ⓗ Ⓘ
236. Ⓐ Ⓑ Ⓒ Ⓓ Ⓔ Ⓕ Ⓖ Ⓗ Ⓘ

Practice Test 5:
U.S. Postal Service Clerk, Distribution Clerk, and Mark-Up Clerk Exam

ADDRESS CHECKING

95 QUESTIONS • 6 MINUTES

Directions: For each question, compare the address in the left column with the address in the right column. If the two addresses are **ALIKE IN EVERY WAY**, darken answer space (A) on your answer sheet. If the two addresses are **DIFFERENT IN ANY WAY**, darken answer space (D) on your answer sheet.

1.	1897 Smicksburg Rd	1897 Smithsburg Rd
2.	3609 E Paseo Aldeano	3909 E Paseo Aldeano
3.	11787 Ornamental Ln	1787 Ornamental Ln
4.	1096 Camino Grande E	1096 Camino Grande E
5.	2544 E Radcliff Ave	2544 E Redcliff Ave
6.	5796 E Narragansett Dr	5796 E Narragasett Dr
7.	12475 Ebbtide Way W	12475 Ebbtide Way W
8.	14396 N Via Armando	14396 S Via Armando
9.	2155 S Del Giorgio Rd	2155 S Del Giorgio Rd
10.	16550 Bainbridge Cir	16505 Bainbridge Cir
11.	1826 Milneburg Rd	1826 Milneburg St
12.	Eureka KS 67045	Eureka KY 67045
13.	4010 Glenaddie Ave	4010 Glenaddie Ave
14.	13501 Stratford Rd	13501 Standford Rd
15.	3296 W 64th St	3296 E 64th St
16.	2201 Tennessee Cir	2201 Tennessee Cir
17.	1502 Avenue M NE	1502 Avenue N NE
18.	1096 SE Longrone Dr	1096 SE Longrone Dr

19.	1267 Darthmouth Ct	1267 Darthmont Ct
20.	825 Ophanage Rd	825 Ophanage Rd
21.	1754 Golden Springs Rd	1754 Golden Springs Road
22.	1015 Tallwoods Ln	1015 Tallwoods Ln
23.	1097 Lambada Dr	1097 Lambadd Dr
24.	Vredenburgh AL 36481	Verdenburgh AL 36481
25.	1800 Monticello Ave	1800 Monticello Ave
26.	1723 Yellowbird Ln	1723 Yellowbird Ct
27.	700 Valca Materials Rd	700 Valca Materials Rd
28.	1569 Ladywood Ln N	1569 Ladywood Ln W
29.	3256 Interurban Dr	3256 Interurban Dr
30.	1507 Haughton Cir	1507 Haughton Ct
31.	8971 Robertson Ave	8971 Robinson Ave
32.	3801 NE 49th Street	3801 NW 49th Street
33.	4102 Chalkville Rd	4102 Chalkview Rd
34.	1709 Ingersoll Cir	1709 Ingersoll Cir
35.	6800 N Nantucket Ln	6800 N Nantucket Ln
36.	12401 Tarrymore Dr	12401 Terrymore Dr
37.	1097 Huntsville Ave	1097 Huntsville Ave
38.	3566 Lornaridge Pl	3566 Lornaridge Pl
39.	2039 Klondike Ave SW	2039 Klondie Ave SW
40.	3267 Mayland Ln	3267 Maryland Ln
41.	12956 Strawberry Ln	12596 Strawberry Ln
42.	De Armanville AL 36257	De Armanville AL 36257
43.	6015 Anniston Dr	6015 Anneston Dr
44.	1525 E 90th St	1525 E 90th St
45.	1299 Chappaque Rd	1266 Chappaque Rd
46.	2156 Juliette Dr	2156 Juliaetta Dr
47.	999 N Hollingsworth St	999 S Hollingsworth St
48.	16901 Odum Crest Ln	19601 Odum Crest Ln
49.	9787 Zellmark Dr	9787 Zealmark Dr

50.	11103 NE Feasell Ave	11103 NE Feasell Ave
51.	51121 N Mattison Rd	51121 S Mattison Rd
52.	8326 Blackjack Ln	8326 Blackjack Blvd
53.	18765 Lagarde Ave	18765 Lagrande Ave
54.	11297 Gallatin Ln	11297 Gallatin Ln
55.	Wormleysburg PA 17043	Wormleysburg, PA 17043
56.	22371 N Sprague Ave	22371 S Sprague Ave
57.	15014 Warrior River Rd	15014 Warrior River Rd
58.	45721 Hucytown Plaza	45721 Hueytowne Plaza
59.	8973 Tedescki Dr	8793 Tedescki Dr
60.	12995 Raimond Muscoda Pl	12995 Raimont Muscoda Pl
61.	Phippsburg CO 80469	Phippsburg CA 80469
62.	52003 W 49th Ave	52003 W 46th Ave
63.	17201 Zenobia Cir	17210 Zenobia Cir
64.	4800 Garrison Cir	4800 Garrison Dr
65.	Los Angeles CA 90070	Los Angeles CA 90076
66.	14798 W 62nd Ave	14198 W 62nd Ave
67.	7191 E Eldridge Way	7191 E Eldridge Way
68.	1279 S Quintard Dr	1279 S Guintard Dr
69.	21899 Dellwood Ave	21899 Dillwood Ave
70.	7191 Zenophone Cir	7191 Zenohone Cir
71.	4301 Los Encinos Way	4301 Los Encinas Way
72.	19700 Ostronic Dr NW	19700 Ostronic Dr NE
73.	23291 Van Velsire Dr	23219 Van Velsire Dr
74.	547 Paradise Valley Rd	547 Paradise Valley Ct
75.	23167 Saltillo Ave	23167 SantilloAve
76.	43001 Mourning Dove Way	43001 Mourning Dove Way
77.	21183 Declaration Ave	21183 Declaration Ave
78.	10799 Via Sierra Ramal Ave	10799 Via Sierra Ramel Ave
79.	16567 Hermosillia Ct	16597 Hermosillia Ct
80.	Villamont VA 24178	Villamont VA24178

81.	18794 Villaboso Ave	18794 Villeboso Ave
82.	24136 Ranthom Ave	24136 Ranthon Ave
83.	13489 Golondrina Pl	13489 Golondrina St
84.	6598 Adamsville Ave	6598 Adamsville Ave
85.	12641 Indals Pl NE	12641 Indals Pl NW
86.	19701 SE 2nd Avenue	19701 NE 2nd Avenue
87.	22754 Cachalote Ln	22754 Cachalott Ln
88.	12341 Kingfisher Rd	12341 Kingsfisher Rd
89.	24168 Lorenzana Dr	24168 Lorenzano Dr
90.	32480 Blackfriar Rd	32480 Blackfriar Rd
91.	16355 Wheeler Dr	16355 Wheelen Dr
92.	5100 Magna Carta Rd	5100 Magna Certa Rd
93.	2341 N Federalist Pl	2341 N Federalist Pl
94.	22200 Timpangos Rd	22200 Timpangos Rd
95.	19704 Calderon Rd	19704 Calderon Rd

STOP End of Address Checking section. If you finish before time is up, check your work on this section only. Do not go to the next section until the signal is given.

MEMORY FOR ADDRESSES

88 QUESTIONS • 5 MINUTES

The questions for this part are based upon the addresses in a set of five boxes. Your task is to darken on your answer sheet the letter of the box in which each question address belongs.

The exam itself provides three practice sessions before the question set that really counts. Practice I and Practice III supply you with the boxes and permit you to refer to them if necessary. Practice II and the Memory for Addresses test itself do not permit you to look at the boxes. The test itself is based on memory.

Practice for Memory for Addresses

Directions: The five boxes below are labelled (A), (B), (C), (D), and (E). In each box are three sets of number spans with names and two names that are not associated with numbers. In the next **THREE MINUTES,** you must try to memorize the box location of each name and number span. The position of a name or number span within its box is not important. You need only remember the letter of the box in which the item is to be found. You will use these names and numbers to answer three sets of practice questions that are NOT scored and one actual test that is scored.

(A)	(B)	(C)	(D)	(E)
8100–8399	6800–6999	7600–8099	8400–8699	7000–7599
Test	Test	Test	Test	Test
Pigeon	Vampire	Octopus	Ghost	Lever
7600–8099	7000–7599	8100–8399	6800–6999	8400–8699
City	City	City	City	City
Webb	Yak	Fleet	Hammer	Nougat
6800–6999	8400–8699	7000–7599	7600–8099	8100–8399
Mark	Mark	Mark	Mark	Mark

PRACTICE I

Directions: Use the next **THREE MINUTES** to darken the answer space on the Practice I answer sheet the letter of the box in which each item that follows is to be found. Try to darken each answer choice without looking back at the boxes. If, however, you get stuck, you may refer to the boxes during this practice exercise. If you find that you must look at the boxes, try to memorize as you do so. This test is for practice only. It will not be scored.

1. 6800-6999 Test

2. 7000-7599 City

3. 8100-8399 Mark

4. Octopus

5. Webb

6. 7000-7599 Test

7. Nougat

8. 7600-8099 Mark

9. 7000-7599 City

10. Fleet

11. Hammer

12. 7000-7599 Mark

13. 7600-8099 City

14. 8400-8699 Test

15. 8400-8699 Mark

16. 7600-8099 City

17. Vampire

18. Lever

19. Ghost

20. 6800-6999 Mark

21. 8100-8399 City

22. 8400-8699 City

23. 8400-8699 Mark

24. Pigeon

25. Fleet

26. 8400-8699 Test

27. 7000-7599 Mark

28. 6800-6999 Test

29. 7600-8099 City

30. Yak

31. Nougat

32. 8100-8399 Test

33. 7000-7599 Test

34. Lever

35. 7000-7599 City

36. 7600-8099 Mark

37. Octopus

38. Webb

39. Hammer

40. 8100-8399 Mark

41. 7600-8099 Test

42. 6800-6999 City

43. 7600-8099 Test

44. Fleet

45. 6800-6999 Mark

46. 8100-8399 City

47. 8400-8699 City

48. 8400-8699 Mark

49. Yak

50. Vampire

51. 7000-7599 Test

52. 8100-8399 Mark

53. 8100-8399 Test

54. Ghost

55. Fleet

56. 6800-6999 Mark

57. 7000-7599 Mark

58. 7000-7599 City

59. Lever

60. Octopus

61. 7600-8099 Test

62. 8400-8699 Test

63. 7600-8099 City

64. Hammer

65. Pigeon

66. 7600-8099 Mark

67. 6800-6999 City

68. 6800-6999 Test

69. 8100-8399 City

70. Webb

71. Nougat

72. 7600-8099 Test

73. 8400-8699 City

74. 8400-8699 Mark

75. 8100-8399 Test

76. 7000-7599 City

77. 7000-7599 Mark

78. Hammer

79. Lever

80. Pigeon

81. 7600-8099 Test

82. 7000-7599 Test

83. 8100-8399 Mark

84. Vampire

85. Fleet

86. 7600-8099 City

87. 6800-6999 Mark

88. 8400-8699 City

PRACTICE II

Directions: The next 88 questions constitute another practice exercise. Darken your answers on the Practice II answer sheet. Again, the time limit is **THREE MINUTES.** This time, however, you must NOT look at the boxes while answering the questions. You must rely on your memory in marking the box location of each item. This practice test will not be scored.

1. 7000-7599 Mark

2. 6800-6999 City

3. 6800-6999 Test

4. Pigeon

5. Nougat

6. 8400-8699 Test

7. 7000-7599 City

8. 6800-6999 Mark

9. Hammer

10. Ghost

11. 7600-8099 City

12. 8100-8399 Mark

13. 7600-8099 Mark

14. 7600-8099 Test

15. Octopus

16. Webb

17. 8100-8399 City

18. 8400-8699 City

19. 6800-6999 Mark

20. Fleet

21. Lever

22. Yak

23. 8100-8399 Test

24. 7000-7599 Test

25. Vampire

26. Octopus

27. 6800-6999 Test

28. 6800-6999 City

29. 6800-6999 Mark

30. Lever

31. Nougat
32. 7000-7599 City
33. 8100-8399 Mark
34. 8100-8399 City
35. 8100-8399 Test
36. 8400-8699 Mark
37. Yak
38. Webb
39. 7600-8099 Test
40. 7000-7599 Mark
41. Fleet
42. 8400-8699 City
43. 7600-8099 City
44. 8400-8699 Test
45. Pigeon
46. Ghost
47. Hammer
48. 7600-8099 Mark
49. 7000-7599 Test
50. 8100-8399 Mark
51. 6800-6999 City
52. 7600-8099 Test
53. Lever
54. Hammer
55. 8100-8399 Test
56. 7000-7599 City
57. 7000-7599 Mark
58. Pigeon
59. Vampire

60. 8100-8399 City
61. 7600-8099 City
62. 7000-7599 Test
63. 6800-6999 Mark
64. Nougat
65. Yak
66. Webb
67. 8400-8699 Mark
68. 7600-8099 Mark
69. 8400-8699 City
70. 6800-6999 Test
71. Ghost
72. Octopus
73. Fleet
74. 8400-8699 Test
75. 7600-8099 Test
76. 6800-6999 Mark
77. 7600-8099 City
78. Nougat
79. Webb
80. 6800-6999 City
81. 6800-6999 Test
82. 7600-8099 Mark
83. Vampire
84. Octopus
85. 7000-7599 Test
86. 8100-8399 City
87. 6800-6999 Mark
88. 8100-8399 Test

Practice III

Directions: The names and addresses are repeated for you in the boxes below. Each name and each number span is in the same box in which you found it in the original set. You will now be allowed **FIVE MINUTES** to study the locations again. Do your best to memorize the letter of the box in which each item is located. This is your last chance to see the boxes.

(A)	(B)	(C)	(D)	(E)
8100–8399	6800–6999	7600–8099	8400–8699	7000–7599
Test	Test	Test	Test	Test
Pigeon	Vampire	Octopus	Ghost	Lever
7600–8099	7000–7599	8100–8399	6800–6999	8400–8699
City	City	City	City	City
Webb	Yak	Fleet	Hammer	Nougat
6800–6999	8400–8699	7000–7599	7600–8099	8100–8399
Mark	Mark	Mark	Mark	Mark

Directions: This is your last practice test. Darken the answer space for the location of each of the 88 items on your answer sheet. You will have **FIVE MINUTES** to answer these questions. Do NOT look back at the boxes. This practice test will not be scored.

1. Fleet
2. Lever
3. 8400-8699 Test
4. 7000-7599 City
5. 6800-6999 Mark
6. Vampire
7. Pigeon
8. 8100-8399 Test
9. 8100-8399 Mark
10. 7000-7599 Test
11. 8100-8399 City
12. Octopus
13. Ghost
14. Yak
15. 6800-6999 City
16. 6800-6999 Test

17. 7600-8099 Mark
18. 7600-8099 City
19. Hammer
20. Nougat
21. 8400-8699 Mark
22. 8400-8699 City
23. 8400-8699 Test
24. 7000-7599 Mark
25. Octopus
26. Fleet
27. 8100-8399 City
28. 8100-8399 Test
29. 7000-7599 City
30. 7000-7599 Test
31. 8100-8399 Test
32. 7000-7599 City

33. 7000-7599 Mark

34. Nougat

35. Ghost

36. 6800-6999 City

37. 7000-7599 Test

38. 8100-8399 Mark

39. Pigeon

40. Webb

41. 7600-8099 City

42. 8100-8399 City

43. 8400-8699 Mark

44. Fleet

45. Vampire

46. 6800-6999 Test

47. 6800-6999 Mark

48. 7600-8099 Mark

49. Hammer

50. Yak

51. 8400-8699 City

52. 8400-8699 Test

53. 7600-8099 Test

54. Lever

55. Octopus

56. 7000-7599 Test

57. 7000-7599 Mark

58. 7000-7599 City

59. 8100-8399 Test

60. Vampire

61. 8100-8399 City

62. Hammer

63. 8100-8399 Mark

64. 7000-7599 Test

65. Ghost

66. Yak

67. 6800-6999 Mark

68. 7600-8099 City

69. Octopus

70. Fleet

71. 8400-8699 City

72. 7000-7599 Mark

73. 7600-8099 Test

74. 7600-8099 Mark

75. 6800-6999 City

76. 6800-6999 Test

77. Webb

78. Pigeon

79. Lever

80. 8400-8699 Test

81. 8400-8699 Mark

82. Nougat

83. 8400-8699 City

84. 7000-7599 City

85. 7000-7599 Test

86. Hammer

87. 6800-6999 Mark

88. Yak

Actual Test

Directions: Darken your answers on the answer sheet in the section headed "ACTUAL TEST." This test will be scored. You are NOT permitted to look at the boxes. Work from memory, as quickly and as accurately as you can.

1. 8400-8699 Test
2. 7000-7599 City
3. 8400-8699 Mark
4. Nougat
5. Pigeon
6. 6800-6999 Test
7. 8100-8399 Test
8. 8400-8699 City
9. 7000-7599 Mark
10. Ghost
11. Hammer
12. Vampire
13. 7600-8099 City
14. 7600-8099 Mark
15. 6800-6999 Mark
16. Octopus
17. Yak
18. 7600-8099 Test
19. 7000-7599 Test
20. 8400-8699 City
21. 8100-8399 Mark
22. Vampire
23. Lever
24. 7600-8099 Test
25. 7600-8099 City
26. 8100-8399 Mark

27. Webb
28. Ghost
29. 6800-6999 Mark
30. 7000-7599 Test
31. 8100-8399 City
32. 8400-8699 City
33. Pigeon
34. Yak
35. 7600-8099 Mark
36. 8400-8699 Mark
37. 8100-8399 Test
38. 6800-6999 City
39. Octopus
40. Hammer
41. Nougat
42. 7000-7599 City
43. 6800-6999 Test
44. 7600-8099 Mark
45. Nougat
46. 8400-8699 City
47. 6800-6999 Mark
48. 7600-8099 Test
49. 7000-7599 City
50. Ghost
51. Fleet
52. Yak

53. 7000-7599 Test
54. 8100-8399 City
55. 7600-8099 City
56. Pigeon
57. Octopus
58. 6800-6999 City
59. 8400-8699 Mark
60. 8100-8399 Mark
61. 8100-8399 Test
62. Webb
63. Hammer
64. 8400-8699 Test
65. 7000-7599 Mark
66. 8100-8399 City
67. Lever
68. Vampire
69. 8100-8399 Test
70. 8400-8699 City

71. 7000-7599 Test
72. 6800-6999 Mark
73. 8100-8399 City
74. 6800-6999 City
75. Yak
76. Nougat
77. Fleet
78. 6800-6999 Test
79. 7000-7599 Mark
80. 7000-7599 City
81. 8100-8399 Test
82. 8100-8399 Mark
83. Pigeon
84. Lever
85. Hammer
86. 8400-8699 Test
87. 8400-8699 Mark
88. 7600-8099 City

STOP   End of Memory for Addresses section. If you finish before time is up, check your work on this section only. Do not go to the next section until the signal is given.

NUMBER SERIES

24 QUESTIONS • 20 MINUTES

> **Directions:** Each number series question consists of a series of numbers that follows some definite order. The numbers progress from left to right according to some rule. One lettered pair of numbers comprises the next two numbers in the series. Study each series to try to find a pattern to the series and to figure the rule that governs the progression. Choose the answer pair that continues the series according to the pattern established and darken the answer space on your answer sheet.

1. 3 8 4 9 5 10 6   **(A)** 7 11   **(B)** 7 8   **(C)** 11 8   **(D)** 12 7   **(E)** 11 7

2. 18 14 19 17 20 20 21   **(A)** 22 24   **(B)** 14 19   **(C)** 24 21   **(D)** 21 23   **(E)** 23 22

3. 6 9 10 7 11 12 8   **(A)** 9 10   **(B)** 9 13   **(C)** 16 14   **(D)** 13 14   **(E)** 14 15

4. 7 5 3 9 7 5 11   **(A)** 13 12   **(B)** 7 5   **(C)** 9 7   **(D)** 13 7   **(E)** 9 9

5. 7 9 18 10 12 18 13   **(A)** 18 14   **(B)** 15 18   **(C)** 14 15   **(D)** 15 14   **(E)** 14 18

6. 2 6 4 8 6 10 8   **(A)** 12 10   **(B)** 6 10   **(C)** 10 12   **(D)** 12 16   **(E)** 6 4

7. 7 9 12 14 17 19 22   **(A)** 25 27   **(B)** 23 24   **(C)** 23 25   **(D)** 24 27   **(E)** 26 27

8. 3 23 5 25 7 27 9   **(A)** 10 11   **(B)** 27 29   **(C)** 29 11   **(D)** 11 28   **(E)** 28 10

9. 1 2 2 3 4 12 5 6   **(A)** 7 8   **(B)** 11 7   **(C)** 11 56   **(D)** 56 7   **(E)** 30 7

10. 1 2 3 6 4 5 6 6 7   **(A)** 6 5   **(B)** 8 9   **(C)** 6 8   **(D)** 7 6   **(E)** 8 6

11. 1 3 40 5 7 37 9   **(A)** 11 39   **(B)** 9 11   **(C)** 34 11   **(D)** 11 34   **(E)** 11 35

12. 25 27 29 31 33 35 37   **(A)** 39 41   **(B)** 38 39   **(C)** 37 39   **(D)** 37 38   **(E)** 39 40

13. 91 85 17 81 75 15 71   **(A)** 74 14   **(B)** 61 51   **(C)** 65 13   **(D)** 65 10   **(E)** 66 33

14. 41 37 46 42 51 47 56   **(A)** 5 170   **(B)** 52 61   **(C)** 41) 60   **(D)** 60 43   **(E)** 55 65

15. 6 6 6 18 18 18 54   **(A)** 54 108   **(B)** 54 162   **(C)** 108 108   **(D)** 10 8 162   **(E)** 54 54

16. 13 23 14 22 15 21 16   **(A)** 17 20   **(B)** 20 17   **(C)** 17 18   **(D)** 20 19   **(E)** 16 20

17. 52 10 48 20 44 30 40   **(A)** 36 50   **(B)** 50 36   **(C)** 36 40   **(D)** 40 36   **(E)** 40 40

18. 94 84 75 67 60 54 49   **(A)** 45 42   **(B)** 49 45   **(C)** 44 40   **(D)** 46 42   **(E)** 45 40

19. 76 38 38 48 24 24 34   **(A)** 34 44   **(B)** 34 34   **(C)** 17 17   **(D)** 34 17   **(E)** 17 27

20. 83 38 84 48 85 58 86   **(A)** 86 68   **(B)** 87 78   **(C)** 59 95   **(D)** 68 88   **(E)** 68 87

21. 19 21 21 24 24 24 28   **(A)** 28 31   **(B)** 28 33   **(C)** 32 36   **(D)** 28 28   **(E)** 28 32

22. 52 45 38 32 26 21 16   **(A)** 16 12   **(B)** 12 8   **(C)** 11 6   **(D)** 11 7   **(E)** 12 9

23. 100 81 64 49 36 25 16   **(A)** 12 10   **(B)** 8 4   **(C)** 8 2   **(D)** 9 4   **(E)** 9 2

24. 4 40 44 5 50 55 6   **(A)** 60 66   **(B)** 6 60   **(C)** 6 66   **(D)** 7 70   **(E)** 70 77

STOP   End of Number Series section. If you finish before time is up, check your work on this section only. Do not go to the next section until the signal is given.

FORMS COMPLETION

30 QUESTIONS • 15 MINUTES

Directions: Read each form and answer the items based on the information provided. Mark your answers on the answer sheet.

QUESTIONS 1–9 REFER TO THE FOLLOWING GRAPHIC.

1. Which of these would be a correct entry for Box 5?

   (A) A check mark
   (B) $13.85
   (C) 12 and 20
   (D) 08530

2. Where would you enter the insurance fee?

   (A) Box 3
   (B) Box 6
   (C) Box 10
   (D) Box 12

3. A check mark would be the correct entry for every box EXCEPT

   (A) Box 6
   (B) Box 7a
   (C) Box 8a
   (D) Box 11b

4. Where would you indicate that the package was delivered?

   (A) Box 16
   (B) Box 18
   (C) Box 19
   (D) Box 22

5. All of the following boxes indicate employee signatures are needed EXCEPT

(A) Box 4
(B) Box 18
(C) Box 21
(D) Box 24

6. Which of these would be a correct entry for Box 13b?

(A) A check mark
(B) 3 lbs. 6 oz.
(C) 4/11
(D) $13.85

7. Which box would you check to show 2nd day delivery to the military?

(A) Box 2a
(B) Box 2b
(C) Box 8a
(D) Box 11a

8. The country code for mail being sent out of the United States is entered in which box?

(A) Box 1
(B) Box 14
(C) Box 15
(D) Box 16

9. Which of these would be the correct entry for Box 15?

(A) A check mark
(B) $1.60
(C) Initials
(D) 6/12/06

QUESTIONS 10-15 REFER TO THE FOLLOWING GRAPHIC.

PS Form **2865**, February 1997 *(Reverse)*

10. Which of these would be a correct entry for Box 9?

(A) Paris, France
(B) Ms. Marie Hrouda
(C) 10/21/06
(D) $100

11. Where would you indicate that the item is Express Mail International?

(A) Box 1a
(B) Box 1b
(C) Box 1c
(D) Box 1f

12. Which of these would be a correct entry for Box 7?

    (A) A check mark
    (B) Computer Programmers Worldwide
    (C) 14 Piccadilly Lane
    (D) 9/30/06

13. How would you indicate that the piece of mail was a letter?

    (A) Check Box 1a
    (B) Check Box 1b
    (C) Write the word in Box 3
    (D) Write the word in Box 5

14. Where would you enter the Article Number?

    (A) Box 2
    (B) Box 3
    (C) Box 4
    (D) Box 6

15. Which of these would be the correct entry for Box 3?

    (A) A check mark
    (B) Peoria, IL
    (C) London, England
    (D) $250

QUESTIONS 16–18 REFER TO THE FOLLOWING GRAPHIC.

16. Where would you enter the check number for the COD package?

    (A) Box 2
    (B) Box 3
    (C) Box 4
    (D) Box 5

17. Which of the following would be a correct entry for Box 2?

    (A) 2/22/06
    (B) A check mark
    (C) #2345
    (D) Mr. Steve Krasowski

18. You could enter a date in each of the following boxes EXCEPT

    (A) Box 1
    (B) Box 4
    (C) Box 5
    (D) Box 6

QUESTIONS 19–21 REFER TO THE FOLLOWING GRAPHIC.

19. Which of these would be a correct
    entry for Box 7?

    (A) A check mark
    (B) $1,000
    (C) Ms. Dy Anne Going
    (D) 3/22/06

20. Where would you stamp the receipt?

    (A) Box 1
    (B) Box 2
    (C) Box 6
    (D) Box 9

21. Where would you indicate that the
    item is being sent to Boston?

    (A) Box 2
    (B) Box 4
    (C) Box 6
    (D) Box 9

QUESTIONS 22–25 REFER TO THE FOLLOWING GRAPHIC.

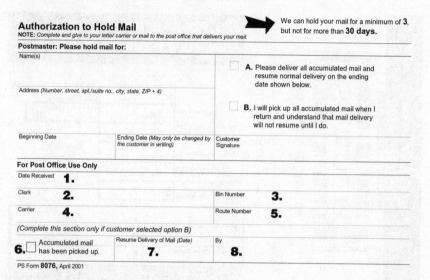

22. Which of these would be a correct entry for Box 5?

   (A) Rural Route 5
   (B) $1.60
   (C) 6/5/06
   (D) Tim Criswell

23. Where would you enter the mail carrier's name?

   (A) Box 1
   (B) Box 2
   (C) Box 3
   (D) Box 4

24. Which of these would be a correct answer for Box 6?

   (A) A check mark
   (B) 5/20/06
   (C) 5/20/06 to 6/1/06
   (D) Michelle McDermott

25. Which of these would be a correct answer for Box 7?

   (A) A check mark
   (B) 1/20/06
   (C) 510 Crescent Boulevard
   (D) 07046

QUESTIONS 26–30 REFER TO THE FOLLOWING GRAPHIC.

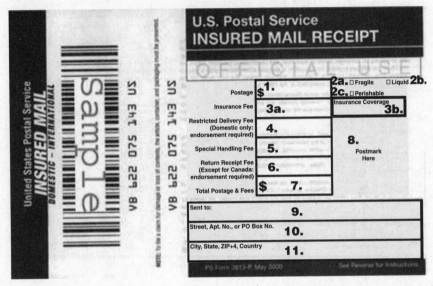

26. Where would you check that the item is perishable?

    (A) Box 2a
    (B) Box 2b
    (C) Box 2c
    (D) Box 3b

27. Where would you enter the total postage and fees?

    (A) Box 1
    (B) Box 3a
    (C) Box 5
    (D) Box 7

28. What would be the correct entry for Box 8?

    (A) A check mark
    (B) A postmark
    (C) $2.50
    (D) 12456

29. If the item was being mailed to a foreign country, which box could NOT be completed?

    (A) Box 1
    (B) Box 3b
    (C) Box 4
    (D) Box 5

30. You could enter fees in all of the following boxes EXCEPT

    (A) Box 1
    (B) Box 2a
    (C) Box 3a
    (D) Box 4

STOP   End of Forms Completion section. If you finish before time is up, check your work on this section only. Do not go to the next section until the signal is given.

CODING

36 QUESTIONS • 6 MINUTES

Directions: Work through items 1 through 36 assigning a code to each item based on the Coding Guide below. Mark your answers on the answer sheet. Work quickly and accurately.

Coding Guide	
Address Range	**Delivery Route**
100–199 N. Broad Avenue 50–250 E. 12th Street 10–25 E. Chestnut Street	**(A)**
200–500 N. Broad Avenue 26–70 E. Chestnut Street	**(B)**
20–35 Rural Route 2 7000–15000 S. Broad Avenue 300–1000 S. Chester Road	**(C)**
All mail that doesn't fall into one of the address ranges listed above.	**(D)**

	Address	**Delivery Route**			
1.	105 N. Broad Avenue	(A)	(B)	(C)	(D)
2.	52 E. Chestnut Street	(A)	(B)	(C)	(D)
3.	220 N. Brook Street	(A)	(B)	(C)	(D)
4.	195 E. 12th Street	(A)	(B)	(C)	(D)
5.	68 E. Chestnut Street	(A)	(B)	(C)	(D)
6.	28 Rural Route 2	(A)	(B)	(C)	(D)
7.	7801 S. Broad Avenue	(A)	(B)	(C)	(D)
8.	10 Rural Route 2	(A)	(B)	(C)	(D)
9.	42 Rural Route 2	(A)	(B)	(C)	(D)
10.	72 E. 12th Street	(A)	(B)	(C)	(D)
11.	152 N. Brook Street	(A)	(B)	(C)	(D)
12.	9500 S. Broad Avenue	(A)	(B)	(C)	(D)
13.	900 S. Chester Road	(A)	(B)	(C)	(D)
14.	1000 N. Broad Avenue	(A)	(B)	(C)	(D)
15.	401 N. Broad Avenue	(A)	(B)	(C)	(D)
16.	76 E. Chestnut Street	(A)	(B)	(C)	(D)
17.	368 N. Broad Avenue	(A)	(B)	(C)	(D)
18.	8620 S. Broad Avenue	(A)	(B)	(C)	(D)

	Address		Delivery Route		
19.	1201 S. Clement Street	(A)	(B)	(C)	(D)
20.	14 Rural Route 2	(A)	(B)	(C)	(D)
21.	15 E. Chestnut Street	(A)	(B)	(C)	(D)
22.	1250 E. 12th Street	(A)	(B)	(C)	(D)
23.	59 W. Chestnut Street	(A)	(B)	(C)	(D)
24.	28 Rural Route 2	(A)	(B)	(C)	(D)
25.	1400 S. Broad Avenue	(A)	(B)	(C)	(D)
26.	305 S. Chester Road	(A)	(B)	(C)	(D)
27.	178 N. Broad Avenue	(A)	(B)	(C)	(D)
28.	15101 N. Broad Avenue	(A)	(B)	(C)	(D)
29.	59 E. Chestnut Street	(A)	(B)	(C)	(D)
30.	99 E. 12th Street	(A)	(B)	(C)	(D)
31.	7000 S. Brook Street	(A)	(B)	(C)	(D)
32.	249 N. Broad Avenue	(A)	(B)	(C)	(D)
33.	30 Rural Route 2	(A)	(B)	(C)	(D)
34.	1049 S. Chester Road	(A)	(B)	(C)	(D)
35.	19 E. Chestnut Street	(A)	(B)	(C)	(D)
36.	1000 S. Broad Avenue	(A)	(B)	(C)	(D)

STOP   End of Coding section. If you finish before time is up, check your work on this section only. Do not go to the next section until the signal is given.

FOLLOWING ORAL INSTRUCTIONS

25 MINUTES

> **Directions:** When you are ready to try this test, give the following instructions to a friend and have the friend read them aloud to you at the rate of 80 words per minute. Do NOT read them to yourself. Your friend will need a watch with a second hand. Listen carefully and do exactly what your friend tells you to do with the worksheet and with the answer sheet. Your friend will tell you what to do with each item on the worksheet. After each set of instructions, your friend will give you time to darken the answer space on the answer sheet. Since B and D sound very much alike, your friend will say "B as in baker" when he or she means B and "D as in dog" when he or she means D.

BEFORE PROCEEDING FURTHER, TEAR OUT THE WORKSHEET ON PAGES 235–236 OF THIS TEST. THEN HAND THIS BOOK TO YOUR FRIEND.

To the person who is to read the instructions: The instructions are to be read at the rate of 80 words per minute. Do not read aloud the material in parentheses. Once you have begun the test itself, do not repeat any instructions. The next three paragraphs consist of approximately 120 words. Read these three paragraphs aloud to the candidate in about one and one-half minutes. You may reread these paragraphs as often as necessary to establish an 80-words-per-minute reading speed.

READ ALOUD TO THE CANDIDATE

On the job, you will have to listen to directions and then do what you have been told to do. In this test, I will read instructions to you. Try to understand them as I read them; I cannot repeat them. Once we begin, you may not ask any questions until the end of the test.

On the job, you won't have to deal with pictures, numbers, and letters like those in the test, but you will have to listen to instructions and follow them. We are using this test to see how well you can follow instructions.

You are to mark your test booklet according to the instructions that I'll read to you. After each set of instructions, I'll give you time to record your answers on the separate answer sheet.

THE ACTUAL TEST BEGINS NOW.

Look at line 1 on your worksheet. (Pause slightly.) Underline the fifth number on line 1. (Pause 2 seconds.) Now, on your answer sheet, find the number you have underlined and mark D as in dog. (Pause 5 seconds.)

Now look at line 2 on your worksheet. (Pause slightly.) In each box that contains a vowel, write that vowel next to the number in the box. (Pause 5 seconds.) Now, on your answer sheet, darken the answer spaces for the number-letter combinations in the box or boxes in which you just wrote. (Pause 10 seconds.)

Look at line 3 on your worksheet. (Pause slightly.) Find the smallest number on line 3 and multiply it by 2. Write the number at the end of line 3. (Pause 5 seconds.) Now, on your answer sheet, darken answer space (C) for that number. (Pause 5 seconds.)

Look at line 3 again. (Pause slightly.) Divide the third number by 10 and write that number at the end of the line. (Pause 2 seconds.) Now, on your answer sheet, darken answer space (A) for the number you just wrote. (Pause 5 seconds.)

Now look at line 4 on your worksheet. (Pause slightly.) Mail for Detroit and Hartford is to be put in box 3. (Pause slightly.) Mail for Cleveland and St. Louis is to be put in box 26. (Pause slightly.) Write C in the box in which you put mail for St. Louis. (Pause 2 seconds.) Now, on your answer sheet, darken the answer space for the number-letter combination that is in the box you just wrote in. (Pause 5 seconds.)

Look at line 5 on your worksheet. (Pause slightly.) Write B as in baker on the line next to the highest number. (Pause 2 seconds.) Now, on your answer sheet, darken the answer space for the number-letter combination in the circle in which you just wrote. (Pause 5 seconds.)

Look at line 5 again. (Pause slightly.) Write the letter C on the line next to the lowest number. (Pause 2 seconds.) Now, on your answer sheet, darken the answer space for the number-letter combination in the circle in which you just wrote. (Pause 5 seconds.)

Look at the boxes and words on line 6 of your worksheet. (Pause 2 seconds.) In Box 1, write the first letter of the third word. (Pause 5 seconds.) In Box 2, write the last letter of the first word. (Pause 5 seconds.) In Box 3, write the last letter of the second word. (Pause 5 seconds.) Now, on your answer sheet, darken answer spaces for the number-letter combinations in all three boxes. (Pause 15 seconds.)

Look at line 7 on your worksheet. (Pause slightly.) Write the number 33 next to the letter in the mid-size circle. (Pause 2 seconds.) Now, on your answer sheet, darken the answer space for the number-letter combination in the circle in which you just wrote. (Pause 5 seconds.)

Look at line 8 on your worksheet. (Pause slightly.) If July comes before June, write D as in dog on the line after the second number; if not, write A on the line after the first number. (Pause 10 seconds.) Now, on your answer sheet, darken the answer space for the number-letter combination you just wrote. (Pause 5 seconds.)

Look at line 9 on your worksheet. (Pause slightly.) The number on each sack represents the number of pieces of mail in that sack. Next to the letter, write the last two figures of the sack containing the most pieces of mail. (Pause 2 seconds.) On your answer sheet, darken the answer space for the number-letter combination in the sack you just wrote in. (Pause 5 seconds.)

Look at line 9 again. (Pause slightly.) Now, write next to the letter the first two figures in the sack containing the fewest pieces of mail. (Pause 2 seconds.) On your answer sheet, darken the answer space for the number-letter combination in the sack you just wrote in. (Pause 5 seconds.)

Look at line 10 on your worksheet. (Pause slightly.) Answer this question: What is the sum of 8 plus 13? (Pause 2 seconds.) If the answer is 25, write 25 in the second box; if not, write the correct answer in the fourth box. (Pause 2 seconds.) Now, on your answer sheet, darken the number-letter combination in the box you just wrote in. (Pause 5 seconds.)

Look at line 10 again. (Pause slightly.) In the fifth box, write the number of ounces in a pound. (Pause 2 seconds.) Now, on your answer sheet, darken the number-letter combination in the box you just wrote in. (Pause 5 seconds.)

Look at line 11 on your worksheet. (Pause slightly.) If the number in the circle is greater than the number in the star, write B as in baker in the triangle; if not, write E in the box. (Pause 5 seconds.) Now, on your answer sheet, darken the number-letter combination in the figure you just wrote in. (Pause 5 seconds.)

Look at line 12 on your worksheet. (Pause slightly.) Draw one line under each P in line 12. (Pause 5 seconds.) Draw two lines under each Q in line 12. (Pause 5 seconds.) Count the number of Ps and the number of Qs. (Pause 5 seconds.) If there are more Ps than Qs, darken 71 (A) on your answer sheet; if there are not more Ps than Qs, darken 71 (C) on your answer sheet. (Pause 5 seconds.)

Look at line 13 on your worksheet. (Pause slightly.) Circle each odd number that falls between 65 and 85. (Pause 10 seconds.) Now, on your answer sheet, darken answer space (D) as in dog for each number that you circled. (Pause 10 seconds.)

Look at line 13 again. (Pause slightly.) Find the number that is evenly divisible by 6 and underline it. (Pause 2 seconds.) Now, on your answer sheet, darken answer space (A) for that number. (Pause 5 seconds.)

Look at line 14 on your worksheet. (Pause slightly.) Each circled time represents a pickup time from a street letter box. Find the pickup time which is furthest from noon and write the last two figures of that time on the line in the circle. (Pause 2 seconds.) Now, on your answer sheet, darken the number-letter combination that is in the circle you just wrote in. (Pause 5 seconds.)

Look at line 14 again. (Pause slightly.) Find the pickup time that is closest to noon and write the last two figures of that time on the line in the circle. (Pause 2 seconds.) Now, on your answer sheet, darken the number-letter combination that is in the circle you just wrote in. (Pause 5 seconds.)

Look at line 15 on your worksheet. (Pause slightly.) Write the highest number in the small box. (Pause 2 seconds.) Write the lowest number in the large box. (Pause 2 seconds.) Now, on your answer sheet, darken the number-letter combinations in the boxes you just wrote in. (Pause 10 seconds.)

Look at line 16 on your worksheet. (Pause slightly.) If, in the alphabet, the fourth letter on line 16 comes before the first letter on line 16, draw a line under the fourth letter (pause 2 seconds); if not, draw a line under the first letter on line 16. (Pause 2 seconds.) Now, on your answer sheet, find number 39 and darken the answer space for the letter you underlined. (Pause 5 seconds.)

Look at line 17 on your worksheet. (Pause slightly.) Find the number that does not belong on line 17 and circle that number. (Pause 2 seconds.) Now, on your answer sheet, darken answer space (D) as in dog for the number you just circled. (Pause 5 seconds.)

Look at line 17 again. (Pause slightly.) Find the number that answers this question: 60 minus 20 equals . . . and draw two lines under that number. (Pause 2 seconds.) Now, on your answer sheet, darken answer space (C) for the number under which you just drew two lines. (Pause 5 seconds.)

Look at line 18 on your worksheet. (Pause slightly.) If 3 is less than 7 and 4 is more than 6, write the number 12 in the first box (pause 5 seconds); if not, write the number 48 in the third box. (Pause 5 seconds.) Now, on your answer sheet, darken the answer space for the number-letter combination in the box you just wrote in. (Pause 5 seconds.)

Look at line 19 on your worksheet. (Pause slightly.) Draw a circle around the number that represents the product of 5 x 6. (Pause 5 seconds.) Now, on your answer sheet, find the number that you just circled and darken answer space (A) for that number. (Pause 5 seconds.)

Worksheet

Directions: Listening carefully to each set of instructions, mark each item on this worksheet as directed. Then complete each question by marking the answer sheet as directed. For each answer you will darken the answer for a number-letter combination. Should you fall behind and miss an instruction, don't become excited. Let that one go and listen for the next one. If, when you start to darken an answer space for a number, you find that you have already darkened another answer space for that number, either erase the first mark and darken the answer space for the new combination, or let the first mark stay and do not darken an answer space for the new combination. Write with a pencil that has a clean eraser. When you finish, you should have no more than one answer space darkened for each number.

1. 6   3   18   90   45   36   12

2.

B	G	E	C	A	D
25 ___	36 ___	5 ___	17 ___	82 ___	13 ___

3. 17   4   30   25   9   41

4.

```
┌──────────────┐      ┌──────────────┐
│      3       │      │      26      │
│   DETROIT    │      │   ST. LOUIS  │
│   HARTFORD   │      │   CLEVELAND  │
│  ─────────   │      │  ─────────   │
└──────────────┘      └──────────────┘
```

5.   (27 ___)   (54 ___)   (31 ___)   (76 ___)   (18 ___)

6.

12 ___	56 ___	87 ___

RED WHITE BLUE

7.   (___ D)   (___ E)   (___ A)

8. 7 ___   64 ___   31 ___

practice test

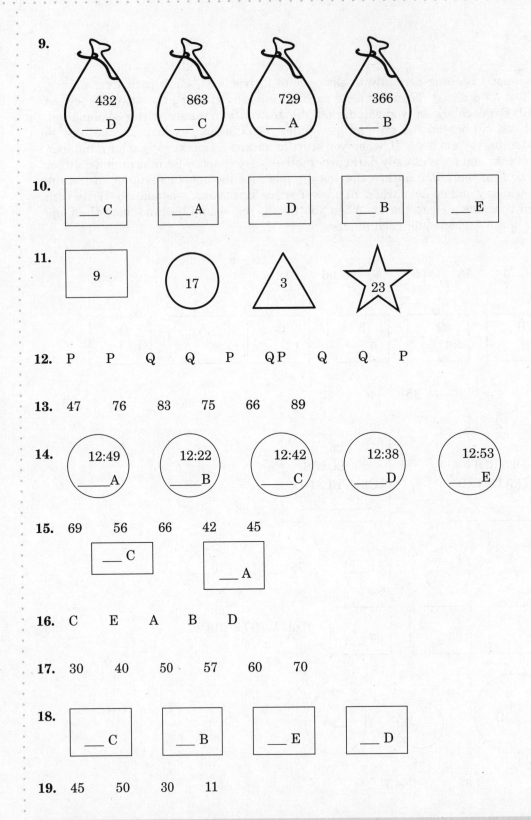

9.

432 __ D   863 __ C   729 __ A   366 __ B

10.

__ C   __ A   __ D   __ B   __ E

11.

9   17   3   23

12. P   P   Q   Q   P   Q P   Q   Q   P

13. 47   76   83   75   66   89

14.

12:49 __ A   12:22 __ B   12:42 __ C   12:38 __ D   12:53 __ E

15. 69   56   66   42   45

__ C   __ A

16. C   E   A   B   D

17. 30   40   50   57   60   70

18.

__ C   __ B   __ E   __ D

19. 45   50   30   11

STOP End of Following Oral Instructions section. If you finish before time is up, check your work on this section only. Do not go to the next section until the signal is given.

PERSONAL CHARACTERISTICS AND EXPERIENCE INVENTORY

236 QUESTIONS • 90 MINUTES

Section 1: Agree/Disagree

Directions: Read each item carefully. Decide which of the four responses ranging from **Strongly Agree** to **Strongly Disagree** fits you best. For some items, more than one response may describe you. Choose the best description and mark only that one answer on the answer sheet. It is important to answer each item, even if you are not certain which response is best for you. Also, try to work at a fairly rapid pace.

1. You like to work at a fast pace.

   (A) Strongly Agree
   (B) Agree
   (C) Disagree
   (D) Strongly Disagree

2. You like a job where you are in contact with people.

   (A) Strongly Agree
   (B) Agree
   (C) Disagree
   (D) Strongly Disagree

3. You like to have others give you directions about what to do.

   (A) Strongly Agree
   (B) Agree
   (C) Disagree
   (D) Strongly Disagree

4. You are very organized about your work and work area.

   (A) Strongly Agree
   (B) Agree
   (C) Disagree
   (D) Strongly Disagree

5. You believe in doing every task to the best of your ability.

   (A) Strongly Agree
   (B) Agree
   (C) Disagree
   (D) Strongly Disagree

6. You like looking for answers to problems.

   (A) Strongly Agree
   (B) Agree
   (C) Disagree
   (D) Strongly Disagree

7. You do not like to vary how you do a task.

   (A) Strongly Agree
   (B) Agree
   (C) Disagree
   (D) Strongly Disagree

8. You like to help others when they are having difficulty doing a task.

   (A) Strongly Agree
   (B) Agree
   (C) Disagree
   (D) Strongly Disagree

9. You never like change in the beginning but adapt to it in time.

   (A) Strongly Agree
   (B) Agree
   (C) Disagree
   (D) Strongly Disagree

10. Because all jobs are stressful, you have figured out how to manage stress.

    (A) Strongly Agree
    (B) Agree
    (C) Disagree
    (D) Strongly Disagree

11. You take on new tasks at work enthusiastically.

    (A) Strongly Agree
    (B) Agree
    (C) Disagree
    (D) Strongly Disagree

12. You need quiet to work effectively.

    (A) Strongly Agree
    (B) Agree
    (C) Disagree
    (D) Strongly Disagree

13. You find details boring.

    (A) Strongly Agree
    (B) Agree
    (C) Disagree
    (D) Strongly Disagree

14. You follow through on whatever tasks you take on.

    (A) Strongly Agree
    (B) Agree
    (C) Disagree
    (D) Strongly Disagree

15. You put other people at ease.

    (A) Strongly Agree
    (B) Agree
    (C) Disagree
    (D) Strongly Disagree

16. You find change exciting.

    (A) Strongly Agree
    (B) Agree
    (C) Disagree
    (D) Strongly Disagree

17. Details are the most important part of a task.

    (A) Strongly Agree
    (B) Agree
    (C) Disagree
    (D) Strongly Disagree

18. You enjoy the feeling of a job well done.

    (A) Strongly Agree
    (B) Agree
    (C) Disagree
    (D) Strongly Disagree

19. You do not like having to ask for additional information to do a task.

    (A) Strongly Agree
    (B) Agree
    (C) Disagree
    (D) Strongly Disagree

20. You never stop until a task is finished to the best of your ability.

    (A) Strongly Agree
    (B) Agree
    (C) Disagree
    (D) Strongly Disagree

21. You like to move around in your job.

    (A) Strongly Agree
    (B) Agree
    (C) Disagree
    (D) Strongly Disagree

22. You like helping other people solve a problem.

    (A) Strongly Agree
    (B) Agree
    (C) Disagree
    (D) Strongly Disagree

23. You like a job that involves physical activity such as lifting or moving things.

    (A) Strongly Agree
    (B) Agree
    (C) Disagree
    (D) Strongly Disagree

24. You like a job that has a number of different tasks.

    (A) Strongly Agree
    (B) Agree
    (C) Disagree
    (D) Strongly Disagree

25. You are very organized in how you do your work.

    (A) Strongly Agree
    (B) Agree
    (C) Disagree
    (D) Strongly Disagree

26. You can explain procedures easily to others.

    (A) Strongly Agree
    (B) Agree
    (C) Disagree
    (D) Strongly Disagree

27. The more complicated a task is the better you like doing it.

    (A) Strongly Agree
    (B) Agree
    (C) Disagree
    (D) Strongly Disagree

28. You do not like having to make decisions about how to get your job done.

    (A) Strongly Agree
    (B) Agree
    (C) Disagree
    (D) Strongly Disagree

29. You find criticism difficult to accept.

    (A) Strongly Agree
    (B) Agree
    (C) Disagree
    (D) Strongly Disagree

30. You like jobs that start early in the morning.

    (A) Strongly Agree
    (B) Agree
    (C) Disagree
    (D) Strongly Disagree

31. You like to work in a place with a lot of other people around.

    (A) Strongly Agree
    (B) Agree
    (C) Disagree
    (D) Strongly Disagree

32. You are comfortable with routine.

    (A) Strongly Agree
    (B) Agree
    (C) Disagree
    (D) Strongly Disagree

33. You like to set your own pace at work.

    (A) Strongly Agree
    (B) Agree
    (C) Disagree
    (D) Strongly Disagree

34. You enjoy finding different ways to accomplish tasks.

    (A) Strongly Agree
    (B) Agree
    (C) Disagree
    (D) Strongly Disagree

35. A leadership role makes you uncomfortable.

    (A) Strongly Agree
    (B) Agree
    (C) Disagree
    (D) Strongly Disagree

36. You like to figure out why something is not working.

    (A) Strongly Agree
    (B) Agree
    (C) Disagree
    (D) Strongly Disagree

37. You find change challenging, but manageable.

    (A) Strongly Agree
    (B) Agree
    (C) Disagree
    (D) Strongly Disagree

38. You always do what you say you will.

    (A) Strongly Agree
    (B) Agree
    (C) Disagree
    (D) Strongly Disagree

39. You prefer to work with a small number of people.

    (A) Strongly Agree
    (B) Agree
    (C) Disagree
    (D) Strongly Disagree

practice test

40. Repeating tasks is boring.

    (A) Strongly Agree
    (B) Agree
    (C) Disagree
    (D) Strongly Disagree

41. You worry whether you did a task as well as you could have.

    (A) Strongly Agree
    (B) Agree
    (C) Disagree
    (D) Strongly Disagree

42. You would rather have someone else in charge.

    (A) Strongly Agree
    (B) Agree
    (C) Disagree
    (D) Strongly Disagree

43. You like to work behind the scenes to get things done.

    (A) Strongly Agree
    (B) Agree
    (C) Disagree
    (D) Strongly Disagree

44. Work-related stress does not bother you.

    (A) Strongly Agree
    (B) Agree
    (C) Disagree
    (D) Strongly Disagree

45. You could be better organized about how you manage your time.

    (A) Strongly Agree
    (B) Agree
    (C) Disagree
    (D) Strongly Disagree

46. You prefer to work alone.

    (A) Strongly Agree
    (B) Agree
    (C) Disagree
    (D) Strongly Disagree

47. You do not mind sitting for long periods of time when you work.

    (A) Strongly Agree
    (B) Agree
    (C) Disagree
    (D) Strongly Disagree

48. You like a job with a number of tasks to complete.

    (A) Strongly Agree
    (B) Agree
    (C) Disagree
    (D) Strongly Disagree

49. You do not find it easy to explain things to others.

    (A) Strongly Agree
    (B) Agree
    (C) Disagree
    (D) Strongly Disagree

50. You like interaction with large numbers of coworkers.

    (A) Strongly Agree
    (B) Agree
    (C) Disagree
    (D) Strongly Disagree

51. A job with a great deal of routine would be boring.

    (A) Strongly Agree
    (B) Agree
    (C) Disagree
    (D) Strongly Disagree

52. You do not mind asking for help when you do not know how to do something.

    (A) Strongly Agree
    (B) Agree
    (C) Disagree
    (D) Strongly Disagree

53. Job satisfaction is not important to you.

    (A) Strongly Agree
    (B) Agree
    (C) Disagree
    (D) Strongly Disagree

54. You like to move from one task to another during a workday.

    (A) Strongly Agree
    (B) Agree
    (C) Disagree
    (D) Strongly Disagree

55. You work well late in the day when others begin to fade.

    (A) Strongly Agree
    (B) Agree
    (C) Disagree
    (D) Strongly Disagree

56. You would rather work past quitting time than ask for help to finish a job.

    (A) Strongly Agree
    (B) Agree
    (C) Disagree
    (D) Strongly Disagree

57. You can pick up the pace if the amount of work increases during certain periods.

    (A) Strongly Agree
    (B) Agree
    (C) Disagree
    (D) Strongly Disagree

58. You leave troubleshooting problems to someone else.

    (A) Strongly Agree
    (B) Agree
    (C) Disagree
    (D) Strongly Disagree

59. You enjoy trying new tasks.

    (A) Strongly Agree
    (B) Agree
    (C) Disagree
    (D) Strongly Disagree

60. You tend to take on too many responsibilities.

    (A) Strongly Agree
    (B) Agree
    (C) Disagree
    (D) Strongly Disagree

61. Feeling productive and appreciated at work is important to you.

    (A) Strongly Agree
    (B) Agree
    (C) Disagree
    (D) Strongly Disagree

62. You find the details of a job uninteresting.

    (A) Strongly Agree
    (B) Agree
    (C) Disagree
    (D) Strongly Disagree

63. You like someone else to set the pace at work.

    (A) Strongly Agree
    (B) Agree
    (C) Disagree
    (D) Strongly Disagree

64. You like to make decisions about how you get your work done.

    (A) Strongly Agree
    (B) Agree
    (C) Disagree
    (D) Strongly Disagree

65. You learn from criticism.

    (A) Strongly Agree
    (B) Agree
    (C) Disagree
    (D) Strongly Disagree

66. You do not like having to stand for a long time when you work.

    (A) Strongly Agree
    (B) Agree
    (C) Disagree
    (D) Strongly Disagree

67. Doing your best is your number-one work priority.

    (A) Strongly Agree
    (B) Agree
    (C) Disagree
    (D) Strongly Disagree

68. You make decisions only when you have all the facts.

- **(A)** Strongly Agree
- **(B)** Agree
- **(C)** Disagree
- **(D)** Strongly Disagree

69. You find out as much information as you can before you begin a new task.

- **(A)** Strongly Agree
- **(B)** Agree
- **(C)** Disagree
- **(D)** Strongly Disagree

70. Speed results in errors.

- **(A)** Strongly Agree
- **(B)** Agree
- **(C)** Disagree
- **(D)** Strongly Disagree

71. You always finish what you start.

- **(A)** Strongly Agree
- **(B)** Agree
- **(C)** Disagree
- **(D)** Strongly Disagree

72. You prefer jobs where you do not have to interact with a number of people.

- **(A)** Strongly Agree
- **(B)** Agree
- **(C)** Disagree
- **(D)** Strongly Disagree

73. You become tense when working under the pressure of a deadline.

- **(A)** Strongly Agree
- **(B)** Agree
- **(C)** Disagree
- **(D)** Strongly Disagree

74. You find it difficult to stop and start tasks because of interruptions.

- **(A)** Strongly Agree
- **(B)** Agree
- **(C)** Disagree
- **(D)** Strongly Disagree

75. You do not like having to deal with angry or frustrated people.

- **(A)** Strongly Agree
- **(B)** Agree
- **(C)** Disagree
- **(D)** Strongly Disagree

76. You appreciate it when a coworker puts a new person at ease.

- **(A)** Strongly Agree
- **(B)** Agree
- **(C)** Disagree
- **(D)** Strongly Disagree

77. You are very good at details.

- **(A)** Strongly Agree
- **(B)** Agree
- **(C)** Disagree
- **(D)** Strongly Disagree

78. You can always find something in the way a task is done that needs improving.

- **(A)** Strongly Agree
- **(B)** Agree
- **(C)** Disagree
- **(D)** Strongly Disagree

79. You find it difficult to ask for help when you do not know how to do something.

- **(A)** Strongly Agree
- **(B)** Agree
- **(C)** Disagree
- **(D)** Strongly Disagree

80. You find it easy to shift from one task to another.

- **(A)** Strongly Agree
- **(B)** Agree
- **(C)** Disagree
- **(D)** Strongly Disagree

81. You like being challenged in your job to find new ways of doing things.

- **(A)** Strongly Agree
- **(B)** Agree
- **(C)** Disagree
- **(D)** Strongly Disagree

82. Working at a fast pace is difficult and uncomfortable for you.

    (A) Strongly Agree
    (B) Agree
    (C) Disagree
    (D) Strongly Disagree

83. You like routine in your job.

    (A) Strongly Agree
    (B) Agree
    (C) Disagree
    (D) Strongly Disagree

84. You become bored if you have to repeat the same tasks.

    (A) Strongly Agree
    (B) Agree
    (C) Disagree
    (D) Strongly Disagree

85. You find working with a large group makes a job easier to do.

    (A) Strongly Agree
    (B) Agree
    (C) Disagree
    (D) Strongly Disagree

86. You enjoy working at difficult tasks.

    (A) Strongly Agree
    (B) Agree
    (C) Disagree
    (D) Strongly Disagree

87. You find it easy to deal with people.

    (A) Strongly Agree
    (B) Agree
    (C) Disagree
    (D) Strongly Disagree

88. You try to make the best of less than perfect situations.

    (A) Strongly Agree
    (B) Agree
    (C) Disagree
    (D) Strongly Disagree

89. When asked to do a new task, you ask very practical questions about how to do it.

    (A) Strongly Agree
    (B) Agree
    (C) Disagree
    (D) Strongly Disagree

90. You prefer doing many tasks at once rather than one after another.

    (A) Strongly Agree
    (B) Agree
    (C) Disagree
    (D) Strongly Disagree

91. You figure out how to accomplish your tasks more quickly and efficiently than others.

    (A) Strongly Agree
    (B) Agree
    (C) Disagree
    (D) Strongly Disagree

92. You adapt easily to changes in how things are done.

    (A) Strongly Agree
    (B) Agree
    (C) Disagree
    (D) Strongly Disagree

93. You are an accurate judge of how long tasks will take you.

    (A) Strongly Agree
    (B) Agree
    (C) Disagree
    (D) Strongly Disagree

94. When your ideas do not work, you can easily admit it.

    (A) Strongly Agree
    (B) Agree
    (C) Disagree
    (D) Strongly Disagree

95. You work well with people on a one-to-one basis.

    (A) Strongly Agree
    (B) Agree
    (C) Disagree
    (D) Strongly Disagree

96. You work against the clock, not against other people.

    (A) Strongly Agree
    (B) Agree
    (C) Disagree
    (D) Strongly Disagree

97. You reexamine how things are done from time to time to see if you can improve on them.

(A) Strongly Agree
(B) Agree
(C) Disagree
(D) Strongly Disagree

98. A slow, steady pace gets the job done.

(A) Strongly Agree
(B) Agree
(C) Disagree
(D) Strongly Disagree

99. You concentrate on one task at a time even if you have several to work on at the same time.

(A) Strongly Agree
(B) Agree
(C) Disagree
(D) Strongly Disagree

100. Most things that go wrong on a job are beyond your control.

(A) Strongly Agree
(B) Agree
(C) Disagree
(D) Strongly Disagree

101. Unclear instructions are the cause of most of your problems on the job.

(A) Strongly Agree
(B) Agree
(C) Disagree
(D) Strongly Disagree

102. The biggest problem on a job is the unrealistic expectations of a supervisor.

(A) Strongly Agree
(B) Agree
(C) Disagree
(D) Strongly Disagree

Section 2: Frequency

Directions: Read each item carefully. Decide which of the four responses ranging from **Very Often** to **Rarely** fits you best. For some items, more than one response may describe you. Choose the best description and mark only that one answer on the answer sheet. It is important to answer each item, even if you are not certain which response is best for you. Also, try to work at a fairly rapid pace.

103. You think things through carefully before making a decision.

(A) Very often
(B) Often
(C) Sometimes
(D) Rarely

104. Whatever you start, you finish.

(A) Very often
(B) Often
(C) Sometimes
(D) Rarely

105. You find it easy to pick up a task if you are interrupted.

(A) Very often
(B) Often
(C) Sometimes
(D) Rarely

106. You put others at ease.

(A) Very often
(B) Often
(C) Sometimes
(D) Rarely

107. You put off making decisions hoping that the problem will solve itself.

(A) Very often
(B) Often
(C) Sometimes
(D) Rarely

108. You accomplish tasks more quickly than coworkers.

(A) Very often
(B) Often
(C) Sometimes
(D) Rarely

109. You ask questions in meetings if you do not understand something.

    (A) Very often
    (B) Often
    (C) Sometimes
    (D) Rarely

110. You are the person who sets the pace at work.

    (A) Very often
    (B) Often
    (C) Sometimes
    (D) Rarely

111. You find criticism helpful in improving your job performance.

    (A) Very often
    (B) Often
    (C) Sometimes
    (D) Rarely

112. Deadlines create stress for you.

    (A) Very often
    (B) Often
    (C) Sometimes
    (D) Rarely

113. You are willing to explain something several times if a person does not understand.

    (A) Very often
    (B) Often
    (C) Sometimes
    (D) Rarely

114. You consider others' points of view in making decisions.

    (A) Very often
    (B) Often
    (C) Sometimes
    (D) Rarely

115. You lose track of the details of a task.

    (A) Very often
    (B) Often
    (C) Sometimes
    (D) Rarely

116. You restate instructions to make sure that you understand what to do.

    (A) Very often
    (B) Often
    (C) Sometimes
    (D) Rarely

117. You carry work stress into your outside life.

    (A) Very often
    (B) Often
    (C) Sometimes
    (D) Rarely

118. You wait for someone else to offer suggestions about how to complete a task.

    (A) Very often
    (B) Often
    (C) Sometimes
    (D) Rarely

119. You become impatient with people who want to do something the same way all the time.

    (A) Very often
    (B) Often
    (C) Sometimes
    (D) Rarely

120. You compliment others on a job well done.

    (A) Very often
    (B) Often
    (C) Sometimes
    (D) Rarely

121. When shown that another way would work better, you stick with the original way.

    (A) Very often
    (B) Often
    (C) Sometimes
    (D) Rarely

122. You shift from task to task without slowing your work pace.

    (A) Very often
    (B) Often
    (C) Sometimes
    (D) Rarely

123. You become impatient with people who make small talk about family and friends during work time.

    (A) Very often
    (B) Often
    (C) Sometimes
    (D) Rarely

124. You take criticism personally.

    (A) Very often
    (B) Often
    (C) Sometimes
    (D) Rarely

125. You overpromise what you can reasonably accomplish in a given period of time.

    (A) Very often
    (B) Often
    (C) Sometimes
    (D) Rarely

126. You ask for help if you cannot finish a task by the deadline.

    (A) Very often
    (B) Often
    (C) Sometimes
    (D) Rarely

127. You lose interest in what you are doing if the task is going well.

    (A) Very often
    (B) Often
    (C) Sometimes
    (D) Rarely

128. You can figure out the problem when others cannot.

    (A) Very often
    (B) Often
    (C) Sometimes
    (D) Rarely

129. You become impatient with others when you are rushing to finish a task.

    (A) Very often
    (B) Often
    (C) Sometimes
    (D) Rarely

130. You become tense when dealing with angry or frustrated people.

    (A) Very often
    (B) Often
    (C) Sometimes
    (D) Rarely

131. If you speed up doing tasks, you make errors.

    (A) Very often
    (B) Often
    (C) Sometimes
    (D) Rarely

132. Without being asked, you offer criticism of coworkers' job performance.

    (A) Very often
    (B) Often
    (C) Sometimes
    (D) Rarely

133. You are the leader in a group.

    (A) Very often
    (B) Often
    (C) Sometimes
    (D) Rarely

134. You worry about your work even after you leave the job.

    (A) Very often
    (B) Often
    (C) Sometimes
    (D) Rarely

135. You become impatient if others do not understand something as quickly as you do.

    (A) Very often
    (B) Often
    (C) Sometimes
    (D) Rarely

136. You try to calm the situation if conflicts develop.

    (A) Very often
    (B) Often
    (C) Sometimes
    (D) Rarely

137. You ask for help if you cannot finish a task by the deadline.

    (A) Very often
    (B) Often
    (C) Sometimes
    (D) Rarely

138. You plan ahead so that you do not miss any details.

    (A) Very often
    (B) Often
    (C) Sometimes
    (D) Rarely

139. You change routines to fit you rather than follow the established process.

    (A) Very often
    (B) Often
    (C) Sometimes
    (D) Rarely

140. You let others try new tasks before you yourself try them.

    (A) Very often
    (B) Often
    (C) Sometimes
    (D) Rarely

141. You become sidetracked by the details of a task.

    (A) Very often
    (B) Often
    (C) Sometimes
    (D) Rarely

142. You ignore conflict when it develops.

    (A) Very often
    (B) Often
    (C) Sometimes
    (D) Rarely

143. You are the first to notice when someone is having a bad day.

    (A) Very often
    (B) Often
    (C) Sometimes
    (D) Rarely

144. You step in to help coworkers solve problems.

    (A) Very often
    (B) Often
    (C) Sometimes
    (D) Rarely

145. You seek out complicated tasks to do.

    (A) Very often
    (B) Often
    (C) Sometimes
    (D) Rarely

146. You figure out for yourself how to accomplish a task rather than follow someone else's directions.

    (A) Very often
    (B) Often
    (C) Sometimes
    (D) Rarely

147. You encourage others to do their best at their jobs.

    (A) Very often
    (B) Often
    (C) Sometimes
    (D) Rarely

148. You lose focus on what you are doing if you do the same thing for a long period of time.

    (A) Very often
    (B) Often
    (C) Sometimes
    (D) Rarely

149. You are the one whom others ask to explain something they do not understand.

    (A) Very often
    (B) Often
    (C) Sometimes
    (D) Rarely

150. You do a job exactly as your supervisor explains the process.

(A) Very often
(B) Often
(C) Sometimes
(D) Rarely

151. You become frustrated if you cannot do a task.

(A) Very often
(B) Often
(C) Sometimes
(D) Rarely

152. Your work area is disorganized.

(A) Very often
(B) Often
(C) Sometimes
(D) Rarely

153. You see the practical issues involved in getting a task done.

(A) Very often
(B) Often
(C) Sometimes
(D) Rarely

154. You complete tasks to the best of your ability.

(A) Very often
(B) Often
(C) Sometimes
(D) Rarely

155. You are one of the crowd rather than the leader.

(A) Very often
(B) Often
(C) Sometimes
(D) Rarely

156. You take on tasks that allow you to work on your own.

(A) Very often
(B) Often
(C) Sometimes
(D) Rarely

157. You increase the pace of your work to outdo your coworkers.

(A) Very often
(B) Often
(C) Sometimes
(D) Rarely

158. You find it difficult to keep up a steady, rapid pace at tasks.

(A) Very often
(B) Often
(C) Sometimes
(D) Rarely

159. You become tense because of stress on the job.

(A) Very often
(B) Often
(C) Sometimes
(D) Rarely

160. You are the first to suggest changes in routines.

(A) Very often
(B) Often
(C) Sometimes
(D) Rarely

161. You get into arguments.

(A) Very often
(B) Often
(C) Sometimes
(D) Rarely

162. You troubleshoot problems rather than ask someone else what is wrong.

(A) Very often
(B) Often
(C) Sometimes
(D) Rarely

163. You accept others' suggestions about how a task can be done.

    (A) Very often
    (B) Often
    (C) Sometimes
    (D) Rarely

164. You set goals for yourself to accomplish certain things each day.

    (A) Very often
    (B) Often
    (C) Sometimes
    (D) Rarely

165. You offer help when someone is having difficulty with a task.

    (A) Very often
    (B) Often
    (C) Sometimes
    (D) Rarely

166. You worry whether you did a task as well as you could have.

    (A) Very often
    (B) Often
    (C) Sometimes
    (D) Rarely

167. You anticipate problems that may arise in doing a task.

    (A) Very often
    (B) Often
    (C) Sometimes
    (D) Rarely

168. You tell others how to do their jobs without their asking.

    (A) Very often
    (B) Often
    (C) Sometimes
    (D) Rarely

169. You volunteer to try out new ways of doing things.

    (A) Very often
    (B) Often
    (C) Sometimes
    (D) Rarely

170. You lose track of what you are doing if you are interrupted while you work.

    (A) Very often
    (B) Often
    (C) Sometimes
    (D) Rarely

171. You make decisions quickly rather than wait for complete information.

    (A) Very often
    (B) Often
    (C) Sometimes
    (D) Rarely

172. You confront conflict when it occurs rather than let it grow.

    (A) Very often
    (B) Often
    (C) Sometimes
    (D) Rarely

173. The details of a task can seem overwhelming to you at times.

    (A) Very often
    (B) Often
    (C) Sometimes
    (D) Rarely

174. You encourage others to try new ways of doing things.

    (A) Very often
    (B) Often
    (C) Sometimes
    (D) Rarely

175. You become impatient if others do not understand your explanation of something.

    (A) Very often
    (B) Often
    (C) Sometimes
    (D) Rarely

176. You are the one whom others turn to for help on the job.

    (A) Very often
    (B) Often
    (C) Sometimes
    (D) Rarely

177. You vary the way you accomplish tasks.

    (A) Very often
    (B) Often
    (C) Sometimes
    (D) Rarely

178. You are not satisfied with how you do your job.

    (A) Very often
    (B) Often
    (C) Sometimes
    (D) Rarely

179. You make sure that you follow through on whatever task you take on.

    (A) Very often
    (B) Often
    (C) Sometimes
    (D) Rarely

180. You ask for help if you do not understand how to do something.

    (A) Very often
    (B) Often
    (C) Sometimes
    (D) Rarely

181. You take on more responsibilities than you can handle comfortably.

    (A) Very often
    (B) Often
    (C) Sometimes
    (D) Rarely

182. You push to get your point of view across in a group.

    (A) Very often
    (B) Often
    (C) Sometimes
    (D) Rarely

183. You become angry if coworkers interrupt your work.

    (A) Very often
    (B) Often
    (C) Sometimes
    (D) Rarely

184. You find alternate ways for completing tasks.

    (A) Very often
    (B) Often
    (C) Sometimes
    (D) Rarely

185. You misjudge how long it will take to accomplish tasks.

    (A) Very often
    (B) Often
    (C) Sometimes
    (D) Rarely

186. You let others ask questions for you.

    (A) Very often
    (B) Often
    (C) Sometimes
    (D) Rarely

practice test

Section 3: Experience

Directions: Read each item carefully. Decide which response best describes your experience. For some items, more than one response may describe you. Choose the best description and mark only that one answer on the answer sheet. It is important to answer each item, even if you are not certain which response is best for you. Also, try to work at a fairly rapid pace.

187. Where do you like to work the most?

   (A) Outdoors most of the time
   (B) Outdoors all the time
   (C) Indoors most of the time
   (D) Indoors all the time
   (E) Splitting time about equally between indoor and outdoor work
   (F) Splitting time so that you work outdoors more than indoors
   (G) Splitting time so that you work indoors more than outdoors
   (H) Would not mind doing any of these

188. Most of your contact with customers has included which of the following?

   (A) Answering customers' questions
   (B) Explaining information to customers
   (C) Selling items to customers
   (D) Do not interact directly with customers
   (E) Not sure

189. Which of the following types of contact do you like the least in the work environment?

   (A) Dealing with customers
   (B) Dealing with other workers
   (C) Dealing with supervisors
   (D) Would not mind any of these
   (E) Not sure

190. Which of the following pattern of work is the most difficult for you?

   (A) Working on one task at a time
   (B) Working on several tasks at once
   (C) Shifting from task to task during a workday
   (D) Being interrupted while you work
   (E) Do not mind any of these

191. With which type of job do you have the most experience?

   (A) Operating machinery
   (B) Customer contact
   (C) Lifting and moving heavy loads of up to 70 pounds
   (D) Lifting and moving lighter loads
   (E) Handling money
   (F) Clerical work
   (G) Driving and making deliveries
   (H) Have no experience

192. When is the best time of day for you to work?

   (A) Early morning
   (B) Day
   (C) Evening
   (D) Night
   (E) Would not mind working any of these
   (F) Not sure

193. What type of work do you like the least?

  (A) Walking around throughout the work day
  (B) Driving for several hours a day
  (C) Standing or sitting in place for hours
  (D) Operating machinery all day
  (E) Lifting and moving loads
  (F) Would not mind any of these
  (G) Not sure

194. Which type of work pace do you like the most?

  (A) Fast pace
  (B) Slow pace
  (C) Steady pace: fast or slow
  (D) Moderate pace
  (E) Not sure

195. What kind of decision making do you want the most in your job?

  (A) Making all the decisions about how you do your work
  (B) Making no decisions about how you do your work
  (C) Making some decisions about how you do your work
  (D) Being asked for suggestions about how your work should be done
  (E) Would not mind any of these

196. In dealing with customers, you are best at which of the following?

  (A) Answering questions
  (B) Explaining instructions
  (C) Making change
  (D) Not sure

197. One of your greatest strengths working with people is which of the following?

  (A) Ignoring conflict
  (B) Calming angry or frustrated coworkers
  (C) Calming angry or frustrated customers
  (D) Confronting a situation before it turns into conflict
  (E) Not sure

198. Which of the following describes how you feel about working with numbers?

  (A) Not something you like to do
  (B) Something you can do but would rather not
  (C) Something you like to do
  (D) Not sure

199. Which of the following types of problem solving do you like the most?

  (A) Troubleshooting problems with machines
  (B) Helping customers with problems
  (C) Figuring out ways to get tasks done
  (D) Prioritizing your workload
  (E) Not sure

200. Which of the following is the best type of supervision for you?

  (A) Be able to set priorities with minimal supervision
  (B) Be able to set work routines with minimal supervision
  (C) Have supervisor set work routines
  (D) Have supervisor set priorities
  (E) Have freedom to change work routines to fit work flow as needed
  (F) Have freedom to change work priorities to fit work flow as needed
  (G) Not sure

201. Which of the following is the least important to you in a work environment?

  (A) Quiet
  (B) A lot of activity around you
  (C) A large number of coworkers
  (D) A small number of coworkers
  (E) Lack of pressure
  (F) Would not mind any of these
  (G) Not sure

202. Which of the following types of work do you find the most difficult to do all day?

    (A) Sit in one place
    (B) Stand in one place
    (C) Drive
    (D) Move and lift loads
    (E) Operate machinery
    (F) Deal with customers
    (G) Walk
    (H) Do not mind any of these
    (I) Not sure

203. Which of the following types of responsibility do you like the least?

    (A) Handling and being accountable for money
    (B) Explaining instructions
    (C) Answering questions
    (D) Operating machinery
    (E) Driving a vehicle
    (F) Routing shipments
    (G) Making work-related decisions
    (H) Would not mind any of these
    (I) Not sure

204. Which of the following would you like the least?

    (A) Being out in all kinds of weather
    (B) Taking the same route every day
    (C) Driving in all kinds of weather
    (D) Working on weekends
    (E) Starting early in the morning
    (F) Walking all day
    (G) Carrying loads
    (H) Would not mind any of these
    (I) Not sure

205. Which of the following tasks do you like the least?

    (A) Handling money
    (B) Dealing with customers
    (C) Memorizing information
    (D) Operating machines
    (E) Working with details
    (F) Sorting items
    (G) Would not mind any of these
    (H) Not sure

206. What amount of responsibility do you like to have in a job?

    (A) Little responsibility
    (B) Moderate amount of responsibility
    (C) Great deal of responsibility
    (D) Does not matter
    (E) Not sure

207. Most of your experience with technology has been with which of the following?

    (A) Cash registers
    (B) Data entry
    (C) Applications of databases
    (D) Word processing
    (E) Spreadsheets
    (F) Internet
    (G) Calculator
    (H) Have no experience with technology

208. How important is physical activity to you in a job?

    (A) No importance
    (B) Little importance
    (C) Moderate importance
    (D) Great importance
    (E) Not sure

209. Most of your experience with motor vehicles has been driving which of the following?

    (A) Cars
    (B) Vans
    (C) Pick-up trucks
    (D) Small trucks
    (E) Tractor-trailers
    (F) Have no experience with motor vehicles

210. Which type of work do you like the most?

    (A) Driving and making deliveries
    (B) Standing or sitting in one place
    (C) Walking around throughout the day
    (D) Operating machinery
    (E) Lifting and moving loads
    (F) Would not mind any of these
    (G) Not sure

211. Which of the following characteristics of a machine-based job do you like the least?

    (A) Working under pressure
    (B) Focusing on a machine all day
    (C) Feeding materials through a machine
    (D) Moving material to and from machines
    (E) Troubleshooting machinery problems
    (F) Machinery noise
    (G) Lack of coworker interaction
    (H) Would not mind any of these
    (I) Not sure

212. Which type of pressure do you like the least?

    (A) Working under a deadline
    (B) Working under a quota system
    (C) Competition from coworkers
    (D) Solving a problem for an angry or frustrated customer
    (E) Troubleshooting a machine problem
    (F) Would not mind any of these
    (G) Not sure

213. Which type of physical activity do you like the least?

    (A) Stretching, reaching, bending
    (B) Lifting and moving heavy loads up to 70 pounds
    (C) Lifting and moving lighter loads
    (D) Packing shipments
    (E) Pushing a handtruck
    (F) Loading goods onto trucks
    (G) Would not mind any of these
    (H) Not sure

214. Which of the following do you like the least about working with numbers?

    (A) Remembering numbers
    (B) Entering data with numbers and letters
    (C) Comparing information that includes numbers
    (D) Handling money
    (E) Coding using numbers and letters
    (F) Have no experience

215. With which of the following do you have the least experience?

    (A) Operating office machines
    (B) Using databases
    (C) Dealing with customers
    (D) Working independently
    (E) Have none of this experience

216. You have most experience working in which of the following situations?

    (A) Working independently without direct day-to-day supervision
    (B) Working as part of a small work team or work group
    (C) Working as one of many workers in a department
    (D) Supervising others
    (E) Not sure

217. What is the perfect size for a work group?

    (A) Alone
    (B) Between 2 and 10
    (C) Between 11 and 25
    (D) More than 25
    (E) Number does not matter
    (F) Not sure

218. Which of the following tasks could you do best under pressure?

    (A) Repetitive tasks
    (B) Operate machinery
    (C) Enter data in a database
    (D) Retrieve information from a database
    (E) Deal with customers
    (F) Could do all of these
    (G) Not sure

219. Which of the following tasks related to instructions do you like the least?

    (A) Reading written instructions
    (B) Following written instructions
    (C) Remembering oral instructions
    (D) Following oral instructions
    (E) Giving oral instructions to others
    (F) Writing instructions for others
    (G) Would not mind any of these
    (H) Not sure

220. Which of the following would you like least about a job?

    (A) Pressure to work quickly
    (B) Working on weekends
    (C) Working at night
    (D) Standing in one place for long periods of time
    (E) Bending, stretching, reaching, lifting, and moving loads
    (F) Troubleshooting problems with machines
    (G) Would not mind any of these
    (H) Not sure

221. Which of the following is the most difficult type of work for you?

    (A) Working with numbers
    (B) Working with details
    (C) Memorizing information
    (D) Dealing with people
    (E) Repeating the same task over and over
    (F) Doing a variety of tasks
    (G) Working quickly
    (H) Not sure

222. Which of the following describes the amount of people contact that you like the least?

    (A) Interacting with the same people on a daily basis
    (B) Interacting with many people daily—customers and coworkers
    (C) Having long periods of time during a day when you work alone
    (D) Always working around and with other people
    (E) Would not mind any of these
    (F) Not sure

223. Which work pattern do you like the most?

    (A) Varying my routine often during the day
    (B) Following the same routine every day
    (C) Having an occasional change in routine during the day
    (D) Would not mind any of these

224. Which of the following is the most likely to create tension for you?

    (A) Deadlines
    (B) Amount of work to be completed within a period of time
    (C) Supervisor's expectations
    (D) Competition from coworkers
    (E) Angry or frustrated customers
    (F) Angry coworkers
    (G) Mechanical problems with machinery
    (H) None of these

225. Which of the following best describes your experience with machines?

    (A) Operate heavy machinery
    (B) Operate light machinery
    (C) Use a computer
    (D) Troubleshoot mechanical problems
    (E) Drive a truck
    (F) Have no experience with machines

226. With which type of work do you have the least experience?

    (A) Customer contact
    (B) Handling money
    (C) Clerical work
    (D) Driving and making deliveries
    (E) Operating machinery
    (F) Lifting and moving heavy loads of up to 70 pounds
    (G) Lifting and moving lighter loads
    (H) Have none of these experiences

227. Which is the most difficult time for you to work?

    (A) Early morning
    (B) Day
    (C) Evening
    (D) Night

228. Which type of work situation do you like the most?

    (A) Interacting only with coworkers
    (B) Dealing with the public
    (C) Interacting with coworkers and the public
    (D) Would not mind any of these
    (E) Not sure

229. Which of the following is the least important to you in a job?

    (A) Steady work pace
    (B) Mix of fast and slow periods
    (C) Steady routine
    (D) Variety of tasks to accomplish
    (E) Only a few tasks to accomplish
    (F) Not sure

230. Which of the following skills is your strongest?

    (A) Working with numbers
    (B) Working with details
    (C) Dealing with people
    (D) Doing repetitive tasks without becoming bored
    (E) Not sure

231. In which type of work environment would you like least to work?

    (A) Loading dock
    (B) Open area with many machines going all day
    (C) Sales counter
    (D) Outdoors in all kinds of weather
    (E) Small work area
    (F) Would not mind any of these
    (G) Not sure

232. Which of the following types of responsibility for doing your job is most important to you?

    (A) Responsibility for setting your priorities
    (B) Responsibility for how you set up your work routine
    (C) Responsibility for how much you accomplish each day
    (D) Responsibility for how long it takes you to do tasks during the day
    (E) Does not matter
    (F) Not sure

233. Which of the following describes how you feel about handling money and making change?

    (A) Not something you like to do
    (B) One of your strengths
    (C) Something you can do but would rather not
    (D) Not sure

234. What type of physical work do you like the least?

    (A) Sitting or standing in one place all day
    (B) Driving and making deliveries
    (C) Walking
    (D) Operating machines
    (E) Lifting and moving loads
    (F) Would not mind any of these
    (G) Not sure

235. How do you prefer to get your job done?

    (A) Following a routine set by someone else
    (B) Making your own routine
    (C) Not having a regular routine in a job
    (D) Would not mind any of these

236. In how large a group do you prefer to work?

    (A) Alone
    (B) With a small group of people
    (C) With a large group of people
    (D) With a small group within a larger group
    (E) Would not mind any of these
    (F) Not sure

STOP   End of Personal Characteristics and Experience Inventory section. If you finish before time is up, check your work on this section only. Do not go to the next section until the signal is given.

ANSWER KEY AND EXPLANATIONS

Address Checking

1. D	20. A	39. D	58. D	77. A
2. D	21. D	40. D	59. D	78. D
3. D	22. A	41. D	60. D	79. D
4. A	23. D	42. A	61. D	80. A
5. D	24. D	43. D	62. D	81. D
6. D	25. A	44. A	63. D	82. D
7. A	26. D	45. D	64. D	83. D
8. D	27. A	46. D	65. D	84. A
9. A	28. D	47. D	66. D	85. D
10. D	29. A	48. D	67. A	86. D
11. D	30. D	49. D	68. D	87. D
12. D	31. D	50. A	69. D	88. D
13. A	32. D	51. D	70. D	89. D
14. D	33. D	52. D	71. D	90. A
15. D	34. A	53. D	72. D	91. D
16. A	35. A	54. A	73. D	92. D
17. D	36. D	55. A	74. D	93. A
18. A	37. A	56. D	75. D	94. A
19. D	38. A	57. A	76. A	95. A

ANALYZING YOUR ERRORS

This Address Checking Test contains 30 address pairs that are exactly alike and 65 address pairs that are different. The chart below shows what kind of difference occurs in each of the addresses that contains a difference. Check your answers against this chart to see which kind of difference you missed most often. Note also the questions in which you thought you saw a difference but there really was none. Becoming aware of your errors will help you to eliminate those errors on the actual exam.

Type of Difference	Question Numbers	Number of Questions You Missed
Difference in NUMBERS	2, 3, 10, 41, 45, 48, 59, 62, 63, 65, 66, 73, 79	
Difference in ABBREVIATIONS	8, 11, 12, 15, 17, 21, 26, 28, 30, 32, 47, 51, 52, 56, 61, 64, 72, 74, 83, 85, 86	
Difference in NAMES	1, 5, 6, 14, 19, 23, 24, 31, 33, 36, 39, 40, 43, 46, 49, 53, 58, 60, 68, 69, 70, 71, 75, 78, 81, 82, 87, 88, 89, 91, 92	
No Difference	4, 7, 9, 13, 16, 18, 20, 22, 25, 27, 29, 34, 35, 37, 38, 42, 44, 50, 54, 55, 57, 67, 76, 77, 80, 84, 90, 93, 94, 95	

Memory for Addresses

PRACTICE I

1. B	19. D	37. C	55. C	72. C
2. B	20. A	38. A	56. A	73. E
3. E	21. C	39. D	57. C	74. B
4. C	22. E	40. E	58. B	75. A
5. A	23. B	41. C	59. E	76. B
6. E	24. A	42. D	60. C	77. C
7. E	25. C	43. C	61. C	78. D
8. D	26. D	44. C	62. D	79. E
9. B	27. C	45. E	63. A	80. A
10. C	28. B	46. B	64. D	81. C
11. D	29. A	47. D	65. A	82. E
12. C	30. B	48. C	66. D	83. E
13. A	31. E	49. B	67. D	84. B
14. D	32. A	50. B	68. B	85. C
15. B	33. E	51. E	69. C	86. A
16. A	34. E	52. E	70. A	87. A
17. B	35. B	53. A	71. E	88. E
18. E	36. D	54. D		

PRACTICE II

1. C	19. A	37. B	55. A	72. C
2. D	20. C	38. A	56. B	73. C
3. B	21. E	39. C	57. C	74. D
4. A	22. B	40. C	58. A	75. C
5. E	23. A	41. C	59. B	76. A
6. D	24. E	42. E	60. C	77. A
7. B	25. B	43. A	61. A	78. E
8. A	26. C	44. D	62. E	79. A
9. D	27. B	45. A	63. A	80. D
10. D	28. D	46. D	64. E	81. B
11. A	29. A	47. D	65. B	82. D
12. E	30. E	48. D	66. A	83. B
13. D	31. E	49. E	67. B	84. C
14. C	32. B	50. E	68. D	85. E
15. C	33. E	51. D	69. E	86. C
16. A	34. C	52. C	70. B	87. A
17. C	35. A	53. E	71. D	88. A
18. E	36. B	54. D		

PRACTICE III

1. C	19. D	37. E	55. C	72. C
2. E	20. E	38. E	56. E	73. C
3. D	21. B	39. A	57. C	74. D
4. B	22. E	40. A	58. B	75. D
5. A	23. D	41. A	59. A	76. B
6. B	24. C	42. C	60. B	77. A
7. A	25. C	43. B	61. C	78. A
8. A	26. C	44. C	62. D	79. E
9. E	27. C	45. B	63. E	80. D
10. E	28. A	46. B	64. E	81. B
11. C	29. B	47. A	65. D	82. E
12. C	30. E	48. D	66. B	83. E
13. D	31. A	49. D	67. A	84. B
14. B	32. B	50. B	68. A	85. E
15. D	33. C	51. E	69. C	86. D
16. B	34. E	52. D	70. C	87. A
17. D	35. D	53. C	71. E	88. B
18. A	36. D	54. E		

ACTUAL TEST

1. D	19. E	37. A	55. A	72. A
2. B	20. E	38. D	56. A	73. C
3. B	21. E	39. C	57. C	74. D
4. E	22. B	40. D	58. D	75. B
5. A	23. E	41. E	59. B	76. E
6. B	24. C	42. B	60. E	77. C
7. A	25. A	43. B	61. A	78. B
8. E	26. E	44. D	62. A	79. C
9. C	27. A	45. E	63. D	80. B
10. D	28. D	46. E	64. D	81. A
11. D	29. A	47. A	65. C	82. E
12. B	30. E	48. C	66. C	83. A
13. A	31. C	49. B	67. E	84. E
14. D	32. E	50. D	68. A	85. D
15. A	33. A	51. C	69. A	86. D
16. C	34. B	52. B	70. C	87. B
17. B	35. E	53. E	71. E	88. A
18. C	36. B	54. C		

answers practice test 5

Number Series

1.	E	6.	A	11.	D	16.	B	20.	E
2.	E	7.	D	12.	A	17.	D	21.	D
3.	D	8.	C	13.	C	18.	A	22.	B
4.	C	9.	E	14.	B	19.	C	23.	D
5.	B	10.	B	15.	E			24.	A

1. **The correct answer is (E).** There are two alternating series, each ascending by +1. One series begins with 3, the other with S.

2. **The correct answer is (E).** The two alternating series progress at different rates. The first, beginning with 18, moves up one number at a time. The alternating series, beginning with 14, increases by +3.

3. **The correct answer is (D).** There are two alternating series, but this time two numbers of one series interpose between steps of the other series. Thus, one series reads 6 7 8 while the other reads 9 10 11 12 13 14.

4. **The correct answer is (C).** Here we have a series of mini-series. The pattern in each mini-series is −2, −2. Then the pattern repeats with the first number of the next mini-series two numbers higher than the first number of the preceding mini-series.

5. **The correct answer is (B).** The series really is +2, +1, with the number 18 appearing between the two numbers at the + 1 phase.

6. **The correct answer is (A).** Two series alternate, both ascending by +2.

7. **The correct answer is (D).** Here the progression is +2, +3; +2, +3; and so on.

8. **The correct answer is (C).** Both alternating series move up by +2.

9. **The correct answer is (E).** The series is essentially 1 2 3 4 5 6 7, but after each two numbers in the series we find the product of the multiplication of those two numbers: 1 × 2 = 2; 3 × 4 = 12; 5 × 6 = 30; 7. . . .

10. **The correct answer is (B).** The series is simply 1 2 3 4 5 6 7 8 9. After each three numbers of the series, we find the number 6.

11. **The correct answer is (D).** There are two series. The ascending series increases by +2. The descending series intervenes after every two members of the ascending series. The descending series moves in steps of −3.

12. **The correct answer is (A).** Weren't you ready for an easy one? There is no catch. The series moves by +2.

13. **The correct answer is (C).** You may feel the rhythm of this series and spot the pattern without playing around with the numbers. If you cannot solve the problem by inspection, then you might see three parallel series. The first series descends by −10 (91 81 71); the second series also descends by minus 10 (85 75 65); the third series descends by −2 (17 15 13). Or, you might see a series of mini-series. Each mini-series begins with a number 10 lower than the first number of the previous mini-series. Within each mini-series the pattern is −6 ÷ 5.

14. **The correct answer is (B).** The pattern is − 4, + 9; − 4, + 9 ... Or, there are two alternating series. The first series ascends at the rate of +5; the alternating series also ascends at the rate of +5.

15. **The correct answer is (E).** Each number appears three times, then is multiplied by 3.

16. **The correct answer is (B).** There are two alternating series. One starts at 13 and moves up by +1, and the other starts at 23 and moves down by −1.

17. **The correct answer is (D).** There are two alternating series. The first series begins with 52 and descends at the rate of −4. The alternating series begins with 10 and ascends at the rate of +10.

18. **The correct answer is (A).** The pattern is: −10, −9, −8, −7, −6, −5, −4, −3.

19. **The correct answer is (C).** The pattern is: ÷ 2, repeat the number, +10 ÷ 2, repeat the number, +10 ÷ 2, repeat the number, +10.

20. **The correct answer is (E).** You see a simple series, 83 84 85 86. . . . After each number in this series you see its mirror image, that is, the mirror image of 83 is 38; the mirror image of 84 is 48; and so forth. Or you might see a series that increases by +1 alternating with a series that increases by +10.

21. **The correct answer is (D).** The pattern is: +2, repeat the number 2 times; +3, repeat the number 3 times; +4, repeat the number 4 times.

22. **The correct answer is (B).** The pattern is −7, −7, −6, −6, −5, −5, −4, −4.

23. **The correct answer is (D).** The series consists of the squares of the whole numbers in descending order.

24. **The correct answer is (A).** You can probably get this one by inspection. If not, notice the series of mini-series. In each mini-series the pattern is 10 times the first number, 11 times the first number.

Forms Completion

1. C	7. D	13. B	19. C	25. B
2. C	8. B	14. C	20. C	26. C
3. A	9. C	15. D	21. D	27. D
4. D	10. A	16. B	22. A	28. D
5. A	11. D	17. A	23. D	29. C
6. B	12. B	18. D	24. A	30. B

1. **The correct answer is (C).** Box 5 requires a date (Month/Day). Therefore, the correct answer is (C), 12 and 20.

2. **The correct answer is (C).** Box 10 is labeled Insurance Fee. Therefore, the correct answer is (C), Box 10.

3. **The correct answer is (A).** Box 6 is labeled Return Receipt Fee. Boxes 7a, 8a, and 11b all have boxes to be checked. Therefore, the correct answer is (A), Box 6.

4. **The correct answer is (D).** Box 22 is labeled Delivery Date. Therefore, the correct answer is (D), Box 22.

5. **The correct answer is (A).** Box 4 is labeled Date Accepted. Boxes 18, 21, and 24 are all labeled Employee Signature. Therefore, the correct answer is (A), Box 4.

6. **The correct answer is (B).** Box 13b is labeled lbs and ozs. Therefore, the correct answer is (B), 3 lbs 6 oz.

7. **The correct answer is (D).** Box 11a is labeled Military 2nd Day. Therefore, the correct answer is (D), Box 11a.

8. **The correct answer is (B).** Box 14 is labeled Int'l Alpha Country Code. Therefore, the correct answer is (B), Box 14.

9. **The correct answer is (C).** Box 15 is labeled Acceptance Emp. Initials. Therefore, the correct answer is (C), Initials.

10. **The correct answer is (A).** Box 9 is labeled Place and Country. Therefore, the correct answer is (A), Paris, France.

11. **The correct answer is (D).** Box 1f is labeled Express Mail International. Therefore, the correct answer is (D), Express Mail International.

12. **The correct answer is (B).** Box 7 is labeled Addressee Name or Firm. Therefore, the correct answer is (B), Computer Programmers Worldwide.

13. **The correct answer is (B).** Box 1b is labeled Letter. Therefore, the correct answer is (B), Check Box 1b.

14. **The correct answer is (C).** Box 4 is labeled Article Number. Therefore, the correct answer is (C), Box 4.

15. **The correct answer is (D).** Box 3 is labeled Insured Value. Therefore, the correct answer is (D), $250.

16. **The correct answer is (B).** Box 3 is labeled Check Number. Therefore, the correct answer is (B), Box 3.

17. **The correct answer is (A).** Box 2 is labeled Date Delivered. Therefore, the correct answer is (A), 2/22/06.

18. **The correct answer is (D).** Box 6 is labeled MO Number(s). Boxes 1, 4, and 5 are require dates. Therefore, the correct answer is (D), Box 6.

19. **The correct answer is (C).** Box 7 is labeled Sent To. Therefore, the correct answer is (C), Ms. Dy Anne Going.

20. **The correct answer is (C).** Box 6 is labeled Postmark Here. Therefore, the correct answer is (C), Box 6.

21. **The correct answer is (D).** Box 9 is labeled City, State, Zip+4. Therefore, the correct answer is (D), Box 9.

22. **The correct answer is (A).** Box 5 is labeled Route Number. Therefore, the correct answer is (A), Rural Route 5.

23. **The correct answer is (D).** Box 4 is labeled Carrier. Therefore, the correct answer is (D), Box 4.

24. **The correct answer is (A).** Box 6 is completed by making a check mark. Therefore, the correct answer is (A), A check mark.

25. **The correct answer is (B).** Box 7 is labeled Resume Delivery of Mail (Date). Therefore, the correct answer is (B), 1/20/06.

26. **The correct answer is (C).** Box 2c is labeled Perishable. Therefore, the correct answer is (C), Box 2c.

27. **The correct answer is (D).** Box 7 is labeled Total Postage and Fees. Therefore, the correct answer is (D), Box 7.

28. **The correct answer is (B).** Box 8 is labeled Postmark Here. Therefore, the correct answer is (B), Box 8.

29. **The correct answer is (C).** Box 4 is labeled Restricted Delivery Fee (Domestic only: endorsement required). Therefore, the correct answer is (C), Box 4.

30. **The correct answer is (B).** Box 2a is labeled Fragile. Therefore, the correct answer is (B), Box 2a.

Coding

1. A	9. D	16. D	23. D	30. A
2. B	10. A	17. B	24. C	31. D
3. D	11. D	18. C	25. D	32. B
4. A	12. C	19. D	26. C	33. C
5. B	13. C	20. D	27. A	34. D
6. C	14. D	21. A	28. D	35. A
7. C	15. B	22. D	29. B	36. D
8. D				

1. **The correct answer is (A).** The address 105 N. Broad Avenue falls in one of the address ranges in the same row as Delivery Route A.

2. **The correct answer is (B).** The address 52 E. Chestnut Street falls in one of the address ranges in the same row as Delivery Route B.

3. **The correct answer is (D).** The address 220 N. Brook Street does not fall into any of the address ranges for Delivery Routes A, B, or C.

4. **The correct answer is (A).** The address 195 E. 12th Street falls in one of the address ranges in the same row as Delivery Route A.

5. **The correct answer is (B).** The address 68 E. Chestnut Street falls in one of the address ranges in the same row as Delivery Route B.

6. **The correct answer is (C).** The address 28 Rural Route 2 falls in one of the address ranges in the same row as Delivery Route C.

7. **The correct answer is (C).** The address 7801 S. Broad Avenue falls in one of the address ranges in the same row as Delivery Route C.

8. **The correct answer is (D).** The address 10 Rural Route 2 does not fall into any of the address ranges for Delivery Routes A, B, or C.

9. **The correct answer is (D).** The address 42 Rural Route 2 does not fall into any of the address ranges for Delivery Routes A, B, or C.

10. **The correct answer is (A).** The address 72 E. 12th Street falls in one of the address ranges in the same row as Delivery Route A.

11. **The correct answer is (D).** The address 152 N. Brook Street does not fall into any of the address ranges for Delivery Routes A, B, or C.

12. **The correct answer is (C).** The address 9500 South Broad Avenue falls in one of the address ranges in the same row as Delivery Route C.

13. **The correct answer is (C).** The address 900 S. Chester Road falls in one of the address ranges in the same row as Delivery Route C.

14. **The correct answer is (D).** The address 1000 N. Broad Avenue does not fall into any of the address ranges for Delivery Routes A, B, or C.

15. **The correct answer is (B).** The address 401 N. Broad Avenue falls in one of the address ranges in the same row as Delivery Route B.

16. **The correct answer is (D).** The address 76 E. Chestnut Street does not fall into any of the address ranges for Delivery Routes A, B, or C.

17. **The correct answer is (B).** The address 368 N. Broad Avenue falls in one of the address ranges in the same row as Delivery Route B.

18. **The correct answer is (C).** The address 8620 S. Broad Avenue falls in one of the address ranges in the same row as Delivery Route C.

19. **The correct answer is (D).** The address 1201 S. Clement Street does not fall into any of the address ranges for Delivery Routes A, B, or C.

20. **The correct answer is (D).** The address 14 Rural Route 2 does not fall into any of the address ranges for Delivery Routes A, B, or C.

21. **The correct address is (A).** The address 15 E. Chestnut Street falls in one of the address ranges in the same row as Delivery Route A.

22. **The correct answer is (D).** The address 1250 E. 12th Street does not fall into any of the address ranges for Delivery Routes A, B, or C.

23. **The correct answer is (D).** The address 59 W. Chestnut Street does not fall into any of the address ranges for Delivery Routes A, B, or C.

24. **The correct address is (C).** The address 28 Rural Route 2 falls in one of the address ranges in the same row as Delivery Route C.

25. **The correct answer is (D).** The address 1400 S. Broad Avenue does not fall into any of the address ranges for Delivery Routes A, B, or C.

26. **The correct answer is (C).** The address 305 S. Chester Road falls in one of the address ranges in the same row as Delivery Route C.

27. **The correct answer is (A).** The address 178 N. Broad Avenue falls in one of the address ranges in the same row as Delivery Route A.

28. **The correct answer is (D).** The address 15101 N. Broad Avenue does not fall into any of the address ranges for Delivery Routes A, B, or C.

29. **The correct answer is (B).** The address 59 E. Chestnut Street falls in one of the address ranges in the same row as Delivery Route B.

30. **The correct answer is (A).** The address 99 E. 12th Street falls in one of the address ranges in the same row as Delivery Route A.

31. **The correct answer is (D).** The address 7000 S. Brook Avenue does not fall into any of the address ranges for Delivery Routes A, B, or C.

32. **The correct answer is (B).** The address 249 N. Broad Avenue falls in one of the address ranges in the same row as Delivery Route B.

33. **The correct answer is (C).** The address 30 Rural Route 2 falls in one of the address ranges in the same row as Delivery Route C.

34. **The correct answer is (D).** The address 1049 S. Chester Road does not fall into any of the address ranges for Delivery Routes A, B, or C.

35. **The correct answer is (A).** The address 19 E. Chestnut Street falls in one of the address ranges in the same row as Delivery Route A.

36. **The correct answer is (D).** The address 1000 S. Broad Avenue does not fall into any of the address ranges for Delivery Routes A, B, or C.

Following Oral Instructions

CORRECTLY FILLED-IN ANSWER SHEET

#	Answer		#	Answer		#	Answer
1.	Ⓐ Ⓑ Ⓒ Ⓓ Ⓔ		31.	Ⓐ Ⓑ Ⓒ Ⓓ Ⓔ		60.	Ⓐ Ⓑ Ⓒ Ⓓ Ⓔ
2.	Ⓐ Ⓑ Ⓒ Ⓓ Ⓔ		32.	Ⓐ Ⓑ Ⓒ Ⓓ Ⓔ		61.	Ⓐ Ⓑ Ⓒ Ⓓ Ⓔ
3.	● Ⓑ Ⓒ Ⓓ Ⓔ		33.	● Ⓑ Ⓒ Ⓓ Ⓔ		62.	Ⓐ Ⓑ Ⓒ Ⓓ Ⓔ
4.	Ⓐ Ⓑ Ⓒ Ⓓ Ⓔ		34.	Ⓐ Ⓑ Ⓒ Ⓓ Ⓔ		63.	Ⓐ Ⓑ ● Ⓓ Ⓔ
5.	Ⓐ Ⓑ Ⓒ Ⓓ ●		35.	Ⓐ Ⓑ Ⓒ Ⓓ Ⓔ		64.	Ⓐ Ⓑ Ⓒ Ⓓ Ⓔ
6.	Ⓐ Ⓑ Ⓒ Ⓓ Ⓔ		36.	Ⓐ ● Ⓒ Ⓓ Ⓔ		65.	Ⓐ Ⓑ Ⓒ Ⓓ Ⓔ
7.	● Ⓑ Ⓒ Ⓓ Ⓔ		37.	Ⓐ Ⓑ Ⓒ Ⓓ Ⓔ		66.	● Ⓑ Ⓒ Ⓓ Ⓔ
8.	Ⓐ Ⓑ ● Ⓓ Ⓔ		38.	Ⓐ Ⓑ Ⓒ Ⓓ Ⓔ		67.	Ⓐ Ⓑ Ⓒ Ⓓ Ⓔ
9.	Ⓐ Ⓑ Ⓒ Ⓓ ●		39.	Ⓐ ● Ⓒ Ⓓ Ⓔ		68.	Ⓐ Ⓑ Ⓒ Ⓓ Ⓔ
10.	Ⓐ Ⓑ Ⓒ Ⓓ Ⓔ		40.	Ⓐ Ⓑ ● Ⓓ Ⓔ		69.	Ⓐ Ⓑ ● Ⓓ Ⓔ
11.	Ⓐ Ⓑ Ⓒ Ⓓ Ⓔ		41.	Ⓐ Ⓑ Ⓒ Ⓓ Ⓔ		70.	Ⓐ Ⓑ Ⓒ Ⓓ Ⓔ
12.	Ⓐ ● Ⓒ Ⓓ Ⓔ		42.	● Ⓑ Ⓒ Ⓓ Ⓔ		71.	Ⓐ Ⓑ ● Ⓓ Ⓔ
13.	Ⓐ Ⓑ Ⓒ Ⓓ Ⓔ		43.	Ⓐ Ⓑ Ⓒ Ⓓ Ⓔ		72.	Ⓐ Ⓑ Ⓒ Ⓓ Ⓔ
14.	Ⓐ Ⓑ Ⓒ Ⓓ Ⓔ		44.	Ⓐ Ⓑ Ⓒ Ⓓ Ⓔ		73.	Ⓐ Ⓑ Ⓒ Ⓓ Ⓔ
15.	Ⓐ Ⓑ Ⓒ Ⓓ Ⓔ		45.	Ⓐ Ⓑ Ⓒ ● Ⓔ		74.	Ⓐ Ⓑ Ⓒ Ⓓ Ⓔ
16.	Ⓐ Ⓑ Ⓒ Ⓓ ●		46.	Ⓐ Ⓑ Ⓒ Ⓓ Ⓔ		75.	Ⓐ Ⓑ Ⓒ ● Ⓔ
17.	Ⓐ Ⓑ Ⓒ Ⓓ Ⓔ		47.	Ⓐ Ⓑ Ⓒ Ⓓ Ⓔ		76.	Ⓐ ● Ⓒ Ⓓ Ⓔ
18.	Ⓐ Ⓑ ● Ⓓ Ⓔ		48.	Ⓐ Ⓑ Ⓒ Ⓓ ●		77.	Ⓐ Ⓑ Ⓒ Ⓓ Ⓔ
19.	Ⓐ Ⓑ Ⓒ Ⓓ Ⓔ		49.	Ⓐ Ⓑ Ⓒ Ⓓ Ⓔ		78.	Ⓐ Ⓑ Ⓒ Ⓓ Ⓔ
20.	Ⓐ Ⓑ Ⓒ Ⓓ Ⓔ		50.	Ⓐ Ⓑ Ⓒ Ⓓ Ⓔ		79.	Ⓐ Ⓑ Ⓒ Ⓓ Ⓔ
21.	Ⓐ ● Ⓒ Ⓓ Ⓔ		51.	Ⓐ Ⓑ Ⓒ Ⓓ Ⓔ		80.	Ⓐ Ⓑ Ⓒ Ⓓ Ⓔ
22.	Ⓐ ● Ⓒ Ⓓ Ⓔ		52.	Ⓐ Ⓑ Ⓒ Ⓓ Ⓔ		81.	Ⓐ Ⓑ Ⓒ Ⓓ Ⓔ
23.	Ⓐ Ⓑ Ⓒ Ⓓ Ⓔ		53.	Ⓐ Ⓑ Ⓒ Ⓓ ●		82.	● Ⓑ Ⓒ Ⓓ Ⓔ
24.	Ⓐ Ⓑ Ⓒ Ⓓ Ⓔ		54.	Ⓐ Ⓑ Ⓒ Ⓓ Ⓔ		83.	Ⓐ Ⓑ Ⓒ ● Ⓔ
25.	Ⓐ Ⓑ Ⓒ Ⓓ Ⓔ		55.	Ⓐ Ⓑ Ⓒ Ⓓ Ⓔ		84.	Ⓐ Ⓑ Ⓒ Ⓓ Ⓔ
26.	Ⓐ Ⓑ ● Ⓓ Ⓔ		56.	Ⓐ Ⓑ Ⓒ ● Ⓔ		85.	Ⓐ Ⓑ Ⓒ Ⓓ Ⓔ
27.	Ⓐ Ⓑ Ⓒ Ⓓ Ⓔ		57.	Ⓐ Ⓑ Ⓒ ● Ⓔ		86.	Ⓐ Ⓑ Ⓒ Ⓓ Ⓔ
28.	Ⓐ Ⓑ Ⓒ Ⓓ Ⓔ		58.	Ⓐ Ⓑ Ⓒ Ⓓ Ⓔ		87.	Ⓐ Ⓑ Ⓒ ● Ⓔ
29.	Ⓐ Ⓑ Ⓒ Ⓓ Ⓔ		59.	Ⓐ Ⓑ Ⓒ Ⓓ Ⓔ		88.	Ⓐ Ⓑ Ⓒ Ⓓ Ⓔ
30.	● Ⓑ Ⓒ Ⓓ Ⓔ						

CORRECTLY FILLED-IN WORKSHEET

1. 6   3   18   90   45   36   12

2.

B	G	E	C	A	D
25 ___	36 ___	5 _E_	17 ___	82 _A_	13 ___

3. 17   4   30   25   9   41   8   3

4.

3 DETROIT HARTFORD _____	26 ST. LOUIS CLEVELAND _C_

5. (27 ___)   (54 ___)   (31 ___)   (76 _B_)   (18 _C_)

6.

12 _B_	56 _D_	87 _E_	RED WHITE BLUE

7.   (___ D)   (___ E)   (33 A)

8. 7 _A_   64 ___   31 ___

9.

432 ___ D	863 63 C	729 ___ A	366 36 B

10.

___ C	___ A	___ D	21 B	16 E

11.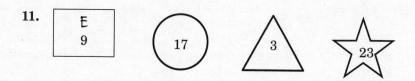

12. P̲   P̲   Q̳   Q̳   P̲   Q̳   P̲   Q̳   Q̳   P̲

13. 47   76   ⊛83⊛   ⊛75⊛   66̲   89

14. (12:49 ___A)   (12:22 22̲ B)   (12:42 ___C)   (12:38 ___D)   (12:53 53̲ E)

15. 69   56   66   42   45

   [69̲ C]   [42̲ A]

16. C   E   A   B̲   D

17. 30   40̳   50   ⊛57⊛   60   70

18. [___C]   [___B]   [48̲ E]   [___D]

19. 45   50   ⦿30⦿   11

Personal Characteristics and Experience Inventory

Answers will vary according to individual characteristics and experiences.

answers practice test 5

ANSWER SHEET PRACTICE TEST 6: U.S. POSTAL SERVICE CLERK-TYPIST EXAM

SEQUENCING

1. Ⓐ Ⓑ Ⓒ Ⓓ Ⓔ
2. Ⓐ Ⓑ Ⓒ Ⓓ Ⓔ
3. Ⓐ Ⓑ Ⓒ Ⓓ Ⓔ
4. Ⓐ Ⓑ Ⓒ Ⓓ Ⓔ
5. Ⓐ Ⓑ Ⓒ Ⓓ Ⓔ
6. Ⓐ Ⓑ Ⓒ Ⓓ Ⓔ
7. Ⓐ Ⓑ Ⓒ Ⓓ Ⓔ

8. Ⓐ Ⓑ Ⓒ Ⓓ Ⓔ
9. Ⓐ Ⓑ Ⓒ Ⓓ Ⓔ
10. Ⓐ Ⓑ Ⓒ Ⓓ Ⓔ
11. Ⓐ Ⓑ Ⓒ Ⓓ Ⓔ
12. Ⓐ Ⓑ Ⓒ Ⓓ Ⓔ
13. Ⓐ Ⓑ Ⓒ Ⓓ Ⓔ
14. Ⓐ Ⓑ Ⓒ Ⓓ Ⓔ

15. Ⓐ Ⓑ Ⓒ Ⓓ Ⓔ
16. Ⓐ Ⓑ Ⓒ Ⓓ Ⓔ
17. Ⓐ Ⓑ Ⓒ Ⓓ Ⓔ
18. Ⓐ Ⓑ Ⓒ Ⓓ Ⓔ
19. Ⓐ Ⓑ Ⓒ Ⓓ Ⓔ
20. Ⓐ Ⓑ Ⓒ Ⓓ Ⓔ

COMPARISONS

21. Ⓐ Ⓑ Ⓒ Ⓓ Ⓔ
22. Ⓐ Ⓑ Ⓒ Ⓓ Ⓔ
23. Ⓐ Ⓑ Ⓒ Ⓓ Ⓔ
24. Ⓐ Ⓑ Ⓒ Ⓓ Ⓔ
25. Ⓐ Ⓑ Ⓒ Ⓓ Ⓔ
26. Ⓐ Ⓑ Ⓒ Ⓓ Ⓔ
27. Ⓐ Ⓑ Ⓒ Ⓓ Ⓔ
28. Ⓐ Ⓑ Ⓒ Ⓓ Ⓔ
29. Ⓐ Ⓑ Ⓒ Ⓓ Ⓔ
30. Ⓐ Ⓑ Ⓒ Ⓓ Ⓔ

31. Ⓐ Ⓑ Ⓒ Ⓓ Ⓔ
32. Ⓐ Ⓑ Ⓒ Ⓓ Ⓔ
33. Ⓐ Ⓑ Ⓒ Ⓓ Ⓔ
34. Ⓐ Ⓑ Ⓒ Ⓓ Ⓔ
35. Ⓐ Ⓑ Ⓒ Ⓓ Ⓔ
36. Ⓐ Ⓑ Ⓒ Ⓓ Ⓔ
37. Ⓐ Ⓑ Ⓒ Ⓓ Ⓔ
38. Ⓐ Ⓑ Ⓒ Ⓓ Ⓔ
39. Ⓐ Ⓑ Ⓒ Ⓓ Ⓔ
40. Ⓐ Ⓑ Ⓒ Ⓓ Ⓔ

41. Ⓐ Ⓑ Ⓒ Ⓓ Ⓔ
42. Ⓐ Ⓑ Ⓒ Ⓓ Ⓔ
43. Ⓐ Ⓑ Ⓒ Ⓓ Ⓔ
44. Ⓐ Ⓑ Ⓒ Ⓓ Ⓔ
45. Ⓐ Ⓑ Ⓒ Ⓓ Ⓔ
46. Ⓐ Ⓑ Ⓒ Ⓓ Ⓔ
47. Ⓐ Ⓑ Ⓒ Ⓓ Ⓔ
48. Ⓐ Ⓑ Ⓒ Ⓓ Ⓔ
49. Ⓐ Ⓑ Ⓒ Ⓓ Ⓔ
50. Ⓐ Ⓑ Ⓒ Ⓓ Ⓔ

SPELLING

51. Ⓐ Ⓑ Ⓒ Ⓓ Ⓔ
52. Ⓐ Ⓑ Ⓒ Ⓓ Ⓔ
53. Ⓐ Ⓑ Ⓒ Ⓓ Ⓔ
54. Ⓐ Ⓑ Ⓒ Ⓓ Ⓔ
55. Ⓐ Ⓑ Ⓒ Ⓓ Ⓔ
56. Ⓐ Ⓑ Ⓒ Ⓓ Ⓔ
57. Ⓐ Ⓑ Ⓒ Ⓓ Ⓔ

58. Ⓐ Ⓑ Ⓒ Ⓓ Ⓔ
59. Ⓐ Ⓑ Ⓒ Ⓓ Ⓔ
60. Ⓐ Ⓑ Ⓒ Ⓓ Ⓔ
61. Ⓐ Ⓑ Ⓒ Ⓓ Ⓔ
62. Ⓐ Ⓑ Ⓒ Ⓓ Ⓔ
63. Ⓐ Ⓑ Ⓒ Ⓓ Ⓔ
64. Ⓐ Ⓑ Ⓒ Ⓓ Ⓔ

65. Ⓐ Ⓑ Ⓒ Ⓓ Ⓔ
66. Ⓐ Ⓑ Ⓒ Ⓓ Ⓔ
67. Ⓐ Ⓑ Ⓒ Ⓓ Ⓔ
68. Ⓐ Ⓑ Ⓒ Ⓓ Ⓔ
69. Ⓐ Ⓑ Ⓒ Ⓓ Ⓔ
70. Ⓐ Ⓑ Ⓒ Ⓓ Ⓔ

answer sheet

COMPUTATIONS

71. Ⓐ Ⓑ Ⓒ Ⓓ Ⓔ
72. Ⓐ Ⓑ Ⓒ Ⓓ Ⓔ
73. Ⓐ Ⓑ Ⓒ Ⓓ Ⓔ
74. Ⓐ Ⓑ Ⓒ Ⓓ Ⓔ
75. Ⓐ Ⓑ Ⓒ Ⓓ Ⓔ

76. Ⓐ Ⓑ Ⓒ Ⓓ Ⓔ
77. Ⓐ Ⓑ Ⓒ Ⓓ Ⓔ
78. Ⓐ Ⓑ Ⓒ Ⓓ Ⓔ
79. Ⓐ Ⓑ Ⓒ Ⓓ Ⓔ
80. Ⓐ Ⓑ Ⓒ Ⓓ Ⓔ

81. Ⓐ Ⓑ Ⓒ Ⓓ Ⓔ
82. Ⓐ Ⓑ Ⓒ Ⓓ Ⓔ
83. Ⓐ Ⓑ Ⓒ Ⓓ Ⓔ
84. Ⓐ Ⓑ Ⓒ Ⓓ Ⓔ
85. Ⓐ Ⓑ Ⓒ Ⓓ Ⓔ

VERBAL ABILITY

86. Ⓐ Ⓑ Ⓒ Ⓓ Ⓔ
87. Ⓐ Ⓑ Ⓒ Ⓓ Ⓔ
88. Ⓐ Ⓑ Ⓒ Ⓓ Ⓔ
89. Ⓐ Ⓑ Ⓒ Ⓓ Ⓔ
90. Ⓐ Ⓑ Ⓒ Ⓓ Ⓔ
91. Ⓐ Ⓑ Ⓒ Ⓓ Ⓔ
92. Ⓐ Ⓑ Ⓒ Ⓓ Ⓔ
93. Ⓐ Ⓑ Ⓒ Ⓓ Ⓔ
94. Ⓐ Ⓑ Ⓒ Ⓓ Ⓔ
95. Ⓐ Ⓑ Ⓒ Ⓓ Ⓔ
96. Ⓐ Ⓑ Ⓒ Ⓓ Ⓔ
97. Ⓐ Ⓑ Ⓒ Ⓓ Ⓔ
98. Ⓐ Ⓑ Ⓒ Ⓓ Ⓔ
99. Ⓐ Ⓑ Ⓒ Ⓓ Ⓔ
100. Ⓐ Ⓑ Ⓒ Ⓓ Ⓔ
101. Ⓐ Ⓑ Ⓒ Ⓓ Ⓔ
102. Ⓐ Ⓑ Ⓒ Ⓓ Ⓔ
103. Ⓐ Ⓑ Ⓒ Ⓓ Ⓔ
104. Ⓐ Ⓑ Ⓒ Ⓓ Ⓔ

105. Ⓐ Ⓑ Ⓒ Ⓓ Ⓔ
106. Ⓐ Ⓑ Ⓒ Ⓓ Ⓔ
107. Ⓐ Ⓑ Ⓒ Ⓓ Ⓔ
108. Ⓐ Ⓑ Ⓒ Ⓓ Ⓔ
109. Ⓐ Ⓑ Ⓒ Ⓓ Ⓔ
110. Ⓐ Ⓑ Ⓒ Ⓓ Ⓔ
111. Ⓐ Ⓑ Ⓒ Ⓓ Ⓔ
112. Ⓐ Ⓑ Ⓒ Ⓓ Ⓔ
113. Ⓐ Ⓑ Ⓒ Ⓓ Ⓔ
114. Ⓐ Ⓑ Ⓒ Ⓓ Ⓔ
115. Ⓐ Ⓑ Ⓒ Ⓓ Ⓔ
116. Ⓐ Ⓑ Ⓒ Ⓓ Ⓔ
117. Ⓐ Ⓑ Ⓒ Ⓓ Ⓔ
118. Ⓐ Ⓑ Ⓒ Ⓓ Ⓔ
119. Ⓐ Ⓑ Ⓒ Ⓓ Ⓔ
120. Ⓐ Ⓑ Ⓒ Ⓓ Ⓔ
121. Ⓐ Ⓑ Ⓒ Ⓓ Ⓔ
122. Ⓐ Ⓑ Ⓒ Ⓓ Ⓔ

123. Ⓐ Ⓑ Ⓒ Ⓓ Ⓔ
124. Ⓐ Ⓑ Ⓒ Ⓓ Ⓔ
125. Ⓐ Ⓑ Ⓒ Ⓓ Ⓔ
126. Ⓐ Ⓑ Ⓒ Ⓓ Ⓔ
127. Ⓐ Ⓑ Ⓒ Ⓓ Ⓔ
128. Ⓐ Ⓑ Ⓒ Ⓓ Ⓔ
129. Ⓐ Ⓑ Ⓒ Ⓓ Ⓔ
130. Ⓐ Ⓑ Ⓒ Ⓓ Ⓔ
131. Ⓐ Ⓑ Ⓒ Ⓓ Ⓔ
132. Ⓐ Ⓑ Ⓒ Ⓓ Ⓔ
133. Ⓐ Ⓑ Ⓒ Ⓓ Ⓔ
134. Ⓐ Ⓑ Ⓒ Ⓓ Ⓔ
135. Ⓐ Ⓑ Ⓒ Ⓓ Ⓔ
136. Ⓐ Ⓑ Ⓒ Ⓓ Ⓔ
137. Ⓐ Ⓑ Ⓒ Ⓓ Ⓔ
138. Ⓐ Ⓑ Ⓒ Ⓓ Ⓔ
139. Ⓐ Ⓑ Ⓒ Ⓓ Ⓔ
140. Ⓐ Ⓑ Ⓒ Ⓓ Ⓔ

DICTATION TRANSCRIPT

1. Ⓐ Ⓑ Ⓒ Ⓓ Ⓔ
2. Ⓐ Ⓑ Ⓒ Ⓓ Ⓔ
3. Ⓐ Ⓑ Ⓒ Ⓓ Ⓔ
4. Ⓐ Ⓑ Ⓒ Ⓓ Ⓔ
5. Ⓐ Ⓑ Ⓒ Ⓓ Ⓔ
6. Ⓐ Ⓑ Ⓒ Ⓓ Ⓔ
7. Ⓐ Ⓑ Ⓒ Ⓓ Ⓔ
8. Ⓐ Ⓑ Ⓒ Ⓓ Ⓔ
9. Ⓐ Ⓑ Ⓒ Ⓓ Ⓔ
10. Ⓐ Ⓑ Ⓒ Ⓓ Ⓔ
11. Ⓐ Ⓑ Ⓒ Ⓓ Ⓔ
12. Ⓐ Ⓑ Ⓒ Ⓓ Ⓔ
13. Ⓐ Ⓑ Ⓒ Ⓓ Ⓔ
14. Ⓐ Ⓑ Ⓒ Ⓓ Ⓔ
15. Ⓐ Ⓑ Ⓒ Ⓓ Ⓔ
16. Ⓐ Ⓑ Ⓒ Ⓓ Ⓔ
17. Ⓐ Ⓑ Ⓒ Ⓓ Ⓔ
18. Ⓐ Ⓑ Ⓒ Ⓓ Ⓔ
19. Ⓐ Ⓑ Ⓒ Ⓓ Ⓔ
20. Ⓐ Ⓑ Ⓒ Ⓓ Ⓔ
21. Ⓐ Ⓑ Ⓒ Ⓓ Ⓔ
22. Ⓐ Ⓑ Ⓒ Ⓓ Ⓔ
23. Ⓐ Ⓑ Ⓒ Ⓓ Ⓔ
24. Ⓐ Ⓑ Ⓒ Ⓓ Ⓔ
25. Ⓐ Ⓑ Ⓒ Ⓓ Ⓔ
26. Ⓐ Ⓑ Ⓒ Ⓓ Ⓔ
27. Ⓐ Ⓑ Ⓒ Ⓓ Ⓔ
28. Ⓐ Ⓑ Ⓒ Ⓓ Ⓔ
29. Ⓐ Ⓑ Ⓒ Ⓓ Ⓔ
30. Ⓐ Ⓑ Ⓒ Ⓓ Ⓔ
31. Ⓐ Ⓑ Ⓒ Ⓓ Ⓔ
32. Ⓐ Ⓑ Ⓒ Ⓓ Ⓔ
33. Ⓐ Ⓑ Ⓒ Ⓓ Ⓔ
34. Ⓐ Ⓑ Ⓒ Ⓓ Ⓔ
35. Ⓐ Ⓑ Ⓒ Ⓓ Ⓔ
36. Ⓐ Ⓑ Ⓒ Ⓓ Ⓔ
37. Ⓐ Ⓑ Ⓒ Ⓓ Ⓔ
38. Ⓐ Ⓑ Ⓒ Ⓓ Ⓔ

39. Ⓐ Ⓑ Ⓒ Ⓓ Ⓔ
40. Ⓐ Ⓑ Ⓒ Ⓓ Ⓔ
41. Ⓐ Ⓑ Ⓒ Ⓓ Ⓔ
42. Ⓐ Ⓑ Ⓒ Ⓓ Ⓔ
43. Ⓐ Ⓑ Ⓒ Ⓓ Ⓔ
44. Ⓐ Ⓑ Ⓒ Ⓓ Ⓔ
45. Ⓐ Ⓑ Ⓒ Ⓓ Ⓔ
46. Ⓐ Ⓑ Ⓒ Ⓓ Ⓔ
47. Ⓐ Ⓑ Ⓒ Ⓓ Ⓔ
48. Ⓐ Ⓑ Ⓒ Ⓓ Ⓔ
49. Ⓐ Ⓑ Ⓒ Ⓓ Ⓔ
50. Ⓐ Ⓑ Ⓒ Ⓓ Ⓔ
51. Ⓐ Ⓑ Ⓒ Ⓓ Ⓔ
52. Ⓐ Ⓑ Ⓒ Ⓓ Ⓔ
53. Ⓐ Ⓑ Ⓒ Ⓓ Ⓔ
54. Ⓐ Ⓑ Ⓒ Ⓓ Ⓔ
55. Ⓐ Ⓑ Ⓒ Ⓓ Ⓔ
56. Ⓐ Ⓑ Ⓒ Ⓓ Ⓔ
57. Ⓐ Ⓑ Ⓒ Ⓓ Ⓔ
58. Ⓐ Ⓑ Ⓒ Ⓓ Ⓔ
59. Ⓐ Ⓑ Ⓒ Ⓓ Ⓔ
60. Ⓐ Ⓑ Ⓒ Ⓓ Ⓔ
61. Ⓐ Ⓑ Ⓒ Ⓓ Ⓔ
62. Ⓐ Ⓑ Ⓒ Ⓓ Ⓔ
63. Ⓐ Ⓑ Ⓒ Ⓓ Ⓔ
64. Ⓐ Ⓑ Ⓒ Ⓓ Ⓔ
65. Ⓐ Ⓑ Ⓒ Ⓓ Ⓔ
66. Ⓐ Ⓑ Ⓒ Ⓓ Ⓔ
67. Ⓐ Ⓑ Ⓒ Ⓓ Ⓔ
68. Ⓐ Ⓑ Ⓒ Ⓓ Ⓔ
69. Ⓐ Ⓑ Ⓒ Ⓓ Ⓔ
70. Ⓐ Ⓑ Ⓒ Ⓓ Ⓔ
71. Ⓐ Ⓑ Ⓒ Ⓓ Ⓔ
72. Ⓐ Ⓑ Ⓒ Ⓓ Ⓔ
73. Ⓐ Ⓑ Ⓒ Ⓓ Ⓔ
74. Ⓐ Ⓑ Ⓒ Ⓓ Ⓔ
75. Ⓐ Ⓑ Ⓒ Ⓓ Ⓔ
76. Ⓐ Ⓑ Ⓒ Ⓓ Ⓔ

77. Ⓐ Ⓑ Ⓒ Ⓓ Ⓔ
78. Ⓐ Ⓑ Ⓒ Ⓓ Ⓔ
79. Ⓐ Ⓑ Ⓒ Ⓓ Ⓔ
80. Ⓐ Ⓑ Ⓒ Ⓓ Ⓔ
81. Ⓐ Ⓑ Ⓒ Ⓓ Ⓔ
82. Ⓐ Ⓑ Ⓒ Ⓓ Ⓔ
83. Ⓐ Ⓑ Ⓒ Ⓓ Ⓔ
84. Ⓐ Ⓑ Ⓒ Ⓓ Ⓔ
85. Ⓐ Ⓑ Ⓒ Ⓓ Ⓔ
86. Ⓐ Ⓑ Ⓒ Ⓓ Ⓔ
87. Ⓐ Ⓑ Ⓒ Ⓓ Ⓔ
88. Ⓐ Ⓑ Ⓒ Ⓓ Ⓔ
89. Ⓐ Ⓑ Ⓒ Ⓓ Ⓔ
90. Ⓐ Ⓑ Ⓒ Ⓓ Ⓔ
91. Ⓐ Ⓑ Ⓒ Ⓓ Ⓔ
92. Ⓐ Ⓑ Ⓒ Ⓓ Ⓔ
93. Ⓐ Ⓑ Ⓒ Ⓓ Ⓔ
94. Ⓐ Ⓑ Ⓒ Ⓓ Ⓔ
95. Ⓐ Ⓑ Ⓒ Ⓓ Ⓔ
96. Ⓐ Ⓑ Ⓒ Ⓓ Ⓔ
97. Ⓐ Ⓑ Ⓒ Ⓓ Ⓔ
98. Ⓐ Ⓑ Ⓒ Ⓓ Ⓔ
99. Ⓐ Ⓑ Ⓒ Ⓓ Ⓔ
100. Ⓐ Ⓑ Ⓒ Ⓓ Ⓔ
101. Ⓐ Ⓑ Ⓒ Ⓓ Ⓔ
102. Ⓐ Ⓑ Ⓒ Ⓓ Ⓔ
103. Ⓐ Ⓑ Ⓒ Ⓓ Ⓔ
104. Ⓐ Ⓑ Ⓒ Ⓓ Ⓔ
105. Ⓐ Ⓑ Ⓒ Ⓓ Ⓔ
106. Ⓐ Ⓑ Ⓒ Ⓓ Ⓔ
107. Ⓐ Ⓑ Ⓒ Ⓓ Ⓔ
108. Ⓐ Ⓑ Ⓒ Ⓓ Ⓔ
109. Ⓐ Ⓑ Ⓒ Ⓓ Ⓔ
110. Ⓐ Ⓑ Ⓒ Ⓓ Ⓔ
111. Ⓐ Ⓑ Ⓒ Ⓓ Ⓔ
112. Ⓐ Ⓑ Ⓒ Ⓓ Ⓔ
113. Ⓐ Ⓑ Ⓒ Ⓓ Ⓔ
114. Ⓐ Ⓑ Ⓒ Ⓓ Ⓔ

answer sheet

115. Ⓐ Ⓑ Ⓒ Ⓓ Ⓔ   119. Ⓐ Ⓑ Ⓒ Ⓓ Ⓔ   123. Ⓐ Ⓑ Ⓒ Ⓓ Ⓔ
116. Ⓐ Ⓑ Ⓒ Ⓓ Ⓔ   120. Ⓐ Ⓑ Ⓒ Ⓓ Ⓔ   124. Ⓐ Ⓑ Ⓒ Ⓓ Ⓔ
117. Ⓐ Ⓑ Ⓒ Ⓓ Ⓔ   121. Ⓐ Ⓑ Ⓒ Ⓓ Ⓔ   125. Ⓐ Ⓑ Ⓒ Ⓓ Ⓔ
118. Ⓐ Ⓑ Ⓒ Ⓓ Ⓔ   122. Ⓐ Ⓑ Ⓒ Ⓓ Ⓔ

Practice Test 6: U.S. Postal Service Clerk-Typist Exam

SEQUENCING

20 QUESTIONS • 3 MINUTES

Directions: For each question there is a name, number, or code in a box at the left and four other names, numbers, or codes in alphabetical or numerical order at the right. Find the correct space for the boxed name or number so that it will be in alphabetical and/or numerical order with the others and darken the answer space of your choice on your answer sheet.

1. | Hackett, Gerald |

(A) →
    Habert, James
(B) →
    Hachett, J.J.
(C) →
    Hachetts, K. Larson
(D) →
    Hachettson, Leroy
(E) →

2. | 159233362 |

(A) →
    58146020
(B) →
    59233162
(C) →
    59233262
(D) →
    59233662
(E) →

3. | MYP-6734 |

(A) →
    NYP-6733
(B) →
    NYS-7412
(C) →
    NZT-4899
(D) →
    PYZ-3636
(E) →

4. Bobbitt, Olivier E.

- **(A)** →
  Bobbitt, D. Olivier
- **(B)** →
  Bobbitt, Olive B.
- **(C)** →
  Bobbitt, Olivia H.
- **(D)** →
  Bobbitt, R. Olivia
- **(E)** →

5. 100102032

- **(A)** →
  00120312
- **(B)** →
  00120323
- **(C)** →
  00120324
- **(D)** →
  00200303
- **(E)** →

6. LPD-6100

- **(A)** →
  LPD-5865
- **(B)** →
  LPD-6001
- **(C)** →
  LPD-6101
- **(D)** →
  LPD-6106
- **(E)** →

7. Vanstory, George

- **(A)** →
  Vanover, Eva
- **(B)** →
  VanSwinderen, Floyd
- **(C)** →
  VanSyckle, Harry
- **(D)** →
  Vanture, Laurence
- **(E)** →

8. Fitzsimmons, Hugh

- **(A)** →
  Fitts, Harold
- **(B)** →
  Fitzgerald, June
- **(C)** →
  FitzGibbon, Junius
- **(D)** →
  FitzSimons, Martin
- **(E)** →

9. | 01066010 |

(A) →
01006040
(B) →
01006051
(C) →
01016053
(D) →
01016060
(E) →

10. | AAZ-2687 |

(A) →
AAA-2132
(B) →
AAS-4623
(C) →
ASA-3216
(D) →
ASZ-5490
(E) →

11. | Pawlowicz, Ruth M. |

(A) →
Pawalek, Edward
(B) →
Pawelek, Flora G.
(C) →
Pawlowski, Joan M.
(D) →
Pawtowski, Wanda
(E) →

12. | NCD-7834 |

(A) →
NBJ-4682
(B) →
NBT-5066
(C) →
NCD-7710
(D) →
NCD-7868
(E) →

13. | 36270013 |

(A) →
36260006
(B) →
36270000
(C) →
36270030
(D) →
36670012
(E) →

14. Freedinberg, Erma T.

(A) →
Freedenberg, Emerson
(B) →
Freedenberg, Erma
(C) →
Freedenburg, Erma E.
(D) →
Freedinburg, Erma F.
(E) →

15. Prouty, Martha

(A) →
Proutey, Margaret
(B) →
Proutey, Maude
(C) →
Prouty, Myra
(D) →
Prouty, Naomi
(E) →

16. 58006021

(A) →
58006130
(B) →
58097222
(C) →
59000599
(D) →
59909000
(E) →

17. EKK-1443

(A) →
EGK-1164
(B) →
EKG-1329
(C) →
EKK-1331
(D) →
EKK-1403
(E) →

18. D'Amato, Vincent

(A) →
Daly, Steven
(B) →
D'Amboise, S. Vincent
(C) →
Daniel, Vail
(D) →
DeAlba, Valentina
(E) →

19. | Schaeffer, Roger D. |

(A) →
Schaffert, Evelyn M.
(B) →
Schaffner, Margaret M.
(C) →
Schafhirt, Milton G.
(D) →
Shafer, Richard E.
(E) →

20. | SPP-4856 |

(A) →
PPS-4838
(B) →
PSP-4921
(C) →
SPS-4906
(D) →
SSP-4911
(E) →

STOP   End of Sequencing section. If you finish before time is up, check your work on this section only. Do not go to the next section until the signal is given.

practice test

COMPARISONS

30 QUESTIONS • 5 MINUTES

Directions: In each line across the page there are three names, addresses, or codes that are very much alike. Compare the three and decide which ones are EXACTLY alike. On your answer sheet, mark:

    (A) if **ALL THREE** names, addresses, or codes are exactly **ALIKE**
    (B) if only the **FIRST** and **SECOND** names, addresses, or codes are exactly **ALIKE**
    (C) if only the **FIRST** and **THIRD** names, addresses, or codes are exactly **ALIKE**
    (D) if only the **SECOND** and **THIRD** names, addresses, or codes are exactly **ALIKE**
    (E) if **ALL THREE** names, addresses, or codes are **DIFFERENT**

21.	Drusilla S. Ridgeley	Drusilla S. Ridgeley	Drusilla S. Ridgeley
22.	Andrei I. Toumantzev	Andrei I. Tourmantzev	Andrei I. Toumantzov
23.	6-78912-e3e42	6-78912-3e3e42	6-78912-e3e42
24.	86529 Dunwoodie Drive	86529 Dunwoodie Drive	85629 Dunwoodie Drive
25.	1592514	1592574	1592574
26.	Ella Burk Newham	Ella Burk Newnham	Elena Burk Newnham
27.	5416R-1952TZ-op	5416R-1952TZ-op	5416R-1952TZ-op
28.	60646 West Touhy Avenue	60646 West Touhy Avenue	60646 West Touhey Avenue
29.	Mardikian & Moore, Inc.	Mardikian and Moore, Inc.	Mardikian & Moore, Inc.
30.	9670243	9670423	9670423
31.	Eduardo Ingles	Eduardo Inglese	Eduardo Inglese
32.	Roger T. DeAngelis	Roger T. D'Angelis	Roger T. DeAngeles
33.	7692138	7692138	7692138
34.	2695 East 3435 South	2695 East 3435 South	2695 East 3435 South
35.	63qs5-95YT3-001	63qs5-95YT3-001	63qs5-95YT3-001
36.	2789350	2789350	2798350
37.	Helmut V. Lochner	Helmut V. Lockner	Helmut W. Lochner
38.	2454803	2548403	2454803
39.	Lemberger, WA 28094-9182	Lemberger, VA 28094-9182	Lemberger, VA 28094-9182
40.	4168-GNP-78852	4168-GNP-78852	4168-GNP-78852
41.	Yoshihito Saito	Yoshihito Saito	Yoshihito Saito
42.	5927681	5927861	5927681

43. O'Reilly Bay, LA 56212   O'Reillys Bay, LA 56212   O'Reilly Bay, LA 56212

44. Francis Ransdell   Frances Ramsdell   Francis Ramsdell

45. 5634-OotV5a-16867   5634-Ootv5a-16867   5634-Ootv5a-16867

46. Dolores Mollicone   Dolores Mollicone   Doloras Mollicone

47. David C. Routzon   David E. Routzon   David C. Routzron

48. 8932 Shimabui Hwy.   8932 Shimabui Hwy.   8932 Shimabui Hwy.

49. 6177396   6177936   6177396

50. A8987-B73245   A8987-B73245   A8987-B73245

STOP End of Comparisons section. If you finish before time is up, check your work on this section only. Do not go to the next section until the signal is given.

SPELLING

20 QUESTIONS • 3 MINUTES

Directions: Find the correct spelling of the word and darken the appropriate space on your answer sheet. If none of the spellings is correct, darken answer space (D).

51. (A) anticipate
    (B) antisipate
    (C) anticapate
    (D) none of these

52. (A) similiar
    (B) simmilar
    (C) similar
    (D) none of these

53. (A) sufficiantly
    (B) suficeintly
    (C) sufficiently
    (D) none of these

54. (A) intelligence
    (B) inteligence
    (C) intellegence
    (D) none of these

55. (A) referance
    (B) referrence
    (C) referense
    (D) none of these

56. (A) conscious
    (B) consious
    (C) conscius
    (D) none of these

57. (A) paralell
    (B) parellel
    (C) parellell
    (D) none of these

58. (A) abundence
    (B) abundance
    (C) abundants
    (D) none of these

59. (A) corregated
    (B) corrigated
    (C) corrugated
    (D) none of these

60. (A) accumalation
    (B) accumulation
    (C) accumullation
    (D) none of these

61. (A) resonance
    (B) resonence
    (C) resonnance
    (D) none of these

62. (A) benaficial
    (B) benefitial
    (C) beneficial
    (D) none of these

63. (A) spesifically
    (B) specificially
    (C) specifically
    (D) none of these

64. (A) elemanate
    (B) elimenate
    (C) elliminate
    (D) none of these

65. (A) collosal
    (B) colosal
    (C) collossal
    (D) none of these

66. (A) auxillary
    (B) auxilliary
    (C) auxiliary
    (D) none of these

67. (A) inimitable
    (B) inimitible
    (C) inimatable
    (D) none of these

68. (A) disapearance
    (B) dissapearance
    (C) disappearence
    (D) none of these

69. **(A)** appelate
    (B) appellate
    (C) apellate
    (D) none of these

70. **(A)** esential
    (B) essential
    (C) essencial
    (D) none of these

S T O P   End of Spelling section. If you finish before time is up, check your work on this section only. Do not go to the next section until the signal is given.

COMPUTATIONS

15 QUESTIONS • 8 MINUTES

Directions: In the following questions, solve each problem and find your answer among the list of suggested answers for that question. Choose (A), (B), (C), or (D) for the answer you obtained, or if your answer is not among these, darken (E) for that question.

71. 83
        − 56

(A) 23
(B) 29
(C) 33
(D) 37
(E) none of these

72. 15
        + 17

(A) 22
(B) 32
(C) 39
(D) 42
(E) none of these

73. 32
        × 7

(A) 224
(B) 234
(C) 324
(D) 334
(E) none of these

74. 39
        × 2

(A) 77
(B) 78
(C) 79
(D) 81
(E) none of these

75. 43
        − 15

(A) 23
(B) 32
(C) 33
(D) 35
(E) none of these

76. 50
        + 49

(A) 89
(B) 90
(C) 99
(D) 109
(E) none of these

77. 6)366

(A) 11
(B) 31
(C) 36
(D) 66
(E) none of these

78. 38
    × 3

(A) 111
(B) 113
(C) 115
(D) 117
(E) none of these

79. 19
   + 21

(A) 20
(B) 30
(C) 40
(D) 50
(E) none of these

80. 13
    − 6

(A) 5
(B) 7
(C) 9
(D) 11
(E) none of these

81. 6)‾180‾

(A) 29
(B) 31
(C) 33
(D) 39
(E) none of these

82. 10
    × 1

(A) 0
(B) 1
(C) 10
(D) 100
(E) none of these

83. 7)‾287‾

(A) 21
(B) 27
(C) 31
(D) 37
(E) none of these

84. 12
   + 11

(A) 21
(B) 22
(C) 23
(D) 24
(E) none of these

85. 85
   − 64

(A) 19
(B) 21
(C) 29
(D) 31
(E) none of these

S T O P End of Computations section. If you finish before time is up, check your work on this section only. Do not go to the next section until the signal is given.

VERBAL ABILITY

55 QUESTIONS • 50 MINUTES

Following Written Instructions

> **Directions:** Questions 86–140 test your ability to follow instructions. Each question directs you to darken a specific number and letter combination on your answer sheet. The questions require your total concentration because the answers that you are instructed to darken are, for the most part, NOT in numerical sequence (i.e., you would not use Number 1 on your answer sheet to answer Question 1; Number 2 for Question 2; etc.). Instead, you must darken the number and space specifically designated in each test question.

86. Look at the letters below. Draw a circle around the letter that comes first in the alphabet. Now, on your answer sheet, find Number 12 and darken the answer space for the letter you just circled.

    E   G   D   Z   B   F

87. Draw a line under the odd number below that is more than 5 but less than 10. Find this number on your answer sheet and darken space E.

    8   10   5   6   11   9

88. Divide the number 16 by 4 and write your answer on the line below. Now find this number on your answer sheet and darken answer space (A).

    _____

89. Write the letter C on the line next to the left-hand number below. Now, on your answer sheet, darken the answer space for the number-letter combination you see.

    5 _____   19 _____   7 _____

90. If in any week Wednesday comes before Tuesday, write the number 15 on the line below. If not, write the number 18. Now, on your answer sheet, darken answer space (A) for the number you just wrote.

    _____

91. Count the number of Bs in the line below and write that number at the end of the line. Now, on your answer sheet, darken answer space (D) for the number you wrote.

    A   D   A   E   B   D   C   A_____

92. Write the letter B on the line with the highest number. Now, on your answer sheet, darken the number-letter combination that appears on that line.

    16 _____   9 _____   20 _____   11 _____

93. If the product of 6 × 4 is greater than the product of 8 × 3, write the letter E on the line below. If not, write the letter C. Now, on your answer sheet find number 8 and darken the answer space for the letter you just wrote.

    _____

94. Write the number 2 in the largest circle below. Now, on your answer sheet, darken the answer space for the number-letter combination in that circle.

95. Write the letter D on the line next to the number that is the sum of 7 + 4 + 4. Now, on your answer sheet, darken the answer space for that number-letter combination.

13 _____   14 _____   15 _____   16 _____   17 _____

96. If 5 × 5 equals 25 and 5 + 5 equals 10, write the number 17 on the line below. If not, write the number 10. Now, on your answer sheet, darken answer space (E) for the number you just wrote.

_____

97. Circle the second letter below. On the line beside that letter write the number that represents the number of days in a week. Now, on your answer sheet, darken the answer space for that number-letter combination.

_____ C   _____ D   _____ B   _____ E

98. If a triangle has more angles than a rectangle, write the number 13 in the circle below. If not, write the number 14 in the square. Now, on your answer sheet, darken the space for the number-letter combination in the figure that you just wrote in.

99. Count the number of Bs below and write that number at the end of the line. Subtract 2 from that number. Now, on your answer sheet, darken answer space (E) for the number that represents 2 less than the number of Bs in the line.

B E A D E C C B B B A E B D _____

100. The numbers below represent morning pick-up times from neighborhood letter boxes. Draw a line under the number that represents the latest pick-up time. Now, on your answer sheet, darken answer space (D) for the number that is the same as the "minutes" of the time that you underlined.

9:19   10:16   10:10

101. If a person who is 6 feet tall is taller than a person who is 5 feet tall and if a pillow is softer than a rock, darken answer space 11 (A) on your answer sheet. If not, darken answer space 6 (B).

102. Write the fourth letter of the alphabet on the line next to the third number below. Now, on your answer sheet, darken that number-letter combination.

10 _____   19 _____   13 _____   4 _____

103. Write the letter B in the box containing the next to smallest number. On your answer sheet, darken the answer space for that number-letter combination.

| 10___ | 19___ | 11___ | 6___ |

104. Directly below you will see three boxes and three words. Write the third letter of the first word on the line in the second box. Now, on your answer sheet, darken the answer space for that number-letter combination.

| 6___ | 19___ | 12___ | BAD   DRAB   ALE |

105. Count the number of points on the figure below. If there are five or more points, darken the answer space for 6 (E) on your answer sheet. If there are fewer than five points, darken answer space 6 (A).

Grammar and Punctuation

Directions: Each question from 106–125 consists of a sentence written in four different ways. Choose the sentence that is most appropriate in grammar, usage, and punctuation to be suitable for a business letter or report, and darken its answer space on your answer sheet.

106. **(A)** Double parking is when you park your car alongside one that is already having been parked.
     (B) When one double parks, you park your car alongside one that is already parked.
     (C) Double parking is parking alongside a car already parked.
     (D) To double park is alongside a car already parked.

107. **(A)** This is entirely among you and he.
     (B) This is completely among him and you.
     (C) This is between you and him.
     (D) This is between he and you.

108. **(A)** As I said, "neither of them are guilty."
     (B) As I said, "neither of them are guilty".
     (C) As I said, "neither of them is guilty."
     (D) As I said, neither of them is guilty.

109. **(A)** I think that they will promote whoever has the best record.
     (B) The firm would have liked to have promoted all employees with good records.
     (C) Such of them that have the best records have excellent prospects of promotion.
     (D) I feel sure they will give the promotion to whomever has the best record.

110. **(A)** The receptionist must answer courteously the questions of all them callers.
   (B) The receptionist must answer courteously the questions what are asked by the callers.
   (C) There would have been no trouble if the receptionist had have always answered courteously.
   (D) The receptionist should answer courteously the questions of all callers.

111. **(A)** Since the report lacked the needed information, it was of no use to them.
   (B) This report was useless to them because there were no needed information in it.
   (C) Since the report did not contain the needed information, it was not real useful to them.
   (D) Being that the report lacked the needed information, they could not use it.

112. **(A)** The company had hardly declared the dividend till the notices were prepared for mailing.
   (B) They had no sooner declared the dividend when they sent the notices to the stockholders.
   (C) No sooner had the dividend been declared than the notices were prepared for mailing.
   (D) Scarcely had the dividend been declared than the notices were sent out.

113. **(A)** The supervisors reprimanded the typists, whom she believed had made careless errors.
   (B) The typists would have corrected the errors had they of known that the supervisor would see the report.
   (C) The errors in the typed reports were so numerous that they could hardly be overlooked.
   (D) Many errors were found in the reports which they typed and could not disregard them.

114. **(A)** "Are you absolutely certain, she asked, that you are right?"
   (B) "Are you absolutely certain," she asked, "that you are right?"
   (C) "Are you absolutely certain," she asked, "That you are right"?
   (D) "Are you absolutely certain", she asked, "That you are right?"

115. **(A)** He goes only to church on Christmas and Easter.
   (B) He only goes to church on Christmas and Easter.
   (C) He goes to only church on Christmas and Easter.
   (D) He goes to church only on Christmas and Easter.

116. **(A)** Most all these statements have been supported by persons who are reliable and can be depended upon.
   (B) The persons which have guaranteed these statements are reliable.
   (C) Reliable persons guarantee the facts with regards to the truth of these statements.
   (D) These statements can be depended on, for their truth has been guaranteed by reliable persons.

117. **(A)** The success of the book pleased both the publisher and authors.
   (B) Both the publisher and they was pleased with the success of the book.
   (C) Neither they or their publisher was disappointed with the success of the book.
   (D) Their publisher was as pleased as they with the success of the book.

118. **(A)** In reviewing the typists' work reports, the job analyst found records of unusual typing speeds.
    (B) It says in the job analyst's report that some employees type with great speed.
    (C) The job analyst found that, in reviewing the typists' work reports, that some unusual typing speeds had been made.
    (D) In the reports of typists' speeds, the job analyst found some records that are kind of unusual.

119. **(A)** Every carrier should always have something to throw; not something to throw at the dog but something what will divert its attention.
    (B) Every carrier should have something to throw—not something to throw at the dog but something to divert its attention.
    (C) Every carrier should always carry something to throw not something to throw at the dog but something that will divert it's attention.
    (D) Every carrier should always carry something to throw, not something to throw at the dog, but, something that will divert its' attention.

120. **(A)** Brown's & Company employees have recently received increases in salary.
    (B) Brown & Company recently increased the salaries of all its employees.
    (C) Recently Brown & Company has increased their employees' salaries.
    (D) Brown & Company have recently increased the salaries of all its employees.

121. **(A)** If properly addressed, the letter will reach my mother and I.
    (B) The letter had been addressed to myself and my mother.
    (C) I believe the letter was addressed to either my mother or I.
    (D) My mother's name, as well as mine, was on the letter.

122. **(A)** One of us have to make the reply before tomorrow.
    (B) Making the reply before tomorrow will have to be done by one of us.
    (C) One of us has to reply before tomorrow.
    (D) Anyone has to reply before tomorrow.

123. **(A)** You have got to get rid of some of these people if you expect to have the quality of the work improve.
    (B) The quality of the work would improve if they would leave fewer people do it.
    (C) I believe it would be desirable to have fewer persons doing this work.
    (D) If you had planned on employing fewer people than this to do the work, this situation would not have arose.

124. **(A)** The paper we use for this purpose must be light, glossy, and stand hard usage as well.
    (B) Only a light and a glossy, but durable, paper must be used for this purpose.
    (C) For this purpose, we want a paper that is light, glossy, but that will stand hard wear.
    (D) For this purpose, paper that is light, glossy, and durable is essential.

125. **(A)** This letter, together with the reports, are to be sent to the postmaster.
    (B) The reports, together with this letter, is to be sent to the postmaster.
    (C) The reports and this letter is to be sent to the postmaster.
    (D) This letter, together with the reports, is to be sent to the postmaster.

Vocabulary

Directions: Each question from 126–133 consists of a sentence containing a word in **boldface** type. Choose the best meaning for the word in **boldface** type and darken its answer space on your answer sheet.

126. Please consult your office **manual** to learn the proper operation of our copying machine. **Manual** means most nearly

   (A) labor
   (B) handbook
   (C) typewriter
   (D) handle

127. There is a specified punishment for each **infraction** of the rules. **Infraction** means most nearly

   (A) violation
   (B) use
   (C) interpretation
   (D) part

128. The order was **rescinded** within the week. **Rescinded** means most nearly

   (A) revised
   (B) canceled
   (C) misinterpreted
   (D) confirmed

129. If you have a question, please raise your hand to **summon** the test proctor. **Summon** means most nearly

   (A) ticket
   (B) fine
   (C) give
   (D) call

130. We dared not prosecute the terrorist for fear of **reprisal**. **Reprisal** means most nearly

   (A) retaliation
   (B) advantage
   (C) warning
   (D) denial

131. The increased use of dictation machines has severely **reduced** the need for office stenographers. **Reduced** means most nearly

   (A) enlarged
   (B) cut out
   (C) lessened
   (D) expanded

132. Frequent use of marijuana may **impair** your judgment. **Impair** means most nearly

   (A) weaken
   (B) conceal
   (C) improve
   (D) expose

133. It is altogether **fitting** that the parent discipline the child. **Fitting** means most nearly

   (A) illegal
   (B) bad practice
   (C) appropriate
   (D) required

Reading Comprehension

Directions: For questions 134–140, read each paragraph and answer the question that follows it by darkening the answer space of the correct answer on your answer sheet.

134. A survey to determine the subjects that have helped students most in their jobs shows that typewriting leads all other subjects in the business group. It also leads among the subjects college students consider most valuable and would take again if they were to return to high school.

The paragraph best supports the statement that

(A) the ability to type is an asset in business and in school
(B) students who return to night school take typing
(C) students with a knowledge of typing do superior work in college
(D) success in business is assured those who can type

135. Telegrams should be clear, concise, and brief. Omit all unnecessary words. The parts of speech most often used in telegrams are nouns, verbs, adjectives, and adverbs. If possible, do without pronouns, prepositions, articles, and copulative verbs. Use simple sentences, rather than complex and compound.

The paragraph best supports the statement that in writing telegrams one should always use

(A) common and simple words
(B) only nouns, verbs, adjectives, and adverbs
(C) incomplete sentences
(D) only words essential to the meaning

136. Since the government can spend only what it obtains from the people, and this amount is ultimately limited by their capacity and willingness to pay taxes, it is very important that the people be given full information about the work of the government.

The paragraph best supports the statement that

(A) governmental employees should be trained not only in their own work, but also in how to perform the duties of other employees in their agency
(B) taxation by the government rests upon the consent of the people
(C) the release of full information on the work of the government will increase the efficiency of governmental operations
(D) the work of the government, in recent years, has been restricted because of reduced tax collections

137. Both the high school and the college should take the responsibility for preparing the student to get a job. Since the ability to write a good application letter is one of the first steps toward this goal, every teacher should be willing to do what he can to help the student learn to write such letters.

The paragraph best supports the statement that

(A) inability to write a good letter often reduces one's job prospects
(B) the major responsibility of the school is to obtain jobs for its students
(C) success is largely a matter of the kind of work the student applies for first
(D) every teacher should teach a course in the writing of application letters

138. Direct lighting is the least satisfactory lighting arrangement. The desk or ceiling light with a reflector that diffuses all the rays downward is sure to cause a glare on the working surface.

The paragraph best supports the statement that direct lighting is least satisfactory as a method of lighting chiefly because

(A) the light is diffused, causing eye strain
(B) the shade on the individual desk lamp is not constructed along scientific lines
(C) the working surface is usually obscured by the glare
(D) direct lighting is injurious to the eyes

139. "White collar" is a term used to describe one of the largest groups of workers in American industry and trade. It distinguishes those who work with the pencil and the mind from those who depend on their hands and the machine. It suggests occupations in which physical exertion and handling of materials are not primary features of the job.

The paragraph best supports the statement that "white collar" workers are

(A) not so strong physically as those who work with their hands
(B) those who supervise workers handling materials
(C) all whose work is entirely indoors
(D) not likely to use machines as much as are other groups of workers

140. In large organizations some standardized, simple, inexpensive method of giving employees information about company policies and rules, as well as specific instructions regarding their duties, is practically essential. This is the purpose of all office manuals of whatever type.

The paragraph best supports the statement that office manuals

(A) are all about the same
(B) should be simple enough for the average employee to understand
(C) are necessary to large organizations
(D) act as constant reminders to the employee of his duties

STOP End of Verbal Ability section. If you finish before time is up, check your work on this section only. Do not go to the next section until the signal is given.

DICTATION

3 MINUTES

> **Directions:** Have someone dictate the sample passage to you. It should take 3 minutes. Take notes on your own paper.

Directions to person dictating: This practice dictation should be dictated at the rate of 80 words a minute. Each pair of lines is dictated in 10 seconds. Do not dictate the punctuation except for periods, but dictate with the expression the punctuation indicates. Use a watch with a second hand to enable you to read the exercise at the proper speed. *Exactly on a minute start dictating. Finish reading each two lines at the number of seconds indicated below.*

In recent years there has been a great	
increase in the need for capable stenographers,	10 sec.
not only in business offices but also	
in public service agencies, both	20 sec.
governmental and private. (Period) The high	
schools and business schools in many parts of	30 sec.
the country have tried to meet this need by	
offering complete commercial courses. (Period)	40 sec.
The increase in the number of persons who	
are enrolled in these courses shows that	50 sec.
students have become aware of the great	
demand for stenographers. (Period) A person	1 min.
who wishes to secure employment in this	
field must be able to take dictation	10 sec.
and to transcribe the notes with both speed	
and accuracy. (Period) The rate of	20 sec.
speed at which dictation is given in most	
offices is somewhat less than that of	30 sec.
ordinary speech. (Period) Thus, one who has	
had a thorough training in shorthand	40 sec.
should have little trouble in taking complete	
notes. (Period) Skill in taking dictation	50 sec.
at a rapid rate is of slight value if	
the stenographer cannot also type the notes	2 min.
in proper form. (Period) A manager	
sometimes dictates a rough draft of the ideas	10 sec.
he/she wishes to have included in a letter,	
and leaves to the stenographer the task	20 sec.
of putting them in good form. (Period)	
For this reason, knowledge of the essentials	30 sec.

of grammar and of composition is as
important as the ability to take   40 sec.
dictation. (Period) In addition, a stenographer
should be familiar with the sources of   50 sec.
general information that are most likely
to be used in office work. (Period)   3 min.

After dictating the test, pause for 15 seconds to permit the test-taker to complete notetaking.

DICTATION TRANSCRIPT

125 QUESTIONS • 30 MINUTES

Directions: The transcript below is the material that was dictated to you in the previous section, except that many of the words have been left out. From your notes, you are to tell what the missing words are. Proceed as follows:

Compare your notes with the transcript and when you come to a blank in the transcript decide what word (or words) belongs there. Look at the word list to see whether you can find the same word there. Notice what letter, (A), (B), (C), or (D), is printed beside it, and write that letter in the blank. (You may also write the word or words, or the shorthand for them, if you wish.) The same word may belong in more than one blank. If the exact answer is not listed, write E in the blank.

ALPHABETIC WORD LIST

Write (E) if the answer is not listed.

also — **(A)**
also in — **(C)**
business — **(C)**
busy — **(D)**
capable — **(A)**
commerce — **(C)**
commercial — **(D)**
county — **(B)**
culpable — **(D)**
decrease — **(A)**
governing — **(D)**
governmental — **(C)**
had been — **(B)**
has been — **(D)**
many — **(A)**
most — **(D)**
need — **(C)**
needy — **(D)**
offending — **(A)**

offering — **(C)**
officials — **(D)**
one — **(C)**
only — **(B)**
parts — **(A)**
private — **(C)**
public — **(D)**
recent — **(B)**
recurrent — **(A)**
school — **(C)**
schools — **(B)**
servant — **(D)**
stenographers — **(D)**
stenos — **(A)**
their — **(D)**
there — **(B)**
tied — **(A)**
to beat — **(C)**
tried — **(B)**

TRANSCRIPT

In _____ years _____ _____ a great _____
    1   2   3   4
in the _____ for _____ _____, not _____ in
       5   6   7   8
_____ _____ but _____ in _____ _____
 9   10   11   12   13
agencies, both _____ and _____. The high
               14   15
_____ and _____ schools in _____ _____ of
 16   17   18   19
the _____ have _____ _____ this _____ by
    20   21   22   23
_____ complete _____ courses.
 24   25

ALPHABETIC WORD LIST

Write (E) if the answer is not listed.

awake — **(C)**	in a — **(B)**
aware — **(B)**	in the — **(A)**
be able — **(A)**	increase — **(C)**
be able to — **(C)**	increment — **(A)**
became — **(B)**	notations — **(B)**
better — **(A)**	notes — **(C)**
both — **(D)**	number — **(C)**
courses — **(D)**	numbers — **(D)**
curses — **(C)**	people — **(A)**
demand — **(C)**	person — **(C)**
demean — **(A)**	seclude — **(C)**
dictation — **(B)**	secure — **(B)**
dictation notes — **(C)**	speech — **(C)**
employing — **(A)**	speed — **(B)**
employment — **(D)**	students — **(C)**
enrolled — **(B)**	studies — **(D)**
enroute — **(D)**	the — **(C)**
feel — **(A)**	this — **(A)**
felt — **(D)**	transcribe — **(C)**
grate — **(D)**	transcript — **(D)**
great — **(A)**	who desires — **(C)**

TRANSCRIPT, CONT'D.

The ____ ____ ____ of ____ who are
    26   27   28   29
____ in these ____ shows ____ ____
30   31   32   33
have ____ ____ of the ____ ____ for
    34   35   36   37
stenographers. A ____ ____ to ____
          38   39   40
____ in ____ ____ must ____ to take
41   42   43   44
____ and to ____ the ____ with ____
45   46   47   48
____ and ____.
49   50

ALPHABETIC WORD LIST

Write (E) if the answer is not listed.

also — **(D)**	rampant — **(B)**
also can — **(B)**	rate — **(C)**
at a — **(A)**	ratio — **(D)**
at the — **(C)**	should — **(D)**
compete — B	should not — **(A)**
complete — **(D)**	sight — **(C)**
dictates — **(B)**	slight — **(B)**
dictation — **(D)**	somehow — **(D)**
firm — **(C)**	speech — **(A)**
form — **(D)**	speed — **(A)**
gained — **(A)**	stenographer — **(C)**
give — **(D)**	taking — **(C)**
has — **(C)**	that — **(D)**
have — **(B)**	thorough — **(C)**
less — **(B)**	through — **(B)**
less than — **(A)**	treble — **(D)**
many — **(A)**	trial — **(A)**
most — **(D)**	typed — **(D)**
note — **(C)**	typewriter — **(A)**
notes — **(B)**	valuate — **(A)**
offices — **(C)**	value — **(C)**
orderly — **(C)**	what — **(C)**
ordinary — **(D)**	which — **(B)**
proffer — **(C)**	who gets — **(A)**
proper — **(A)**	who had — **(C)**

TRANSCRIPT, CONT'D.

The ____ of ____ at ____ dictation is
    51   52   53
____ in ____ ____ is ____ ____ than
54   55   56   57   58
____ of ____ ____. Thus, one ____ had
59   60   61   62
a ____ ____ in shorthand ____ ____
   63   64   65   66
little ____ in ____ ____ ____. Skill in
      67   68   69   70
____ ____ ____ ____ ____ is of
71   72   73   74   75
____ ____ if the ____ cannot ____
76   77   78   79
____ the ____ in ____ ____.
80   81   82   83

ALPHABETIC WORD LIST

Write (E) if the answer is not listed.

ability — **(B)**
adding — **(C)**
addition — **(A)**
are — **(D)**
as — **(A)**
composing — **(A)**
composition — **(C)**
dictates — **(B)**
essence — **(B)**
essentials — **(C)**
form — **(A)**
familial — **(C)**
familiar — **(A)**
general — **(C)**
generous — **(A)**
good — **(C)**
grammatical — **(D)**
great — **(A)**
had — **(A)**
have — **(B)**
ideals — **(C)**
ideas — **(A)**
included — **(C)**
inclusive — **(A)**
information — **(D)**
important — **(B)**
impotent — **(A)**
knowledge — **(B)**
knowledgeable — **(C)**
leaves — **(B)**
lets — **(C)**

letter — **(D)**
like — **(A)**
likely — **(C)**
manager — **(A)**
management — **(B)**
of the — **(D)**
of these — **(A)**
office — **(A)**
official — **(B)**
put in — **(D)**
putting — **(C)**
reasoning — **(B)**
rough — **(A)**
roughly — **(D)**
sauces — **(A)**
shall — **(D)**
should — **(B)**
some times — **(A)**
somethings — **(D)**
source — **(D)**
stenographic — **(A)**
take — **(D)**
task — **(D)**
this — **(A)**
to — **(A)**
to be — **(B)**
used — **(C)**
useful — **(A)**
wished — **(D)**
wishes — **(A)**
with the — **(D)**

You will now have ten minutes to transfer your answers to the answer sheet.

TRANSCRIPT, CONT'D.

A ____ ____ ____ a ____ ____ ____
   84 85 86   87 88 89
____ s/he ____ to ____ ____ in a
90   91   92 93
____, and ____ to the ____ the ____ of
94   95   96   97
____ them in ____ ____. For ____
98   99 100   101
____, ____ ____ ____ of ____ and of
102 103 104 105   106
____ is ____ ____ ____ ____ to
107   108 109 110 111
____ dictation. In ____, ____ stenogra-
112   113   114
pher ____ be ____ ____ ____ of ____
115   116 117 118   119
____ that ____ most ____ ____ ____
120   121   122 123 124
in ____ work.
   125

STOP End of Dictation section. If you finish before time is up, check your work on this section only. Do not go to the next section until the signal is given.

ANSWER KEY AND EXPLANATIONS

Sequencing

1. E	5. A	9. E	13. C	17. E
2. D	6. C	10. C	14. D	18. B
3. A	7. B	11. C	15. C	19. A
4. D	8. D	12. D	16. A	20. C

1. **The correct answer is (E).** Hachettson; Hackett

2. **The correct answer is (D).** 59233262; 59233362

3. **The correct answer is (A).** MYP; NYP

4. **The correct answer is (D).** Olivia H.; Olivier E.; R. Olivia

5. **The correct answer is (A).** 0010; 0012

6. **The correct answer is (C).** 6001; 6100; 6101

7. **The correct answer is (B).** Vanover; Vanstory; VanSwinderen

8. **The correct answer is (D).** FitzGibbon; Fitzsimmons; FitzSimons

9. **The correct answer is (E).** 01016060; 01066010

10. **The correct answer is (C).** AAS; AAZ; ASA

11. **The correct answer is (C).** Pawelek; Pawlowicz; Pawlowski

12. **The correct answer is (D).** 7710; 7834; 7868

13. **The correct answer is (C).** 36270000; 36270013; 36270030

14. **The correct answer is (D).** Freedenberg; Freedenburg; Freedinberg; Freedinburg

15. **The correct answer is (C).** Proutey; Prouty, Martha; Prouty, Myra

16. **The correct answer is (A).** 58006021; 58006130

17. **The correct answer is (E).** EKK-1403; EKK-1443

18. **The correct answer is (B).** Daly; D'Amato; D'Amboise

19. **The correct answer is (A).** Schaeffer; Schaffert

20. **The correct answer is (C).** PSP; SPP; SPS

Comparisons

21.	A	27.	A	33.	A	39.	D	45.	D
22.	E	28.	B	34.	A	40.	A	46.	B
23.	C	29.	C	35.	A	41.	A	47.	E
24.	B	30.	D	36.	B	42.	C	48.	A
25.	D	31.	D	37.	E	43.	C	49.	C
26.	E	32.	E	38.	C	44.	E	50.	A

21. **The correct answer is (A).**

Drusilla S. Ridgeley; Drusilla S. Ridgeley; Drusilla S. Ridgeley

22. **The correct answer is (E).**

Andrei I. Toumantzev; Andrei I. Tourmantzev; Andrei I. Toumantzov

23. **The correct answer is (C).**

6-78912-e3e42; 6-78912-3e3e42; 678912-e3e42

24. **The correct answer is (B).**

86529 Dunwoodie Drive; 86529 Dunwoodie Drive; 85629 Dunwoodie Drive

25. **The correct answer is (D).**

1592514; 1592574; 1592574

26. **The correct answer is (E).**

Ella Burk Newham; Ella Burk Newnham; Elena Burk Newnham

27. **The correct answer is (A).**

5416R-1952TZ-op; 5416R-1952TZ-op; 5416R-1952TZ-op

28. **The correct answer is (B).**

60646 West Touhy Avenue; 60646 West Touhy Avenue; 60646 West Touhey Avenue

29. **The correct answer is (C).**

Mardikian & Moore, Inc.; Mardikian and Moore, Inc.; Mardikian & Moore, Inc.

30. **The correct answer is (D).**

9670243; 9670423; 9670423

31. **The correct answer is (D).**

Eduardo Ingles ; Eduardo Inglese; Eduardo Inglese

32. **The correct answer is (E).**

Roger T. DeAngelis; Roger T. D'Angelis; Roger T. DeAngeles

33. **The correct answer is (A).**

7692138; 7692138; 7692138

34. **The correct answer is (A).**

2695 East 3435 South; 2695 East 3435 South; 2695 East 3435 South

35. **The correct answer is (A).**

   63qs5-95YT3-001; 63qs5-95YT3-001; 63qs5-95YT3-001

36. **The correct answer is (B).**

   2789350; 2789350; 2798350

37. **The correct answer is (E).**

   Helmut V. Lochner; Helmut V. Lockner; Helmut W. Lochner

38. **The correct answer is (C).**

   2454803; 2548403; 2454803

39. **The correct answer is (D).**

   Lemberger, WA 28094-9182; Lemberger, VA 28094-9182; Lemberger, VA 28094-9182

40. **The correct answer is (A).**

   4168-GNP-78852; 4168-GNP-78852; 4168-GNP-78852

41. **The correct answer is (A).**

   Yoshihito Saito; Yoshihito Saito; Yoshihito Saito

42. **The correct answer is (C).**

   5927681; 5927861; 5927681

43. **The correct answer is (C).**

   O'Reilly Bay, LA 56212; O'Reillys Bay, LA 56212; O'Reilly Bay, LA 56212

44. **The correct answer is (E).**

   Francis Ransdell; Frances Ramsdell; Francis Ramsdell

45. **The correct answer is (D).**

   5634-OotV5a-16867; 5634-Ootv5a-16867; 5634-Ootv5a-16867

46. **The correct answer is (B).**

   Dolores Mollicone; Dolores Mollicone; Doloras Mollicone

47. **The correct answer is (E).**

   David C. Routzon; David E. Routzon; David C. Routzron

48. **The correct answer is (A).**

   8932 Shimabui Hwy.; 8932 Shimabui Hwy.; 8932 Shimabui Hwy.

49. **The correct answer is (C).**

   6177396; 6177936; 6177396

50. **The correct answer is (A).**

   A8987-B373245; A8987-B373245; A8987-B373245

answers practice test 6

Spelling

51. A	55. D	59. C	63. C	67. A
52. C	56. A	60. B	64. D	68. D
53. C	57. D	61. A	65. D	69. B
54. A	58. B	62. C	66. C	70. B

51. **The correct answer is (A).** anticipate

52. **The correct answer is (C).** similar

53. **The correct answer is (C).** sufficiently

54. **The correct answer is (A).** intelligence

55. **The correct answer is (D).** reference

56. **The correct answer is (A).** conscious

57. **The correct answer is (D).** parallel

58. **The correct answer is (B).** abundance

59. **The correct answer is (C).** corrugated

60. **The correct answer is (B).** accumulation

61. **The correct answer is (A).** resonance

62. **The correct answer is (C).** beneficial

63. **The correct answer is (C).** specifically

64. **The correct answer is (D).** eliminate

65. **The correct answer is (D).** colossal

66. **The correct answer is (C).** auxiliary

67. **The correct answer is (A).** inimitable

68. **The correct answer is (D).** disappearance

69. **The correct answer is (B).** appellate

70. **The correct answer is (B).** essential

Computation

71.	E	74.	B	77.	E	80.	B	83.	E
72.	B	75.	B	78.	E	81.	E	84.	C
73.	A	76.	C	79.	C	82.	C	85.	B

71. The correct answer is (E).

$$\begin{array}{r} 83 \\ -\,56 \\ \hline 27 \end{array}$$

72. The correct answer is (B).

$$\begin{array}{r} 15 \\ +\,17 \\ \hline 32 \end{array}$$

73. The correct answer is (A).

$$\begin{array}{r} 32 \\ \times\,7 \\ \hline 224 \end{array}$$

74. The correct answer is (B).

$$\begin{array}{r} 39 \\ \times\,2 \\ \hline 78 \end{array}$$

75. The correct answer is (B).

$$\begin{array}{r} 43 \\ -\,15 \\ \hline 28 \end{array}$$

76. The correct answer is (C).

$$\begin{array}{r} 50 \\ +\,49 \\ \hline 99 \end{array}$$

77. The correct answer is (E).

$$6\overline{)366} = 61$$

78. The correct answer is (E).

$$\begin{array}{r} 38 \\ \times\,3 \\ \hline 114 \end{array}$$

79. The correct answer is (C).

$$\begin{array}{r} 19 \\ +\,21 \\ \hline 40 \end{array}$$

80. The correct answer is (B).

$$\begin{array}{r} 13 \\ -\,6 \\ \hline 7 \end{array}$$

81. **The correct answer is (E).**

$$6\overline{)180}$$ with quotient 30

82. **The correct answer is (C).**

$$\begin{array}{r} 10 \\ \times\ 1 \\ \hline 10 \end{array}$$

83. **The correct answer is (E).**

$$7\overline{)287}$$ with quotient 41

84. **The correct answer is (C).**

$$\begin{array}{r} 12 \\ +\ 11 \\ \hline 23 \end{array}$$

85. **The correct answer is (B).**

$$\begin{array}{r} 85 \\ -\ 64 \\ \hline 21 \end{array}$$

Verbal Ability

86. D	97. B	108. D	119. B	130. A
87. C	98. D	109. A	120. B	131. C
88. E	99. A	110. D	121. D	132. A
89. A	100. D	111. A	122. C	133. C
90. C	101. D	112. C	123. C	134. A
91. E	101. E	113. C	124. D	135. D
92. D	101. A	114. B	125. D	136. B
93. C	104. D	115. D	126. B	137. A
94. E	105. B	116. D	127. A	138. C
95. B	106. C	117. D	128. B	139. D
96. A	107. C	118. A	129. D	140. C

Questions 86–105. If you made any errors in the *Following Written Instructions* portion, go back and reread those questions more carefully.

106. **The correct answer is (C).** Sentence (C) is the best expression of the idea. Sentence (A) has two grammatical errors: the use of *when* to introduce a definition and the unacceptable verb form *is already having been parked*. Sentence (B) incorrectly shifts subjects from *one* to *you*. Sentence (D) does not make sense.

107. **The correct answer is (C).** Choice (B) is incorrect because only two persons are involved in this statement. *Between* is used when there are only two, *among* is reserved for three or more. (A) makes a similar error. In addition, both (A) and (D) use the pronoun *he*. The object of a preposition, in this case *between,* must be in the objective case, hence *him.*

108. **The correct answer is (D).** Punctuation aside, both (A) and (B) incorrectly place the verb in the plural, *are*. *Neither* is a singular indefinite pronoun. It means *not one and not the other* and requires a singular verb. The choice between (C) and (D) is more difficult, but basically this is a simple statement and not a direct quote.

109. **The correct answer is (A).** Whoever is the subject of the phrase *whoever has the best record.* Hence (A) is the correct answer and (D) is wrong. Both (B) and (C) are wordy and awkward.

110. **The correct answer is (D).** All the other choices contain obvious errors.

111. **The correct answer is (A).** Choice (B) uses the plural verb *were* with the singular subject *report*. (C) and (D) are colloquial and incorrect even for informal speech. They have no place in business writing.

112. **The correct answer is (C).** Choices (A) and (B) use adverbs incorrectly; choice (B) is awkward and unidiomatic.

113. **The correct answer is (C).** Choices (B) and (D) are obviously incorrect. In (A), the pronoun *who* should be the subject of the phrase, *who had made careless errors.*

114. **The correct answer is (B).** Only the quoted material should appear enclosed by quotation marks, so (A) is incorrect. Only the first word of a sentence should begin with a capital letter, so both (C) and (D) are wrong. In addition, only the quoted material itself is a question; the entire sentence is a statement. Therefore, the question mark must be placed inside the quotes.

115. **The correct answer is (D).** Choices (A) and (B) imply that he stays in church all day on Christmas and Easter and goes nowhere else. Choice (C) makes the same implication and in addition splits the infinitive awkwardly. In (D) the modifier *only* is correctly placed to tell us that the only times he goes to church are on Christmas and Easter.

116. **The correct answer is (D).** Choice (A) might state either *most* or *all* but not both; choice (B) should read *persons who;* choice (C) should read *with regard to . . .*

117. **The correct answer is (D).** Choice (A) is incorrect because *both* can refer to only two, but the publisher and authors implies at least three; choice (B) requires the plural verb *were;* choice (C) requires the correlative construction *neither . . . nor.*

118. **The correct answer is (A).** Choices (C) and (D) are glaringly poor. Choice (B) is not incorrect, but choice (A) is far better.

119. **The correct answer is (B).** Choice (A) incorrectly uses a semicolon to separate a complete clause from a sentence fragment. Additionally, (A) incorrectly uses *what* in place of *that.* Choice (C) is a run-on sentence that also misuses an apostrophe: *It's* is the contraction for *it is,* not the possessive of *it.* Choice (D) uses commas indiscriminately; it also misuses the apostrophe.

120. **The correct answer is (B).** In choice (A) the placement of the apostrophe is inappropriate; choices (C) and (D) use the plural, but there is only one company.

121. **The correct answer is (D).** Choices (A) and (C) are incorrect in use of the subject form *I* instead of the object of the preposition *me.* Choice (B) incorrectly uses the reflexive *myself.* Only I can address a letter to myself.

122. **The correct answer is (C).** Choice (A) incorrectly uses the plural verb form *have* with the singular subject *one.* (B) is awkward and wordy. (D) incorrectly changes the subject from *one of us* to *anyone.*

123. **The correct answer is (C).** (A) is wordy. In (B), the correct verb should be *have* in place of *leave.* In (D), the word *arose* should be *arisen.*

124. **The correct answer is (D).** The first three sentences lack parallel construction. All the words that modify *paper* must appear in the same form.

125. **The correct answer is (D).** The phrase, *together with* . . . is extra information and not a part of the subject; therefore, both (A) and (B) represent similar errors of agreement. Choice (C) also presents disagreement in number between subject and verb, but in this case the compound subject, indicated by the use of the conjunction, *and,* requires a plural verb.

126. **The correct answer is (B).** Even if you do not recognize the root *manu* meaning *hand* and relating directly to *handbook,* you should have no trouble getting this question right. If you substitute each of the choices in the sentence, you will readily see that only one makes sense.

127. **The correct answer is (A).** Within the context of the sentence, the thought of a specified punishment for use, interpretation, or an edition of the rules does not make too much sense. *Fraction* gives a hint of *part,* but you must also contend with the negative prefix *in.* Since it is reasonable to expect punishment for negative behavior with relation to the rules, *violation,* which is the meaning of INFRACTION, is the proper answer.

128. **The correct answer is (B).** The prefix should help you narrow your choices. The prefix *re* meaning *back* or *again* narrows the choices to (A) or (B). To RESCIND is to *take back* or to *cancel.*

129. **The correct answer is (D).** First eliminate (C) since it does not make sense in the sentence. Your experience with the word *summons* may be with relation to *tickets* and *fines,* but tickets and fines have nothing to do with asking questions while taking a test. Even if you are unfamiliar with the word SUMMON, you should be able to choose *call* as the best synonym in this context.

130. **The correct answer is (A).** REPRISAL means injury done for injury received or *retaliation.*

131. **The correct answer is (C).** To REDUCE is to *make smaller* or to *lessen.*

132. **The correct answer is (A).** To IMPAIR is to *make worse,* to *injure,* or to *weaken.*

133. **The correct answer is (C).** FITTING in this context means *suitable* or *appropriate.*

134. **The correct answer is (A).** The survey showed that of all subjects typing has helped most in business. It was also considered valuable by college students in their schoolwork.

135. **The correct answer is (D).** See the second sentence.

136. **The correct answer is (B).** According to the paragraph, the government can spend only what it obtains from the people. The government obtains money from the people by taxation. If the people are unwilling to pay taxes, the government has no source of funds.

137. **The correct answer is (A).** Step one in the job application process is often the application letter. If the letter is not effective, the applicant will not move on to the next step and job prospects will be greatly lessened.

138. **The correct answer is (C).** The second sentence states that direct lighting causes glare on the working surface.

139. **The correct answer is (D).** While all the answer choices are likely to be true, the answer suggested by the paragraph is that "white collar" workers work with their pencils and their minds rather than with their hands and machines.

140. **The correct answer is (C).** All the paragraph says is that office manuals are a necessity in large organizations.

Dictation Transcript

1. B	26. C	51. C	76. B	101. A
2. B	27. A	52. A	77. C	102. E
3. D	28. C	53. B	78. C	103. B
4. E	29. E	54. E	79. D	104. D
5. C	30. B	55. D	80. E	105. C
6. A	31. D	56. C	81. B	106. E
7. D	32. E	57. E	82. A	107. C
8. B	33. C	58. B	83. D	108. A
9. C	34. E	59. D	84. A	109. B
10. E	35. B	60. D	85. E	110. E
11. A	36. A	61. A	86. B	111. B
12. D	37. C	62. E	87. A	112. D
13. E	38. C	63. C	88. E	113. A
14. C	39. E	64. E	89. D	114. E
15. C	40. B	65. D	90. A	115. B
16. B	41. D	66. B	91. A	116. A
17. C	42. A	67. E	92. B	117. D
18. A	43. E	68. C	93. C	118. E
19. A	44. A	69. D	94. D	119. C
20. E	45. B	70. B	95. B	120. D
21. E	46. C	71. C	96. E	121. D
22. E	47. C	72. D	97. D	122. C
23. C	48. D	73. A	98. C	123. B
24. C	49. B	74. E	99. C	124. C
25. D	50. E	75. C	100. A	125. A

answers practice test 6

Correctly Filled-In Transcript

In __B__ years __B__ __D__ a great __E__
   1   2   3   4

in the __C__ For __A__ __D__ , not __B__ B
     5   6   7   8

in __C__ __E__ but __A__ in __D__ __E__
   9   10   11   12   13

agencies, both __C__ and __C__ . The high
               14   15

__B__ and __C__ schools in __A__ __A__ of
16   17   18   19

the __E__ have __E__ __E__ this __C__ by
   20   21 22   23

__C__ complete __D__ courses.
24   25

The __C__ __A__ __C__ of __E__ who are
    26   27   28   29

__B__ in these __D__ shows __E__ __C__
30   31   32   33

have __E__ __B__ of the __A__ __C__ for
    34   35   36   37

stenographers. A __C__ __E__ to __B__
              38   39   40

__D__ in __A__ __E__ must __A__ to take
41   42   43   44

__B__ and to __C__ the __C__ with __D__
45   46   47   48

__B__ and __E__ .
49   50

The __C__ of __A__ at __B__ dictation is
    51   52   53

__E__ in __D__ __C__ is __E__ __B__
54   55   56   57   58

than __D__ of __D__ __A__ . Thus, one
      59   60   61

__E__ had a __C__ __E__ in shorthand
62   63   64

__D__ __B__ little __E__ in __C__ __D__
65   66   67   68   69

__B__ . Skill in __C__ __D__ __A__ __E__
70   71   72   73   74

__C__ is of __B__ __C__ if the __C__
75   76   77   78

cannot __D__ __E__ the __B__ in __A__
       79   80   81   82

__D__ .
83

Practice Test 6: U.S. Postal Service Clerk-Typist Exam 307

A <u>A</u> <u>E</u> <u>B</u> a <u>A</u> <u>E</u>
  84   85   86   87   88

<u>D</u> <u>A</u> s/he <u>A</u> to <u>B</u> <u>C</u>
  89   90   91   92   93

in a <u>D</u> , and <u>B</u> to the <u>E</u> the
     94   95   96

<u>D</u> of <u>C</u> them in <u>C</u> <u>A</u> . For
  97   98   99   100

<u>A</u> <u>E</u> , <u>B</u> <u>D</u> <u>C</u> of
101   102   103   104   105

<u>E</u> and of <u>C</u> is <u>A</u> <u>B</u> <u>E</u>
106   107   108   109   110

<u>B</u> to <u>D</u> dictation. In <u>A</u> , <u>E</u>
111   112   113   114

stenographer <u>B</u> be <u>A</u> <u>D</u> <u>E</u>
                115   116   117   118

of <u>C</u> <u>D</u> that <u>D</u> most <u>C</u>
    119   120   121   122

<u>B</u> <u>C</u> in <u>A</u> work.
123 124   125

ANSWER SHEET PRACTICE TEST 7: SENIOR OFFICE TYPIST EXAM (COURT SYSTEM)

SPELLING

1. Ⓐ Ⓑ Ⓒ Ⓓ Ⓔ   8. Ⓐ Ⓑ Ⓒ Ⓓ Ⓔ   15. Ⓐ Ⓑ Ⓒ Ⓓ Ⓔ
2. Ⓐ Ⓑ Ⓒ Ⓓ Ⓔ   9. Ⓐ Ⓑ Ⓒ Ⓓ Ⓔ   16. Ⓐ Ⓑ Ⓒ Ⓓ Ⓔ
3. Ⓐ Ⓑ Ⓒ Ⓓ Ⓔ   10. Ⓐ Ⓑ Ⓒ Ⓓ Ⓔ   17. Ⓐ Ⓑ Ⓒ Ⓓ Ⓔ
4. Ⓐ Ⓑ Ⓒ Ⓓ Ⓔ   11. Ⓐ Ⓑ Ⓒ Ⓓ Ⓔ   18. Ⓐ Ⓑ Ⓒ Ⓓ Ⓔ
5. Ⓐ Ⓑ Ⓒ Ⓓ Ⓔ   12. Ⓐ Ⓑ Ⓒ Ⓓ Ⓔ   19. Ⓐ Ⓑ Ⓒ Ⓓ Ⓔ
6. Ⓐ Ⓑ Ⓒ Ⓓ Ⓔ   13. Ⓐ Ⓑ Ⓒ Ⓓ Ⓔ   20. Ⓐ Ⓑ Ⓒ Ⓓ Ⓔ
7. Ⓐ Ⓑ Ⓒ Ⓓ Ⓔ   14. Ⓐ Ⓑ Ⓒ Ⓓ Ⓔ

GRAMMAR SKILLS

21. Ⓐ Ⓑ Ⓒ Ⓓ Ⓔ   26. Ⓐ Ⓑ Ⓒ Ⓓ Ⓔ   31. Ⓐ Ⓑ Ⓒ Ⓓ Ⓔ
22. Ⓐ Ⓑ Ⓒ Ⓓ Ⓔ   27. Ⓐ Ⓑ Ⓒ Ⓓ Ⓔ   32. Ⓐ Ⓑ Ⓒ Ⓓ Ⓔ
23. Ⓐ Ⓑ Ⓒ Ⓓ Ⓔ   28. Ⓐ Ⓑ Ⓒ Ⓓ Ⓔ   33. Ⓐ Ⓑ Ⓒ Ⓓ Ⓔ
24. Ⓐ Ⓑ Ⓒ Ⓓ Ⓔ   29. Ⓐ Ⓑ Ⓒ Ⓓ Ⓔ   34. Ⓐ Ⓑ Ⓒ Ⓓ Ⓔ
25. Ⓐ Ⓑ Ⓒ Ⓓ Ⓔ   30. Ⓐ Ⓑ Ⓒ Ⓓ Ⓔ

CLERICAL SKILLS

35. Ⓐ Ⓑ Ⓒ Ⓓ Ⓔ   41. Ⓐ Ⓑ Ⓒ Ⓓ Ⓔ   46. Ⓐ Ⓑ Ⓒ Ⓓ Ⓔ
36. Ⓐ Ⓑ Ⓒ Ⓓ Ⓔ   42. Ⓐ Ⓑ Ⓒ Ⓓ Ⓔ   47. Ⓐ Ⓑ Ⓒ Ⓓ Ⓔ
37. Ⓐ Ⓑ Ⓒ Ⓓ Ⓔ   43. Ⓐ Ⓑ Ⓒ Ⓓ Ⓔ   48. Ⓐ Ⓑ Ⓒ Ⓓ Ⓔ
38. Ⓐ Ⓑ Ⓒ Ⓓ Ⓔ   44. Ⓐ Ⓑ Ⓒ Ⓓ Ⓔ   49. Ⓐ Ⓑ Ⓒ Ⓓ Ⓔ
39. Ⓐ Ⓑ Ⓒ Ⓓ Ⓔ   45. Ⓐ Ⓑ Ⓒ Ⓓ Ⓔ   50. Ⓐ Ⓑ Ⓒ Ⓓ Ⓔ
40. Ⓐ Ⓑ Ⓒ Ⓓ Ⓔ

RECORD-KEEPING SKILLS

51. Ⓐ Ⓑ Ⓒ Ⓓ Ⓔ   56. Ⓐ Ⓑ Ⓒ Ⓓ Ⓔ   61. Ⓐ Ⓑ Ⓒ Ⓓ Ⓔ
52. Ⓐ Ⓑ Ⓒ Ⓓ Ⓔ   57. Ⓐ Ⓑ Ⓒ Ⓓ Ⓔ   62. Ⓐ Ⓑ Ⓒ Ⓓ Ⓔ
53. Ⓐ Ⓑ Ⓒ Ⓓ Ⓔ   58. Ⓐ Ⓑ Ⓒ Ⓓ Ⓔ   63. Ⓐ Ⓑ Ⓒ Ⓓ Ⓔ
54. Ⓐ Ⓑ Ⓒ Ⓓ Ⓔ   59. Ⓐ Ⓑ Ⓒ Ⓓ Ⓔ   64. Ⓐ Ⓑ Ⓒ Ⓓ Ⓔ
55. Ⓐ Ⓑ Ⓒ Ⓓ Ⓔ   60. Ⓐ Ⓑ Ⓒ Ⓓ Ⓔ   65. Ⓐ Ⓑ Ⓒ Ⓓ Ⓔ

answer sheet

READING COMPREHENSION

66. Ⓐ Ⓑ Ⓒ Ⓓ Ⓔ   76. Ⓐ Ⓑ Ⓒ Ⓓ Ⓔ   86. Ⓐ Ⓑ Ⓒ Ⓓ Ⓔ
67. Ⓐ Ⓑ Ⓒ Ⓓ Ⓔ   77. Ⓐ Ⓑ Ⓒ Ⓓ Ⓔ   87. Ⓐ Ⓑ Ⓒ Ⓓ Ⓔ
68. Ⓐ Ⓑ Ⓒ Ⓓ Ⓔ   78. Ⓐ Ⓑ Ⓒ Ⓓ Ⓔ   88. Ⓐ Ⓑ Ⓒ Ⓓ Ⓔ
69. Ⓐ Ⓑ Ⓒ Ⓓ Ⓔ   79. Ⓐ Ⓑ Ⓒ Ⓓ Ⓔ   89. Ⓐ Ⓑ Ⓒ Ⓓ Ⓔ
70. Ⓐ Ⓑ Ⓒ Ⓓ Ⓔ   80. Ⓐ Ⓑ Ⓒ Ⓓ Ⓔ   90. Ⓐ Ⓑ Ⓒ Ⓓ Ⓔ
71. Ⓐ Ⓑ Ⓒ Ⓓ Ⓔ   81. Ⓐ Ⓑ Ⓒ Ⓓ Ⓔ   91. Ⓐ Ⓑ Ⓒ Ⓓ Ⓔ
72. Ⓐ Ⓑ Ⓒ Ⓓ Ⓔ   82. Ⓐ Ⓑ Ⓒ Ⓓ Ⓔ   92. Ⓐ Ⓑ Ⓒ Ⓓ Ⓔ
73. Ⓐ Ⓑ Ⓒ Ⓓ Ⓔ   83. Ⓐ Ⓑ Ⓒ Ⓓ Ⓔ   93. Ⓐ Ⓑ Ⓒ Ⓓ Ⓔ
74. Ⓐ Ⓑ Ⓒ Ⓓ Ⓔ   84. Ⓐ Ⓑ Ⓒ Ⓓ Ⓔ   94. Ⓐ Ⓑ Ⓒ Ⓓ Ⓔ
75. Ⓐ Ⓑ Ⓒ Ⓓ Ⓔ   85. Ⓐ Ⓑ Ⓒ Ⓓ Ⓔ   95. Ⓐ Ⓑ Ⓒ Ⓓ Ⓔ

Practice Test 7: Senior Office Typist Exam (Court System)

SPELLING

95 QUESTIONS • 3 HOURS

Directions: Choose the word that is correctly spelled and darken its letter on your answer sheet.

1. (A) apellate
   (B) appelate
   (C) appeallate
   (D) appellate

2. (A) presumption
   (B) presoumption
   (C) presumsion
   (D) presumptsion

3. (A) litigiant
   (B) litigent
   (C) litigant
   (D) litigint

4. (A) committment
   (B) commitment
   (C) comittment
   (D) comitment

5. (A) affidavid
   (B) afidavis
   (C) affidavit
   (D) afidavit

6. (A) arraign
   (B) arrain
   (C) arreign
   (D) areign

7. (A) cumalative
   (B) cummuletive
   (C) cummalative
   (D) cumulative

8. (A) sevarance
   (B) severance
   (C) severence
   (D) severants

9. (A) adjurnment
   (B) adjuornment
   (C) ajournment
   (D) adjournment

10. (A) comenced
    (B) commentced
    (C) commenced
    (D) commensced

Directions: Each question consists of three sentences with one underlined word. One of the underlined words might be spelled incorrectly. On your answer sheet, darken the letter of the sentence which contains the incorrectly spelled word. If no sentence contains a misspelled word, darken answer space (D).

11. **(A)** Punishment must be a planned part of a comprehensive program of treating delinquency.
    (B) It is easier to spot inexperienced check forjers than other criminals.
    (C) Even young vandals and hooligans can be reformed if given adequate attention.
    (D) No error.

12. **(A)** The court officer does not have authority to make exceptions.
    (B) Usually the violations are the result of illegal and dangerous driving behavior.
    (C) The safety division is required to investigate if the dispatcher files a complaint.
    (D) No error.

13. **(A)** Comic books that glorify the criminal have a distinct influence in producing young criminals.
    (B) Some of the people behind bars are innocent people who have been put there by mistake.
    (C) Educational achievment is closely associated with delinquency.
    (D) No error.

14. **(A)** Disciplinary action is most effective when it is taken promptly.
    (B) Release on "personal recognizance" refers to release without bail.
    (C) Parole violators forfeit their freedom.
    (D) No error.

15. **(A)** Some responsibilities take precedence over preservation of evidence.
    (B) Objects should not be touched unless there is some compelling reason.
    (C) The detension system works unfairly against people who are single and unemployed.
    (D) No error.

16. **(A)** Evidence is inmaterial if it does not prove the truth of a fact at issue.
    (B) Without qualms the offender will lie and manipulate others.
    (C) If spectators become disorderly, the court officer may threaten to cite them for contempt of court.
    (D) No error.

17. **(A)** Under certain conditions, circumstantial evidence may be admissible.
    (B) Just because evidence is circumstantial does not mean that it is irrelevant.
    (C) An aggressive offender may appear to be very hostile.
    (D) No error.

18. **(A)** A victim of assault may want to take revenge.
    (B) The result of the trial was put in doubt when the prosecuter produced a surprise witness.
    (C) The court officer must maintain order and decorum in the courtroom.
    (D) No error.

19. **(A)** A person whose accident record can be explained by a correctable physical defect cannot be called "accident-prone."
    (B) A litigant should not be permitted to invoke the aid of technical rules.
    (C) Refusal to waive immunity automatically terminates employment.
    (D) No error.

20. **(A)** Court employees may be fired for malfeasance.
    (B) A common tactic used by defense lawyers is embarrassment of the witness.
    (C) The criminal justice system may be called an "adversary system."
    (D) No error.

GRAMMAR SKILLS

Directions: Choose the sentence that is grammatically **incorrect** and darken its letter on your answer sheet.

21. **(A)** One of us has to reply before tomorrow.
    (B) All employees who had served from 40 to 51 years were retired.
    (C) The personnel office takes care of employment, dismissals, and etc.
    (D) We often come across people with whom we disagree.

22. **(A)** The jurors have been instructed to deliver a sealed verdict.
    (B) The court may direct the convict to be imprisoned in a county penitentiary instead of a state prison.
    (C) Conveying self-confidence is displaying assurance.
    (D) He devotes as much, if not more, time to his work than the rest of the employees.

23. **(A)** In comparison with that kind of pen, this kind is more preferable.
    (B) The jurors may go to dinner only with the permission of the judge.
    (C) There was neither any intention to commit a crime nor any injury incurred.
    (D) It is the sociological view that all weight should be given to the history and development of the individual.

24. **(A)** The supervisor makes the suggestions for improvement, not the employee.
    (B) Violations of traffic laws and illegal and dangerous driving behavior constitutes bad driving.
    (C) Cynics take the position that the criminal is rarely or never reformed.
    (D) The ultimate solution to the housing problem of the hardcore slum does not lie in code enforcement.

25. **(A)** No crime can occur unless there is a written law forbidding the act or omission in question.
    (B) If one wants to prevent crime, we must deal with the possible criminals before they reach the prison.
    (C) One could reasonably say that the same type of correctional institution is not desirable for the custody of all prisoners.
    (D) When you have completed the report, you may give it to me or directly to the judge.

26. **(A)** The structure of an organization should be considered in determining the organization's goals.
    (B) Complaints are welcomed because they frequently bring into the open conditions and faults in service that should be corrected.
    (C) The defendant had a very unique alibi, so the judge dismissed the case.
    (D) Court officers must direct witnesses to seats when the latter present themselves in court to testify.

27. **(A)** The clerk promptly notified the judge of the fire for which he was highly praised.
    (B) There is justice among thieves; the three thieves divided the goods equally among themselves.
    (C) If he had been notified promptly, he might have been here on time.
    (D) Though doubt may exist about the mailability of some matter, the sender is fully liable for law violation if such matter should be nonmailable.

Directions: Choose the sentence that is grammatically **correct** and darken its letter on your answer sheet.

28. **(A)** In high-visibility crimes, it is apparent to all concerned that they are criminal acts at the time when they are committed.
    (B) Statistics tell us that more people are killed by guns than by any kind of weapon.
    (C) Reliable persons guarantee the facts with regards to the truth of these statements.
    (D) The errors in the typed report were so numerous that they could hardly be overlooked.

29. **(A)** She suspects that the service is not so satisfactory as it should be.
    (B) The court officer goes to the exhibit table and discovered that Exhibit B is an entirely different document.
    (C) The jurors and alternates comprise a truly diverse group.
    (D) Our aim should be not merely to reform law breakers but striking at the roots of crime.

30. **(A)** Close examination of traffic accident statistics reveal that traffic accidents are frequently the result of violations of traffic laws.
    (B) If you had planned on employing fewer people than this to do the work, this situation would not have arose.
    (C) As far as good looks and polite manners are concerned, they are both alike.
    (D) If a murder has been committed with a bow and arrow, it is irrelevant to show that the defendant was well acquainted with firearms.

31. **(A)** An individual engages in criminal behavior if the number of criminal patterns which he or she has acquired exceeds the number of noncriminal patterns.
    (B) Every person must be informed of the reason for their arrest unless arrested in the actual commission of a crime.
    (C) The one of the following motorists to which it would be most desirable to issue a summons is the one which was late for an important business appointment.
    (D) The officer should glance around quickly but with care to determine whether his entering the area will damage any evidence.

32. **(A)** The typist would of corrected the errors had she realized that the supervisor would see the report.
    (B) If the budget allows, we are likely to reemploy anyone whose training fits them to do the work.
    (C) Since the report lacked the needed information, it was of no value to me.
    (D) There would have been no trouble if the receptionist would have always answered courteously.

33. (A) Due to the age of the defendant, the trial will be heard in Juvenile Court and the record will be sealed.

(B) Calculate the average amount stolen per incident by dividing the total value by the amount of offenses.

(C) The combination to the office safe is known only to the chief clerk and myself.

(D) Hearsay is evidence based on repeating the words told by another and not based on personal observation or knowledge.

34. (A) A court officer needs specific qualifications that are different than those required of police officers.

(B) Understanding how one's own work contributes to the effort of the entire agency indicates an appreciation for the importance of that job.

(C) If only one guard was assigned to the jury room, the chances of wrongdoing would be heightened.

(D) One should not use an improved method for performing a task until you have obtained approval of the supervisor.

CLERICAL SKILLS

Directions: For each question, compare the name/address/number listings in all three columns. Then darken answer space:

- **(A)** if the listings in **ALL THREE** columns are exactly **ALIKE**
- **(B)** if only the listings in **COLUMNS 1** and **3** are exactly **ALIKE**
- **(C)** if only the listings in **COLUMNS 1** and **2** are exactly **ALIKE**
- **(D)** if the listings in **ALL THREE** columns are **DIFFERENT**

Column 1	Column 2	Column 3
35. John H. Smith 238 N. Monroe Street Phila., PA 19147 176-54-326 5578-98765-33	John H. Smith 238 N. Monroe Street Phila, PA 19147 176-54-326 5578-98765-33	John H. Smith 238 N. Monroe Street Phila., PA 19147 176-54-326 5578-98765-33
36. Evan A. McKinley 2872 Broadway East Amherst, NY 14051 212-883-5184 9803-115-6848	Evan A. McKinley 2872 Broadway East Amherst, NY 14051 212-883-5184 9083-115-6848	Evan A. McKinley 2872 Broadway East Amherst, NV 14051 212-883-5184 9083-115-6848
37. Luigi Antonio Cruz, Jr. 2695 East 3435 South Salt Lake City, UT 84109 801-485-1563, x.233 013-5589734-9	Luigi Antonio Cruz, Jr. 2695 East 3435 South Salt, Lake City, UT 84109 801-485-1563, x.233 013-5589734-9	Luigi Antonio Cruz, Jr. 2695 East 3435 South Salt Lake City, UT 84109 801-485-1563, x.233 013-5589734-9
38. Educational Records Inst. P.O. Box 44268a Atlanta, Georgia 30337 18624-40-9128 63qs5-95YT3-001	Educational Records Inst. P.O. Box 44268a Atlanta, Georgia 30337 18624-40-9128 63qs5-95YT3-001	Educational Records Inst. P.O. Box 44286a Atlanta, Georgia 30337 18624-40-9128 63qs5-95YT3-001
39. Sr. Consultant, Labor Rel. Benner Mgmt. Group 86408 W. 3rd Ave. Trowbridge, MA 02178 617-980-1136	Sr. Consultant, Labor Rel. Banner Mgmt. Group 86408 W. 3rd Ave. Trowbridge, MA 02178 617-980-1136	Sr. Consultant, Labor Rel. Benner Mgmt. Group 84608 W. 3rd Ave. Trowbridge, MA 02178 617-980-1136
40. Marina Angelika Salvis P.O.B. 11283 Gracie Sta. Newtown, PA 18940-0998 215-382-0628 4168-GNP-78852	Marina Angelika Salvis P.O.B. 11283 Gracie Sta. Newtown, PA 18940-0998 215-382-0628 4168-GNP-78852	Marina Angelika Salvis PO.B. 11283 Gracie Sta. Newtown, PA 18940-0998 215-382-0628 4168-GNP-78852
41. Durham Reichard, III 8298 Antigua Terrace Gaithersburg, MD 20879 301-176-9887-8 0-671-843576-X	Durham Reichard, III 8298 Antigua Terrace Gaithersburg, MD 20879 301-176-9887-8 0-671-843576-X	Durham Reichard, III 8298 Antigua Terrace Gaithersberg, MD 20879 301-176-9887-8 0-671-843576-X

Column 1	Column 2	Column 3
42. L. Chamberlain Smythe Mardikian & Moore, Inc. Cor. Mott Street at Pell San Francisco, Calif. 58312-398401-25	L. Chamberlain Smythe Mardikian and Moore, Inc. Cor. Mott Street at Pell San Francisco, Calif. 58312-398401-25	L. Chamberlain Smythe Mardikian & Moore, Inc. Cor. Mott Street at Pell San Francisco, Calif. 58312-398401-25
43. Ramona Fleischer-Chris 60646 West Touhy Avenue Sebastopol, CA 95472 707-998-0104 0-06-408632-0	Ramona Fleisher-Chris 60646 West Touhy Avenue Sebastopol, CA 95472 707-998-0104 0-06-408632-0	Ramona Fleischer-Chris 60646 West Touhey Avenue Sebastopol, CA 95472 707-998-0104 0-06-408632-0
44. George Sebastian Barnes Noble/Encore/Dalton 43216 M Street, NE Washington, DC 20036 202-222-1272	George Sebastian Barnes Noble/Encore/Dalton 43216 M. Street, NE Washington, DC 20036 202-222-1272	George Sebastian Barnes Noble/Encore/Dalton 43216 M Street, NE Washington, DC 20036 202-222-1272
45. Baldwin Algonquin, III 2503 Bartholemew Way Lemberger, VA 28094-9182 9-1-303-558-8536 683-64-0828	Baldwin Algonquin, III 2503 Bartholemew Way Lemberger, VA 28094-9182 9-1-303-558-8536 683-64-0828	Baldwin Algonquin, III 2503 Bartholomew Way Lemberger, VA 28094-9182 9-l-303-558-8536 683-64-0828
46. Huang Ho Cheung 612 Gallopade Gallery, E. Seattle, WA 98101-2614 001-206-283-7722 5416R-1952TZ-op	Huang Ho Cheung 612 Gallopade Gallery, E. Seattle, WA 98101-2614 001-206-283-7722 5416R-1952TZ-op	Huang Ho Cheung 612 Gallopade Gallery, E. Seattle, WA 98101-2614 001-206-283-7722 5416R-1952TZ-op
47. Hilliard H. Hyacinth 86529 Dunwoodie Drive Kanakao, HI 91132 808-880-8080 6-78912-e3e42	Hilliard H. Hyacinth 86529 Dunwoodie Drive Kanakao, HI 91132 808-880-8080 6-78912-3e3e42	Hilliard H. Hyacinth 85629 Dunwoodie Drive Kanakao, HI 91132 808-880-8080 6-78912-e3e42
48. Anoko Kawamoto 8932 Shimabui Hwy. O'Reilly Bay, LA 56212 713-864-7253-4984 5634-Ootv5a-16867	Anoko Kawamoto 8932 Shimabui Hwy. O'Reillys Bay, LA 56212 713-864-7253-4984 5634-Ootv5a-16867	Anoko, Kawamoto 8932 Shimabui Hwy. O'Reilly Bay, LA 56212 713-864-7253-4984 5634-Ootv5a-16867
49. Michael Chrzanowski 312 Colonia del Valle 4132 ES, Mexico DF 001-45-67265 A8987-B73245	Michael Chrzanowski 312 Colonia del Valle 4132 ES, Mexico DF 001-45-67265 A8987-B73245	Michael Chrzanowski 312 Colonia del Valle 4132 ES, Mexico D.F 001-45-67265 A8987-B73245
50. Leonard Wilson-Wood 6892 Grand Boulevard, W. St. Georges South, DE 302-333-4273 0-122365-3987	Leonard Wilson-Wood 6892 Grand Boulevard, W. St. Georges South, DE 302-333-4273 0-122365-3987	Leonard Wilson-Wood 6892 Grand Boulevard, W. St. Georges South, DE 302-333-4273 0-122365-3987

RECORD-KEEPING SKILLS

Directions: Study the information given in the tables and combine the information as indicated. Answer the multiple-choice questions in accordance with the information on the tables. You are NOT permitted to use a calculator to arrive at totals.

DAILY LOG OF CASES

MONDAY				
Judge	*Date Filed*	*Sum at Issue*	*Disposition*	*Award*
Baron	6/5/98	$ 9,500	adjourned	X
Lee	4/2/99	20,000	dismissed	X
Conlon	12/8/97	12,000	settled	X
Ramos	3/31/99	5,500	settled	X
Lee	10/81/98	10,000	dismissed	X
Jones	1/5/99	14,000	found for plaintiff	$15,000
Baron	5/1/00	7,600	adjourned	X

TUESDAY				
Judge	*Date Filed*	*Sum at Issue*	*Disposition*	*Award*
Ramos	2/2/99	$ 3,000	found for plaintiff	$3,375
Amati	8/6/99	8,000	dismissed	X
Moro	4/8/98	11,500	found for plaintiff	9,000
Jones	11/17/97	12,000	adjourned	X
Conlon	12/4/97	4,500	adjourned	X
Amati	6/12/98	2,000	settled	X

WEDNESDAY				
Judge	*Date Filed*	*Sum at Issue*	*Disposition*	*Award*
Conlon	1/7/00	$10,000	dismissed	X
Baron	5/3/99	5,000	adjourned	X
Ramos	6/22/98	7,500	found for plaintiff	$ 6,000
Moro	2/15/00	22,000	settled	X
Lee	9/7/99	8,000	settled	X
Conlon	11/30/97	16,000	found for plaintiff	17,250
Amati	7/10/99	10,000	found for plaintiff	10,850

THURSDAY				
Judge	*Date Filed*	*Sum at Issue*	*Disposition*	*Award*
Jones	5/18/99	$ 7,500	found for plaintiff	$ 6,000
Amati	3/6/98	9,250	settled	X
Conlon	3/31/99	6,000	adjourned	X
Moro	8/28/98	12,000	adjourned	X
Conlon	10/30/97	4,600	found for plaintiff	5,000

FRIDAY				
Judge	*Date Filed*	*Sum at Issue*	*Disposition*	*Award*
Lee	4/12/99	$ 6,000	adjourned	X
Baron	1/28/00	9,500	dismissed	X
Ramos	7/17/99	28,000	found for plaintiff	$20,000
Amati	12/2/98	15,000	settled	X
Lee	2/21/99	8,000	found for plaintiff	8,625
Moro	5/9/98	22,000	settled	X
Baron	8/25/98	11,000	dismissed	X
Jones	11/4/97	5,500	settled	X

DAILY BREAKDOWN OF CASES						
	Mon.	*Tue.*	*Wed.*	*Thurs.*	*Fri.*	*Total*
Case Status						
Dismissed	2	1	1	0	2	6
Adjourned						
Settled						
Found for Plaintiff						
Total Cases						
	Mon.	*Tue.*	*Wed.*	*Thurs.*	*Fri.*	*Total*
Cases Filed by Year						
1997	1	2	1	1	1	6
1998						
1999						
2000						
Total Cases						

SUMMARY OF CASES					
Judge	*Dismissed*	*Adjourned*	*Settled*	*Found for Plaintiff*	*Total*
Amati	1		3	1	5
Baron					
Conlon					
Jones					
Lee					
Moro					
Ramos					

51. The judge scheduled to hear the greatest number of cases in this week was

(A) Amati
(B) Lee
(C) Conlon
(D) Ramos

52. The judge who determined no cash awards in this week was

(A) Moro
(B) Jones
(C) Baron
(D) Lee

53. How many judges were assigned to hear more than one case in one day?

(A) 1
(B) 2
(C) 3
(D) 4

54. In how many cases was the sum finally awarded lower than the sum at issue?

(A) 2
(B) 3
(C) 4
(D) 5

55. How many of the cases filed in 1997 were dismissed?

(A) 0
(B) 1
(C) 2
(D) 3

56. Of the cases adjourned, the greatest number were filed in

(A) 1997
(B) 1998
(C) 1999
(D) 2000

57. Which two judges were scheduled to sit on only three days?

(A) Jones and Baron
(B) Baron and Lee
(C) Lee and Moro
(D) Ramos and Jones

58. In which month was the greatest number of cases filed?

(A) February
(B) May
(C) August
(D) November

59. The total amount of money awarded on Wednesday was

(A) $33,500
(B) $34,100
(C) $35,300
(D) $45,000

60. The total amount of money awarded by Jones was

(A) $39,000
(B) $21,500
(C) $21,000
(D) $17,500

61. The amount at issue in the cases that were adjourned on Thursday was

- **(A)** $12,100
- **(B)** $18,000
- **(C)** $21,350
- **(D)** $29,250

62. When the amount of an award is greater than the sum at issue, the higher award represents an additional sum meant to cover plaintiff's costs in the suit. The total amount awarded this week to cover costs was

- **(A)** $ 4,500
- **(B)** $ 4,850
- **(C)** $ 9,000
- **(D)** $13,500

63. If all the plaintiffs who filed cases in 2000 were awarded exactly the sums for which they sued, they would have received a total of

- **(A)** $41,500
- **(B)** $45,100
- **(C)** $48,600
- **(D)** $49,100

64. The total amount awarded to plaintiffs who filed their cases in 1997 was

- **(A)** $ 1,650
- **(B)** $20,600
- **(C)** $22,250
- **(D)** $22,650

65. Comparing cases filed in 1998 with cases filed in 1999,

- **(A)** four more of the 1998 cases were settled than 1999 cases
- **(B)** two fewer 1999 cases were settled than 1998 cases
- **(C)** an equal number of cases was settled from the two years
- **(D)** three more of the 1998 cases were settled than 1999 cases

READING COMPREHENSION

Directions: Each passage below contains 15 numbered blanks. Read the passage once quickly to get the overall idea. Below each passage are listed sets of words numbered to match the blanks. Read the passage through a second time, more slowly, and choose the word from each set which makes the most sense both in the sentence and the total paragraph. Darken the letter of that word on your answer sheet.

A large proportion of people _____ bars are _____ convicted criminals, _____ people who
                                 66   67   68
have been arrested and are being _____ until _____ trial in _____. Experts have often
                                      69   70   71
pointed out that this _____ system does not operate fairly. For instance, a person who can
                          72
afford to pay bail usually will not get locked up. The theory of the bail system is that the
person will make sure to show up in court when he or she is supposed to; _____, bail will be
                                                                  73
forfeited—the person will _____ the _____ that was put up. Sometimes a person _____ can
                             74   75   76
show that he or she is a stable _____ with a job and a family will be released on "Personal
                                 77
recognizance" (without bail). The result is that the well-to-do, the _____, and the family men
                                                                        78
can often _____ the detention system. The people who do wind up in detention tend to _____
                    79   80
the poor, the unemployed, the single, and the young.

66. (A) under
    (B) at
    (C) tending
    (D) behind

67. (A) always
    (B) not
    (C) hardened
    (D) very

68. (A) but
    (B) and
    (C) also
    (D) although

69. (A) hanged
    (B) freed
    (C) held
    (D) judged

70. (A) your
    (B) his
    (C) daily
    (D) their

71. (A) jail
    (B) court
    (C) fire
    (D) judgment

72. (A) school
    (B) court
    (C) detention
    (D) election

73. (A) otherwise
    (B) therefore
    (C) because
    (D) then

74. (A) save
    (B) spend
    (C) lose
    (D) count

75. (A) wall
    (B) money
    (C) front
    (D) pretense

76. (A) whom
    (B) which
    (C) what
    (D) who

77. (A) citizen
    (B) horse
    (C) cleaner
    (D) clown

78. (A) handsome
    (B) athletic
    (C) employed
    (D) alcoholic

79. (A) survive
    (B) avoid
    (C) provide
    (D) institute

80. (A) become
    (B) help
    (C) be
    (D) harm

_____ acts are classified according to _____ standards. One is whether the _____ is major or
  81   82   83

minor. A major offense, such as murder, would be _____ a felony, _____ a minor offense, such
                                             84   85

as reckless driving, would be considered a misdemeanor. _____ standard of classification is
                                               86

the specific kind of crime committed. Examples are burglary and robbery, which are _____
                                                           87

often used incorrectly by individuals who are _____ aware of the actual _____ as defined by
                                       88   89

law. A person who breaks _____ a building to commit a _____ or other major crime is _____
                           90   91   92

of burglary, while robbery is the felonious taking of an individual's _____ from his person or
                                                         93

_____ his immediate _____ by the use of violence or threat.
  94   95

81. (A) People's
    (B) Criminal
    (C) Felonious
    (D) Numerous

82. (A) decent
    (B) published
    (C) community
    (D) several

83. (A) crime
    (B) act
    (C) offender
    (D) standard

84. (A) labeled
    (B) convicted
    (C) executed
    (D) tried

85. (A) moreover
    (B) because
    (C) whereas
    (D) hence

86. (A) Gold
    (B) Juried
    (C) Another
    (D) My

87. (A) crimes
    (B) terms
    (C) verdicts
    (D) sentences

88. (A) sometimes
    (B) very
    (C) not
    (D) angrily

89. (A) difference
    (B) definitions
    (C) crimes
    (D) victims

90. (A) down
    (B) into
    (C) apart
    (D) from

91. (A) felony
    (B) burglary
    (C) robbery
    (D) theft

92. (A) accused
    (B) convicted
    (C) freed
    (D) guilty

93. (A) life
    (B) liberty
    (C) property
    (D) weapon

94. (A) throughout
    (B) in
    (C) by
    (D) for

95. (A) lifetime
    (B) home
    (C) presence
    (D) concern

ANSWER KEY AND EXPLANATIONS

Spelling

1. D	5. C	9. D	13. C	17. D
2. A	6. A	10. C	14. D	18. B
3. C	7. D	11. B	15. C	19. A
4. B	8. B	12. D	16. A	20. D

1. **The correct answer is (D).** appellate

2. **The correct answer is (A).** presumption

3. **The correct answer is (C).** litigant

4. **The correct answer is (B).** commitment

5. **The correct answer is (C).** affidavit

6. **The correct answer is (A).** arraign

7. **The correct answer is (D).** cumulative

8. **The correct answer is (B).** severance

9. **The correct answer is (D).** adjournment

10. **The correct answer is (C).** commenced

11. **The correct answer is (B).** forgers

12. **The correct answer is (D).** no error

13. **The correct answer is (C).** achievement

14. **The correct answer is (D).** no error

15. **The correct answer is (C).** detention

16. **The correct answer is (A).** immaterial

17. **The correct answer is (D).** no error

18. **The correct answer is (B).** prosecutor

19. **The correct answer is (A).** correctible

20. **The correct answer is (D).** no error

Grammar Skills

21. C	24. B	27. A	30. D	33. D
22. D	25. B	28. D	31. A	34. B
23. A	26. C	29. C	32. C	

21. **The correct answer is (C).** There should be no "and" before the "etc." at the end of a series of words.

22. **The correct answer is (D).** This is an incomplete comparison. It should read: "He devotes as much *as*, if not more, time to his work than do the rest of the employees."

23. **The correct answer is (A).** (A) "More preferable" is a redundancy. "Preferable" alone is quite adequate.

24. **The correct answer is (B).** The compound subject requires the plural form of the verb—constitute.

25. **The correct answer is (B).** This sentence shifts point of view midstream. It could read either "If one wants to prevent crime, one must deal . . ." or "If we want to prevent crime, we must deal . . ."

26. **The correct answer is (C).** "Unique" means that there is only one; therefore, the word can take no qualifier.

27. **The correct answer is (A).** This is an ambiguous statement. Was the judge praised for the fire? Was the clerk praised for the fire? It would be better to say, "The clerk was highly praised for promptly notifying the judge of the fire."

28. **The correct answer is (D).** (A) reads as if all concerned are criminal acts. Since guns are a kind of weapon, (B) would have to read . . . than any *other* kind of weapon." In (C), "regards" is the wrong word. The word required is "regard."

29. **The correct answer is (C).** In (A) the idiomatic form is "*as* satisfactory." (B) confuses two tenses in the same sentence. It would be correct to say the court officer *went* and discovered. (D) requires a parallel construction, either "reforming and striking" or "to reform and to strike."

30. **The correct answer is (D).** In (A) "examination" being singular requires the singular verb, "reveals." In (B) we need "would not have *arisen*." As for (C), the word "alike" obviously includes "both," so the word "both" is redundant.

31. **The correct answer is (A).** In (B) every person is singular and therefore must be informed for the reason for *his* (or *her*) arrest. In (C), a motorist is a person, not a thing, so use *who* and *to whom* rather than *which*. In (D) we need the parallelism of "quickly but carefully."

32. **The correct answer is (C).** In (A) we need the auxiliary verb <u>have</u> in place of the incorrect <u>of</u>. In (B) "anyone" is singular so the referent pronoun must also be singular. In (D), the construction is awkward. ". . . if the receptionist had always answered . . ." is sufficient and accurate.

33. **The correct answer is (D).** (A) is incorrect because it is poor form to begin a sentence with "due to." In (B) what is meant is the *number* of offenses. In (C) we need a simple objective case pronoun, ". . . is known only to the chief clerk and *me*."

34. **The correct answer is (B).** In (A) the correct idiomatic form is "different *from*." (C) requires a subjunctive form because the statement is contrary to fact. "If only one guard *were* . . . ." (D) shifts point of view. For consistency the pronoun throughout may be either "one" or "you."

Clerical Skills

35. B	39. D	42. B	45. C	48. B
36. D	40. A	43. D	46. A	49. C
37. A	41. C	44. B	47. D	50. A
38. C				

35. **The correct answer is (B).** In Column 2, Phila, PA 19147 differs from Phila., PA 19147.

36. **The correct answer is (D).** In Column 3, East Amherst, NV 14051 differs from East Amherst, NY 14051. In Column 2, 9083-115-6848 differs from 9803-115-6848.

37. **The correct answer is (A).** All columns are alike.

38. **The correct answer is (C).** In Column 3, P.O. Box 44286a differs from P.O. Box 44268a.

39. **The correct answer is (D).** In Column 2, Banner differs from Benner. In Column 3, 84608 differs from 86408.

40. **The correct answer is (A).** All columns are alike.

41. **The correct answer is (C).** In Column 3, Gaithersberg differs from Gaithersburg.

42. **The correct answer is (B).** In Column 2, the word *and* is spelled out; in Column 1, the same effect is gained with &.

43. **The correct answer is (D).** In Column 2, Fleisher differs from Fleischer. In Column 3, Touhey differs from Touhy.

44. **The correct answer is (B).** In Column 2, 43216 M. Street, NE differs from 43216 M Street, NE.

45. **The correct answer is (C).** In Column 3, Bartholomew differs from Bartholemew.

46. **The correct answer is (A).** All columns are alike.

47. **The correct answer is (D).** In Column 3, 85629 Dunwoodie Drive differs from 86529 Dunwoodie Drive. In Column 2, 6-78912-3e3e42 differs from 6-78912-e3e42.

48. **The correct answer is (B).** In Column 2, O'Reillys Bay differs from O'Reilly Bay.

49. **The correct answer is (C).** In Column 3, Mexico D.F. differs from Mexico DF.

50. **The correct answer is (A).** All columns are alike.

Record-Keeping Skills

51. C	54. C	57. B	60. C	63. D
52. C	55. A	58. B	61. B	64. C
53. D	56. C	59. B	62. A	65. B

51. **The correct answer is (C).** Conlon was scheduled to hear six cases, Amati and Lee were scheduled for five apiece, and Ramos was scheduled for four.

52. **The correct answer is (C).** Of the cases Baron was scheduled to hear, three were adjourned and two were dismissed. Jones gave cash awards in two cases, and Moro and Lee gave cash awards in one each.

53. **The correct answer is (D).** Lee and Baron were both scheduled for two trials on Monday and Friday, Amati was scheduled for two on Tuesday, and Conlon was scheduled for two on Wednesday and Thursday.

54. **The correct answer is (C).** On Tuesday, Moro awarded $9,000 in a suit for $11,500; on Wednesday, Ramos awarded $6,000 in a suit for $7,500; on Thursday, Jones awarded $6,000 in a suit for $7,500; and on Friday, Ramos awarded $20,000 in a suit for $28,000.

55. **The correct answer is (A).** Of the six cases filed in 1997, two were settled, two were adjourned, and two were adjudicated. None was dismissed.

56. **The correct answer is (C).** Three of the 1999 cases were adjourned, one 2000 case was adjourned, and two each of 1997 and 1998 cases were adjourned.

57. The correct answer is (B). Lee and Baron each sat on Monday, Wednesday, and Friday. Jones sat on Monday, Tuesday, Thursday, and Friday. Moro sat on Tuesday, Wednesday, Thursday, and Friday. Ramos sat on Monday, Tuesday, Wednesday, and Friday.

58. The correct answer is (B). Four cases were filed in May. Three cases were filed in each of February, August, and November.

59. The correct answer is (B). $6,000 + $17,250 + $10,850 = $34,100

60. The correct answer is (C). $15,000 + $6,000 = $21,000

61. The correct answer is (B). $6,000 + $12,000 = $18,000

62. The correct answer is (A).

```
$15,000 − $14,000 = $1,000   (Jones on Monday)
 $3,375 −  $3,000 =   $375   (Ramos on Tuesday)
$17,250 − $16,000 = $1,250   (Conlon on Wednesday)
$10,850 − $10,000 =   $850   (Amati on Wednesday)
 $5,000 −  $4,600 =   $400   (Conlon on Thursday)
 $8,625 −  $8,000 =   $625   (Lee on Friday)
                    $4,500
```

63. The correct answer is (D).

```
5/1/00     $ 7,600
1/7/00      10,000
2/15/00     22,000
1/28/00  +   9,500
           $49,100
```

64. The correct answer is (C).

On Wednesday, Conlon awarded $17,250 in a 11/30/97 case.

On Thursday, Conlon awarded　　5,000 in a 10/30/97 case.

$22,250

65. The correct answer is (B). Four 1998 cases were settled; only two 1999 cases were settled.

Reading Comprehension

66.	B	72.	C	78.	C	84.	A	90.	B
67.	B	73.	A	79.	B	85.	C	91.	D
68.	A	74.	C	80.	C	86.	C	92.	D
69.	C	75.	B	81.	B	87.	B	93.	C
70.	D	76.	D	82.	D	88.	C	94.	B
71.	B	77.	A	83.	A	89.	A	95.	C

Correct answers for questions 66–80, completed paragraph:

A large proportion of people <u>behind</u> bars are <u>not</u> convicted criminals, <u>but</u> people who have
        66   67   68
been arrested and are being <u>held</u> until <u>their</u> trial in <u>court</u>. Experts have often pointed out that
                             69   70   71
this <u>detention</u> system does not operate fairly. For instance, a person who can afford to pay bail
      72
usually will not get locked up. The theory of the bail system is that the person will make sure
to show up in court when he or she is supposed to; <u>otherwise</u>, bail will be forfeited—the person
                                                    73
will <u>lose</u> the <u>money</u> that was put up. Sometimes a person <u>who</u> can show that he or she is a
      74   75   76
stable <u>citizen</u> with a job and a family will be released on "personal recognizance" (without
        77
bail). The result is that the well-to-do, the <u>employed</u>, and the family men can often <u>avoid</u> the
                                               78   79
detention system. The people who do wind up in detention tend to <u>be</u> the poor, the
                                                                    80
unemployed, the single, and the young.

Correct answers for questions 81–95, completed paragraph:

<u>Criminal</u> acts are classified according to <u>several</u> standards. One is whether the <u>crime</u> is
 81   82   83
major or minor. A major offense, such as murder, would be <u>labeled</u> a felony, <u>whereas</u> a
                                                            84   85
minor offense, such as reckless driving, would be considered a misdemeanor. <u>Another</u>
                                                                             86
standard of classification is the specific kind of crime committed. Examples are burglary
and robbery, which are <u>terms</u> often used incorrectly by individuals who are <u>not</u> aware of the
                        87   88
actual <u>difference</u> as defined by law. A person who breaks <u>into</u> a building to commit a <u>theft</u>
        89   90   91
or other major crime is <u>guilty</u> of burglary, while robbery is the felonious taking of an
                         92
individual's <u>property</u> from his person or <u>in</u> his immediate <u>presence</u> by the use of violence
              93   94   95
or threat.

ANSWER SHEET PRACTICE TEST 8: MUNICIPAL OFFICE AIDE EXAM

1. Ⓐ Ⓑ Ⓒ Ⓓ Ⓔ
2. Ⓐ Ⓑ Ⓒ Ⓓ Ⓔ
3. Ⓐ Ⓑ Ⓒ Ⓓ Ⓔ
4. Ⓐ Ⓑ Ⓒ Ⓓ Ⓔ
5. Ⓐ Ⓑ Ⓒ Ⓓ Ⓔ
6. Ⓐ Ⓑ Ⓒ Ⓓ Ⓔ
7. Ⓐ Ⓑ Ⓒ Ⓓ Ⓔ
8. Ⓐ Ⓑ Ⓒ Ⓓ Ⓔ
9. Ⓐ Ⓑ Ⓒ Ⓓ Ⓔ
10. Ⓐ Ⓑ Ⓒ Ⓓ Ⓔ
11. Ⓐ Ⓑ Ⓒ Ⓓ Ⓔ
12. Ⓐ Ⓑ Ⓒ Ⓓ Ⓔ
13. Ⓐ Ⓑ Ⓒ Ⓓ Ⓔ
14. Ⓐ Ⓑ Ⓒ Ⓓ Ⓔ
15. Ⓐ Ⓑ Ⓒ Ⓓ Ⓔ
16. Ⓐ Ⓑ Ⓒ Ⓓ Ⓔ
17. Ⓐ Ⓑ Ⓒ Ⓓ Ⓔ
18. Ⓐ Ⓑ Ⓒ Ⓓ Ⓔ
19. Ⓐ Ⓑ Ⓒ Ⓓ Ⓔ
20. Ⓐ Ⓑ Ⓒ Ⓓ Ⓔ
21. Ⓐ Ⓑ Ⓒ Ⓓ Ⓔ
22. Ⓐ Ⓑ Ⓒ Ⓓ Ⓔ
23. Ⓐ Ⓑ Ⓒ Ⓓ Ⓔ
24. Ⓐ Ⓑ Ⓒ Ⓓ Ⓔ
25. Ⓐ Ⓑ Ⓒ Ⓓ Ⓔ
26. Ⓐ Ⓑ Ⓒ Ⓓ Ⓔ
27. Ⓐ Ⓑ Ⓒ Ⓓ Ⓔ

28. Ⓐ Ⓑ Ⓒ Ⓓ Ⓔ
29. Ⓐ Ⓑ Ⓒ Ⓓ Ⓔ
30. Ⓐ Ⓑ Ⓒ Ⓓ Ⓔ
31. Ⓐ Ⓑ Ⓒ Ⓓ Ⓔ
32. Ⓐ Ⓑ Ⓒ Ⓓ Ⓔ
33. Ⓐ Ⓑ Ⓒ Ⓓ Ⓔ
34. Ⓐ Ⓑ Ⓒ Ⓓ Ⓔ
35. Ⓐ Ⓑ Ⓒ Ⓓ Ⓔ
36. Ⓐ Ⓑ Ⓒ Ⓓ Ⓔ
37. Ⓐ Ⓑ Ⓒ Ⓓ Ⓔ
38. Ⓐ Ⓑ Ⓒ Ⓓ Ⓔ
39. Ⓐ Ⓑ Ⓒ Ⓓ Ⓔ
40. Ⓐ Ⓑ Ⓒ Ⓓ Ⓔ
41. Ⓐ Ⓑ Ⓒ Ⓓ Ⓔ
42. Ⓐ Ⓑ Ⓒ Ⓓ Ⓔ
43. Ⓐ Ⓑ Ⓒ Ⓓ Ⓔ
44. Ⓐ Ⓑ Ⓒ Ⓓ Ⓔ
45. Ⓐ Ⓑ Ⓒ Ⓓ Ⓔ
46. Ⓐ Ⓑ Ⓒ Ⓓ Ⓔ
47. Ⓐ Ⓑ Ⓒ Ⓓ Ⓔ
48. Ⓐ Ⓑ Ⓒ Ⓓ Ⓔ
49. Ⓐ Ⓑ Ⓒ Ⓓ Ⓔ
50. Ⓐ Ⓑ Ⓒ Ⓓ Ⓔ
51. Ⓐ Ⓑ Ⓒ Ⓓ Ⓔ
52. Ⓐ Ⓑ Ⓒ Ⓓ Ⓔ
53. Ⓐ Ⓑ Ⓒ Ⓓ Ⓔ

54. Ⓐ Ⓑ Ⓒ Ⓓ Ⓔ
55. Ⓐ Ⓑ Ⓒ Ⓓ Ⓔ
56. Ⓐ Ⓑ Ⓒ Ⓓ Ⓔ
57. Ⓐ Ⓑ Ⓒ Ⓓ Ⓔ
58. Ⓐ Ⓑ Ⓒ Ⓓ Ⓔ
59. Ⓐ Ⓑ Ⓒ Ⓓ Ⓔ
60. Ⓐ Ⓑ Ⓒ Ⓓ Ⓔ
61. Ⓐ Ⓑ Ⓒ Ⓓ Ⓔ
62. Ⓐ Ⓑ Ⓒ Ⓓ Ⓔ
63. Ⓐ Ⓑ Ⓒ Ⓓ Ⓔ
64. Ⓐ Ⓑ Ⓒ Ⓓ Ⓔ
65. Ⓐ Ⓑ Ⓒ Ⓓ Ⓔ
66. Ⓐ Ⓑ Ⓒ Ⓓ Ⓔ
67. Ⓐ Ⓑ Ⓒ Ⓓ Ⓔ
68. Ⓐ Ⓑ Ⓒ Ⓓ Ⓔ
69. Ⓐ Ⓑ Ⓒ Ⓓ Ⓔ
70. Ⓐ Ⓑ Ⓒ Ⓓ Ⓔ
71. Ⓐ Ⓑ Ⓒ Ⓓ Ⓔ
72. Ⓐ Ⓑ Ⓒ Ⓓ Ⓔ
73. Ⓐ Ⓑ Ⓒ Ⓓ Ⓔ
74. Ⓐ Ⓑ Ⓒ Ⓓ Ⓔ
75. Ⓐ Ⓑ Ⓒ Ⓓ Ⓔ
76. Ⓐ Ⓑ Ⓒ Ⓓ Ⓔ
77. Ⓐ Ⓑ Ⓒ Ⓓ Ⓔ
78. Ⓐ Ⓑ Ⓒ Ⓓ Ⓔ
79. Ⓐ Ⓑ Ⓒ Ⓓ Ⓔ

answer sheet

Practice Test 8: Municipal Office Aide Exam

79 QUESTIONS • 3½ HOURS

Directions: Choose the best answer to each question and darken its letter on the answer sheet.

1. Assume that a few co-workers meet near your desk and talk about personal matters during working hours. Lately, this practice has interfered with your work. In order to stop this practice, the best action for you to take *first* is to

   (A) ask your supervisor to put a stop to the co-workers' meeting near your desk.
   (B) discontinue any friendship with this group.
   (C) ask your co-workers not to meet near your desk.
   (D) request that your desk be moved to another location.

2. To maintain office coverage during working hours, your supervisor has scheduled your lunch hour from 1 p.m. to 2 p.m. and your co-worker's lunch hour from 12 p.m. to 1 p.m. Lately, your co-worker has been returning late from lunch each day. As a result you don't get a full hour, since you must return to the office by 2 p.m. Of the following, the best action for you to take *first* is to

   (A) explain to your co-worker in a courteous manner that his or her lateness is interfering with your right to a full hour for lunch.
   (B) tell your co-worker that his lateness must stop or you will report him to your supervisor.
   (C) report your co-worker's lateness to your supervisor.
   (D) leave at 1 p.m. for lunch, whether your co-worker has returned or not.

3. Assume that, as an office worker, one of your jobs is to open mail sent to your unit, read the mail for content, and send the mail to the appropriate person for handling. You accidentally open and begin to read a letter marked "personal" addressed to a co-worker. Of the following, the best action for you to take is to

   (A) report to your supervisor that your co-worker is receiving personal mail at the office.
   (B) destroy the letter so that your co-worker doesn't know you saw it.
   (C) reseal the letter and place it on the co-worker's desk without saying anything.
   (D) bring the letter to your co-worker and explain that you opened it by accident.

4. Suppose that in evaluating your work your supervisor gives you an overall good rating, but states that you sometimes turn in work with careless errors. The best action for you to take would be to

   (A) ask a co-worker who is good at details to proofread your work.
   (B) take time to do a careful job, paying more attention to detail.
   (C) continue working as usual since occasional errors are to be expected.
   (D) ask your supervisor if he or she would mind correcting your errors.

5. Assume that you are taking a telephone message for a co-worker who is not in the office at the time. Of the following, the least important item to write on the message is the

   (A) length of the call.
   (B) name of the caller.
   (C) time of the call.
   (D) telephone number of the caller.

Directions: Questions 6–13. Examine each sentence considering grammar, punctuation, spelling, and capitalization. If the English usage in the underlined parts of the sentence given is better than any of the changes in the underlined words suggested in choice (B), (C), or (D), choose choice (A). If the changes in the underlined words suggested in choice (B), (C), or (D) would make the sentence correct, choose the correct choice. Do not select a choice that will change the meaning of the sentence.

6. This <u>Fall</u> the office will be closed on <u>Columbus Day, October</u> 9th.

   (A) Correct as is
   (B) fall . . . Columbus Day, October
   (C) Fall . . . columbus day, October
   (D) fall . . . Columbus Day, october

7. This manual <u>discribes the duties</u> <u>performed</u> by an office aide.

   (A) Correct as is
   (B) describe the duties performed
   (C) discribe the duties performed
   (D) describes the duties performed

8. There <u>weren't no</u> paper in the supply closet.

   (A) Correct as is
   (B) weren't any
   (C) wasn't any
   (D) wasn't no

9. The new employees left <u>there</u> office to attend a meeting.

   (A) Correct as is
   (B) they're
   (C) their
   (D) thier

10. The office worker started working at <u>8;30 a.m.</u>

    (A) Correct as is
    (B) 8:30 a.m.
    (C) 8;30 a,m.
    (D) 8;30 am.

11. The <u>alphabet, or A to Z sequence are</u> the basis of most filing systems.

    (A) Correct as is
    (B) alphabet, or A to Z sequence, is
    (C) alphabet, or A to Z, sequence are
    (D) alphabet, or A too Z sequence, is

12. <u>Those</u> file cabinets are five <u>feet</u> tall.

    (A) Correct as is
    (B) Them . . . feet
    (C) Those . . . foot
    (D) Them . . . foot

13. The office aide checked the <u>register</u> <u>and finding</u> the date of the meeting.

    (A) Correct as is
    (B) regaster and finding
    (C) register and found
    (D) regaster and found

Directions: Questions 14–21 have two lists of numbers. Each list contains three sets of numbers. Check each of the three sets in the list on the right to see if they are the same as the corresponding set in the list on the left. Darken answer space:

(A) if **NONE** of the sets in the right list are the **SAME** as those in the left list
(B) if **ONLY ONE** of the sets in the right list is the **SAME** as those in the left list
(C) if **ONLY TWO** of the sets in the right list are the **SAME** as those in the left list
(D) if ALL **THREE** sets in the right list are the **SAME** as those in the left list

14. 7354183476   7354983476
     4474747744   4474747774
     57914302311   57914302311

15. 7143592185   7143892185
     8344517699   8344518699
     9178531263   9178531263

16. 2572114731   257214731
     8806835476   8806835476
     8255831246   8255831246

17. 331476853821   331476858621
     6976658532996   6976655832996
     3766042113715   3766042113745

18. 8806663315   8806663315
     74477138449   74477138449
     211756663666   211756663666

19. 990006966996   99000696996
     53022219743   53022219843
     4171171117717   4171171177717

20. 24400222433004   24400222433004
     5300030055000355 5300030055500355
     20000075532002022 20000075532002022

21. 611166640660001116   61116664066001116
     7111300117001100733   7111300117001100733
     26666446664476518   26666446664476518

Directions: Questions 22–25 have two lists of names and addresses. Each list contains three sets of names and addresses. Check each of the three sets in the list on the right to see if they are the same as the corresponding set in the list on the left. Darken answer space:

    (A) if **NONE** of the sets in the right list are the **SAME** as those in the left list
    (B) if **ONLY ONE** of the sets in the right list is the **SAME** as those in the left list
    (C) if **ONLY TWO** of the sets in the right list are the **SAME** as those in the left list
    (D) if **ALL THREE** sets in the right list are the **SAME** as those in the left list

22.

Mary T. Berlinger 2351 Hampton St. Monsey, N.Y. 20117	Mary T. Berlinger 2351 Hampton St. Monsey, N.Y. 20117
Eduardo Benes 473 Kingston Avenue Central Islip, N.Y. 11734	Eduardo Benes 473 Kingston Avenue Central Islip, N.Y. 11734
Alan Carrington Fuchs 17 Gnarled Hollow Road Los Angeles, California 91635	Alan Carrington Fuchs 17 Gnarled Hollow Road Los Angeles, California 91685

23.

David John Jacobson 178 35 St. Apt. 4C New York, N.Y. 00927	David John Jacobson 178 53 St. Apt. 4C New York, N.Y. 00927
Ann-Marie Calonella 7243 South Ridge Blvd. Bakersfield, California 96714	Ann-Marie Calonella 7243 South Ridge Blvd. Bakersfield, California 96714
Pauline M. Thompson 872 Linden Ave. Houston, Texas 70321	Pauline M. Thomson 872 Linden Ave. Houston, Texas 70321

24.

Chester LeRoy Masterton 152 Lacy Rd. Kankakee, Ill. 54532	Chester LeRoy Masterson 152 Lacy Rd. Kankakee, Ill. 54532
William Maloney S. LaCrosse Pla. Wausau, Wisconsin 52146	William Maloney S. LaCross Pla. Wausau, Wisconsin 52146
Cynthia V. Barnes 16 Pines Rd. Greenpoint, Mississippi 20376	Cynthia V. Barnes 16 Pines Rd. Greenpoint, Mississippi 20376

25.

Marcel Jean Frontenac 6 Burton On The Water Calender, Me. 01471	Marcel Jean Frontenac 6 Burton On The Water Calender, Me. 01471
J. Scott Marsden 174 S. Tipton St. Cleveland, Ohio	J. Scott Marsden 174 Tipton St. Cleveland, Ohio
Lawrence T. Haney 171 McDonough St. Decatur, Ga. 31304	Lawrence T. Haney 171 McDonough St. Decatur, Ga. 31304

Directions: Base your answers to questions 26–30 on the information in the following passage.

In an experiment, several people were put in an airtight room. The air soon became warm and moist. The amount of carbon dioxide increased, and the amount of oxygen decreased. Everyone felt very uncomfortable. Then, without letting in any fresh air, an electric fan was turned on. Almost as soon as the air was set in motion, everyone became comfortable again.

This, and many other experiments, show that the moisture, temperature, and movement of indoor air are of more importance than the amount of oxygen or carbon dioxide that it contains. Air that contains little more than the usual amount of carbon dioxide is not dangerous to breathe. Air that contains a little less than the usual amount of oxygen is not dangerous to breathe.

Without proper ventilation, the air of a room in winter may become as dry as that of the Sahara Desert. In very dry air, the temperature must be 80 degrees Fahrenheit or more before we feel comfortably warm. Dry air causes the skin and the linings of the nose, throat, and air tubes to become dry. When this happens, germs are able to break through these linings very easily.

26. When several people were kept in an airtight room, the

  (A) oxygen increased; carbon dioxide decreased.
  (B) oxygen decreased; the air became dry.
  (C) carbon dioxide increased; oxygen decreased.
  (D) air became cool and dry.

27. Without proper ventilation, the air in a room

  (A) becomes dangerous.
  (B) becomes 80° Fahrenheit.
  (C) becomes a desert.
  (D) becomes dry.

28. According to this article, what made the people comfortable again?

  (A) moving the air
  (B) reducing the oxygen
  (C) increasing the temperature
  (D) increasing carbon dioxide

29. We become more susceptible to germs when the linings of our nose and throat are

  (A) moist.
  (B) hot.
  (C) cost.
  (D) dry.

30. The best title for this selection might be

  (A) "Stopping Germs."
  (B) "Oxygen and Carbon Dioxide."
  (C) "Pollution."
  (D) "Indoor Air."

31. People do not feel comfortably warm in very dry air unless

  (A) the temperature is 60° Fahrenheit or more.
  (B) the temperature is 80° Fahrenheit or more.
  (C) the air has more than the usual amount of oxygen.
  (D) the air has less than the usual amount of oxygen.

Directions: For questions 32–35, select the choice that is closest in meaning to the underlined word.

32. A central file eliminates the need to **retain** duplicate material. The word **retain** most nearly means

    (A) keep
    (B) change
    (C) locate
    (D) process

33. Filing is a **routine** office task. **Routine** most nearly means

    (A) proper
    (B) regular
    (C) simple
    (D) difficult

34. Sometimes a word, phrase, or sentence must be **deleted** to correct an error. **Deleted** most nearly means

    (A) removed
    (B) added
    (C) expanded
    (D) improved

35. Your supervisor will **evaluate** your work. **Evaluate** most nearly means

    (A) judge
    (B) list
    (C) assign
    (D) explain

practice test 8

Code Table

T	M	V	D	S	P	R	G	B	H
1	2	3	4	5	6	7	8	9	0

Directions: For questions 36–43, the code table above shows 10 letters with matching numbers. For each question, there are three sets of letters. Each set of letters is followed by a set of numbers which may or may not match their correct letter according to the code table. For each question, check all three sets of letters and numbers and darken answer space:

- **(A)** if **NO PAIRS** are **CORRECTLY MATCHED**
- **(B)** if only **ONE PAIR** is **CORRECTLY MATCHED**
- **(C)** if only **TWO PAIRS** are **CORRECTLY MATCHED**
- **(D)** if **ALL THREE PAIRS** are **CORRECTLY MATCHED**

36. RSBMRM — 759262
    GDSRVH — 845730
    VDBRTM — 349713

37. TGVSDR — 183247
    SMHRDP — 520647
    TRMHSR — 172057

38. DSPRGM — 456782
    MVDBHT — 234902
    HPMDBT — 062491

39. BVPTRD — 936184
    GDPHMB — 807029
    GMRHMV — 827032

40. MGVRSH — 283750
    TRDMBS — 174295
    SPRMGV — 567283

41. SGBSDM — 489542
    MGHPTM — 290612
    MPBMHT — 269301

42. TDPBHM — 146902
    VPBMRS — 369275
    GDMBHM — 842902

43. MVPTBV — 236194
    PDRTMB — 647128
    BGTMSM — 981232

Directions: For questions 44–49, each provides the names of four people. For each question, choose as your answer the one that should be filed first according to the usual system of alphabetical filing of names, as described in the paragraph below.

In filing names, you must start with the last name. Names are filed in order of the first letter of the last name, then the second letter, etc. Therefore, BAILY would be filed before BROWN, which would be filed before COLT. A name with fewer letters of the same type comes first; i.e., Smith comes before Smithe. If the last names are the same, the names are filed alphabetically by the first name. If the first name is an initial, the initial would come before a first name that starts with the same letter as the initial. Therefore, I. BROWN would come before IRA BROWN. Finally, if the last name and first name of two people are the same, the name would be filed alphabetically by the middle name, once again an initial coming before a middle name that starts with the same letter as the initial. If there is no middle name at all, the name comes before those with middle initials or names.

44. **(A)** Scott Biala
    (B) Mary Byala
    (C) Martin Baylor
    (D) Francis Bauer

45. **(A)** Howard J. Black
    (B) Howard Black
    (C) J. Howard Black
    (D) John H. Black

46. **(A)** Theodora Garth Kingston
    (B) Theadore Barth Kingston
    (C) Thomas Kingston
    (D) Thomas T. Kingston

47. **(A)** Paulette Mary Huerta
    (B) Paul M. Huerta
    (C) Paulette L. Huerta
    (D) Peter A. Huerta

48. **(A)** Martha Hunt Morgan
    (B) Martin Hunt Morgan
    (C) Mary H. Morgan
    (D) Martine H. Morgan

49. **(A)** James T. Meerschaum
    (B) James M. Mershum
    (C) James F. Mearshaum
    (D) James N. Meshum

Directions: For questions 50–53, choose the best answer to each question and darken its letter on the answer sheet.

50. Which one of the following statements about proper telephone usage is *not* always correct? When answering the telephone, you should

    (A) know who you are speaking to.
    (B) give the caller your undivided attention.
    (C) identify yourself to the caller.
    (D) obtain the information the caller wishes before you do your other work.

51. Assume that, as a member of a Worker's Safety Committee in your agency, you are responsible for encouraging other employees to follow correct safety practices. While you are working on your regular assignment, you observe an employee violating a safety rule. Of the following, the best action for you to take *first* is to

    (A) speak to the employee about safety practices and order him or her to stop violating the safety rule.
    (B) speak to the employee about safety practices and point out the safety rule he or she is violating.
    (C) bring the matter up in the next committee meeting.
    (D) report this violation of the safety rule to the employee's supervisor.

52. Assume that you have been temporarily assigned by your supervisor to do a job that you do not want to do. The best action for you to take is to

    (A) discuss the job with your supervisor explaining why you don't want to do it.
    (B) discuss the job with your supervisor and tell him or her that you will not do it.
    (C) ask a co-worker to take your place on this job.
    (D) do some other job that you like; your supervisor may give the job you don't like to someone else.

53. Assume that you keep the confidential personnel files of employees in your unit. A friend asks you to obtain information from the file of one of your co-workers. The best action to take is to

    (A) ask the co-worker if you can give the information to your friend.
    (B) ask your supervisor if you can give the information to your friend.
    (C) give the information to your friend.
    (D) refuse to give the information to your friend.

Directions: For questions 54–56, answer the questions *solely* on the basis of the information contained in the following passage.

The city government is committed to providing a safe and healthy work environment for all city employees. An effective agency safety program reduces accidents by educating employees about the types of careless acts that can cause accidents. Even in an office, accidents can happen. If each employee is aware of possible safety hazards, the number of accidents on the job can be reduced.

Careless use of office equipment can cause accidents and injuries. For example, file cabinet drawers that are filled with papers can be so heavy that the entire cabinet could tip over from the weight of one open drawer.

The bottom drawers of desks and file cabinets should never be left open, since employees could easily trip over open drawers and injure themselves.

When reaching for objects on a high shelf, an employee should use a strong, sturdy object, such as a stepstool, to stand on. Makeshift platforms made out of books, papers, or boxes can easily collapse. Even chairs can slide out from underfoot, causing serious injury.

Even at an employee's desk, safety hazards can occur. Frayed or cut wires should be repaired or replaced immediately.

54. The goal of an effective safety program is to

   (A) reduce office accidents.
   (B) stop employees from smoking on the job.
   (C) encourage employees to continue their education.
   (D) eliminate high shelves in offices.

55. Desks and file cabinets can become safety hazards when

   (A) their drawers are left open.
   (B) they are used as wastebaskets.
   (C) they are makeshift.
   (D) they are not anchored securely to the floor.

56. Accidents are likely to occur when

   (A) employees' desks are cluttered with books and papers.
   (B) employees are not aware of safety hazards.
   (C) employees close desk drawers.
   (D) stepstools are used to reach high objects.

practice test 8

Directions: For questions 57–63, choose the best answer to each question and darken its letter on the answer sheet.

57. Assume that part of your job as a worker in the accounting division of a city agency is to answer the telephone. When you first answer the telephone, it is *least* important to tell the caller

    (A) your title.
    (B) your name.
    (C) the name of your unit.
    (D) the name of your agency.

58. Assume that you are assigned to work as a receptionist and your duties are to answer phones, greet visitors, and do other general office work. You are busy with a routine job when several visitors approach your desk. The best action to take is to

    (A) ask the visitors to have a seat and assist them after your work is completed.
    (B) tell the visitors that you are busy and they should return at a more convenient time.
    (C) stop working long enough to assist the visitors.
    (D) continue working and wait for the visitors to ask you for assistance.

59. Assume that your supervisor has chosen you to take a special course during working hours to learn a new payroll procedure. Although you know that you were chosen because of your good work record, a co-worker, who feels that he or she should have been chosen, has been telling everyone in your unit that the choice was unfair. Of the following, the best way to handle this situation *first* is to

    (A) suggest to the co-worker that everything in life is unfair.
    (B) contact your union representative in case your co-worker presents a formal grievance.
    (C) tell your supervisor about your co-worker's complaints and let him or her handle the situation.
    (D) tell the co-worker that you were chosen because of your superior work record.

60. Assume that while you are working on an assignment that must be completed quickly, a supervisor from another unit asks you to obtain information for her. Of the following, the best way to respond to her request is to

    (A) tell her to return in an hour, since you are busy.
    (B) give her the names of some people in her own unit who could help her.
    (C) tell her you are busy and refer her to a co-worker.
    (D) tell her that you are busy, and ask her if she could wait until you finish your assignment.

61. A co-worker in your unit is often out because of illness. Your supervisor assigns the co-worker's work to you when she is not there. Lately, doing her work has interfered with your own job. The best action for you to take first is to

(A) discuss the problem with your supervisor.

(B) complete your own work before starting your co-worker's work.

(C) ask other workers in your unit to assist you.

(D) work late in order to get the jobs done.

62. During the month of June, 40,587 people attended a city-owned swimming pool. In July, 13,014 more people attended the swimming pool than the number that had attended in June. In August, 39,655 people attended the swimming pool. The total number of people who attended the swimming pool during the months of June, July, and August was

(A) 80,242.

(B) 93,256.

(C) 133,843.

(D) 210,382.

63. Assume a city agency has 775 office workers. If 2 out of 25 office workers were absent on a particular day, how many office workers reported to work on that day?

(A) 713

(B) 744

(C) 750

(D) 773

> **Directions:** For questions 64–71, answer the questions *solely* on the basis of the information contained in the following passage.

The telephone directory is made up of two books. The first book consists of the introductory section and the alphabetical listing of names section. The second book is the classified directory (also known as the Yellow Pages). Many people who are familiar with one book do not realize how useful the other can be. The efficient office worker should become familiar with both books in order to make the best use of this important source of information.

The introductory section gives general instructions for finding numbers in the alphabetical listing and classified directory. This section also explains how to use the telephone company's many services, including the operator and information services; gives examples of charges for local and long-distance calls; and lists area codes for the entire country. In addition, this section provides a useful postal ZIP code map.

The alphabetical listing of names section lists the names, addresses, and telephone numbers of subscribers in an area. Guide names, or "telltales," are on the top corner of each page. These guide names indicate the first and last name to be found on that page. "Telltales" help locate any particular name quickly. A cross-reference spelling is also given to help locate names which are spelled several different ways.

City, state, and federal government agencies are listed in the blue pages of the alphabetical book under the major government heading, For example, an agency of the federal government would be listed under "United States Government."

The classified directory, or Yellow Pages, is a separate book. In this section are advertising services, public transportation line maps, shopping guides, and listings of businesses arranged by the type of product or services they offer. This book is most useful when looking for the name or phone number of a business when all that is known is the type of product offered and the address, or when trying to locate a particular type of business in an area. Businesses listed in the classified directory can usually be found in the alphabetical listing of names section. When the name of the business is known, you will find the address or phone number more quickly in the alphabetical listing of names section.

64. The introductory section provides

  (A) shopping guides.
  (B) government listings.
  (C) business listings.
  (D) information services.

65. Advertising services would be found in the

  (A) introductory section.
  (B) alphabetical listing of names section.
  (C) classified directory.
  (D) information services.

66. According to the information in the passage for locating government agencies, the Information Office of the Department of Consumer Affairs of New York City government would be alphabetically listed first under

  (A) "I" for Information Office.
  (B) "D" for Department of Consumer Affairs.
  (C) "N" for New York City.
  (D) "G" for government.

67. When the name of a business is known, the quickest way to find the phone number is to look in the

  (A) classified directory.
  (B) introductory section.
  (C) alphabetical listing of names section.
  (D) advertising service section.

68. The quickest way to find the phone number of a business when the type of service a business offers and its address is known, is to look in the

(A) classified directory.
(B) alphabetical listing of names section.
(C) introductory section.
(D) information service.

69. What is a "telltale"?

(A) An alphabetical listing
(B) A guide name
(C) A map
(D) A cross-reference listing

70. The best way to find a postal ZIP code is to look in the

(A) classified directory.
(B) introductory section.
(C) alphabetical listing of names section.
(D) government heading.

71. To help find names that have several different spellings, the telephone directory provides

(A) cross-reference spelling.
(B) "telltales."
(C) spelling guides.
(D) advertising services.

Directions: For questions 62–79, choose the best answer to each question and darken its letter on the answer sheet.

72. Assume that your agency has been given $2,025 to purchase file cabinets. If each file cabinet costs $135, how many file cabinets can your agency purchase?

(A) 8
(B) 10
(C) 15
(D) 16

73. Assume that your unit ordered 14 staplers at a total cost of $30.20 and each stapler costs the same amount. The cost of one stapler was most nearly

(A) $1.02.
(B) $1.61.
(C) $2.16.
(D) $2.26.

74. Assume that you are responsible for counting and recording licensing fees collected by your department. On a particular day, your department collected in fees 40 checks in the amount of $6 each; 80 checks in the amount of $4 each; 45 $20 bills; 30 $10 bills; 42 $5 bills; and 186 $1 bills. The total amount in fees collected on that day was

(A) $1,406.
(B) $1,706.
(C) $2,156.
(D) $2,356.

75. Assume that you are responsible for your agency's petty cash fund. During the month of February, you pay out seven subway fares at $1.25 each and one taxi fare for $7.30; you pay out nothing else from the fund. At the end of February, you count the money left in the fund and find three $1 bills, four quarters, five dimes, and four nickels. The amount of money you had available in the petty cash fund at the *beginning* of February was

(A) $4.70.
(B) $11.35.
(C) $16.05.
(D) $20.75.

76. You overhear your supervisor criticize a co-worker for handling equipment in an unsafe way. You feel that the criticism may be unfair. Of the following, it would be best for you to

   (A) take your co-worker aside and tell him or her how you feel about your supervisor's comments.

   (B) interrupt the discussion and defend your co-worker to your supervisor.

   (C) continue working as if you had not overheard the discussion.

   (D) make a list of other workers who have violated safety rules and give it to your supervisor.

77. Assume that you have been assigned to work on a long-term project with an employee who is known for being uncooperative. In beginning to work with this employee, it would be *least* desirable for you to

   (A) understand why the person is uncooperative.

   (B) act in a calm manner rather than an emotional manner.

   (C) be appreciative of the co-worker's work.

   (D) report the co-worker's lack of cooperation to your supervisor.

78. Assume that you are assigned to sell tickets at a city-owned ice skating rink. An adult ticket costs $3.75 and a children's ticket costs $2.00. At the end of a day, you find that you have sold 36 adult tickets and 80 children's tickets. The total amount of money you collected for that day was

   (A) $285.50.

   (B) $295.00.

   (C) $298.75.

   (D) $301.00.

79. If each office worker files 487 index cards in one hour, how many cards can 26 office workers file in one hour?

   (A) 10,662

   (B) 12,175

   (C) 12,662

   (D) 14,266

ANSWER KEY AND EXPLANATIONS

1. C	17. A	33. B	49. C	65. C
2. A	18. D	34. A	50. D	66. C
3. D	19. A	35. A	51. B	67. C
4. B	20. C	36. B	52. A	68. A
5. A	21. C	37. B	53. D	69. B
6. B	22. C	38. C	54. A	70. B
7. D	23. B	39. A	55. A	71. A
8. C	24. B	40. D	56. B	72. C
9. C	25. C	41. A	57. A	73. C
10. B	26. C	42. D	58. C	74. C
11. B	27. D	43. A	59. C	75. D
12. A	28. A	44. D	60. D	76. C
13. C	29. D	45. B	61. A	77. D
14. B	30. D	46. B	62. C	78. B
15. B	31. B	47. B	63. A	79. C
16. C	32. A	48. A	64. D	

Questions 1–5 rely on your common sense and good judgment in interpersonal relations.

6. **The correct answer is (B).** The seasons are not capitalized, but names of holidays and months are.

7. **The correct answer is (D).** The subject of the sentence, the manual, is singular, so the verb must be singular as well. The correct spelling is *describes*.

8. **The correct answer is (C).** "Paper" is a singular noun taking the singular verb "was." The construction ". . . n't no" constitutes an unacceptable double negative.

9. **The correct answer is (C).** "Their" is the possessive. "They're" is the contraction for "they are." "There" refers to a place. Choice (D) is a misspelling.

10. **The correct answer is (B).** The correct way to express time is 8:30 A.M.

11. **The correct answer is (B).** The "alphabet," singular, "is." The phrase "or A to Z sequence" is extra information about the alphabet, so it is enclosed by commas. "Too" means "also" or "excessive" and is the incorrect spelling of *to*.

12. **The correct answer is (A).** "Five" is plural, so use the plural "feet."

13. **The correct answer is (C).** "Checked and found"—both verbs must be in the past tense. The correct spelling is *register*.

For questions 14–25, we have circled the areas of difference.

14. **The correct answer is (B).** The numbers are alike in only one set.

7354①83476	7354⑨83476
44747477④4	44747477⑦4
57914302311	57914302311

15. **The correct answer is (B).** The numbers are alike in only one set.

7143⑤92185	7143⑧92185
834451⑦699	834451⑧699
9178531263	9178531263

16. **The correct answer is (C).** The numbers are alike in two sets.

2572(114)731	2572(14)731
8806835476	8806835476
8255831246	8255831246

17. **The correct answer is (A).** None of the sets are alike.

33147685(38)21	33147685(86)21
69766(585)32996	69766(558)32996
39660421137①5	37660421137④5

18. **The correct answer is (D).** All of the sets are exactly alike.

19. **The correct answer is (A).** None of the sets are alike.

9900069(669)96	9900069(69)96
53022219⑦43	53022219⑧43
417117(1117)717	417117(117)7717

20. **The correct answer is (C).** The numbers are alike in two sets.

24400222433004	24400222433004
530003005(500)0355	530003005(550)0355
20000075532002022	20000075532002022

21. **The correct answer is (C).** The numbers are alike in two sets.

611166640660(001)116	611166640660(01)116
7111300117001100733	7111300117001100733
26666446664476518	26666446664476518

22. **The correct answer is (C).** The names and addresses are exactly alike in two sets.

Mary T. Berlinger	Mary T. Berlinger
2351 Hampton St.	2351 Hampton St.
Monsey, N.Y. 20117	Monsey, N.Y. 20117
Eduardo Benes	Eduardo Benes
473 Kingston Avenue	473 Kingston Avenue
Central Islip, N.Y. 11734	Central Islip, N.Y. 11734
Alan Carrington Fuchs	Alan Carrington Fuchs
17 Gnarled Hollow Road	17 Gnarled Hollow Road
Los Angeles, California 916(35)	Los Angeles, California 91611(85)

23. **The correct answer is (B).** The names and addresses are alike in only one set.

David John Jacobson
178(35) St. Apt. 4C
New York, N.Y. 00927

David John Jacobson
178(53) St. Apt. 4C
New York, N.Y. 00927

Ann-Marie Calonella
7243 South Ridge Blvd.
Bakersfield, California 96714

Ann-Marie Calonella
7243 South Ridge Blvd.
Bakersfield, California 96714

Pauline M. Tho(mps)on
872 Linden Ave.
Houston, Texas 70321

Pauline A Tho(ms)on
872 Linden Ave.
Houston, Texas 70321

24. **The correct answer is (B).** The names and addresses are alike in only one set.

Chester LeRoy Master(t)on
152 Lacy Rd.
Kankakee, Ill. 54532

Chester LeRoy Master(s)on
152 Lacy Rd.
Kankakee, Ill. 54532

William Maloney
S. LaCros(se) Pla.
Wausau, Wisconsin 52146

William Maloney
S. LaCros(s) Pla.
Wausau, Wisconsin 52146

Cynthia V. Barnes
16 Pines Rd.
Greenpoint, Mississippi 20376

Cynthia V. Barnes
16 Pines Rd.
Greenpoint, Mississippi 20376

25. **The correct answer is (C).** The names and addresses are exactly alike in two sets.

Marcel Jean Frontenac
6 Burton On The Water
Calender, Me. 01471

Marcel Jean Frontenac
6 Burton On The Water
Calender, Me. 01471

J. Scott Marsden
174 (S.) Tipton St.
Cleveland, Ohio

J. Scott Marsden
174 ( ) Tipton St.
Cleveland, Ohio

Lawrence T. Haney
171 McDonough St.
Decatur, Ga. 31304

Lawrence T. Haney
171 McDonough St.
Decatur, Ga. 31304

26. **The correct answer is (C).** Carbon dioxide increased; oxgen decreased, as stated in the first paragraph of the passage.

27. **The correct answer is (D).** Choice (D) becomes dry. The last paragraph of the passage states that the air becomes very dry without proper ventilation.

28. **The correct answer is (A).** In the first paragraph, you read that people in the room became comfortable after an electric fan was turned on. The fan moved the air.

29. **The correct answer is (D).** The last paragraph states that when the linings of the nose, throat, and air tubes become dry, germs can more easily break through these linings.

30. **The correct answer is (D).** A title should reflect the overall subject matter, and indoor air is the subject matter of this passage. Choices (A) and (B) relate to indoor air, but neither is the main subject. Pollution (C) is not described or discussed in the passage at all.

31. **The correct answer is (B).** The last paragraph states that people feel comfortably warm in very dry air when the temperature is 80° Fahrenheit or more.

For questions 32–36, if you made errors consult a dictionary.

For questions 36–43, the areas of miscoding are marked.

36. **The correct answer is (B).** Only one set is correctly coded.

    RSBM(R)M — 7592(6)2
    GDSRVH — 845730
    VDBRT(M) — 34971(3)

37. **The correct answer is (B).** Only one set is correctly coded.

    TGV(S)DR — 183(2)47
    SMH(R)D(P) — 520(6)4(7)
    TRMHSR — 172057

38. **The correct answer is (C).** Two sets are correctly coded.

    DSPRGM — 456782
    MVDBH(T) — 23490(2)
    HPMDBT — 062491

39. **The correct answer is (A).** No sets are correctly coded.

    BVPT(R)D — 9361(8)4
    G(DP)HMB — 8(07)0029
    GMRH(MV) — 8270(32)

40. **The correct answer is (D).** All three sets are correctly coded.

41. **The correct answer is (A).** No sets are correctly coded.

    (S)GBSDM — (4)89542
    M(G)HPTM — 2(9)0612
    MPB(M)HT — 269(3)01

42. **The correct answer is (D).** All three sets are correctly coded.

43. **The correct answer is (A).** No sets are correctly coded.

    MVPTB(V) — 23619(4)
    PDRTM(B) — 64712(8)
    BGTM(S)M — 9812(3)2

44. **The correct answer is (D).** Bauer—Baylor—Biala—Byala

45. **The correct answer is (B).** Howard—Howard J—J. Howard—John H.

46. **The correct answer is (B).** Theadore—Theodora—Thomas—Thomas T.

47. **The correct answer is (B).** Paul M.—Paulette L.—Paulette Mary—Peter A.

48. **The correct answer is (A).** Martha—Martin—Martine—Mary

49. **The correct answer is (C).** Mearshaum—Meerschaum—Mershum—Meshum

50. **The correct answer is (D).** You must always identify yourself, find out to whom you are speaking, and be courteous to the caller, but sometimes a return call could give information at a later hour or date.

51. **The correct answer is (B).** The first thing to do is speak to the employee who may not even be aware of the rule.

52. **The correct answer is (A).** Be "up front" with your supervisor. Refusing to do a distasteful task or trying to hand it off to someone else is not proper business procedure.

53. **The correct answer is (D).** Confidential means "private."

54. **The correct answer is (A).** See the first paragraph.

55. **The correct answer is (A).** See the third paragraph.

56. **The correct answer is (B).** See the first paragraph.

57. **The correct answer is (A).** Think of what the caller needs to know. He or she needs to know what agency has been reached and to whom he or she is speaking. Your title is irrelevant.

58. **The correct answer is (C).** A receptionist receives visitors.

59. **The correct answer is (C).** No matter how you approach the co-worker, you are likely to create ill feeling. Let your supervisor handle this tricky office morale problem.

60. **The correct answer is (D).** Your own work comes first, but you do want to be helpful. Tactfully offer to help out when your own work is completed, and let the supervisor ask for a referral if she needs the information more quickly.

61. **The correct answer is (A).** The supervisor does the assigning and is responsible for having the work done. Let the supervisor know what the problem is.

62. **The correct answer is (C).**

June		40,587
July	$40,587 + 13,014 =$	53,601
+ August		39,655
Total		133,842

63. **The correct answer is (A).**

$775 \div 25 = $ 31 groups of 25 workers in the agency.

$31 \times 2 = $ 62 absent that day (2 from each group of 25)

$775 - 62 = 713$ present

64. **The correct answer is (D).** See the second paragraph.

65. **The correct answer is (C).** See the last paragraph.

66. **The correct answer is (C).** See the fourth paragraph.

67. **The correct answer is (C).** See the third paragraph.

68. **The correct answer is (A).** See the last paragraph.

69. **The correct answer is (B).** See the second sentence of the third paragraph.

70. **The correct answer is (B).** See the second paragraph.

71. **The correct answer is (A).** See the last sentence of the third paragraph.

72. **The correct answer is (C).** $\$2,025 \div \$135 = \$15$

73. **The correct answer is (C).** $\$30.20 \div 14 = \$2.157 = \$2.16$

74. **The correct answer is (C).**

40 checks	@ $6 =	$240
80 checks	@ 4 =	320
45 bills	@ 20 =	900
30 bills	@ 10 =	300
42 bills	@ 5 =	210
+ 186 bills	@ 1 =	186
Total		$2,156

75. **The correct answer is (D).**

7 fares	@ = $1.25 =	$8.75
+ 1 fare	@ = 7.30 =	7.30
Total spent		$16.05

3 dollar bills =	$3.00
4 quarters =	1.00
5 dimes =	.50
+ 4 nickels =	.20
Amount left	$4.70

Amount spent	$16.05
+ Amount left	4.70
Amount to begin	$20.75

76. **The correct answer is (C).** The remarks were not meant for your ears. Do your own work and mind your own business.

77. **The correct answer is (D).** You've just begun to work, and the co-worker has not had a chance to prove cooperative or uncooperative. There is nothing to report.

78. **The correct answer is (B).**

36 adults	@ $3.75 =	$135
+ 80 children	@ 2.00 =	160
Total		$295

79. **The correct answer is (C).** 487 x 26 = 12,662

Practice Test 9: Private Sector Clerical Exam

FILING SKILLS

25 QUESTIONS

> **Directions:** Arrange the names in each question in proper alphabetical order for filing.

1. Adam Dunn
   E. Dunn
   A. Duncan
   Edward Robert Dunn

   1. _____
      _____
      _____
      _____

2. Paul Moore
   William Moore
   Paul A. Moore
   William Allen Moore

   2. _____
      _____
      _____
      _____

3. William Carver
   Howard Cambell
   Arthur Chambers
   Charles Banner

   3. _____
      _____
      _____
      _____

4. George Peters
   Eric Petersen
   G. Peters
   E. Petersen

   4. _____
      _____
      _____
      _____

5. Edward Hallam
   Jos. Frank Hamilton
   Edward A. Hallam
   Joseph F. Hamilton

   5. _____
      _____
      _____
      _____

6. William O'Hara
   Arthur Gordon
   James DeGraff
   Anne von Glatin

   6. _____
      _____
      _____
      _____

7. Theodore Madison
   Timothy McGill
   Thomas MacLane
   Thomas A. Madison

   7. _____
   _____
   _____
   _____

8. Dr. Chas. D. Peterson
   Miss Irene F. Petersen
   Lawrence E. Peterson
   Prof. N. A. Petersen

   8. _____
   _____
   _____
   _____

9. Edward La Gabriel
   Marie Doris Gabriel
   Marjorie N. Gabriel
   Mrs Marian Gabriel

   9. _____
   _____
   _____
   _____

10. Herbert Restman
    H. Restman
    Harry Restmore
    H. Restmore

    10. _____
    _____
    _____
    _____

11. Timothy Macalan
    Fred McAlden
    Thomas MacAllister
    Mrs. Frank McAllen

    11. _____
    _____
    _____
    _____

12. Peter La Vance
    George Van Meer
    Wallace De Vance
    Leonard Vance

    12. _____
    _____
    _____
    _____

13. Devine, Sarah
    Devine, S.
    Devine, Sara H.
    Devin, Sarah

    13. _____
    _____
    _____
    _____

14. Bennet, C.,
    Benett, Chuck
    Bennet, Chas.
    Bennett, Charles

    14. _____
    _____
    _____
    _____

15. Rivera, Ilena
    Riviera, Ilene
    Rivere, I.
    Riviera Ilana

    15. _____
    _____
    _____
    _____

16. Corral, Dr. Robert
    Carrale, Prof Robert
    Corren, R.
    Corret, Ron

    16. _____
    _____
    _____
    _____

17. Chas. A. Levine
    Kurt Levene
    Charles Levine
    Kurt E. Levene

17. _____
    _____
    _____
    _____

18. Prof. Geo. Kinkaid
    Mr. Alan Kinkaid
    Dr. Albert A. Kinkade
    Kincade, Lillian

18. _____
    _____
    _____
    _____

19. Charles Green
    Chas. T. Greene
    Charles Thomas Greene
    Wm. A. Greene

19. _____
    _____
    _____
    _____

20. Doris MacAllister
    D. McAllen
    Lewis T. MacBride
    Lewis McBride

20. _____
    _____
    _____
    _____

21. Robert B. Pierce
    R. Bruce Pierce
    Ronald Pierce
    Robert Bruce Pierce

21. _____
    _____
    _____
    _____

22. Charlotte Stair
    C. B. Stare
    Charles B. Stare
    Elaine La Stella

22. _____
    _____
    _____
    _____

23. James Borenstein
    Frieda Albrecht
    Samuel Brown
    George Appelman

23. _____
    _____
    _____
    _____

24. James McCormack
    Ruth MacNamara
    Kathryn McGillicuddy
    Frances Mason

24. _____
    _____
    _____
    _____

25. A. S. Martinson
    Albert Martinson
    Albert S. Martinson
    M. Martanson

25. _____
    _____
    _____
    _____

practice test

SPELLING

90 QUESTIONS

Directions: In the following list, some words are spelled correctly and some words are misspelled. On the line to the right, write the correct spelling of each misspelled word. If a word is spelled correctly, write "Correct as written."

1. professor   1. _____
2. sabbatical   2. _____
3. associate   3. _____
4. dictater   4. _____
5. accidently   5. _____
6. bureau   6. _____
7. auxilary   7. _____
8. synthesis   8. _____
9. receiveable   9. _____
10. facsimile   10. _____
11. proxey   11. _____
12. negotiable   12. _____
13. confidential   13. _____
14. pertainent   14. _____
15. corrective   15. _____
16. satisfactorally   16. _____
17. accomplishment   17. _____
18. bookeeping   18. _____
19. beforhand   19. _____
20. supervisor   20. _____
21. manifest   21. _____
22. machinary   22. _____
23. harassment   23. _____
24. bankrupcy   24. _____
25. requisition   25. _____
26. pollish   26. _____

27. acknowledgment   27. _____
28. typograpfical   28. _____
29. codify   29. _____
30. performance   30. _____
31. weight   31. _____
32. occasionally   32. _____
33. carefuly   33. _____
34. deceit   34. _____
35. efficiently   35. _____
36. scheduling   36. _____
37. distorsion   37. _____
38. exemplify   38. _____
39. chronological   39. _____
40. liability   40. _____
41. courtesy   41. _____
42. notarary   42. _____
43. memmoranda   43. _____
44. ellimination   44. _____
45. clogging   45. _____
46. refered   46. _____
47. aggressive   47. _____
48. shelfs   48. _____
49. personnel   49. _____
50. initiative   50. _____
51. occurance   51. _____
52. guage   52. _____
53. resources   53. _____
54. appearence   54. _____
55. rehearsal   55. _____
56. departmental   56. _____
57. sacrilegious   57. _____
58. subdivision   58. _____

practice test

59.	self-evident	59.	_____
60.	over-charge	60.	_____
61.	primery	61.	_____
62.	cessation	62.	_____
63.	obediance	63.	_____
64.	employees	64.	_____
65.	conspicuous	65.	_____
66.	assinement	66.	_____
67.	thier	67.	_____
68.	effectual	68.	_____
69.	acreage	69.	_____
70.	frequently	70.	_____
71.	commisioner	71.	_____
72.	alien	72.	_____
73.	embarassment	73.	_____
74.	conference	74.	_____
75.	have'nt	75.	_____
76.	admissible	76.	_____
77.	allowance	77.	_____
78.	wellcome	78.	_____
79.	salarys	79.	_____
80.	proffitable	80.	_____
81.	engineerred	81.	_____
82.	interview	82.	_____
83.	procedure	83.	_____
84.	nineth	84.	_____
85.	simultanous	85.	_____
86.	handicaped	86.	_____
87.	foriegner	87.	_____
88.	italicize	88.	_____
89.	overhear	89.	_____
90.	evaluation	90.	_____

GRAMMAR SKILLS

35 QUESTIONS

Directions: Some of the following sentences are correct as written. Others contain an error of grammar, punctuation, or capitalization. On the lines beside each sentence, rewrite the sentence correctly. If the sentence contains no error, write "Correct as written."

1. He was not informed, that he would have to work overtime.

   1. _____

   _____

2. The wind blew several papers off of his desk.

   2. _____

   _____

3. Charles Dole, who is a member of the committee, was asked to confer with commissioner Wilson.

   3. _____

   _____

4. Miss Bell will issue a copy to whomever asks for one.

   4. _____

   _____

   _____

5. Most employees, and he is no exception do not like to work overtime.

   5. _____

   _____

   _____

6. This is the man whom you interviewed last week.

   6. _____

   _____

   _____

7. Of the two cities visited, White Plains is the cleanest.

   7. _____

   _____

   _____

8. Although he was willing to work on other holidays, he refused to work on labor day.

   8. _____

   _____

9. If an employee wishes to attend the conference, he should fill out the necessary forms.

   9. _____

   _____

   _____

10. The division chief reports that an engineer and an inspector is needed for this special survey.

10. _____
     _____
     _____

11. The work was assigned to Miss Green and me.

11. _____
     _____
     _____

12. The staff regulations state that an employee,who is frequently tardy, may receive a negative evaluation.

12. _____
     _____
     _____

13. He is the kind of person who is always willing to undertake difficult assignments.

13. _____
     _____
     _____

14. Mr. Wright's request cannot be granted under no conditions.

14. _____
     _____

15. George Colt a new employee was asked to deliver the report to the Domestic Relations Court.

15. _____
     _____
     _____

16. The supervisor entered the room and said, "The work must be completed today."

16. _____
     _____
     _____

17. The employees were given their assignments and, they were asked to begin work immediately.

17. _____
     _____
     _____

18. The letter will be sent to the United States senate this week.

18. _____
     _____

19. When the supervisor entered the room, he noticed that the book was laying on the desk.

19. _____
     _____
     _____

20. All the clerks, including those who have been appointed recently are required to work on the new assignment.

20. _____
     _____
     _____

21. One of our clerks were promoted yesterday.

21. _____
_____
_____

22. Between you and me, I would prefer not going there.

22. _____
_____
_____

23. The National alliance of Businessmen is trying to persuade private businesses to hire youth in the summertime.

23. _____
_____
_____

24. The supervisor who is on vacation, is in charge of processing vouchers.

24. _____
_____
_____

25. The activity of the committee at its conferences is always stimulating.

25. _____
_____
_____

26. After checking the addresses again, the letters went to the mailroom.

26. _____
_____
_____

27. The director, as well as the employees, are interested in sharing the dividends.

27. _____
_____
_____

28. Mrs. Black the supervisor of the unit, has many important duties.

28. _____
_____
_____

29. We spoke to the man whom you saw yesterday.

29. _____
_____
_____

30. When a holiday falls on sunday, it is officially celebrated on monday.

30. _____
_____
_____

31. Neither Mr. Smith nor Mr. Jones was able to finish his assignment on time.

31. _____
_____

practice test

32. The task of filing these cards is to be divided equally between you and he.

32. _____
_____
_____

33. He is an employee whom we consider to be efficient.

33. _____
_____
_____

34. I believe that the new employees are not as punctual as us.

34. _____
_____
_____

35. The employees, working in this office, are to be congratulated for their work.

35. _____
_____

PROOFREADING SKILLS

73 QUESTIONS

Directions: The letter that follows contains far more errors than you are likely to encounter in anything that you will proofread in a work situation. Read through the letter and make your corrections directly on the page, between the lines and in the margins. Then type the letter, incorporating all of your corrections.

january 24th, 2007

Mr Steven p Anderson
Alacon Manufacturin Comp. Inc
387 Bramson Bullevard
Waltham, MA., 02154

Re: Red worsted wool
Die lot no 68423

My Dear Mr. Andreson,

My knitting store Wooly crafts of 12 Myrtle Ln., Beloit, Wisconsin, tole me to right to you to tell you, about my disapointtion with you're wool. I bought sevin skeins of wool to make a sweater in decembr of 2005. After a few month's i put the work a side. last week i buyed another skien of the same die lot 64823 to finnish the the sweater. The red does'nt match, it is not the same.

Mrs Browne the store Manager said that "The yarn is two old. That may be so, but i read on the rapper that you offer a garantee. The garante says this wool will not fade." Be sure to match die lots. satisfaction is garanteed. "

The hole sweater is know good. I am non satisfied. You could:

1. send me a refund for all nine skeins of wool
2. send me new wool

I am wait for you'r reply as to how you plan to handel my complain?

Very Truly Yours:
Mollie Jones Customer

ANSWERS AND EXPLANATIONS

Filing Skills

Correct alphabetical filing is made much easier when all names are placed in reverse order; that is, with last name first.

1. Duncan, A.
   Dunn, Adam
   Dunn, E.
   Dunn, Edward Robert

2. Moore, Paul
   Moore, Paul A.
   Moore, William
   Moore, William Allen

3. Banner, Charles
   Cambell, Howard
   Carver, William
   Chambers, Arthur

4. Peters, G.
   Peters, George
   Petersen, E.
   Petersen, Eric

5. Hallam, Edward
   Hallam, Edward A.
   Hamilton, Joseph F.
   Hamilton, Jos. Frank

6. DeGraff, James
   Gordon, Arthur
   O'Hara, William
   von Glatin, Anne

7. MacLane, Thomas
   Madison, Theodore
   Madison, Thomas A.
   McGill, Timothy

8. Petersen, Irene F., Miss
   Petersen, N. A., Prof.
   Peterson, Chas. D., Dr.
   Peterson, Lawrence E.

9. Gabriel, Marian, Mrs.
   Gabriel, Marie Doris
   Gabriel, Marjorie N.
   La Gabriel, Edward

10. Restman, H.
    Restman, Herbert
    Restmore, H.
    Restmore, Harry

11. Macalan, Timothy
    MacAllister, Tomas
    McAlden, Fred
    McAllen, Frank, Mrs.

12. De Vance, Wallace
    La Vance, Peter
    Vance, Leonard
    Van Meer, George

13. Devin, Sarah
    Devine, S.
    Devine, Sara H.
    Devine, Sarah

14. Benett, Chuck
    Bennet, C.
    Bennet, Chas.
    Bennett, Charles

15. Rivera, Ilena
    Rivere, I.
    Riviera, Ilana
    Riviera, Ilene

16. Carrale, Robert, Prof.
    Corral, Robert, Dr.
    Corren, R.
    Corret, Ron

17. Levene, Kurt
    Levene, Kurt E.
    Levine, Charles
    Levine, Chas. A.

18. Kincade, Lillian
    Kinkade, Albert A., Dr.
    Kinkaid, Alan, Mr.
    Kinkaid, Geo., Prof.

19. Green, Charles
    Greene, Chas. T.
    Greene, Charles Thomas
    Greene, Wm. A.

20. MacAllister, Doris
    MacBride, Lewis T.
    McAllen, D.
    McBride, Lewis

21. Pierce, R. Bruce
Pierce, Robert B.
Pierce, Robert Bruce
Pierce, Ronald

22. La Stella, Elaine
Stair, Charlotte
Stare, C. B.
Stare, Charles B.

23. Albrecht, Frieda
Appelman, George
Borenstein, James
Brown, Samuel

24. MacNamara, Ruth
Mason, Frances
McCormack, James
McGillicudy, Kathryn

25. Martanson, M.
Martinson, A. S.
Martinson, Albert
Martinson, Albert S.

Spelling

1. Correct as written.
2. Correct as written.
3. Correct as written.
4. The correct spelling is: dictator
5. The correct spelling is: accidentally
6. Correct as written.
7. The correct spelling is: auxiliary
8. Correct as written.
9. The correct spelling is: receivable
10. Correct as written.
11. The correct spelling is: proxy
12. Correct as written.
13. Correct as written.
14. The correct spelling is: pertinent
15. Correct as written.
16. The correct spelling is: satisfactorily
17. Correct as written.
18. The correct spelling is: bookkeeping
19. The correct spelling is: beforehand
20. Correct as written.
21. Correct as written.
22. The correct spelling is: machinery
23. Correct as written.
24. The correct spelling is: bankruptcy
25. Correct as written.

26. **The correct spelling is:** polish
27. **Correct as written.**
28. **The correct spelling is:** typographical
29. **Correct as written.**
30. **The correct spelling is:** performance
31. **Correct as written.**
32. **Correct as written.**
33. **The correct spelling is:** carefully
34. **Correct as written.**
35. **Correct as written.**
36. **Correct as written.**
37. **The correct spelling is:** distortion
38. **Correct as written.**
39. **Correct as written.**
40. **Correct as written.**
41. **Correct as written.**
42. **The correct spelling is:** notary
43. **The correct spelling is:** memoranda
44. **The correct spelling is:** elimination
45. **Correct as written.**
46. **The correct spelling is:** referred
47. **Correct as written.**
48. **The correct spelling is:** shelves
49. **Correct as written.**
50. **Correct as written.**
51. **The correct spelling is:** occurrence
52. **The correct spelling is:** gauge
53. **Correct as written.**
54. **The correct spelling is:** appearance
55. **Correct as written.**
56. **Correct as written.**
57. **Correct as written.**
58. **Correct as written.**
59. **Correct as written.**
60. **The correct spelling is:** overcharge

61. **The correct spelling is:** primary
62. **Correct as written.**
63. **The correct spelling is:** obedience
64. **Correct as written.**
65. **Correct as written.**
66. **The correct spelling is:** assignment
67. **The correct spelling is:** their
68. **Correct as written.**
69. **Correct as written.**
70. **Correct as written.**
71. **The correct spelling is:** commissioner
72. **Correct as written.**
73. **The correct spelling is:** embarrassment
74. **Correct as written.**
75. **The correct spelling is:** haven't
76. **Correct as written.**
77. **Correct as written.**
78. **The correct spelling is:** welcome
79. **The correct spelling is:** salaries
80. **The correct spelling is:** profitable
81. **The correct spelling is:** engineered
82. **Correct as written.**
83. **Correct as written.**
84. **The correct spelling is:** ninth
85. **The correct spelling is:** simultaneous
86. **The correct spelling is:** handicapped
87. **The correct spelling is:** foreigner
88. **Correct as written.**
89. **Correct as written.**
90. **Correct as written.**

Grammar Skills

1. He was not informed <u>that</u> he would have to work overtime. There is no reason for a comma between the <u>verb</u> and its object.

2. The wind blew several papers <u>off his</u> desk. <u>Off of</u> is unacceptable usage.

3. Charles Dole, who is a member of the committee, was asked to confer with Commissioner Wilson. *Commissioner Wilson* is a specific commissioner, so the *C* must be capitalized.

4. Miss Bell will issue a copy to <u>whoever</u> asks for one. *Whoever* is the subject of the verb *asks*.

5. Most employees, and he is no exception<u>,</u> do not like to work overtime. A parenthetical expression must *always* be enclosed by commas.

6. This sentence is correct.

7. Of the two cities visited, White Plains is the <u>cleaner</u>. The comparative *er* is used when only two items are being compared. *Est* requires three or more items.

8. Although he was willing to work on other holidays, he refused to work on Labor <u>D</u>ay. *Labor Day* is a proper name; it must have initial caps.

9. This sentence is correct.

10. The division chief reports that an engineer and an inspector <u>are</u> needed for this special survey. A plural subject requires a plural verb.

11. This sentence is correct.

12. The staff regulations state that an emplo<u>yee who</u> is frequently tard<u>y may</u> receive a negative evaluation. A restrictive clause; <u>that is</u>, a clause that is vital to the meaning of a sentence, should not be set off by commas.

13. This sentence is correct.

14. Mr. Wright's request cannot be granted under <u>any</u> conditions. Use of a double negative is not permitted.

15. George Col<u>t, a new employee,</u> was asked to deliver the report to the Domestic Relations Court. "*A new employee*" is an appositive and must be set off by commas.

16. This sentence is correct.

17. The employees were given their assignment<u>s,</u> and they were asked to begin work immediately. Two independent clauses connected by *and* must be separated by a comma placed before the *and*.

18. The letter will be sent to the United States <u>S</u>enate this week. This is very specific. *Senate* must begin with a capital letter.

19. When the supervisor entered the room, he noticed that the book was <u>lying</u> on the desk. The verb *to lay* should be used only when it could be replaced with the verb *to put*. At all other times, use a form of the verb *to lie*.

20. All the clerks, including those who have been appointed recentl<u>y,</u> are required to work on the new assignment. Omitting the clause "*including those who have been appointed recently*" does not change the meaning of the remaining words. Therefore, this is a nonrestrictive clause and should be set off by commas.

21. One of our clerks *was* promoted yesterday. The subject of the sentence is *one,* which takes a singular verb.

22. This sentence is correct.

23. The National <u>A</u>lliance of Businessmen is trying to persuade private businesses to hire youth in the <u>s</u>ummertime. Each important word in the name of the organization must begin with a capital letter.

24. The supervisor<u>,</u> who is on vacation<u>,</u> <u>is</u> in charge of processing vouchers, OR The supervis<u>or who</u> is on vacation <u>is</u> in charge of processing vouchers. The first version indicates that there is only one supervisor and that supervisor happens to be on vacation. In this case, "who is on vacation" is a nonrestrictive clause and is set off by commas. The second version indicates that there are several supervisors, but the one in charge of processing vouchers is on vacation. In this case, "who is on vacation" is a restrictive clause and should not be set off by commas. The sentence is correct with either two commas or with no commas, depending on the meaning intended, but one comma is definitely wrong.

25. The sentence is correct.

26. <u>After the addresses were checked again,</u> the letters went to the mailroom. As the sentence was originally written, the letters did the checking of the addresses.

27. The director, as well as the employees, <u>is</u> interested in sharing the dividends. The *director* is the subject of the sentence and requires a singular verb.

28. Mrs. Black<u>,</u> the supervisor of the unit<u>,</u> has many important duties. *The supervisor of the unit* is an appositive and must be set off by commas.

29. This sentence is correct.

30. When a holiday falls on <u>S</u>unday, it is officially celebrated on <u>M</u>onday. Days of the week must be capitalized.

31. This sentence is correct.

32. The task of filing these cards is to be divided equally between you and <u>him</u>. *Him* is an object of the preposition *between.*

33. This sentence is correct.

34. I believe that the new employees are not as punctual as <u>we</u>. *As* is an adverb and so does not take an object. You can check your answer in such an instance by silently finishing off the sentence "... *as we are.*"

35. The employees <u>working in this office</u> <u>are</u> to be congratulated for their work. *Working in this office* is a restrictive clause so must not be set off by commas.

Proofreading Skills
The Correctly Typed Letter

                                                                    January 24, 2007
                                                                       1   2

Mr. Steven P. Anderson
 3   4   5
Alacon Manufacturing Co. Inc.
                  6   7   8
387 Bramson Boulevard
                    9
Waltham, MA_02154
           10,11

                              Re: Red worsted wool

                              Dye lot no. 68423
                              12   13

My dear Mr. Anderson:
    14   15 16

        My knitting store, Wooly Crafts , of 12 Myrtle Lane, Beloit, Wisconsin, told me to write to
                      17   18 19   20   21   22
you to tell you about my disappointment with your wool.
              23   24   25

____ I bought seven skeins of wool to make a sweater in December of 2005. After a few months
 26   27   28
29 I put the work aside. Last week I bought another skein of the same dye lot 68423 to finish the
 30   30   31 32   33 34   35   36   37   38
39 sweater. The red doesn't match; it is not the same.
                  40   41

        Mrs. Browne, the store manager, said that the yarn is too old. That may be so, but I read
        42   43   44 45   46   47   48
on the wrapper that you offer a guarantee. The guarantee says, " This wool will not fade. Be
        49   50   51   52 53 54   55
sure to match dye lots. Satisfaction is guaranteed."
              56   57   58   59
The whole sweater is no good. I am not satisfied. You could:
    60   61   62

        1. send me a refund for all eight skeins of wool
                                    63

        2. send me new wool.
        64

I am waiting for your reply as to how you plan to handle my complaint.
    65   66   67   68 69

                                                            Very truly yours ,
                                                                 70   71 72
                                                            Mollie Jones, Customer
                                                                 73

Explanations to the Correctly Typed Letter

1. Capitalize days of the week, months of the year, and holidays.
2. When typing a full date, do not use *th* or *rd*.
3. Use a period after an abbreviation.
4. Capitalize all proper names. The initial stands for the name.
5. Use a period after the initial in a person's name.
6. Spelling error.
7. The abbreviation of *Company* is *Co.* There may or may not be a comma between *Co.* and *Inc.,* depending upon the actual company name. An error cannot be assumed.
8. Use a period after an abbreviation.
9. Spelling error.
10. Do not use a period after official Postal Service two-letter state name designations.
11. Do not use a comma between Postal Service two-letter state name designation and zip code.
12. Incorrect word choice. The word referring to color is "dye."
13. Use a period after an abbreviation.
14. Capitalize only first and last words, titles, and proper names in the salutation.
15. Spelling error. See inside address, above.
16. Use a colon after the salutation in a business letter.
17. An appositive must be set off by commas.
18. Capitalize all proper names, including, but not limited to, names of people.
19. An appositive must be set off by commas. (See #17)
20. Abbreviate *street, road, lane,* etc., only on the envelope and the inside address.
21. Spelling error.
22. Wrong word choice.
23. Comma is not needed here.
24. The word, as written, does not exist.
25. *You're* is the contraction for *you are.* The correct possessive of *you* is *your.*
26. Begin a new paragraph for a new thought.
27. Spelling error.
28. Capitalize days of the week and months of the year. Also spelling error here.
29. This should not be a possessive. The plural of *month* is *months.*
30. Capitalize the letter *I* when it stands alone.
31. One word.
32. Capitalize the first word of a complete sentence.
33. Capitalize the letter *I* when it stands alone.

34. The past tense of *buy* is *bought*.

35. Spelling error.

36. Incorrect word choice. (See #12)

37. Typographical error. Check against dye lot number in reference line.

38. Spelling error.

39. Repeated word.

40. In a contraction, insert an apostrophe in place of the omitted letter or letters. Here, does + not = doesn't.

41. A semicolon may be used to join two short, related independent clauses. As originally written, this is a comma splice.

42. Use a period after an abbreviation.

43. An appositive must be set off by commas.

44. A nonspecific title should not be capitalized.

45. An appositive must be set off by commas. (See #43)

46. The word "that" introduces an indirect quote. An indirect quote should not be enclosed by quotation marks.

47. Wrong word choice. The word meaning "excessively" is *too*.

48. Capitalize the letter *I* when it stands alone.

49. Spelling error.

50. Spelling error.

51. Spelling error.

52. A comma separates a short direct quotation from the speaker.

53. All directly quoted material must be enclosed by quotation marks.

54. Capitalize the first word of a complete sentence.

55. The quotation does not end here.

56. Word choice. (See #12 and #36)

57. Capitalize the first word of a complete sentence.

58. Spelling error.

59. A period always goes inside the quotation marks, whether the quotation marks are used to denote quoted material, to set off titles, or to isolate words used in a special sense.

60. Wrong word choice. The word meaning "entire" is *whole*.

61. Wrong word choice. The negative is *no*.

62. Spelling error.

63. Look back at the letter to be sure all facts are accurate and internally consistent. 7 + 1 = 8.

64. Internal style must be consistent too. The figure *1)* must be followed by *2); a)* and *b)* would be equally acceptable.

65. Word ending omitted.

66. The correct possessive form of *you* is *your*.
67. Spelling error.
68. Spelling error.
69. Do not use a question mark after an indirect question; use a period.
70. Capitalize only the first word in a complimentary closing.
71. Capitalize only the first word in a complimentary closing.
72. The complimentary close of a letter is followed by a comma.
73. Use a comma to separate a name from a title.

APPENDIXES

Where to Look for Clerical Jobs

Very often, finding a job is a matter of luck. However, if you know where to look and when to seize an opportunity, you'll be more likely to find the position you want, especially when it comes to federal, state, and local clerical positions. We'd like to help you make your job search about more than luck. Below are some suggestions to help you get started. Don't stop here, though—the more you search, the more you'll uncover. There's a wealth of job information out there just waiting for you to find it.

FEDERAL EMPLOYMENT

Nearly half the jobs in the federal civil service are clerical, and the government's demand for clerical workers often exceeds the supply. Agencies have not been able to fill all the positions for competent stenographers, typists, office machine operators, and file clerks.

In government, the title "clerk" describes more positions than it does in private industry. For example, an editor or a writer may be called an editorial clerk; a purchasing agent with fairly important responsibilities may be called a purchasing clerk; an accountant may be called a cost accounting clerk. Other clerical job titles include: correspondence clerk, shorthand reporter, mail clerk, file clerk, and record clerk.

Clerical salaries have risen sharply in recent years and in many cases exceed average salaries for similar jobs in private industry. You can usually find good opportunities for advancement in the federal service, and a federal clerical job can be the start of a real career in the government.

The U.S. Office of Personnel Management (OPM) is a good place to start your job search. The OPM updates its list of job openings daily and publishes the quarterly *Federal Exam Announcement*. The OPM Web site is http://www.usajobs.opm.gov/. Here you'll find a complete application for federal employment and instructions on how to fill it out. The site also provides explanations of federal job categories and specific job descriptions. You can search by geographic area or alphabetically to find out which positions are currently open and exactly where the openings are located. The individual

appendix a

listings refer you to full vacancy announcements, including qualifications requirements and application procedures and deadlines. You can download announcements and application forms, and you can even apply online for open positions. Forms and information are available by telephone or mail as well. Call the OPM at 703-724-1850 or TDD 978-461-8404. These are automated numbers that are available seven days a week, 24 hours a day.

Another excellent source for a federal job search is the *Federal Jobs Digest,* a biweekly newspaper that lists thousands of government jobs in the United States and in foreign countries. On the *Federal Jobs Digest* Web site, you'll find thousands of job listings: http://www.jobsfed.com. You can also call at 610-965-5825.

If you don't have ready access to the Internet, another option is to look under the heading "U.S. Government" in the blue pages of your local telephone directory. Look for a listing for the OPM or Federal Job Information Center in your area. A call to these numbers may provide you with automated information or tell you where you can pick up printed information.

Federal Employment Web Sites

- Employment Index (www.employmentindex.com/govjob.html): Links to Web sites of government agencies throughout the United States. Site lists public- and private-sector jobs.

- Federal Jobs Digest (www.jobsfed.com): Listings for U.S. government jobs in the United States and in foreign countries.

- Federal Job Search (www.federaljobsearch.com): Listings for 40,000 U.S. jobs in the United States.

- FedWorld (www.fedworld.gov): Provides searchable abstracts of federal government jobs.

- HRS Federal Job Search (www.hrsjobs.com): A subscription job search and e-mail delivery service.

- The Internet Job Source (www.statejobs.com): The federal jobs section of this site links users to job listings at a variety of federal agencies and also to on-line newspapers listing federal job opportunities.

- Public Services Employees Network (www.pse-net.com): A guide to government employment, including job listings.

- U.S. Office of Personnel Management (www.opm.gov/forms): All forms and applications relating to federal employment from the U.S. Office of Personnel Management.

- U.S. Postal Service (www.usps.gov/employment): Listing of all available positions with the U.S. Postal Service.

- USAJOBS (www.usajobs.opm.gov): The official site for federal employment listings from the U.S. Office of Personnel Management.

STATE AND LOCAL EMPLOYMENT

Many state constitutions require that appointments and promotions in the state civil service and all its civil divisions be made according to merit and fitness, which is determined, whenever possible, through competitive exams. Entry-level positions are all filled competitively by appointment from appropriate civil service eligibility lists. When a vacancy higher than the entrance level is to be filled, the appointment must be made, if possible, by promotion from within. This increases opportunities for entry-level employees to advance to higher-level positions, while emphasizing the importance of recruiting well-trained, intelligent people for these entrance positions.

You'll probably find that civil service in the state, county, and local levels seems much less intimidating than attempting to find a federal job. The application process is often simpler, and the paperwork demands may be easier depending on the hiring agency and the particular position. Yet all of the opportunities are still there: State and local governments provide a large and expanding source of jobs in a wide variety of occupational fields. More than 12 million people work for state and local agencies in the United States; nearly three-fourths of these work in local government, such as counties, municipalities, towns, and school districts.

Clerical, administrative, maintenance, and custodial work make up a large portion of employment in most government agencies. Among the workers involved in these activities are clerk-typists, stenographers, secretaries, and bookkeepers. Here are a few more examples of clerical jobs in state and local government:

- Messengers sort and carry mail, documents, or other materials between offices or buildings.

- Clerks perform basic clerical duties, such as gathering and providing information, sorting, filing, and checking materials.

- Clerk-typists perform typing and clerical duties, such as providing information, composing short letters and memos, sorting, filing, and checking materials.

- Clerk-stenographers take dictation and transcribe notes. Other duties may include typing, providing information, composing letters and memos, sorting, and filing materials.

- Secretary-typists perform secretarial duties, which usually involve typing correspondence, reports, and statistical material while acting as a secretary for one or more employees.

- Executive secretaries perform highly responsible secretarial work as staff assistants to executive directors. They may also supervise a small clerical staff.

- Library assistants perform clerical work in a library, such as maintaining files and records, sorting and shelving books, and checking materials for accuracy.

Almost every state has its own Web site. Here's a very simple way to access the state systems via the Internet: Enter www.state._____.us. In the blank, enter the two-letter postal abbreviation for the state. For example, to reach the Arizona state Web site, enter www.state.az.us. For West Virginia, enter www.state.wv.us. See the list of latest URLs for the state sites below. Although the site addresses may change from time to time, you'll usually be redirected to the correct address if you use this formula.

If the state also has a Job Bank, you can find that Web site in much the same way. This time, you enter www.ajb.org/_____, entering the state's two-letter abbreviation in the blank space. The list of state Job Bank Web sites also appears in the table below.

You may also find city and county employment information on the Internet through your state's home page. Or, if you're living in a large city, you might find it on that city's Web site. Try using some of the most popular search engines, such as Google.com and Yahoo.com to locate other job-related Web sites. Use search terms like *jobs, employment, labor, business, help wanted,* and so on. If you add a specific city or state, you'll likely find more targeted results—and you'll be amazed at the number of suggested job sites you'll find.

State Internet Sites

Alabama	www.state.al.us/	Michigan	www.state.mi.us/
Alaska	www.state.ak.us/	Minnesota	www.state.mn.us/
Arizona	www.state.az.us/	Mississippi	www.state.ms.us/
Arkansas	www.state.ar.us/	Missouri	www.state.mo.us/
California	www.state.ca.us/	Montana	www.state.mt.us/
Colorado	www.state.co.us/	Nebraska	www.state.ne.us/
Connecticut	www.state.ct.us/	Nevada	www.state.nv.us/
Delaware	www.state.de.us/	New Hampshire	www.state.nh.us/
District of		New Jersey	www.state.nj.us/
Columbia	www.dchomepage.net/	New Mexico	www.state.nm.us/
Florida	www.state.ca.us/	New York	www.state.ny.us/
Georgia	www.state.ca.us/	North Carolina	www.state.nc.us/
Hawaii	www.state.hi.us/	North Dakota	www.ajb.org/nd
Idaho	www.state.id.us/	Ohio	www.ajb.org/oh
Illinois	www.state.il.us/	Oklahoma	www.state.ok.us/
Indiana	www.state.in.us/	Oregon	www.state.or.us/
Iowa	www.state.ia.us/	Pennsylvania	www.state.pa.us/
Kansas	www.state.ks.us/	Rhode Island	www.state.ri.us/
Kentucky	www.state.ky.us/	South Carolina	www.state.sc.us/
Louisiana	www.state.la.us/	South Dakota	www.state.sd.us/
Maine	www.state.me.us/	Tennessee	www.state.tn.us/
Maryland	www.state.md.us/	Texas	www.state.tx.us/
Massachusetts	www.state.ma.us/		

State Job Bank Sites

Alabama	www.ajb.org/al	Michigan	www.michigan.gov/mdcs
Alaska	www.jobs.state.ak.us/	Minnesota	www.ajb.org/mn
Arizona	www.ajb.org/az	Mississippi	www.ajb.org/ms
Arkansas	www.ajb.org/ar	Missouri	www.ajb.org/mo
California	www.ajb.org/ca	Montana	www.ajb.org/mt
Colorado	www.ajb.org/co	Nebraska	www.ajb.org/ne
Connecticut	www.ajb.org/ct	Nevada	www.ajb.org/nv
Delaware	www.ajb.org/de	New Hampshire	www.nhworks.org/
District of Columbia	www.ajb.org/dc	New Jersey	www.ajb.org/nj
Florida	www.ajb.org/fl	New Mexico	www.ajb.org/nm
Georgia	www.ajb.org/ga	New York	www.ajb.org/ny
Hawaii	www.ajb.org/hi	North Carolina	www.ajb.org/nc
Idaho	www.ajb.org/id	North Dakota	www.ajb.org/nd
Illinois	www.ajb.org/il	Ohio	www.ajb.org/oh
Indiana	www.ajb.org/in	Oklahoma	www.ajb.org/ok
Iowa	www.ajb.org/ia	Oregon	www.oregon.gov/worksource/
Kansas	www.ajb.org/ks	Pennsylvania	www.ajb.org/pa
Kentucky	www.ajb.org/ky	Rhode Island	www.ajb.org/ri
Louisiana	www.ajb.org/la	South Carolina	www.ajb.org/sc
Maine	www.ajb.org/me	South Dakota	www.ajb.org/sd
Maryland	www.ajb.org/md	Tennessee	www.ajb.org/tn
Massachusetts	www.ajb.org/ma	Texas	www.ajb.org/tx

It's also a good idea to investigate whether your city has a local civil service publication that lists job announcements. For example, in New York City, *The Chief-Leader* is the primary source of listings for local civil service job openings, with a print issue and a Web site at www.thechief-leader.com. You'll also find information about state and federal jobs in the local newspaper and its Web site, if it has one.

APPLYING FOR A GOVERNMENT JOB

Now that you know where to look for civil service clerical jobs, it's important to understand the procedure involved in getting these jobs. The process varies little from job to job and from one level of government to another. Of course, details may vary, but in general, certain steps are common to all.

When you find a *Notice of Examination* (it may be called an Announcement instead), read it very carefully. Carefully review all the details. The notice will provide the title of the job, a brief job description, and a listing of duties and responsibilities. Based on what you read, you can decide whether you want to try for the job.

If the job sounds appealing, here are a few areas you need to concentrate on to give yourself a better chance of success.

Education and Experience Requirements

If you cannot meet the requirements listed in the job description, do not apply. Government service is very popular and many people apply. The government has more than enough applicants from whom to choose, so it will not waive requirements for you.

Age Requirements

Discrimination on the basis of an applicant's age is illegal, but a number of civil service jobs demand so much sustained physical effort (such as firefighting) that they require retirement at an early age. For these positions, you'll see an entry age limit.

If you are already beyond that age, do not apply. If you are too young to meet the requirements, ask about the time lag between applying and hiring. It's possible that you will reach the minimum age requirement by the time the position is to be filled.

Citizenship Requirements

Many jobs are open to all people who are eligible to work in the United States. However, all law enforcement jobs and most federal jobs are limited to U.S. citizens. If you are well on the way to becoming a U.S. citizen and you expect to be naturalized soon, ask about your exact status with respect to the job opening you're interested in.

Residency Requirements

If the position mentions a residency requirement, you must live within the prescribed limits or be willing to move into that area. If you are not willing or able to move to that area, do not apply for the position.

Required Forms to File

The notice or announcement of the position for which you are applying will specify the form of application required. For most federal jobs, you may submit either the Optional Application for Federal Employment (OF 612) or a resume that fulfills the requirements listed in the pamphlet *Applying for a Federal Job* (OF 510). Both of these forms can be downloaded from www.opm.gov/forms/html/of.asp.

For other than federal jobs, the Notice of Examination may tell you where you must go or whom to contact to get the necessary form or forms. Be sure you get all the forms you need to apply. The application may be a simple form that asks nothing more than name, address, citizenship, and Social Security number, or it may be a complex form that requires you to supply a great deal of information about your education, job training and experience, and life experience.

Filing Dates, Place, and Fee

These aspects of job applications vary greatly. For some positions, you can file your application at any time. Others have a first and last day filing date, and if you file too early or late, your application will not be considered. Sometimes it is sufficient to have your application postmarked by the last day for filing; more often, your application must be received by the last date. Occasionally, in-person filing is required, so be sure to check the directions carefully. If you are mailing your application, allow at least five full business days for it to reach its destination. The address for where to file is usually stated on the notice or announcement. Double-check the address to be sure you get it right.

Federal and postal positions do not require a filing fee, but for most other government job openings, you will be charged a fee for processing your application. The fee and the method of payment are not always the same from position to position. Be sure to check these out. If the notice or announcement specifies "money order only," purchase a money order and be sure it's made out properly. If you send or present a personal check or cash, your application will be rejected without consideration.

How to Qualify

This portion of the notice or announcement will tell you the basis on which a candidate will be chosen. Some examination scores consist of a total of weighted education and experience factors. This type of examination, called an "unassembled exam" (because you do not go to one place to take the exam), is based on your responses on the application and on supplementary forms. Obviously, you need to be sure these forms are complete so you get full credit for all you have learned and accomplished.

The notice or announcement may tell you about a qualifying exam—an exam that you must pass in addition to scoring well on an unassembled, written, or performance test. Or it may tell you about a competitive exam requirement, a written performance exam requirement, or both. The competitive exam might be described in very general terms or it might be outlined in detail. If the date of the exam has been set, that date will also appear on the notice. Mark the date on your calendar to help you remember your deadline.

Filing Your Application

Once you have all the required application forms for a position, it's a good idea to photocopy them and then fill out the photocopied versions first. This way, you'll be able to correct mistakes, change the order of information, or add or delete information. Think of them as a worksheet for the final version of your applications.

Don't exaggerate your experience or accomplishments, but be sure to give yourself sufficient credit. Include any responsibilities you assumed, cost-saving ideas that you may have given a previous employer, or any accomplishments beyond your regular duties and responsibilities. Be clear and thorough when you relate what you have learned and what your skills are.

When you're satisfied with the draft, copy the information onto the original forms. Be sure to include any backup material requested, but do not send more "evidence" than is truly necessary to support your claims of qualification. Your application must be complete according to the requirements of the notice or announcement, but you don't want to overwhelm the hirer or hirers with information. Your goal is to command attention by conforming exactly to requirements.

Once you complete the forms, check over them again for neatness and make sure they are complete. Sign wherever indicated, attach the fee (if required), and mail or personally file the application on time.

TAKING AN EXAMINATION

If you are currently employed, *do not* give your notice right away. The time lag between applying for a government job and actual employment is always many months; it may even be a year or two. However, if the Notice of Examination states that a competitive exam will be administered and gives information about subjects included on the exam, you should begin studying as soon as possible.

Once the civil service commission or personnel office to which you submitted your application receives it, a representative will date, stamp, and log the application, and will open a file on you. The office may acknowledge receipt of the application with more forms, sample exam questions, or simply a receipt slip. You may hear nothing at all for several months. Eventually, however, you will receive notice of a testing date or an interview appointment. Write these on your calendar so you don't let the dates slip by or forget to prepare. Write the address to which you are to report in the same place. If you receive an admission ticket for an exam, put it in a safe place, but keep it in sight so that you will not forget to take it with you to the exam.

With notice of the exam date, you should also receive information about the exam. Time may be short between the date you receive notice of the exam and the date you are scheduled to take it, so it's smart to begin studying and preparing right away if you have not already done so.

The exam might be either a paper-and-pencil test or a performance exam—it depends on the nature of the job. For example, an applicant for a locksmith position may be asked to cut some complicated keys and to repair a broken lock, but an applicant for a position as a clerk-stenographer will likely be asked to take dictation and a typing test, along with a multiple-choice test of general clerical abilities. Applicants for most jobs will take only a written test. This is most frequently a multiple-choice test in which the test-taker chooses the best of four or five answer choices and marks the number on a separate answer sheet.

Multiple-choice tests are machine scored. Machine scoring ensures accuracy and objectivity: No one can misinterpret your answers. Machine scoring also allows for many applicants to be rated at the same time, so it speeds up the process (although if you're waiting to hear about the job, you may doubt this!).

Occasionally, the written test will consist of an essay portion along with or instead of the multiple-choice section. Essays usually appear at levels above initial entry level where there are fewer applicants and therefore fewer exams to score. On an essay test, examiners look for indications that you can organize your thoughts and express them effectively in writing.

If you are contacted for an exam, arrive promptly and dress appropriately and comfortably. Neatness is always appropriate; however, you do not need to dress up for a performance exam or for a written exam. If you will be doing manual work for your performance exam, wear clean work clothes. For a written exam, neat, casual clothing is fine.

Working for the Department of Homeland Security

The U.S. Department of Homeland Security (DHS) is an executive department of the federal government responsible for protecting the security of the United States. Its primary missions are to prevent terrorist attacks within the United States, reduce the United States' vulnerability to terrorism, and minimize the damage from potential attacks and natural disasters.

The DHS was created by the Department of Homeland Security Act of 2002 as an outgrowth of the Office of Homeland Security established after the events of September 11, 2001. The third-largest executive department in the federal government, the DHS is comprised of twenty-two agencies that were formerly in the Departments of Agriculture, Commerce, Defense, Energy, Health and Human Services, Justice, Transportation, and Treasury or in independent bodies. The new department is an "umbrella" for a broad range of nonmilitary government agencies responsible for aspects of U.S. security. More than 87,000 different governmental jurisdictions at the federal, state, and local levels have homeland security responsibilities. The strategy of the DHS is to develop a complementary system that connects all levels of U.S. government without duplicating effort.

Although the DHS undergoes periodic revisions and reorganization, it is presently made up of the following components.

- **Directorate for Preparedness.** This department works with state, local, and private sector partners to identify threats, determine vulnerabilities, and target resources where risk is greatest. The goal is to safeguard borders, seaports, bridges and highways, and critical information systems.

- **Science and Technology Directorate**. This department is the main research and development arm of the DHS. It provides federal, state, and local officials with technology and other tools needed for U.S. security.

- **Management Directorate.** This department is in charge of budgets and appropriations, expenditure of funds, accounting and finance, procurement; human resources, information technology systems, facilities and equipment, and the identification and tracking of performance measurements.

- **Office of Policy Directorate.** Policy formulation and coordination for the DHS are handled in this department.

- **Federal Emergency Management (FEMA) Directorate.** National hazards and federal response and recovery efforts following national incidents or natural disasters are the responsibility of this department.

Other offices under the DHS include:

- Office of Intelligence and Analysis

- Office of Operations Coordination

- Domestic Nuclear Detection Office

- Transportation Security Administration (TSA)

- U.S. Customs and Border Protection

- U.S. Immigration and Customs Enforcement

- Federal Law Enforcement Training Center

- U.S. Citizenship and Immigration Services

- U.S. Coast Guard

- U.S. Secret Service

CAREER OPPORTUNITY AREAS

The DHS's three primary missions are: to prevent terrorist attacks within the United States, reduce America's vulnerability to terrorism, and minimize the damage from potential attacks and natural disasters. Homeland Security employees help secure borders, airports, seaports, and waterways; research and develop security technologies; respond to natural disasters or terrorist attacks; and analyze intelligence reports.

Among the many career opportunities in the DHS are jobs in security analysis, human resources, administration, budgeting and accounting, procurement, information technology, research and development, intelligence gathering and analysis, law, engineering, fraud and criminal investigation, immigration and customs processing, law enforcement, environmental protection, trade regulation enforcement, disaster preparedness and recovery, aviation support, and forensics.

FINDING AND APPLYING FOR A DHS JOB

If you are interested in working for the Department of Homeland Security, your first step should be to visit the USAJobs Web site: *http://jobsearch.usajobs.opm.gov/dhscareers/*. Search for current DHS employment opportunities by job category, location, salary, and other categories.

When you find a job announcement that interests you, review it carefully for information about qualifications, duties, salary range, location, benefits, and security requirements. All DHS jobs require that you be a U.S. citizen. Most will also require completion of a full background investigation and submission to a drug test.

Follow instructions for applying for the job of your choice. Make sure you submit all required documents and pay close attention to the application due date and application procedures. These will vary depending on the job you are applying for.

Applicants who are disabled and who hold a certification eligibility letter from a State Vocational Rehabilitation Office or the Department of Veterans Affairs may apply for DHS employment opportunities through one of several special hiring authorities, or directly to a Homeland Security Selective Placement Coordinator. You can find more information by visiting the U.S. Office of Personnel Management's Federal Employment of People with Disabilities Web site, *http://www.opm.gov/disability/*. Or you can contact a Homeland Security Selective Placement Coordinator. They are listed on the DHS Web site, *http://www.dhs.gov*.

Your application and those of other qualified candidates will be forwarded to the supervisor or hiring official for the position you are interested in. If you are one of the best-qualified candidates, you may be called for an interview in person or by telephone. In rare cases you may be hired without an interview. As with other federal civil service hiring offices, DHS supervisors and hiring officials must comply with federal civil service laws to ensure that all applicants receive fair and equal treatment in the hiring process.

JOB BENEFITS

Jobs with the DHS feature competitive starting salaries and opportunities for performance-based salary increases. Employment benefits include:

- A choice of health insurance programs

- Personal leave days for vacation, illness, and family care

- Ten paid holidays per year

- Paid training

- A portable Thrift Savings Plan, similar to a 401(k)

- Nontaxable Flexible Spending Accounts for out-of-pocket medical or dependent care expenses

- Transportation subsidies

- Defined benefit retirement plan

- Flexible work schedules

- Employee recognition program

- Life and long-term care insurance

- Employee Assistance Programs

- Tuition reimbursement

Other benefits may include an allowance for uniforms, health and wellness programs, access to fitness centers, and the opportunity to telecommute (work from home).

PAY SCALE

In 2005, the DHS announced a new Human Resources Management System that includes implementation of a pay-for-performance program. This program will replace the General Schedule used by many other federal government agencies. The new pay schedule is based on private-sector pay bands, in which employees receive salary raises according to performance and/or competency rather than longevity on the job. Occupational "clusters" within the DHS are based on similarity of work, employee qualifications, marketplace rates, and employee competence. Conversion to the new pay system began in 2006.

Peterson's
Book Satisfaction Survey

Give Us Your Feedback

Thank you for choosing Peterson's as your source for personalized solutions for your education and career achievement. Please take a few minutes to answer the following questions. Your answers will go a long way in helping us to produce the most user-friendly and comprehensive resources to meet your individual needs.

When completed, please tear out this page and mail it to us at:

Publishing Department
Peterson's, a Nelnet company
2000 Lenox Drive
Lawrenceville, NJ 08648

You can also complete this survey online at **www.petersons.com/booksurvey**.

1. **What is the ISBN of the book you have purchased? (The ISBN can be found on the book's back cover in the lower right-hand corner.)** _____

2. **Where did you purchase this book?**
   - ❑ Retailer, such as Barnes & Noble
   - ❑ Online reseller, such as Amazon.com
   - ❑ Petersons.com
   - ❑ Other (please specify) _____

3. **If you purchased this book on Petersons.com, please rate the following aspects of your online purchasing experience on a scale of 4 to 1 (4 = Excellent and 1 = Poor).**

	4	3	2	1
Comprehensiveness of Peterson's Online Bookstore page	❑	❑	❑	❑
Overall online customer experience	❑	❑	❑	❑

4. **Which category best describes you?**
   - ❑ High school student
   - ❑ Parent of high school student
   - ❑ College student
   - ❑ Graduate/professional student
   - ❑ Returning adult student
   - ❑ Teacher
   - ❑ Counselor
   - ❑ Working professional/military
   - ❑ Other (please specify) _____

5. **Rate your overall satisfaction with this book.**

Extremely Satisfied	Satisfied	Not Satisfied
❑	❑	❑

6. Rate each of the following aspects of this book on a scale of 4 to 1 (4 = Excellent and 1 = Poor).

	4	3	2	1
Comprehensiveness of the information	❑	❑	❑	❑
Accuracy of the information	❑	❑	❑	❑
Usability	❑	❑	❑	❑
Cover design	❑	❑	❑	❑
Book layout	❑	❑	❑	❑
Special features (e.g., CD, flashcards, charts, etc.)	❑	❑	❑	❑
Value for the money	❑	❑	❑	❑

7. This book was recommended by:
- ❑ Guidance counselor
- ❑ Parent/guardian
- ❑ Family member/relative
- ❑ Friend
- ❑ Teacher
- ❑ Not recommended by anyone—I found the book on my own
- ❑ Other (please specify) _____

8. Would you recommend this book to others?

Yes	Not Sure	No
❑	❑	❑

9. Please provide any additional comments.

_____

_____

_____

_____

Remember, you can tear out this page and mail it to us at:

Publishing Department
Peterson's, a Nelnet company
2000 Lenox Drive
Lawrenceville, NJ 08648

or you can complete the survey online at **www.petersons.com/booksurvey.**

Your feedback is important to us at Peterson's, and we thank you for your time!

If you would like us to keep in touch with you about new products and services, please include your e-mail here: _____